Beginning PyQt

A Hands-on Approach to GUI
Programming with PyQt6

Second Edition

Joshua M Willman

Apress®

Beginning PyQt: A Hands-on Approach to GUI Programming with PyQt6

Joshua M Willman
Sunnyvale, CA, USA

ISBN-13 (pbk): 978-1-4842-7998-4   ISBN-13 (electronic): 978-1-4842-7999-1
https://doi.org/10.1007/978-1-4842-7999-1

Managing Director, Apress Media LLC: Welmoed Spahr
Acquisitions Editor: Celestin Suresh John
Development Editor: James Markham
Coordinating Editor: Divya Modi

Cover designed by eStudioCalamar

Cover image designed by Pixabay

Distributed to the book trade worldwide by Springer Science+Business Media New York, 1 New York Plaza, New York, NY 10004. Phone 1-800-SPRINGER, fax (201) 348-4505, e-mail orders-ny@springer-sbm.com, or visit www.springeronline.com. Apress Media, LLC is a California LLC and the sole member (owner) is Springer Science + Business Media Finance Inc (SSBM Finance Inc). SSBM Finance Inc is a **Delaware** corporation.

For information on translations, please e-mail booktranslations@springernature.com; for reprint, paperback, or audio rights, please e-mail bookpermissions@springernature.com.

Apress titles may be purchased in bulk for academic, corporate, or promotional use. eBook versions and licenses are also available for most titles. For more information, reference our Print and eBook Bulk Sales web page at http://www.apress.com/bulk-sales.

Any source code or other supplementary material referenced by the author in this book is available to readers on GitHub via the book's product page, located at https://github.com/Apress/Beginning-PyQt--second-edition. For more detailed information, please visit http://www.apress.com/source-code.

Printed on acid-free paper

To my daughter, Kalani.

Table of Contents

About the Author

Joshua Willman is a software engineer with more than 12 years of experience developing applications in mainly Python and C++. His career has allowed him to participate in many different fields, from robotics, machine learning, and computer vision to UI development, game development, and more. His first experience with PyQt was building an interface for simplifying the labeling process of datasets for machine learning. Ever since then, he's been hooked!

In recent years, his passion for programming and all things visual has allowed him to participate in numerous projects. These include designing educational courses for mobile robotics and computer vision using Arduino and Raspberry Pi, building GUI applications, and working as a solo indie game developer. He currently works as a robotics engineer, a technical writer, and a content creator (learning web development in his spare time in order to build his own platform, redhuli.io). When he's not working, he enjoys tinkering on robotics projects and spending time with his wonderful wife and daughter.

He is also the author of two books with Apress:

- *Beginning PyQt: A Hands-on Approach to GUI Programming (1st Edition)*

- *Modern PyQt: Create GUI Applications for Project Management, Computer Vision, and Data Analysis*

About the Technical Reviewers

Vikas Kumar has more than seven years of combined experiences in avionics, aerospace, automotive, and healthcare industries in R&D and software development activities. He has been programming and developing desktop applications with C++, Qt, PyQt/PySide, Python, Java, and SQL since the beginning. He holds a Bachelor of Technology in Computer Science and Engineering from Biju Patnaik University of Technology, Odisha, India.

He has worked with various Indian defense clients for the development of avionics test suite for the testing of components of various military aircrafts. He has worked with Airbus as a client for the development of various software responsible for structural and computational analysis of various commercial aircrafts. He has worked with Mercedes-Benz for the development of software responsible for data analysis, simulation, modeling, and validation of high-voltage electric battery used in Mercedes-Benz electric vehicles.

His technical skills include C++, Qt, PyQt/PySide, Python, Java, MySQL, and desktop application development in Linux and Windows.

He currently works as Senior Software Engineer with GE Healthcare India for developing host software for MRI scanners.

Saumitra Jagdale is the founder of Open Cloudware and Global AI Ambassador focusing on the current trends in technology. He is a recognized technical author for various established media houses like OpenSystems Media, CNX Software, AspenCore, Electronics-Lab, and IoT Tech Trends. Additionally, he is a Senior Engineer – Cloud Services and Software at L&T Infotech with expertise in the field of CRM and ERP applications. Being an open source Python developer, he also leads the TensorFlow Community India for promoting deep learning methodologies in the community.

Acknowledgments

I am beyond grateful to Divya Modi, Celestin Suresh John, and the wonderful team at Apress for granting me the opportunity to write the second edition of this book. My deepest appreciation goes to Divya for being there every step along the way.

A special thanks to Andrea Casadei whose inquiries greatly helped to improve this edition.

An immense thanks to the Python, PyQt, and Qt communities. I would also really like to thank Phil Thompson, the creator of PyQt.

I owe an enormous amount of gratitude to Richard Bronosky for giving me a chance when I needed it the most.

Ashish Naik, thank you for all of the support you provided my family and me from the very beginning.

Thanks to my mother, Valorie, and my sisters, Teesha and Jazzmin, for the support you have always given me.

I am deeply thankful to my wife, Evelyn Ye, whose continued patience with me makes these books possible.

To Kalani, you continue to be my motivation and inspiration.

Once again, thank you to the readers. I truly hope that ideas found within this book will fuel your creativity and benefit you in some way.

Introduction

With new PyQt versions come new tools to play with. The latest edition aims to explore some of those ideas while still being aimed toward beginners. You will explore how to use the Python programming language, along with the PyQt6 toolkit, to create graphical user interfaces (GUIs).

Just getting started is more important than anything else. Coding a GUI can be considered a combination of programming and graphic design skills. An awareness of a user's needs is also crucial for better usability and graphical appearance. Programming a GUI is often a matter of selecting the right component, referred to as widgets in PyQt, to complete a task and then applying the necessary programming skills to make them operational.

One goal is to balance the theory behind good design practices with more hands-on, learn-as-you-go style coding examples. New concepts and PyQt classes are introduced in each chapter, and later chapters sometimes build upon previous ones.

Who Should Read This Book

This book is targeted to Python developers who are looking to begin creating graphical user interfaces and want to utilize the latest version of PyQt to get started. Having prior knowledge of PyQt or other Python GUI toolkits is not necessary to begin using this book. It is, however, recommended that you understand the fundamentals of Python and Python syntax and are comfortable using Object-Oriented Programming (OOP).

How This Book Is Organized

The latest edition of *Beginning PyQt* begins by introducing you to the basic ideas behind GUI development. **Chapter 1** will get you on your way to installing and understanding how to use the latest version of PyQt.

Chapters 2 and **3** teach how to add widgets to your applications, thereby adding more and more functionality to your projects. Both chapters introduce different widgets, such as QLabel, QCheckBox, and QLineEdit, and give examples and ideas for using them. **Chapter 3** will also introduce you to PyQt's signals and slots mechanism for handling events.

Chapter 4 focuses on layout managers for arranging widgets.

After learning about different widgets and layouts, **Chapter 5** guides you through examples that help you to create classical GUIs with menus and toolbars.

Chapter 6 presents style sheets for altering the look of your applications.

Chapter 7 discusses how to handle events that occur in a GUI, such as a user clicking on the mouse. You'll also discover how to create your own signals and how to reimplement event handlers.

Since Qt also includes its own graphical user interface to help you create GUIs, we will take a look at how to use Qt Designer in **Chapter 8**.

From there, we'll start learning more advanced concepts.

Chapter 9 introduces you to using the clipboard to copy and paste information between applications.

Chapter 10 shows how to handle data using PyQt's item-based convenience classes. You'll also find out how to add basic drag-and-drop functionality to widgets.

Chapter 11 introduces you to painting, graphics, and animation.

Customization is important in PyQt. **Chapter 12** shows you how to build and use your own custom widgets.

Chapter 13 talks about Qt Quick for building fluid and dynamic applications.

Chapter 14 shows how to use build user interfaces that handle data with SQL databases and PyQt's Model/View architecture.

Chapter 15 discusses multithreaded programming to avoid your applications from freezing.

Chapter 16 contains extra example projects to help you continue to gain extra practice and insight into creating applications with PyQt.

The **Appendix** includes additional information about different PyQt modules and classes. An additional coding example can also be found in the Appendix.

Understanding the Structure and Code of the Chapters

Code for the latest edition is generally broken apart into smaller pieces (unless the program is already a short example). This makes the code easier to digest and understand and also prevents users from code dumps (copying and pasting entire sections). You can always refer to the GitHub repository (link found in the "Links to the Source Code" section) to see the code examples in their entirety.

Also, be sure to pay close attention to the listing titles above each piece of code when following along. They give hints about each section as well as help you know what code example you are viewing. For example, Chapter 2 introduces labels. The code for explaining how to use labels is broken into two parts, Listing 1 and Listing 2. The first listing's header appears like the following lines:

Listing 1. Setting up the main window to show how to use QLabel widgets

```
# labels.py
```

The second part of the application is listed as

Listing 2. The setUpMainWindow() method for displaying text and image labels

```
# labels.py
```

If a code snippet does not contain a listing number, then that code provides additional information but is not located in any of the files.

In addition, where necessary, important differences between PyQt5 and PyQt6 are pointed out in the text.

Another important note is that PyQt is designed to be cross-platform. No world is perfect though, and sometimes, additional explanations are given for developers to get their code running on Windows, macOS, or Linux (Ubuntu). Be sure to take a look at the comments or notes for clarity when running an application.

Finally, as you are reading along, keywords use **bold** font. File names, Python and PyQt module and class names, and bits of the code that are mentioned in the text are displayed using a different font, for example, QPushButton.

Links to the Source Code

The source code for *Beginning PyQt: A Hands-on Approach to GUI Programming with PyQt6* can be found on GitHub at `https://github.com/Apress/Beginning-PyQt--second-edition`.

Reader Feedback

Your feedback, questions, and ideas are always welcome. If you have any questions about this book, PyQt version 5 or 6, or GUI development or would just like to leave a comment, you can always find me at `redhuli.comments@gmail.com`.

CHAPTER 1

Getting Started with PyQt

Hello! Welcome to *Beginning PyQt: A Hands-on Approach to GUI Programming*. You are probably here because you would like to learn how to build applications and need some help getting started. Maybe you have a personal program you need to build, or perhaps you would like to build a custom software application for others to use. Whatever your reason may be, you'll need to figure out where is the best place to start.

The goal of this book is to take a practical approach to coding user interfaces. You'll be able to follow along and code numerous examples, both simple and complex. You'll also gain knowledge through visualization and practice that show how to use fundamental concepts you need to build your own applications. In many cases, those concepts will then be applied to larger projects.

In this chapter, you will

- Learn about the PyQt toolkit for creating user interfaces

- Set up Python 3 and download the latest version of PyQt6

- Consider some fundamental concepts for building user-friendly interfaces

- Create your first application with PyQt

Let's begin this journey by finding out more about PyQt.

The PyQt Framework

The **PyQt** toolkit is a set of Python bindings for the Qt cross-platform widget toolkit and application framework. What does that mean?

First, **Qt** is used for the development of user interfaces and other applications and is being developed by The Qt Company. The framework is significant because it can run on numerous software and hardware systems such as Windows, macOS, Linux, Android, or embedded systems with little to no change to the underlying code and is still able to

1

© Joshua M Willman 2022
J. M. Willman, *Beginning PyQt*, https://doi.org/10.1007/978-1-4842-7999-1_1

maintain capabilities and speed of the system on which it is being run. So in general, you'll be able to make some amazing cross-platform applications without having to worry about the user's platform.

Second, this all means that PyQt combines all the advantages of the Qt C++ cross-platform widget toolkit with Python, the powerful and simple, cross-platform interpreted language. It's worth noting that while PyQt has its own documentation, the Qt documentation tends to be more complete. If you have never used C++ before, this can seem like a daunting task. We'll discuss this topic a little further in this chapter's first application.

For more information about Qt, have a look at `www.qt.io`.

For more information about PyQt, check out `www.riverbankcomputing.com/news`.

Why Choose PyQt?

PyQt is capable of more than just creating graphical interfaces, as it also has access to Qt classes that cover mechanics such as XML handling, SQL databases, network communication, graphics and animations, and many other technologies. Take the capabilities of Qt and combine them with the number of extension modules that Python provides and you have the ability to create new applications that can build upon these preexisting libraries.

PyQt also includes Qt Designer, which allows for anyone to assemble a GUI much faster using a simple drag-and-drop graphical interface designer. Qt Designer is discussed in detail in Chapter 8.

Using PyQt's **signal and slot** mechanism, you can create an extremely interactive interface and customize how different PyQt components interact. This will be covered in more detail in Chapters 3 and 7.

There are, of course, other toolkits available for creating applications with GUIs using Python, such as Tkinter, wxPython, and PySide, and they all have their own advantages. For example, Tkinter comes bundled with Python, meaning that you can find an abundance of helpful resources by doing a quick search on the Internet. PySide is the Python binding of Qt managed by The Qt Company itself. Despite this, PyQt still has a larger following thanks to its age and awesome community of developers.

It is worth noting that if you choose to use PyQt to create commercial applications, you will need to get a license. Applications created in this book will leverage the **GNU General Public License** (**GPL**).

Ultimately, it all comes down to choosing the toolkit that works the best for your project.

PyQt5 vs. PyQt6

The latest version of Qt has brought more focus on 2D and 3D capabilities. There are also quite a few changes in the latest version of PyQt. Since this book's aim is to introduce the fundamentals of developing applications with PyQt, we will take a look at the changes that will impact you the most at this stage of your journey:

- As you dive more into PyQt, you'll definitely use **enums**, **flags**, and other identifiers in the **Qt Namespace**. They are useful for setting the properties of the different classes in PyQt. What's important to understand now is that the fully qualified names are now used for these items rather than the shorthand ones used in PyQt5. For example, PyQt5 used `Qt.AlignCenter` to center text, but PyQt6 uses the full name, `Qt.AlignmentFlag.Center`. You will see numerous examples of this throughout the book, and we'll discuss this more in later chapters.

- Some classes and methods have been deprecated, such as `QDesktopWidget`, while others have been moved, such as the `QAction` class is now located in the `QtGui` module.

- The `exec()` method is now used in PyQt6 to start the event loop of your application rather than `exec_()`.

This is not an exhaustive list, and you will find out more about these and other topics as you follow along. If you are interested to see more of the new changes in PyQt6, have a look at `www.riverbankcomputing.com/static/Docs/PyQt6/pyqt5_differences.html`.

Installing Python 3 and PyQt6

So that all readers are on the same page, let's begin by installing or updating your version of Python.

Checking Your Version of Python

In order to use PyQt, you will first need to have **Python 3.7 or higher** installed.

Note   When PyQt6 was first released, it was compatible with Python 3.6.1 or higher. However, that was scheduled to be discontinued at some point in the future. You should have Python 3.7 or higher on your system just to be on the safe side.

To check which version of Python 3 you have installed on your system, open your system's **shell**, and run the command

```
$ python3 --version
```

Change python3 to python on Windows. This will return your system's Python 3 version. If yours happens to be lower than Python 3.7 or you don't have Python installed, then have a look at www.python.org/downloads/ to get the latest version.

Tip   For those readers that might not want to remove their current version of Python and would like to manage multiple Python versions on their system, have a look at the Python version management tool, pyenv.

Installing PyQt6

Since PyQt does not come included with your Python installation, the next step is to use pip to install the PyQt6 package from the **Python Package Index** (**PyPI**). To create the bindings between Python and C++, the **SIP** binding generator tool is used. When downloading PyQt6 from PyPI, the sip module will automatically be downloaded too.

To install PyQt6, enter the following command into your shell:

```
$ pip3 install PyQt6
```

If you are using Windows, you will probably need to change pip3 to pip. To make sure PyQt is downloaded properly, open up the Python 3 interpreter by entering python3 (python for Windows) into the command line. Then enter the following command:

```
>>> import PyQt6
```

Tip   Throughout the course of this book, you'll create a number of PyQt GUIs. For those readers who are interested in managing their different PyQt projects and their dependencies, have a look at using **virtual environments** and the Python module, venv.

If no errors are returned, we can now move on and learn a little bit more about user interfaces.

Introduction to User Interfaces

The **user interface** (**UI**) has become a key part of our everyday lives, becoming the intermediary between us and our ever-growing number of machines. A UI is designed to facilitate in human-computer interaction. The human needs to operate and control the machine to serve some purpose; meanwhile, the machine needs to simultaneously provide feedback and a means to interact with it in order to aid the human's decision-making process. UIs are everywhere, from the mobile applications on our phones to web browsers, to heavy machinery controls, and even on the appliances in our kitchens. Of course, the ways in which we interact with technology is not merely limited to our hands, as many UIs also allow interaction with our other sensory organs.

A good UI is tasked with helping a person produce a desired result while also allowing for easier, more efficient, and more friendly operation of a machine. Think about the photo editing apps on your phone. Editing the size, color, or exposure is practically effortless as you slide your fingers across the screen and watch the images change almost instantly. The user provides minimal input to achieve the desired output.

What Is a Graphical User Interface?

For this book, we will be focusing on creating desktop **graphical user interfaces** (**GUI**) that take advantage of a computer's graphics capabilities to create visual applications. Decades ago, users would have to use the command line and text commands to interact with the computer. Tasks such as opening, deleting and moving files, and searching through directories were all done by typing in certain commands. However, these were not very user-friendly or simple-to-use interfaces for the general public. So GUIs were created to allow users to interact with electronic devices using graphical controls, rather than command-line interfaces.

These graphical control elements, or **widgets**, such as buttons, menus, and windows, make such tasks effortless. Interaction now becomes as simple as moving your mouse or touching the screen depending upon your device and clicking on the widget.

Concepts for Creating Good Interface Design

This, first and foremost, is a technical book written to help those of you who want to learn how to create and code your own GUI with PyQt and Python. That being said, if you plan to design any kind of UI that other people will use, then you are no longer creating a UI just to solve your own problems. You must also begin to consider other users of the application as well. Think about what you want them to accomplish, or how the application can help them. Sometimes, when we are trying to solve a problem, we get so caught up in trying to create a product that we forget about the people who actually have to interact with them.

The following is a list of concepts to consider when designing your own UI. They are not set rules and by no means a complete list, but rather ideas that you should consider when designing your own applications.

1. Clarity – Using clear language, hierarchy, and flow with visual elements to avoid ambiguity. One of the ways this can be achieved is by considering visual importance to the human eye, laying out widgets with bigger sizes, darker colors, etc., in such a manner that we can visually understand the UI.

2. Conciseness – Simplifying the layout to include only what the user needs to see or interact with at a given time in order to be brief, but also comprehensive. Adding more labels or buttons in your window just to give the user more options is not always better.

3. Consistency – Design the UI so that there is consistency across the application. This helps users to recognize patterns in the visual elements and layout and can be seen in typography that improves the navigation and readability of the application, image styles, or even color schemes.

4. Efficiency – Utilizing good design and shortcuts to help the user improve productivity. If a task can be accomplished in two steps, why design your GUI so that the work has to be completed in five?

5. Familiarity – Consider elements that users normally see in other UIs and how they would expect them to perform in your applications. For example, think about how weird it would be to have to enter your login information, only to find the password entry field is above the username. It is not wrong, but now you are unnecessarily making users think about their actions and slowing them down.

6. Responsive – Give the user feedback, for example, a toggle that changes color to "on" or "off," a small message to notify the user if their input is correct or incorrect, or even a sound effect to verify a completed action. The user should never be left wondering if their action was successful or not.

Creating Your First GUI: An Empty Window

A GUI application generally consists of a main window and possibly one or more dialog boxes. The **main window** is where the user will spend most of their time when using your application and can consist of a menu bar, a status bar, and other widgets. **Dialog boxes** typically are made up of text, maybe one or more widgets for collecting information, and buttons. They appear to the user when necessary to communicate information and prompt them for input. An alert window that pops up asking you if you want to save changes to your document is an example of a dialog. Dialog boxes will be covered further in Chapter 3.

For your first project, seen in Figure 1-1, we'll consider

- How to create an empty window in PyQt6

- The basic classes and modules needed to set up your GUI

- How to modify the main window's size and title

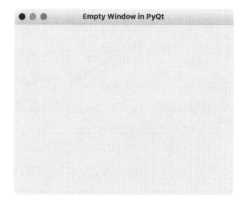

Figure 1-1. *Empty window created with PyQt6*

This application will serve as the foundation for all other programs found in this book.

Explanation for Creating an Empty Window

The code found in Listing 1-1 is all you need to create a window in PyQt6. Examples throughout this book will take advantage of **object-oriented programming** (**OOP**), a programming paradigm that focuses on using classes to create **instances** of those classes, or **objects**, with their own properties and behaviors and modeling the relationships between other objects.

Listing 1-1. Creating an empty window in PyQt

```
# basic_window.py
# Import necessary modules
import sys
from PyQt6.QtWidgets import QApplication, QWidget

class EmptyWindow(QWidget):

    def __init__(self):
        """ Constructor for Empty Window Class """
        super().__init__()
        self.initializeUI()
```

```
    def initializeUI(self):
        """Set up the application."""
        self.setGeometry(200, 100, 400, 300)
        self.setWindowTitle("Empty Window in PyQt")
        self.show() # Display the window on the screen

# Run the program
if __name__ == '__main__':
    app = QApplication(sys.argv)
    window = EmptyWindow()
    sys.exit(app.exec())
```

Your initial window should look similar to the one in Figure 1-1 depending upon your operating system.

Walking through the code, we first start by importing the sys and PyQt6 modules that we need to create a window. The sys module can be used in PyQt to pass command line arguments to our applications and to close them.

The QtWidgets module provides the widget classes that you will need to create desktop-style GUIs. From the QtWidgets module, we import two classes: QApplication and QWidget. You only need to create a single instance of the QApplication class, no matter how many windows or dialog boxes exist in an application. QApplication is responsible for managing the application's main event loop and widget initialization and finalization. The **main event loop** is where user interactions in the GUI window, such as clicking on a button, are managed. Take a quick look at

```
    app = QApplication(sys.argv)
```

QApplication takes as an argument sys.argv. You can also pass in an empty list if you know that your program will not be taking any command line arguments using

```
    app = QApplication([])
```

Tip   Always create your GUI's QApplication object before any other object belonging to the GUI, including the main window. This concept is demonstrated in Listing 1-2.

Next, we create a window object that inherits from the class we created, EmptyWindow. Our class actually inherits from QWidget, which is the base class for which all other user interface objects, such as widgets and windows, are derived.

Tip When creating windows in PyQt, you will generally create a main class that inherits from either QMainWindow, QWidget, or QDialog. You'll find out more about each of these classes and when to use them to create windows and dialog boxes in later chapters.

We need to call the show() method on the window object to display it to the screen. This is located inside the initializeUI() function in our EmptyWindow class. You can see app.exec() being passed as an argument to sys.exit() in the final line of Listing 1-1. The method exec() starts the application's event loop and will remain here until you quit the application. The function sys.exit() ensures a clean exit.

The steps for creating a window are better illustrated in Listing 1-2 using **procedural programming**, a programming paradigm where the computer follows a set of sequential commands to perform a task.

Listing 1-2. Minimum code needed for creating an empty window in PyQt without OOP

```
# procedural.py
# 1. Import necessary modules
import sys # use sys to accept command line arguments
from PyQt6.QtWidgets import QApplication, QWidget

app = QApplication(sys.argv) # 2. Create QApplication object
window = QWidget() # 3. Create window from QWidget object
window.show() # 4. Call show to display GUI window
# 5. Start the event loop. Use sys.exit to close the program
sys.exit(app.exec())
```

The next section demonstrates how to use built-in PyQt methods to change the main window's size and set the window's title.

Modifying the Window

The EmptyWindow class in Listing 1-1 contains a method, initializeUI(), that creates the window based upon the parameters we specify. The initializeUI() function is reproduced in the following code snippet:

```
def initializeUI(self):
    """Initialize the window and display its contents to
    the screen."""
    self.setGeometry(200, 100, 400, 300)
    self.setWindowTitle('Empty Window in PyQt')
    self.show()
```

The method setGeometry() defines the location of the window on your computer screen and its dimensions, width and height. So the window we just created is located at x=200, y=100 in the window and has width=400 and height=300. The setWindowTitle() method is used to set the title of the window. Take a moment to modify the geometry values or title text and see how your changes affect the window. You could also comment out the two methods and see how PyQt uses default parameter settings for both the size and window title.

We will look at further customization of the window's layout in Chapter 4 and appearance in Chapter 6.

Summary

In this chapter, we took a look at getting you set up to build GUIs using PyQt6. Creating user-friendly GUIs is important, and there are a few notions you should keep in mind when designing your applications, such as consistency and clarity, to help users understand your application's purpose and features. Finally, we took a look at the basic classes and methods needed for creating and modifying a simple main window.

In the next chapter, you will learn more about GUI development. You'll find out how to add text and images to GUIs using the widget QLabel while also learning one method for arranging widgets in your windows.

11

CHAPTER 2

Building a Simple GUI

Hello again! GUIs are designed to handle specific tasks, such as writing and editing documents or playing videos. Creating any kind of UI can seem like a formidable task with all the different widgets there are to consider. Widgets are the buttons, checkboxes, sliders, and other components that users use to interact with the GUI.

In order to help you learn about the different kinds of widgets and understand when you might want to use them, each chapter will utilize different widgets and apply them to one or more GUI projects. Whenever a new widget is introduced, you will also apply that component in a smaller practical application before using them in larger GUIs. For some larger applications, we will also discuss the process for designing and arranging the widgets in the application's window.

In this chapter, you will

- Begin learning about widgets in PyQt and find out how to use them in your GUIs

- Consider the design process for a simple GUI application

- Build basic GUIs with primarily the QLabel widget

- See how to organize widgets in a GUI using the move() method

Let's begin by learning about a very fundamental widget.

The QLabel Widget

After learning how to create a window in Chapter 1, we can move forward and add more functionality with widgets. For this chapter, we will focus mainly on using **QLabel** as it is a widget that you will use in almost every GUI you develop. A QLabel object acts as a non-editable placeholder to display plain or rich text, hyperlinks, images, or GIFs. It is also useful for creating labels around other widgets to specify their roles or give them titles.

13

© Joshua M Willman 2022
J. M. Willman, *Beginning PyQt*, https://doi.org/10.1007/978-1-4842-7999-1_2

The GUI you will make, seen in Figure 2-1, demonstrates how to use QLabel to create both text and image labels and will act as your *Hello World* for adding widgets in PyQt.

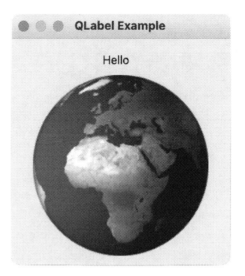

Figure 2-1. *Example of using QLabel widgets to place images and text in a window*

Note   For this and other examples in this chapter, you will need to download the images folder and its contents from the GitHub repository.

Explanation for Using QLabel

Let's begin by using the empty window script you created in Chapter 1 and use it as the foundation for creating Listing 2-1.

Note   As applications in this book grow in complexity, programs will be broken up into more manageable parts and built piece by piece to promote learning and understanding of the code. Many of the programs will start by using the empty window script from Chapter 1 as a starting point. If you get an error because a method or variable is missing while running a section of code, don't fear. Keep coding and following along with each section of code to build the complete application. For example, you will need the code from Listings 2-1 to 2-2 to complete this program.

Listing 2-1. Setting up the main window to show how to use QLabel widgets

```python
# labels.py
# Import necessary modules
import sys
from PyQt6.QtWidgets import QApplication, QWidget, QLabel
from PyQt6.QtGui import QPixmap

class MainWindow(QWidget):

    def __init__(self):
        super().__init__()
        self.initializeUI()

    def initializeUI(self):
        """Set up the application's GUI."""
        self.setGeometry(100, 100, 250, 250)
        self.setWindowTitle("QLabel Example")

        self.setUpMainWindow()
        self.show()

if __name__ == '__main__':
    app = QApplication(sys.argv)
    window = MainWindow()
    sys.exit(app.exec())
```

First, let's import the modules we need. To create the window, we need to import another PyQt class from the QtWidgets module, the QLabel class.

This time we also need to import the QtGui module. The QtGui module handles numerous graphic elements used in GUIs. **QPixmap** is a Qt class that is optimized for showing images on the screen and is useful for displaying an image on a QLabel object.

You'll need to create a `MainWindow` class that inherits from the `QWidget`. If you copied the script from Chapter 1, simply change the name of the `EmptyWindow` class to `MainWindow`. Next, initialize the size of the window with `setGeometry()` and set the title of our GUI using `setWindowTitle()`.

Note   Qt is filled with numerous class methods called **accessors**, also referred to as **getters**, for retrieving values and **mutators**, also called **setters**, for changing values. You have already seen two setter examples. To change the size of a widget or widget, you can use the setter `setGeometry()`. If you wanted to retrieve that value at any time, you could use the getter `geometry()`. Setter and getter methods follow that pattern in PyQt, where setters have the word *set* in the method name, and the getter removes the word *set* and replaces the first letter with a lowercase one.

Next, call the method `setUpMainWindow()`, which is used for not only setting up and arranging the widgets in the main window but for structuring the code as well. This method is created in Listing 2-2. Then we use the `show()` method to display the window. To set up the application, first create a `QApplication` object. Then initiate the `window`. Next, use `exec()` to begin the event loop. Finally, `sys.exit()` is used to handle safely closing the program.

The next thing to do is to create the `MainWindow` method, `setUpMainWindow()`.

Note   Going by PEP 8, the Style Guide for Python Code, function names should be lowercase and separated with an underscore. The guidelines also state that mixedCase is also allowed if that is the prevailing style. This book will use mixedCase for function and method names to follow along with styles used in Qt and PyQt. More information about PEP 8 can be found at `www.python.org/dev/peps/pep-0008/#prescriptive-naming-conventions`.

Listing 2-2. The setUpMainWindow() method for displaying text and image labels

```
# labels.py
    def setUpMainWindow(self):
        """Create QLabel to be displayed in the main window."""
        hello_label = QLabel(self)
        hello_label.setText("Hello")
        hello_label.move(105, 15)

        image = "images/world.png"
        try:
            with open(image):
                world_label = QLabel(self)
                pixmap = QPixmap(image)
                world_label.setPixmap(pixmap)
                world_label.move(25, 40)
        except FileNotFoundError as error:
            print(f"Image not found.\nError: {error}")
```

First, you must create a QLabel object. By passing self as a parameter to QLabel, you set the MainWindow class as the parent of the label. This will be helpful for displaying and arranging the widget in the parent object. Next, specify what the label will say using setText(). Here, the text is set to "Hello". In the following line, we use the move() method to arrange the label in the window.

PyQt has a number of layout techniques, including horizontal layouts, grid layouts, and **absolute positioning**. We'll take an in-depth look at those classes in Chapter 4. For the programs created in this chapter, we will be using absolute positioning with the move() method. With move(), you only need to specify the x and y pixel values of where you want to place the widgets.

Imagine the main window as a graph where its upper-left corner is point (0,0). The x and y values you choose in move() refer to the point where the widget's top-left corner is placed in the main window. For our text label, we specify the values to be x=105 and y=15. This is definitely not the best method for arranging widgets in a window for a number of reasons. For one, it is complicated and involves using trial and error for setting your widget's position. Another reason has to deal with resizing a window. If you were to adjust the size of the window by dragging on the bottom-right corner, you'll notice that the widgets don't move or stretch. Qt's layout classes are great for handling this and other issues. We'll discuss using the layout classes in Chapter 4.

You might think learning using move() is a waste of time, but it can be very useful to understand how to use pixel values to manipulate widgets, especially when we begin dealing with more advanced topics like animations and graphics classes.

The image is loaded in a similar fashion, creating a world_label object to be placed in the main window. Then we construct a QPixmap of the image and use setPixmap() to set the image displayed onto the world_label. The image's absolute location is set using move(). An exception is thrown if the image cannot be found.

Each of PyQt's different classes has their own methods that can be used to customize and change their look and functionality. In the Appendix, you can find a list of the widgets used in this book along with some of the more common methods you are likely to use to modify them.

Once you run the program, you should see a window like Figure 2-1 appear on your screen. In the next section, you'll build a slightly more complex GUI using QLabel widgets.

Project 2.1 – User Profile GUI

A user profile is used to visually display personal data. The data in the profile helps to associate certain characteristics with that user and assists others in learning more about that individual. Depending upon the goal of the application, the information and appearance of the profile will change.

User profiles like the one displayed in Figure 2-2 often have a number of parameters that are either mandatory or optional and allow for some level of customization to fit the preferences of the user, such as a profile image or background colors. Many of them contain similar features, such as the user's name or an "About" section.

Figure 2-2. *The User Profile GUI that displays a user's information*

In the next section, we'll break apart Figure 2-2 and think about how the label widgets will be arranged in the window.

Designing the User Profile GUI

Typical user profile applications often use a combination of different elements, both interactive and static. The schematic in Figure 2-3 focuses on utilizing solely static QLabel widgets for displaying information in the window.

If you compare Figure 2-3 with Figure 2-2, you will notice the similarity with how they are arranged. The user interface can be divided into two parts. The upper portion uses QLabel objects that display a profile image that lies on top of a background image.

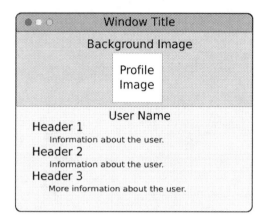

Figure 2-3. *Schematic for the User Profile GUI*

The bottom portion shows the user's information with multiple QLabel widgets, with the textual information arranged vertically and broken down into smaller sections, delineated by the use of different font sizes.

Explanation for the User Profile GUI

Similar to the last application, we'll begin by using the template GUI from Chapter 1 as the foundation for the User Profile's main window in Listing 2-3.

Listing 2-3. Code for setting up the User Profile GUI's main window

```
# user_profile.py
# Import necessary modules
import sys
from PyQt6.QtWidgets import QApplication, QWidget, QLabel
from PyQt6.QtGui import QFont, QPixmap
class MainWindow(QWidget):

    def __init__(self):
        super().__init__()
        self.initializeUI()
```

```
def initializeUI(self):
    """Set up the application's GUI."""
    self.setGeometry(50, 50, 250, 400)
    self.setWindowTitle("2.1 - User Profile GUI")

    self.setUpMainWindow()
    self.show()

# Run program
if __name__ == '__main__':
    app = QApplication(sys.argv)
    window = MainWindow()
    sys.exit(app.exec())
```

For the User Profile GUI, import the same classes and modules as the earlier application along with the addition of one new class, the QFont class from the QtGui module, which allows for us to modify the size and types of fonts in our application. This is perfect for creating the different header sizes.

Before creating setUpMainWindow(), let's create a separate method in MainWindow, seen in Listing 2-4, that will handle loading the different images and creating QLabel objects to display them.

Listing 2-4. Code for createImageLabels() in the User Profile GUI

```
# user_profile.py
    def createImageLabels(self):
        """Open image files and create image labels."""
        images = ["images/skyblue.png",
                    "images/profile_image.png"]

        for image in images:
            try:
                with open(image):
                    label = QLabel(self)
                    pixmap = QPixmap(image)
                    label.setPixmap(pixmap)
```

```
            if image == "images/profile_image.png":
                label.move(80, 20)
        except FileNotFoundError as error:
            print(f"Image not found.\nError: {error}")
```

The images list contains the specific file locations that will be used for both the blue background and the user's profile image in the top part of the window. Using a for loop, iterate through the list's items, create a QLabel object for each, instantiate a QPixmap object, set the pixmap for the label, and if the image is the profile image, center it in the window using move(). Using move() and absolute positioning, you can easily overlap images, but you will need to load the images in order from the bottom-most image to the top-most.

We can now create the MainWindow method setUpMainWindow() in Listing 2-5 where createImageLabels() will be called.

Listing 2-5. Code for the User Profile GUI's setUpMainWindow() method

```
# user_profile.py
    def setUpMainWindow(self):
        """Create the labels to be displayed in the window."""
        self.createImageLabels()

        user_label = QLabel(self)
        user_label.setText("John Doe")
        user_label.setFont(QFont("Arial", 20))
        user_label.move(85, 140)

        bio_label = QLabel(self)
        bio_label.setText("Biography")
        bio_label.setFont(QFont("Arial", 17))
        bio_label.move(15, 170)

        about_label = QLabel(self)
        about_label.setText("I'm a Software Engineer with 10 years\
            experience creating awesome code.")
        about_label.setWordWrap(True)
        about_label.move(15, 190)
```

After the image labels are created, several QLabel objects for showing text are instantiated. For example, the user_label displays the user's name using setText() in the window. You can set a QLabel widget's font with the method setFont(). Be sure to pass a QFont object and specify the type of font and its size. The user_label is then centered in the window using move(). Other labels are created in a similar manner.

Listing 2-6 continues to create and arrange QLabel widgets in the main window.

Listing 2-6. Arranging more labels in the setUpMainWindow() method

```
# user_profile.py
        skills_label = QLabel(self)
        skills_label.setText("Skills")
        skills_label.setFont(QFont("Arial", 17))
        skills_label.move(15, 240)

        languages_label = QLabel(self)
        languages_label.setText("Python  |  PHP  |  SQL  |  JavaScript")
        languages_label.move(15, 260)
```

More labels are created. Notice how the x value in move() stays at 15, leaving a small space on the left side of the window, and the y value gradually increases, placing each subsequent label lower. More labels are added to the GUI in Listing 2-7.

Listing 2-7. Arranging even more labels in the setUpMainWindow() method

```
# user_profile.py
        experience_label = QLabel(self)
        experience_label.setText("Experience")
        experience_label.setFont(QFont("Arial", 17))
        experience_label.move(15, 290)

        developer_label = QLabel(self)
        developer_label.setText("Python Developer")
        developer_label.move(15, 310)

        dev_dates_label = QLabel(self)
        dev_dates_label.setText("Mar 2011 - Present")
        dev_dates_label.setFont(QFont("Arial", 10))
        dev_dates_label.move(15, 330)
```

```
driver_label = QLabel(self)
driver_label.setText("Pizza Delivery Driver")
driver_label.move(15, 350)

driver_dates_label = QLabel(self)
driver_dates_label.setText("Aug 2015 - Dec 2017")
driver_dates_label.setFont(QFont("Arial", 10))
driver_dates_label.move(15, 370)
```

Running the application now, you will see a window appear like the one in Figure 2-2.

Summary

In this chapter, we discovered how to add and arrange widgets in a GUI window. The QLabel widget is a fundamental class and is not only great for displaying text but can also be used with other PyQt classes, such as QPixmap for displaying images or QFont for changing the label's text style or size. Each one of the PyQt classes includes various methods for extending their capabilities and appearance. Examples of those can be found in the Appendix.

In the next chapter, we'll explore a number of different widget classes, including QPushButton and QLineEdit, that will allow users to interact with the applications that you develop.

CHAPTER 3

Adding More Functionality with Widgets

What good is a user interface if it isn't interactive? This chapter is all about learning how to use widgets to make responsive user interfaces that react to a user's interaction, handle different events, and relay important information back to the user. We will take a look at a few common widgets and see how to use them to design and build GUI applications.

In this chapter, you will

- Be introduced to event handling and Qt's signals and slots mechanism

- Build GUIs using new widget classes, including `QPushButton`, `QLineEdit`, `QCheckBox`, and `QMessageBox`

- Learn about useful methods for aligning text and adjusting widget sizes

- Discover more about windows and dialog boxes and see how to create classes that inherit from `QDialog`

- Create an application that teaches how to handle multiple windows

Before jumping into any code, let's learn a little about event handling in PyQt.

Event Handlers and Signals and Slots

GUIs are **event driven**, meaning that they respond to events that are created by the user, from a keyboard or a mouse, or by events caused by the system, such as a timer or when connecting to Bluetooth. In Qt, special kinds of events are even generated to handle

25

© Joshua M Willman 2022
J. M. Willman, *Beginning PyQt*, https://doi.org/10.1007/978-1-4842-7999-1_3

communication between widgets. No matter how they are generated, the application needs to listen for those events and respond to them appropriately. This is known as **event handling**. When exec() is called, the application begins listening for events until the program is closed.

In PyQt, event handling is handled in one of two ways – either through event handlers or with signals and slots. **Event handlers** take care of events. There are different types of events that can be handled, such as paintEvent() for repainting the look of a widget or keyPressEvent() that handles key presses. In Qt, events are objects created from the QEvent class.

The communication between objects in Qt, such as widgets, is handled by signals and slots. **Signals** are generated whenever an event occurs, such as when a button is clicked or a checkbox is toggled on or off. Those signals then need to be handled in some way. **Slots** are the methods that are connected to an event and executed in response to the signal. Slots can either be built-in PyQt functions or Python functions that you create yourself.

Each PyQt class has its own assortment of signals, and many of them are inherited from parent classes. Let's look at an example. Whenever a user clicks a button in the window, that button click will send out, or **emit**, a signal:

```
button.clicked.connect(self.buttonClicked)
```

Here, button is a widget, and clicked is the signal. In order to make use of that signal, we must use connect() to call some function, which in this case is buttonClicked(), which is the slot. The buttonClicked() method could then perform some action, such as opening a new window. Many signals also pass along additional information to the slot, such as a Boolean value that tells whether or not the button was pressed.

Signals and slots, and even making custom signals, will be covered in Chapter 7. For now, let's take a look at a widget that is perfect for demonstrating signals and slots.

The QPushButton Widget

The **QPushButton** widget can be used to perform actions and make choices. When you click on the QPushButton widget, it sends out a signal that can be connected to a function. While you might typically encounter buttons with text that say OK, Next, Cancel, Close, Yes, or No, you can also create your own buttons with descriptive text or icons.

Note   There are different kinds of button classes with different usages, such as `QToolButton` for selecting items in toolbars and `QRadioButton` for creating groups of buttons where only a single selection can be made.

In this first example, you are going to set up a `QPushButton` that, when clicked, uses signals and slots to change the text of a `QLabel` widget and shows how to handle closing an application's main window.

Let's take a look at how to build the GUI.

Explanation for Using QPushButton

Open a new file and copy the code from the empty window script from Chapter 1 into it. As you can see in Listing 3-1, you'll need to import a few more classes, including the `QPushButton` class from `QtWidgets`. The `QtCore` module contains a bunch of non-GUI-related classes. The `Qt` class refers to the **Qt Namespace**, which contains many identifiers used for setting the properties of widgets and other classes.

Listing 3-1. Setting up the main window for using QPushButton widgets

```python
# buttons.py
# Import necessary modules
import sys
from PyQt6.QtWidgets import (QApplication, QWidget, QLabel,
    QPushButton)
from PyQt6.QtCore import Qt

class MainWindow(QWidget):

    def __init__(self):
        super().__init__()
        self.initializeUI()
```

```python
    def initializeUI(self):
        """Set up the application's GUI."""
        self.setGeometry(100, 100, 250, 150)
        self.setWindowTitle("QPushButton Example")

        self.setUpMainWindow()
        self.show()

if __name__ == '__main__':
    app = QApplication(sys.argv)
    window = MainWindow()
    sys.exit(app.exec())
```

Be sure to set the main window's starting x and y positions and size using setGeometry(). Then set the window's title and call the setUpMainWindow() method which we'll create in Listing 3-2.

Listing 3-2. The setUpMainWindow() method for using buttons

```python
# buttons.py
    def setUpMainWindow(self):
        """Create and arrange widgets in the main window."""
        self.times_pressed = 0

        self.name_label = QLabel(
            "Don't push the button.", self)
        self.name_label.setAlignment(
            Qt.AlignmentFlag.AlignCenter)
        self.name_label.move(60, 30)

        self.button = QPushButton("Push Me", self)
        self.button.move(80, 70)
        self.button.clicked.connect(self.buttonClicked)
```

The variable times_pressed will be used to keep track of how many times button is pressed. The window for this application only contains a QLabel and a QPushButton. Rather than using setText() to assign the text for name_label, we can instead pass the text we want to display as the first argument when instantiating the QLabel object.

It is possible to align the contents of widgets that display text. To do so, use setAlignment(), and because we're using PyQt6, be sure to pass the full enum type, Qt. AlignmentFlag. There are different kinds of alignment flags, some of which are

- AlignLeft – Aligns text to the left edge

- AlignRight – Aligns text to the right edge

- AlignHCenter and AlignVCenter – Centers text horizontally and vertically, respectively

- AlignTop and AlignBottom – Aligns text to the top and bottom, respectively

Here, let's use AlignCenter, which is a combination of AlignVCenter and AlignHCenter. Use move() to set the absolute position of the widget.

Note   Instead of using setters, many of the properties for widgets can be set by passing them as arguments to a widget instance. For example, rather than using setAlignment(), you could set the alignment for the label by passing the keyword argument alignment=Qt.AlignmentFlag.AlignCenter after self.

Next, create the QPushButton object, and pass the button's text and self, a reference to the MainWindow class, as arguments. Clicking on the button will emit the clicked signal, which is connected to the buttonClicked() slot (shown in Listing 3-3).

Listing 3-3. Code for the buttonClicked() slot

```python
# buttons.py
    def buttonClicked(self):
        """Handle when the button is clicked.
        Demonstrates how to change text for widgets,
        update their sizes and locations, and how to
        close the window due to events."""
        self.times_pressed += 1

        if self.times_pressed == 1:
            self.name_label.setText("Why'd you press me?")
        if self.times_pressed == 2:
```

```
            self.name_label.setText("I'm warning you.")
            self.button.setText("Feelin' Lucky?")
            self.button.adjustSize()
            self.button.move(70, 70)
        if self.times_pressed == 3:
            print("The window has been closed.")
            self.close()
```

In buttonClicked(), we'll first update the variable times_pressed. Next, there are a series of if statements that depend upon the value of times_pressed. You can update text values for widgets even after they have been created. If times_pressed equals 1, change the text for name_label using setText().

For a value of 2, change the text for both name_label and button. For button, you will also need to adjust its size to fit the longer text value. Since QPushButton inherits QWidget, we can use the QWidget method adjustSize() to change the size of name_label in order to fit the longer text. Since absolute positioning is being used to arrange widgets, you'll also need to use move() to center button in the window. You can see examples of the text changing in Figure 3-1.

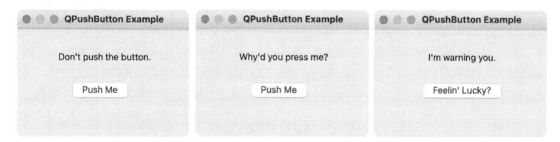

Figure 3-1. *Clicking on the QPushButton will change the label's text and, eventually, the button's text*

Finally, for 3, the QWidget method close() is used to close widgets. In this case, self.close() is referring to the main window and closes the application. We'll look more at closing events later in the "Project 3.1 – Login GUI and Registration Dialog" section.

Next, we'll look at a widget that is useful for collecting user input.

The QLineEdit Widget

It is often necessary for a user to input a single line of text, such as a username or a password. With the **QLineEdit** widget, you can collect data from someone. QLineEdit also supports normal text editing functions such as cut, copy, and paste, and redo or undo. There are also additional capabilities for hiding text when it is entered, using placeholder text, or even setting a limit on the length of the text.

Tip   If you need multiple lines for a user to enter text, use the QTextEdit widget instead.

The GUI you will build in Figure 3-2 demonstrates how to set up and use QLineEdit widgets. You can use other widgets, such as QPushButton, along with signals and slots to retrieve the text in a QLineEdit object or clear its text.

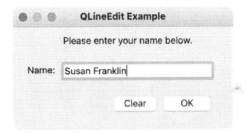

Figure 3-2. *QLineEdit and QPushButton widgets used for collecting and clearing text*

In the next section, you'll find out how to use QLineEdit.

Explanation for Using QLineEdit

Listing 3-4 sets up the main window seen in Figure 3-2. You'll need to import different widget classes, including QLabel, QLineEdit, and QPushButton, as well as Qt from the QtCore module into the empty window script from Chapter 1.

Listing 3-4. Setting up the main window for using QLineEdit widgets

```python
# line_edits.py
# Import necessary modules
import sys
from PyQt6.QtWidgets import (QApplication, QWidget,
    QLabel, QLineEdit, QPushButton)
from PyQt6.QtCore import Qt

class MainWindow(QWidget):

    def __init__(self):
        super().__init__()
        self.initializeUI()

    def initializeUI(self):
        """Set up the application's GUI."""
        self.setMaximumSize(310, 130)
        self.setWindowTitle("QLineEdit Example")

        self.setUpMainWindow()
        self.show()

if __name__ == '__main__':
    app = QApplication(sys.argv)
    window = MainWindow()
    sys.exit(app.exec())
```

Previous examples have used setGeometry() for setting the location and size of a window on the screen. One thing you can do is restrict the size of the window. Here, let's use the QWidget method setMaximumSize() and pass the maximum width and height for MainWindow. Some other methods for setting window sizes include the following:

- setMinimumSize() – Sets the widget's minimum size

- setMinimumHeight() and setMinimumWidth() – Sets the widget's minimum height and width, respectively

- setMaximumHeight() and setMaximumWidth() – Sets the widget's maximum height and width, respectively

- setFixedSize() – Sets the maximum and minimum sizes for the widget, preventing it from changing sizes

Tip   These methods are useful for not only setting the size constraints of windows but for widget objects as well, since they all inherit `QWidget`.

To set up the widgets in the `setUpMainWindow()` method in Listing 3-5, we'll first create two `QLabel` objects, then a `QLineEdit` widget, and two `QPushButton` objects.

Listing 3-5. The setUpMainWindow() method for using line editing widgets

```python
# line_edits.py
    def setUpMainWindow(self):
        """Create and arrange widgets in the main window."""
        QLabel("Please enter your name below.",
                self).move(70, 10)
        name_label = QLabel("Name:", self)
        name_label.move(20, 50)

        self.name_edit = QLineEdit(self)
        self.name_edit.resize(210, 20)
        self.name_edit.move(70, 50)

        clear_button = QPushButton("Clear", self)
        clear_button.move(140, 90)
        clear_button.clicked.connect(self.clearText)

        accept_button = QPushButton("OK", self)
        accept_button.move(210, 90)
        accept_button.clicked.connect(self.acceptText)
```

The two `QLabel` objects are just examples of creating widgets. You can create widgets and arrange them within your GUI without having to assign them to a variable.

The `QLineEdit` object, name_edit, is an example of how to modify a widget's size using the `resize()` method. You'll need to specify the widget's desired height and width values.

The clear_button and accept_button objects are connected to the `clearText()` and `acceptText()` slots, created in Listing 3-6.

Listing 3-6. Code for clearText() and acceptText() slots

```python
# line_edits.py
    def clearText(self):
        """Clear the QLineEdit input field."""
        self.name_edit.clear()

    def acceptText(self):
        """Accept the user's input in the QLineEdit
        widget and close the program."""
        print(self.name_edit.text())
        self.close()
```

When `clear_button` is clicked, it emits a signal that is connected to the `clearText()` slot, and the `name_edit` widget will react to the signal and clear its current text. If the user clicks `accept_button`, the text in `name_edit` is read using the getter `text()` and printed in your computer's shell. The application then closes.

Let's take a look at another commonly found widget in desktop applications.

The QCheckBox Widget

The **QCheckBox** widget is a selectable button that generally has two states: on and off. This makes them perfect for representing features in your GUI that can either be enabled or disabled, or for selecting from a list of options like in a survey.

The application in Figure 3-3 shows a basic questionnaire GUI. The user is allowed to select all checkboxes that apply to them, and each time the user clicks a checkbox, we call a method to show how to determine the widget's current state.

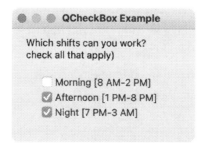

Figure 3-3. *Example that uses QCheckBox widgets*

Note   The checkboxes in QCheckBox are not **mutually exclusive**, meaning you can select more than one checkbox at a time. To make them mutually exclusive, add the checkboxes to a QButtonGroup object or consider using QRadioButton.

The QCheckBox class can also be used in dynamic applications, where a series of checkbox widgets could be used to select or change a GUI's text, appearance, or even state (by enabling or disabling interactivity).

Explanation for Using QCheckBox

Begin creating the MainWindow class like before by using the empty window script from Chapter 1 as a template. For this application, import QCheckBox and other classes shown in Listing 3-7.

Listing 3-7. Setting up the main window for using QCheckBox widgets

```
# checkboxes.py
# Import necessary modules
import sys
from PyQt6.QtWidgets import (QApplication, QWidget, QCheckBox,
    QLabel)
from PyQt6.QtCore import Qt

class MainWindow(QWidget):

    def __init__(self):
        super().__init__()
        self.initializeUI()

    def initializeUI(self):
        """Set up the application's GUI."""
        self.setGeometry(100, 100, 250, 150)
        self.setWindowTitle("QCheckBox Example")

        self.setUpMainWindow()
        self.show()
```

```
if __name__ == '__main__':
    app = QApplication(sys.argv)
    window = MainWindow()
    sys.exit(app.exec())
```

In Listing 3-8, we set up the method for arranging widgets in the window.

Listing 3-8. The setUpMainWindow() method for using checkboxes

```
# checkboxes.py
    def setUpMainWindow(self):
        """Create and arrange widgets in the main window."""
        header_label = QLabel("Which shifts can you work? \
                        (Please check all that apply)", self)
        header_label.setWordWrap(True)
        header_label.move(20, 10)

        # Set up the checkboxes
        morning_cb = QCheckBox("Morning [8 AM-2 PM]", self)
        morning_cb.move(40, 60)
        #morning_cb.toggle() # Uncomment to start checked
        morning_cb.toggled.connect(self.printSelected)

        after_cb = QCheckBox("Afternoon [1 PM-8 PM]", self)
        after_cb.move(40, 80)
        after_cb.toggled.connect(self.printSelected)

        night_cb = QCheckBox("Night [7 PM-3 AM]", self)
        night_cb.move(40, 100)
        night_cb.toggled.connect(self.printSelected)
```

A QLabel widget is used to display a question to the user, helping the user to understand the purpose of the GUI. For labels with longer text that won't fit on one line, use the setWordWrap() method.

Three QCheckBox objects are also created, each with a variable name that is representative of the widget's purpose. The text displayed next to each checkbox is passed as the first argument. The QCheckBox method toggle() can be used to toggle the checkbox on or off. When a checkbox is selected, rather than using the clicked signal like with QPushButton, use toggled to emit a signal that is connected to the slot printSelected(), shown in Listing 3-9.

Tip   It is possible to connect multiple signals to the same slot.

Listing 3-9. Code for the printSelected() slot

```
# checkboxes.py
    def printSelected(self, checked):
        """Print the text of a QCheckBox object when selected
        or deselected. Use sender() to determine which widget
        is sending the signal."""
        sender = self.sender()
        if checked:
            print(f"{sender.text()} Selected.")
        else:
            print(f"{sender.text()} Deselected.")
```

The toggled() signal also passes along additional information, checked, which returns True if the checkbox is selected. Otherwise, it returns False.

With so many widgets connected to the same slot, it can be hard to determine which widget is being interacted with and emitting the signal. Thankfully, the QObject method sender() returns which object (the widget) is sending the signal. (All widgets inherit the QObject class.) For this example, use the getter text() to get the checkbox object's text and print its value in the shell. An example of the output to the terminal can be seen in Figure 3-4.

```
            MacBook-Pro-3 Chapter03 % python3 checkboxes.py
Afternoon [1 PM-8 PM] Selected.
Night [7 PM-3 AM] Selected.
Afternoon [1 PM-8 PM] Deselected.
Night [7 PM-3 AM] Deselected.
Afternoon [1 PM-8 PM] Selected.
Night [7 PM-3 AM] Selected.
```

Figure 3-4. *Output to the shell when the different checkboxes are selected or deselected*

Let's take a look at one more very important class for creating interactive and user-friendly GUIs.

The QMessageBox Dialog

When a user closes an application or saves their work, or an error occurs, they will typically see a dialog box pop up and display some sort of key information. The user can then interact with that dialog box, often by clicking a button to respond to the prompt. Dialog boxes are a very important form of **feedback**, or methods of monitoring and communicating changes back to the user.

The **QMessageBox** class can be used to not only alert the user to a situation but also to decide how to handle the matter. For example, when closing a document you just modified, you might get a dialog box with buttons asking you to Save, Don't Save, or Cancel. Four common types of predefined QMessageBox widgets in PyQt are shown in Table 3-1.

Table 3-1. *Four types of static QMessageBox dialogs in PyQt. Images from* `www.riverbankcomputing.com`

QMessageBox Icons	Types	Details
	Question	Ask the user a question
	Information	Display information during general operations
	Warning	Report noncritical errors
	Critical	Report critical errors

Windows vs. Dialogs

Applications will typically consist of one main window. A **window** is used to visually separate applications from each other and generally consists of menus, a toolbar, and other kinds of widgets that can often act as the main interface for a GUI application. Windows in Qt are typically considered widgets that appear on the screen and don't have a parent widget.

A **dialog box**, or simply **dialog**, pops up and displays options or information while a user is working in the main window. Most kinds of dialog boxes will have a parent window that will be used to determine the position of the dialog with respect to its owner. This also means that communication occurs between the window and the dialog box and dialogs can be used to update the main window.

There are two kinds of dialog boxes. **Modal dialogs** block user interaction from the rest of the program until the dialog box is closed. **Modeless dialogs** allow the user to interact with both the dialog and the rest of the application.

Explanation for Using QMessageBox

The QMessageBox class produces a modal dialog box, and in the following example, we will take a look at how to use three of the predefined QMessageBox message types: question, information, and warning.

Note   For this example, you will also need the authors.txt file found in the files folder of this chapter's repository on GitHub.

This application's main window can be seen in Figure 3-5, and a couple of QMessageBox dialogs are shown in Figure 3-6.

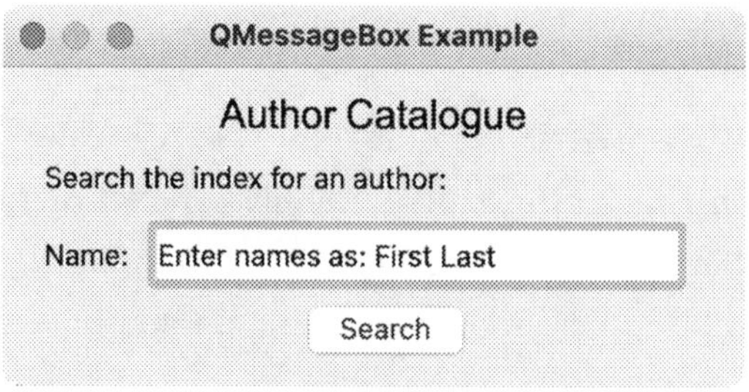

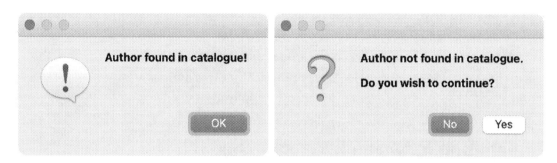

Figure 3-5. *Main window for the QMessageBox example where the user can search for an author's name in a text file*

Figure 3-6. *Information dialog (left) that lets the user know that their search was successful. Question dialog (right) that asks if the user wants to continue searching if the author wasn't found*

For Listing 3-10, you will need to import a few additional classes, including the QMessageBox class from QtWidgets, into the empty window script from Chapter 1.

Listing 3-10. Setting up the main window for using QMessageBox dialogs

```python
# message_boxes.py
# Import necessary modules
import sys
from PyQt6.QtWidgets import (QApplication, QWidget, QLabel,
    QMessageBox, QLineEdit, QPushButton)
from PyQt6.QtGui import QFont

class MainWindow(QWidget):

    def __init__(self):
        super().__init__()
        self.initializeUI()
```

```python
def initializeUI(self):
    """Set up the application's GUI."""
    self.setGeometry(100, 100, 340, 140)
    self.setWindowTitle("QMessageBox Example")

    self.setUpMainWindow()
    self.show()

if __name__ == '__main__':
    app = QApplication(sys.argv)
    window = MainWindow()
    sys.exit(app.exec())
```

To build the window seen in Figure 3-5, you'll need to create a few QLabel objects, a QLineEdit widget for the user to enter an author's name, and a QPushButton object that emits a signal when pressed and searches for the text in a text file. This is all handled in Listing 3-11.

Listing 3-11. The setUpMainWindow() method for using message boxes

```python
# message_boxes.py
    def setUpMainWindow(self):
        """Create and arrange widgets in the main window."""
        catalogue_label = QLabel("Author Catalogue", self)
        catalogue_label.move(100, 10)
        catalogue_label.setFont(QFont("Arial", 18))

        search_label = QLabel(
            "Search the index for an author:", self)
        search_label.move(20, 40)

        # Create author QLabel and QLineEdit widgets
        author_label = QLabel("Name:", self)
        author_label.move(20, 74)

        self.author_edit = QLineEdit(self)
        self.author_edit.move(70, 70)
        self.author_edit.resize(240, 24)
        self.author_edit.setPlaceholderText(
            "Enter names as: First Last")
```

```
# Create the search QPushButton
search_button = QPushButton("Search", self)
search_button.move(140, 100)
search_button.clicked.connect(self.searchAuthors)
```

The widgets catalogue_label and search_label are used to convey information to the user. In PyQt, QLabel widgets are often placed next to QLineEdit and other input widgets as tags. The labels can then be linked to the input widgets as **buddies**. Here, the author_label and author_edit are simply placed next to each other.

Placeholder text can be used to give the user extra information about a QLineEdit widget's purpose or for how to format input text. This is done with setPlaceholderText(). An example of this is seen in Figure 3-5.

Lastly, search_button emits a signal that calls the slot searchAuthors() in Listings 3-12 and 3-13.

Listing 3-12. First part of the code for the searchAuthors() slot

```
# message_boxes.py
    def searchAuthors(self):
        """Search through a catalogue of names.
        If a name is found, display the Author Found dialog.
        Otherwise, display Author Not Found dialog."""
        file = "files/authors.txt"

        try:
            with open(file, "r") as f:
                authors = [line.rstrip("\n") for line in f]

            # Check for name in authors list
            if self.author_edit.text() in authors:
                QMessageBox.information(self, "Author Found",
                    "Author found in catalogue!",
                    QMessageBox.StandardButton.Ok)
```

When the user clicks on search_button, the program will try to open the authors.
txt file and store its contents in the authors list. If the user enters a name in author_
edit that is contained in the authors.txt file, an information dialog appears like the
first image in Figure 3-6.

To create a QMessageBox dialog from one of the predefined types, first, create a
QMessageBox object and call one of the static functions, in this case, information. Next,
pass the parent widget. Then set the dialog's title, "Author Found", and the text that will
appear inside the dialog that provides feedback, possibly with information about actions
a user could take. This is followed by the types of standard buttons that will appear in the
dialog. Multiple buttons can be used and separated with a pipe key, |. Standard buttons
include Open, Save, Cancel, Reset, Yes, and No. The Appendix lists other QMessageBox.
StandardButton types.

Note On macOS, when a message box appears, the title is generally ignored due
to macOS Guidelines. If you are using an Apple computer and don't see a title in
the dialog boxes, don't fear! You haven't done anything wrong.

Listing 3-13. Second part of the code for the searchAuthors() slot

```python
# message_boxes.py
        else:
            answer = QMessageBox.question(self,
                "Author Not Found",
                """<p>Author not found in catalogue.</p>
                <p>Do you wish to continue?</p>""",
                QMessageBox.StandardButton.Yes | \
                QMessageBox.StandardButton.No,
                QMessageBox.StandardButton.No)

        if answer == QMessageBox.StandardButton.No:
            print("Closing application.")
            self.close()
    except FileNotFoundError as error:
        QMessageBox.warning(self, "Error",
            f"""<p>File not found.</p>
```

```
        <p>Error: {error}</p>
        Closing application.""",
        QMessageBox.StandardButton.Ok)
    self.close()
```

If the author is not found, a `question` dialog (second image in Figure 3-6) appears asking the user if they want to search again or quit the program. The standard buttons Yes and No appear in the window. The final argument is used to specify which button you want to highlight in the dialog and set as the default button.

Note   PyQt text widgets are able to display rich text using a subset of the **HyperText Markup Language** (**HTML**) and **Cascading Style Sheets** (**CSS**). This topic is explored more in Chapter 6, but for now, we'll use HTML to arrange the text that is placed between the HTML tags `<p>` and `</p>` into paragraphs.

If an error occurs and the file is not found, the `warning` dialog in Figure 3-7 appears.

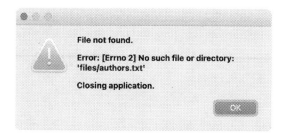

Figure 3-7. *Warning dialog that informs the user that the authors.txt file was not found*

With everything you have learned up to this point, it is a good time to practice creating a larger project.

Project 3.1 – Login GUI and Registration Dialog

A login user interface is probably one of the most common interfaces you interact with on a regular basis – signing into your computer, your online bank account, or your email or social media accounts; logging into your phone; or even signing up for some new app. The login interface is everywhere.

For this example, you will create three different windows. The first window that will appear is the login GUI in Figure 3-8.

Figure 3-8. *The Login window*

This project also demonstrates how to open and close other windows and dialogs and begins looking at how to use event handlers. The first time someone uses your applications, you may want them to sign up and create their own username and password. The Registration dialog in Figure 3-9 appears when a user clicks the Sign Up button in Figure 3-8.

Figure 3-9. *The Registration dialog for creating a new user*

If a user successfully logs in, they will be greeted to the window in Figure 3-10 that simply displays a QLabel widget with the image of a kingfisher.

Figure 3-10. *The application's main window that appears if a user successfully logs in. The image of the kingfisher is from* https://pixabay.com

The next section discusses the different windows, widgets, and their functionalities in this application.

Designing the Login GUI and Registration Dialog

When designing a login interface, you want to create a GUI that clearly labels its widgets, differentiates between the login and signup fields, and helps users to better navigate through potential errors, such as if caps lock is on or if the username is incorrect. While the look and layout of the login GUI may change between platforms, they generally have a few key components that are common throughout, such as

- Username and password entry fields

- Checkboxes that may remember the user's login information or reveal the password when checked

- Buttons that users can click to log in or even register new accounts

For the Login window in Figure 3-8, two separate QLineEdit widgets are used for users to enter their username and password. Under the password QLineEdit widget, there is a checkbox to toggle if the password is hidden or not. There are also two QPushButton widgets: one that the user can click to log in and the other to register a new account.

When the user clicks the Login button, a signal is emitted. The connected slot is used to check if input is correct. QMessageBox dialogs are used to provide feedback if the user exists or does not exist, or as an error message if the users.txt file does not exist. If a successful login does occur, then the main window in Figure 3-10 will appear. You can find users.txt in the files folder of this chapter's GitHub repository.

If a user wants to register a new account, they can click the Sign Up button in the Login window and the *modal* dialog in Figure 3-9 appears. The user cannot interact with the Login window unless the Registration dialog is closed.

Finally, this example also demonstrates how to handle the event when the user closes the window. Rather than just closing the application with close(), you will see how to use the event handler closeEvent() to customize how your programs can close.

The Login GUI is what the user first sees, so let's begin there.

Explanation for Creating the Login GUI

The widgets and concepts learned throughout Chapters 1, 2, and 3 will be applied in this project. Listing 3-14 starts the project by using the empty window script from Chapter 1 to begin building the LoginWindow class. Go ahead and import many of the widget and other classes you have seen before as well as the NewUserDialog class you'll create later in the "Explanation for Creating the Registration Dialog" section.

Listing 3-14. Setting up the window for the Login GUI

```
# login_gui.py
# Import necessary modules
import sys
from PyQt6.QtWidgets import (QApplication, QWidget, QLabel,
    QLineEdit, QPushButton, QCheckBox, QMessageBox)
from PyQt6.QtGui import QFont, QPixmap
from PyQt6.QtCore import Qt
from registration import NewUserDialog

class LoginWindow(QWidget):

    def __init__(self):
        super().__init__()
        self.initializeUI()
```

```python
    def initializeUI(self):
        """Set up the application's GUI."""
        self.setFixedSize(360, 220)
        self.setWindowTitle("3.1 - Login GUI")

        self.setUpWindow()
        self.show()

if __name__ == '__main__':
    app = QApplication(sys.argv)
    window = LoginWindow()
    sys.exit(app.exec())
```

The LoginWindow class is not this application's main window. The class could inherit the QDialog class, the base class for creating dialogs, but we don't need to worry about window modality here, so simply inheriting QWidget will work. Also, setFixedSize() is used to stop the window from growing or shrinking.

Listing 3-15 begins setting up the setUpWindow() method for the LoginWindow class.

Listing 3-15. First part of the setUpWindow() method for the Login GUI

```python
# login_gui.py
    def setUpWindow(self):
        """Create and arrange widgets in the main window."""
        self.login_is_successful = False

        login_label = QLabel("Login", self)
        login_label.setFont(QFont("Arial", 20))
        login_label.move(160, 10)

        # Create widgets for username and password
        username_label = QLabel("Username:", self)
        username_label.move(20, 54)

        self.username_edit = QLineEdit(self)
        self.username_edit.resize(250, 24)
        self.username_edit.move(90, 50)
```

```
password_label = QLabel("Password:", self)
password_label.move(20, 86)

self.password_edit = QLineEdit(self)
self.password_edit.setEchoMode(
    QLineEdit.EchoMode.Password)
self.password_edit.resize(250, 24)
self.password_edit.move(90, 82)
```

The login_is_successful variable keeps track of whether or not the user has logged in. A couple of QLabel and QLineEdit input widgets are created for entering a username and a password. The widgets are then arranged side by side. The setEchoMode() method provided by QLineEdit is very useful for hiding text as it is being input. The Password flag is used here to mask characters while entering the password. Listing 3-16 continues creating and arranging widgets in LoginWindow.

Listing 3-16. Second part of the setUpWindow() method for the Login GUI

```
# login_gui.py
        # Create QCheckBox for displaying password
        self.show_password_cb = QCheckBox(
            "Show Password", self)
        self.show_password_cb.move(90, 110)
        self.show_password_cb.toggled.connect(
            self.displayPasswordIfChecked)

        # Create QPushButton for signing in
        login_button = QPushButton("Login", self)
        login_button.resize(320, 34)
        login_button.move(20, 140)
        login_button.clicked.connect(self.clickLoginButton)

        # Create sign up QLabel and QPushButton
        not_member_label = QLabel("Not a member?", self)
        not_member_label.move(20, 186)

        sign_up_button = QPushButton("Sign Up", self)
        sign_up_button.move(120, 180)
        sign_up_button.clicked.connect(self.createNewUser)
```

Create a QCheckBox called show_password_cb that, when toggled, will emit a signal that calls the displayPasswordIfChecked() slot. The login_button uses the clicked signal to call the clickLoginButton() slot. The sign_up_button opens up a dialog to register new users and calls the createNewUser() slot when clicked.

The next step is to create the various slots. We'll start in Listing 3-17 with clickLoginButton() used by login_button.

Listing 3-17. First part of the clickLoginButton() slot

```
# login_gui.py
    def clickLoginButton(self):
        """Check if username and password match any existing
        entries in users.txt.
        If found, show QMessageBox and close the program.
        If they don't, display a warning QMessageBox."""
        users = {} # Dictionary to store user information
        file = "files/users.txt"

        try:
            with open(file, "r") as f:
                for line in f:
                    user_info = line.split(" ")
                    username_info = user_info[0]
                    password_info = user_info[1].strip("\n")
                    users[username_info] = password_info

            # Collect user and password information
            username = self.username_edit.text()
            password = self.password_edit.text()
```

This method, which is continued in Listing 3-18, first checks to see if the users.txt file exists. If it does, the user's information is collected from the file, and username_info and password_info values are added to the users dictionary. Next, the text values for username_edit and password_edit are collected using text().

Listing 3-18. Second part of the clickLoginButton() slot

```python
# login_gui.py
            if (username, password) in users.items():
                QMessageBox.information(self,
                    "Login Successful!",
                    "Login Successful!",
                    QMessageBox.StandardButton.Ok,
                    QMessageBox.StandardButton.Ok)
                self.login_is_successful = True
                self.close() # Close the login window
                self.openApplicationWindow()
            else:
                QMessageBox.warning(self, "Error Message",
                    "The username or password is incorrect.",
                    QMessageBox.StandardButton.Close,
                    QMessageBox.StandardButton.Close)
        except FileNotFoundError as error:
            QMessageBox.warning(self, "Error",
                f"""<p>File not found.</p>
                <p>Error: {error}</p>""",
                QMessageBox.StandardButton.Ok)
            # Create file if it doesn't exist
            f = open(file, "w")
```

The Python `dict` method `items()` returns a list of key-value pairs as tuples that can be used to check for a matching `username-password` pair in `users`.

If a match is found, the top `QMessageBox` in Figure 3-11 pops up. Then `login_is_successful` is set to `True`, and the current window closes. The example's main window appears by calling `openApplicationWindow()`, which is created in the "Explanation for Creating the Main Window" section. It is worth noting that `close()` does not actually close the window like you may think. The window is merely hidden from view. This is explored further in the "Using Event Handlers to Close a Window" subsection.

Figure 3-11. *The information dialog (top) that informs the user that their input was correct. The warning dialog (bottom) that informs the user of an error*

Otherwise, a warning QMessageBox, the bottom image in Figure 3-11, is displayed if the username or password is incorrect.

The following subsections finish creating the LoginWindow class.

Hiding Input for QLineEdit

The toggled signal used by show_password_cb in Listing 3-16 is connected to the displayPasswordIfChecked() slot in Listing 3-19.

Listing 3-19. Code for the displayPasswordIfChecked() slot

```
# login_gui.py
    def displayPasswordIfChecked(self, checked):
        """If QCheckButton is enabled, view the password.
        Else, mask the password so others can not see it."""
        if checked:
            self.password_edit.setEchoMode(
                QLineEdit.EchoMode.Normal)
        elif checked == False:
            self.password_edit.setEchoMode(
                QLineEdit.EchoMode.Password)
```

If show_password_cb is checked, then the password's characters can be seen using setEchoMode() and passing the enum QLineEdit.EchoMode with the Normal flag. Otherwise, if unchecked, the password's text is masked so others cannot see the characters. An example of this can be seen in Figure 3-8. Flags also exist for hiding the password completely, NoEcho, and for displaying only the character being entered and masking others, PasswordEchoOnEdit.

How to Open a New Window or Dialog

It is possible to have multiple windows and dialogs open at the same time in PyQt. Opening a QMessageBox is relatively easy – simply create a QMessageBox instance when needed. However, for custom dialogs and windows, you will also need to call a method to display them.

The sign_up_button, when clicked, emits a signal that is connected to the createNewUser() method seen in Listing 3-20.

Listing 3-20. Code for the createNewUser() slot and openApplicationWindow() method

```
# login_gui.py
    def createNewUser(self):
        """Open a dialog for creating a new account."""
        self.create_new_user_window = NewUserDialog()
        self.create_new_user_window.show()

    def openApplicationWindow(self):
        """Open a mock main window after the user logs in."""
        self.main_window = MainWindow()
        self.main_window.show()
```

In createNewUser(), create an instance of NewUserDialog from the registration module. To display the modal dialog, call show(). Take a look at the "Explanation for Creating the Registration Dialog" section for creating the class. It is a similar pattern for opening the main window after the user logs in.

Using Event Handlers to Close a Window

A good practice when quitting a program is to present a dialog box, like the one in Figure 3-12, confirming whether the user really wants to quit or not. In most programs, this will prevent the user from forgetting to save their latest work.

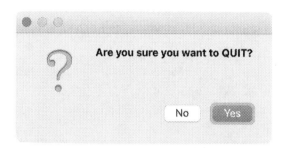

Figure 3-12. *QMessageBox that appears before quitting the application*

When an event occurs, an event object is created depending upon the type of event, and that object is passed to the appropriate object, such as a widget. Event handlers are then used to take care of the event if accepted. Otherwise, the event can be ignored.

When a QWidget is closed in PyQt, a QCloseEvent object is generated. However, widgets and windows are not actually closed. Rather, they are hidden from view if the event is accepted. The reason that the application actually quits when the LoginWindow instance is closed is due to a signal that is emitted when the last main window (one with no parent) is no longer visible. That signal is QApplication.lastWindowClosed(), which is already handled by PyQt.

In order to change how the closeEvent() method is handled, in this case, for the LoginWindow class, you will need to reimplement the closeEvent(). An example of this is shown in Listing 3-21.

Listing 3-21. Modifying the closeEvent() event handler

```
# login_gui.py
    def closeEvent(self, event):
        """Reimplement the closing event to display a
        QMessageBox before closing."""
        if self.login_is_successful == True:
            event.accept()
        else:
```

```
answer = QMessageBox.question(
    self, "Quit Application?",
    "Are you sure you want to QUIT?",
    QMessageBox.StandardButton.No | \
    QMessageBox.StandardButton.Yes,
    QMessageBox.StandardButton.Yes)
if answer == QMessageBox.StandardButton.Yes:
    event.accept()
if answer == QMessageBox.StandardButton.No:
    event.ignore()
```

If the window was closed after login was successful, the event is accepted using the accept() method. If the window is closed for some other reason, a QMessageBox asks the user if they are sure about quitting. If the response from the question QMessageBox is Yes, the close event is accepted, and the program is closed. Otherwise, the event is ignored using ignore().

The next section creates the MainWindow class.

Explanation for Creating the Main Window

The main window used in this project is a very basic example, but the purpose here is to demonstrate how to work with more than one window. In the same Python script as the LoginWindow class, create a new class, MainWindow, that inherits QWidget. This new class can be seen in Listing 3-22.

Listing 3-22. The MainWindow class

```
# login_gui.py
class MainWindow(QWidget):

    def __init__(self):
        super().__init__()
        self.initializeUI()

    def initializeUI(self):
        """Set up the application's GUI."""
        self.setMinimumSize(640, 426)
        self.setWindowTitle('3.1 - Main Window')
```

```
        self.setUpMainWindow()

    def setUpMainWindow(self):
        """Create and arrange widgets in the main window."""
        image = "images/background_kingfisher.jpg"

        try:
            with open(image):
                main_label = QLabel(self)
                pixmap = QPixmap(image)
                main_label.setPixmap(pixmap)
                main_label.move(0, 0)
        except FileNotFoundError as error:
            print(f"Image not found.\nError: {error}")
```

The size of the window is set using setMinimumSize(). One thing to note is that there is no show() method called in initializeUI(). This is because the window will only appear after a successful login (seen in Listing 3-18). The main window in Figure 3-10 presents a simple window with a QLabel.

The classes you create can inherit a majority of PyQt's classes, including ones for dialogs, as you shall see in the next section.

Explanation for Creating the Registration Dialog

Customization is one of the greatest benefits of using PyQt to build GUIs. When the user wants to register a new user, the dialog in Figure 3-9 appears. For the Registration dialog in Listings 3-23 to 3-27, create a separate Python script to keep the code organized and to demonstrate how to import your own custom classes into your projects.

Listing 3-23. Code for setting up the Registration dialog that inherits QDialog

```
# registration.py
# Import necessary modules
import sys
from PyQt6.QtWidgets import (QApplication, QDialog, QLabel,
    QPushButton, QLineEdit, QMessageBox)
from PyQt6.QtGui import QFont, QPixmap
```

```python
class NewUserDialog(QDialog):

    def __init__(self):
        super().__init__()
        self.setModal(True)
        self.initializeUI()

    def initializeUI(self):
        """Set up the application's GUI."""
        self.setFixedSize(360, 320)
        self.setWindowTitle("3.1 - Registration GUI")
        self.setUpWindow()
```

The Registration dialog contains two QLabel widgets for the header and user image in Figure 3-10. These are created in Listing 3-24.

Listing 3-24. Adding labels in the Registration dialog's setUpWindow() method

```python
# registration.py
    def setUpWindow(self):
        """Create and arrange widgets in the window for
        collecting new account information."""
        login_label = QLabel("Create New Account", self)
        login_label.setFont(QFont("Arial", 20))
        login_label.move(90, 20)

        # Create QLabel for image
        user_image = "images/new_user_icon.png"

        try:
            with open(user_image):
                user_label = QLabel(self)
                pixmap = QPixmap(user_image)
                user_label.setPixmap(pixmap)
                user_label.move(150, 60)
        except FileNotFoundError as error:
            print(f"Image not found. Error: {error}")
```

Next, four `QLineEdit` widgets and their corresponding labels are created in Listing 3-25.

Listing 3-25. Adding labels and line editing widgets in the Registration dialog's setUpWindow() method

```python
# registration.py
        # Create name QLabel and QLineEdit widgets
        name_label = QLabel("Username:", self)
        name_label.move(20, 144)

        self.name_edit = QLineEdit(self)
        self.name_edit.resize(250, 24)
        self.name_edit.move(90, 140)

        full_name_label = QLabel("Full Name:", self)
        full_name_label.move(20, 174)

        full_name_edit = QLineEdit(self)
        full_name_edit.resize(250, 24)
        full_name_edit.move(90, 170)

        # Create password QLabel and QLineEdit widgets
        new_pswd_label = QLabel("Password:", self)
        new_pswd_label.move(20, 204)

        self.new_pswd_edit = QLineEdit(self)
        self.new_pswd_edit.setEchoMode(
            QLineEdit.EchoMode.Password)
        self.new_pswd_edit.resize(250, 24)
        self.new_pswd_edit.move(90, 200)

        confirm_label = QLabel("Confirm:", self)
        confirm_label.move(20, 234)

        self.confirm_edit = QLineEdit(self)
        self.confirm_edit.setEchoMode(
            QLineEdit.EchoMode.Password)
        self.confirm_edit.resize(250, 24)
        self.confirm_edit.move(90, 230)
```

These widgets are used for collecting the user's username, full name, password, and an extra QLineEdit widget for ensuring that the password is entered correctly. The button for confirming the data is set up in Listing 3-26.

Listing 3-26. Adding a signup button in the Registration dialog's setUpWindow() method

```
# registration.py
        # Create sign up QPushButton
        sign_up_button = QPushButton("Sign Up", self)
        sign_up_button.resize(320, 32)
        sign_up_button.move(20, 270)
        sign_up_button.clicked.connect(self.confirmSignUp)
```

The sign_up_button emits a signal when clicked that calls the confirmSignUp() slot in Listing 3-27.

Tip   QDialog has its own standard buttons that can be added to a custom dialog class using the QDialogButtonBox class.

Listing 3-27. Code for the confirmSignUp() slot

```
# registration.py
    def confirmSignUp(self):
        """Check if user information is entered and correct.
        If so, append username and password text to file."""
        name_text = self.name_edit.text()
        pswd_text = self.new_pswd_edit.text()
        confirm_text = self.confirm_edit.text()

        if name_text == "" or pswd_text == "":
            # Display QMessageBox if passwords don't match
            QMessageBox.warning(self, "Error Message",
                "Please enter username or password values.",
                QMessageBox.StandardButton.Close,
                QMessageBox.StandardButton.Close)
```

```
    elif pswd_text != confirm_text:
        # Display QMessageBox if passwords don't match
        QMessageBox.warning(self, "Error Message",
            "The passwords you entered do not match.",
            QMessageBox.StandardButton.Close,
            QMessageBox.StandardButton.Close)
    else:
        # Return to login window if passwords match
        with open("files/users.txt", 'a+') as f:
            f.write("\n" + name_text + " ")
            f.write(pswd_text)
        self.close()
```

The confirmSignUp() slot first reads the text from name_edit, new_pswd_edit, and confirm_edit. Next, a series of checks are performed to test if name_text or pswd_text is empty and then to see if pswd_text and confirm_text are the same. One of the two QMessageBox dialogs in Figure 3-13 will pop up if either of the conditions are met.

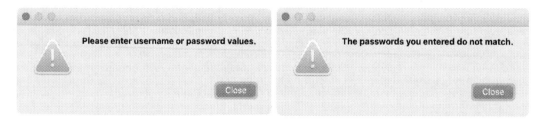

Figure 3-13. *A warning dialog that handles if the username or password fields are empty (left) and another that lets the user know the passwords don't match (right)*

If the user clicks the sign_up_button and all of the data is entered correctly, name_text and pswd_text are saved on a new line in the users.txt file separated by a space that can be seen in Figure 3-14. If the user closes the dialog before completing the form, the dialog will close, but the Login window will still remain open.

Figure 3-14. *The original users.txt file (left) and the updated one (right)*

If the form was completed, the user can try to enter their new username and password into the Login GUI to log in.

Summary

In this chapter, you experienced building GUIs using a variety of widgets – QPushButton, QLineEdit, QCheckBox, and QMessageBox. With the different widgets, you were also able to learn about other important concepts for building GUIs in PyQt, namely, event handling, communication between widgets with signals and slots, the difference between windows and dialogs, and how to create applications with multiple windows. All of these concepts in this chapter lay the framework for creating larger, more responsive, GUIs.

However, there are still a few more concepts that are essential to learn for creating GUI applications. In the next chapter, you will learn about another one of those fundamental topics – layout management.

CHAPTER 4

Learning About Layout Management

As applications grow in size, organizing and managing all of the widgets' locations and sizes in a user interface can become difficult to handle. The good news is that PyQt makes the process for arranging widgets relatively simple thanks to built-in **layout managers**, or classes that handle most of the nitty-gritty details for organizing widgets in GUIs.

In this chapter, you will

- Learn about PyQt's layout manager classes and apply them in numerous GUIs

- Consider which layout manager is best for your application

- Find out how to create complex layouts with nested layouts

- Explore a few different techniques for managing widgets in layout managers, such as adding spaces or working with size policies

- Use a variety of new classes, including QComboBox, QSpinBox, QDoubleSpinBox, QButtonGroup, QTextEdit, QDateEdit, and more, to expand your toolkit and knowledge about creating incredible GUIs

- Expand your experience with previously learned widget classes while building practical applications

Let's get to know more about layout managers and how to use them in PyQt.

© Joshua M Willman 2022
J. M. Willman, *Beginning PyQt*, https://doi.org/10.1007/978-1-4842-7999-1_4

Using Layout Managers in PyQt

Layout management is the useful practice of arranging widgets in GUIs. When organizing widgets, you'll need to consider a number of situations, including a widget's size and position relative to other widgets, what to do if the window is resized, and how to handle widgets when they are added or removed. Layout management is also very important to consider from the user's perspective. Arranging your widgets intuitively can help a user quickly navigate a GUI and perform tasks more easily.

The layout manager classes make organizing widgets simpler and allow for child and parent widgets to communicate, ensuring that widgets utilize the space in a window more efficiently whenever changes occur. Each layout manager manages widgets and space differently, but there is a general pattern for setting up and adding widgets to a layout.

Let's look at a brief example. Suppose you wanted to arrange a QLabel widget above a QLineEdit widget. First, create your two widget objects:

```
label = QLabel("Name")
line_edit = QLineEdit()
```

Notice how neither a parent widget nor the parameter name self is passed as an argument when creating the widgets. This is because a layout manager will automatically take care of reparenting widgets to be associated with the parent widget. Or put more simply, layout managers set the parents for the child widgets.

Next, create an instance of the layout manager for arranging widgets vertically, QVBoxLayout:

```
v_box = QVBoxLayout() # Create layout manager instance
v_box.addWidget(label) # Add widgets to the layout
v_box.addWidget(line_edit)
parent_widget.setLayout(v_box) # Set the layout for the parent
```

To add widgets to the layout, use the addWidget() method and pass the widget to be added. Then apply the layout used in the parent widget by calling the QWidget method setLayout(). The parent widget could be a widget, a window, or even a dialog. *Layout managers cannot be parents for widgets; only widgets can be parents for other widgets.*

Instead of using setLayout(), you can also pass the parent widget to the layout manager, like so:

```
v_box = QVBoxLayout(parent_widget)
```

Finally, you can also add layouts to other layouts to create a **nested layout**. To add a layout, create a new layout instance and use the method addLayout() to pass the layout to the parent layout:

```
h_box = QHBoxLayout()
v_box.addLayout(h_box)
```

Here, h_box is the child layout and v_box is the parent, and h_box becomes an **inner layout**, or a child of a parent layout. This topic is covered later in the "Creating Nested Layouts" section.

Before moving on, let's recap what absolute positioning is and its purpose.

Absolute Positioning

One method for arranging widgets in an interface is absolute positioning, and it involves specifying the size and position values for a child widget within its parent. This idea was introduced and used in Chapters 2 and 3 using the QWidget method move(). The reasoning behind this was so you could gain a fundamental understanding of how to use the space in a window and also so you can see firsthand the usefulness of using layout managers.

So why would you want to use absolute positioning? Absolute positioning can be most useful for setting the position and size values of widgets that are contained within other widgets, or perhaps for repositioning a window's location on the desktop.

If you do decide to use absolute positioning, there are a few drawbacks to keep in mind. First, resizing the main window will not cause the widgets in it to adjust their size or position. Second, the differences between operating systems, such as fonts and font sizes, could drastically change the look and layout of the widgets in an interface on different platforms. Finally, using absolute positioning is expensive in terms of a developer's time, as they will need to calculate the exact size and position of each widget while also tackling issues such as window resizing and the addition or removal of widgets in the GUI.

In the next section, you'll look at your first layout manager for arranging widgets either horizontally or vertically.

Horizontal and Vertical Layouts with Box Layouts

Imagine you have a group of widgets that you want to arrange in your window, either by stacking them on top of one another in a column or by displaying them next to each other in a single row. The layout manager **QBoxLayout** is great for handling either of these situations. QBoxLayout uses the space it is provided from a parent to assign each widget a box with a certain amount of space. The amount of space is based on a number of different factors, such as the widget's minimum allowed size.

While you could use QBoxLayout, PyQt also has two separate convenience classes that derive from QBoxLayout and deliver functionality based on the desired orientation of the widgets:

- QHBoxLayout – Arranges widgets horizontally from left to right or vice versa

- QVBoxLayout – Arranges widgets vertically from top to bottom or vice versa

Optional parameters can be passed to the addWidget() method for the box layouts as seen in the following line:

```
addWidget(widget, stretch, alignment)
```

The stretch parameter refers to the **stretch factor**, or how much the widgets will stretch in relation to other widgets in the row or column. The value for stretch is an int, where 0 uses a widget's default parameters to set the stretch factor. Widgets are laid out proportionally, and ones with larger stretch values will use more space. Widgets can also be aligned in a row or column using the alignment argument.

The following applications provide separate examples for using QHBoxLayout and QVBoxLayout. They also use signals and slots to create complete, practical programs.

Explanation for QHBoxLayout

For this project, the GUI in Figure 4-1 consists of three basic widgets: QLabel, QLineEdit, and QPushButton. These widgets are arranged horizontally using QHBoxLayout.

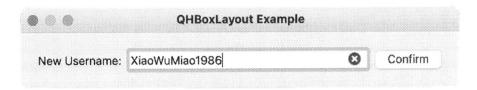

Figure 4-1. *A simple QHBoxLayout example with each widget arranged horizontally in the GUI*

The application in Listings 4-1 to 4-3 allows for a user to enter a username into the QLineEdit widget. Editing the text emits a signal that will check if the input is of a certain length and contains only alphabetical or numerical characters.

To get started, create a new script and copy the code in the basic_window.py script from Chapter 1 into your new file.

Listing 4-1. Setting up the main window for using QHBoxLayout

```python
# horizontal_box.py
# Import necessary modules
import sys
from PyQt6.QtWidgets import (QApplication, QWidget, QLabel,
    QLineEdit, QPushButton, QHBoxLayout)

class MainWindow(QWidget):

    def __init__(self):
        super().__init__()
        self.initializeUI()

    def initializeUI(self):
        """Set up the application's GUI."""
        self.setMinimumWidth(500)
        self.setFixedHeight(60)
        self.setWindowTitle("QHBoxLayout Example")

        self.setUpMainWindow()
        self.show()
```

```
if __name__ == '__main__':
    app = QApplication(sys.argv)
    window = MainWindow()
    sys.exit(app.exec())
```

Be sure to import the widget classes along with QHBoxLayout from QtWidgets. Although the layout manager classes are in the QtWidgets module, they are not widgets and do not inherit QWidget. Instead, they derive from **QLayout**, the base class for layout managers.

You can use a combination of methods to determine how a window can resize. Here, the window's minimum width is set with setMinimumWidth() so that it can be resized horizontally, but the height is fixed using setFixedHeight().

In Listing 4-2, begin by creating the three widgets in setUpMainWindow().

Listing 4-2. The setUpMainWindow() method for using QHBoxLayout

```
# horizontal_box.py
    def setUpMainWindow(self):
        """Create and arrange widgets in the main window."""
        name_label = QLabel("New Username:")

        name_edit = QLineEdit()
        name_edit.setClearButtonEnabled(True)
        name_edit.textEdited.connect(self.checkUserInput)

        self.accept_button = QPushButton("Confirm")
        self.accept_button.setEnabled(False)
        self.accept_button.clicked.connect(self.close)

        main_h_box = QHBoxLayout()
        main_h_box.addWidget(name_label)
        main_h_box.addWidget(name_edit)
        main_h_box.addWidget(self.accept_button)
        self.setLayout(main_h_box)
```

For QLineEdit widgets, the setClearButtonEnabled() method is useful for displaying a clear button when there is text in the editor field. An example of the clear button is shown in Figure 4-1.

Some widgets, such as QPushButton, can be enabled or disabled using the QWidget method setEnabled(). The accept_button object in this program begins disabled. Signals and slots can then be used to check if certain parameters are met in order to switch the widget's states. An example of this is seen in Listing 4-3, where the checkUserInput() slot is connected to the clicked signal for accept_button.

Before moving on, take a look at how the QHBoxLayout instance is set up. With layout managers, widgets are added sequentially. So the first widget added with addWidget() in QHBoxLayout, name_label, will be the left-most widget. This is followed by name_edit and accept_button.

Listing 4-3. Code for the checkUserInput() slot

```python
# horizontal_box.py
    def checkUserInput(self, text):
        """Check the length and content of name_edit."""
        if len(text) > 0 \
            and all(t.isalpha() or t.isdigit() for t in text):
            self.accept_button.setEnabled(True)
        else: self.accept_button.setEnabled(False)
```

When the user edits text in name_edit, the textEdited signal will trigger checkUserInput(). This signal gives us access to the current text. If the length of text is at least 1 and only contains letters or numbers, then accept_button is enabled.

You can now run the application, and as a test, you should readjust the size of the window and see how the widgets also stretch to utilize the space. Let's take a look at QVBoxLayout next.

Explanation for QVBoxLayout

Creating a survey like the one in Figure 4-2 to collect data from users can be very useful for businesses or for research. In the following program, we will take a look at how to use the QVBoxLayout class to create a simple window that displays a question to the user and allows them to select an answer.

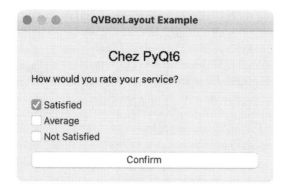

Figure 4-2. *A simple QVBoxLayout example with each widget arranged vertically in the GUI*

While building the GUI in Listings 4-4 to 4-6, we'll also take a look at how to organize and manage groups of buttons. For this GUI, we'll begin with the basic_window.py script from Chapter 1.

Listing 4-4. Setting up the main window for using QVBoxLayout

```python
# vertical_box.py
# Import necessary modules
import sys
from PyQt6.QtWidgets import (QApplication, QWidget, QLabel,
    QCheckBox, QPushButton, QButtonGroup, QVBoxLayout)
from PyQt6.QtCore import Qt
from PyQt6.QtGui import QFont

class MainWindow(QWidget):

    def __init__(self):
        super().__init__()
        self.initializeUI()

    def initializeUI(self):
        """Set up the application's GUI."""
        self.setMinimumSize(350, 200)
        self.setWindowTitle("QVBoxLayout Example")

        self.setUpMainWindow()
        self.show()
```

```
if __name__ == '__main__':
    app = QApplication(sys.argv)
    window = MainWindow()
    sys.exit(app.exec())
```

Be sure to import the necessary classes and set up the main window.

Each of the widgets in Figure 4-2 is arranged vertically in the window. What we'll do is start by setting up the text and alignment for the header and question labels in Listing 4-5.

Listing 4-5. The setUpMainWindow() method for using QVBoxLayout, part 1

```
# vertical_box.py
    def setUpMainWindow(self):
        """Create and arrange widgets in the main window."""
        header_label = QLabel("Chez PyQt6")
        header_label.setFont(QFont("Arial", 18))
        header_label.setAlignment(
            Qt.AlignmentFlag.AlignCenter)
        question_label = QLabel(
            "How would you rate your service?")
        question_label.setAlignment(Qt.AlignmentFlag.AlignTop)
```

The QCheckBox widgets are also arranged in the window using a layout manager, but we'll need to first discuss how to manage groups of related buttons.

The QButtonGroup Class

You may often have a few checkboxes or buttons that need to be grouped together to make it easier to manage them. Thankfully, PyQt has the **QButtonGroup** class to help manage associated buttons while also making them mutually exclusive. This can be helpful if you only want one checkbox to be checked at a time.

To add buttons to QButtonGroup and to a window, you can use the following order:

1. Create a QButtonGroup instance and make it a member of a class, meaning create an instance variable of the class, that is, self. button_group, or pass a parent object as an argument, that is, button_group = QButtonGroup(self).

2. Create the button or checkbox objects that will be added to the button group from step 1.

3. Add the buttons from step 2 to the button group using the QButtonGroup method addButton().

4. Connect all buttons in a group to one signal, such as the QButtonGroup signal buttonClicked.

5. Add the widgets created in step 2 to a layout manager.

QButtonGroup is not actually a widget, but an abstract container around the buttons added to it. Therefore, you can't actually add QButtonGroup to a layout. The procedure for adding checkboxes to QButtonGroup is demonstrated in Listing 4-6.

Listing 4-6. The setUpMainWindow() method for using QVBoxLayout, part 2

```python
# vertical_box.py
        ratings = ["Satisfied", "Average", "Not Satisfied"]
        ratings_group = QButtonGroup(self)
        ratings_group.buttonClicked.connect(
            self.checkboxClicked)

        self.confirm_button = QPushButton("Confirm")
        self.confirm_button.setEnabled(False)
        self.confirm_button.clicked.connect(self.close)

        main_v_box = QVBoxLayout()
        main_v_box.addWidget(header_label)
        main_v_box.addWidget(question_label)

        for cb in range(len(ratings)):
            rating_cb = QCheckBox(ratings[cb])
            ratings_group.addButton(rating_cb)
            main_v_box.addWidget(rating_cb)

        main_v_box.addWidget(self.confirm_button)
        self.setLayout(main_v_box)
```

```
def checkboxClicked(self, button):
    """Check if a QCheckBox in the button group has
    been clicked."""
    print(button.text())
    self.confirm_button.setEnabled(True)
```

Here, we create a QButtonGroup, ratings_group, to manage the three QCheckBox widgets. If any of the mutually exclusive checkboxes are selected, it'll emit a signal that triggers checkboxClicked(). The slot simply demonstrates how to check which checkbox is checked and enables confirm_button.

The QCheckBox objects are created by iterating over the values in the ratings list. They are also added to both the button group and the window's layout manager, main_v_box, in the same loop.

Creating Nested Layouts

Sometimes, a single layout manager won't be able to suit all of your needs as your interfaces become more complex. Fortunately, handling this matter isn't too difficult with PyQt as you can arrange layouts inside of other layouts to solve intricate arrangement issues.

Previous examples have demonstrated how to apply layouts to a widget using the setLayout() method, thereby creating the parent layout. For the GUI in Figure 4-3, you'll notice how some widgets are arranged vertically, while others are arranged horizontally. The widgets arranged side by side are placed in inner layouts, and those layouts are then added to the parent layout using the layout manager method addLayout().

Figure 4-3. *Widgets arranged using a combination of layout managers*

While this example focuses on using the box layout managers, it is important to also keep in mind that you can combine any of the layout managers to create your own nested layouts.

Explanation for Nested Layouts

In addition to constructing nested layouts in this program, you will also learn about two new types of widgets, the spin box and the combo box, that are both useful for selecting a single option from a set of values.

Listing 4-7 begins by importing the classes we'll need and setting up the MainWindow class.

Listing 4-7. Setting up the main window for using nested layouts

```python
# nested.py
# Import necessary modules
import sys
from PyQt6.QtWidgets import (QApplication, QWidget, QLabel,
    QComboBox, QSpinBox, QHBoxLayout, QVBoxLayout)
from PyQt6.QtCore import Qt
from PyQt6.QtGui import QFont

class MainWindow(QWidget):

    def __init__(self):
        super().__init__()
        self.initializeUI()

    def initializeUI(self):
        """Set up the application's GUI."""
        self.setMinimumSize(400, 160)
        self.setWindowTitle("Nested Layout Example")

        self.setUpMainWindow()
        self.show()
```

```
if __name__ == '__main__':
    app = QApplication(sys.argv)
    window = MainWindow()
    sys.exit(app.exec())
```

With the MainWindow class started, let's begin building the setUpMainWindow()
method and look at two new widgets that we'll use in this GUI.

The QSpinBox and QComboBox Widgets

Rather than using a QLineEdit widget for inputting information, sometimes, you
may want a user to only be allowed to select from a list of predetermined values or
numerical ranges.

QSpinBox creates an object that is similar to a text box but allows the user to select
integer values by either typing a value into the widget or by clicking on up and down
arrows. You can also edit the range of the values, set the step size when the arrow
is clicked, set a starting value, or even add prefixes or suffixes in the box. There are
classes similar to QSpinBox that provide similar functionality for different situations.
QDoubleSpinBox is used for selecting floating-point numbers. **QDateTimeEdit** or one of
its variations is useful for selecting date and time values.

The **QComboBox** widget displays a drop-down list of options for the user to select
when a user clicks on the widget's arrow button. Combo boxes are handy for displaying a
large amount of options in the least amount of space.

In Listing 4-8, we will take a look at how to create both kinds of widgets in the
setUpMainWindow() method.

Listing 4-8. Creating the widgets in setUpMainWindow()

```
# nested.py
    def setUpMainWindow(self):
        """Create and arrange widgets in the main window."""
        info_label = QLabel(
            "Select 2 items for lunch and their prices.")
        info_label.setFont(QFont("Arial", 16))
        info_label.setAlignment(Qt.AlignmentFlag.AlignCenter)
```

```
# Create a list of food items and two separate
# QComboBox widgets to display all of the items
food_list = ["egg", "turkey sandwich", "ham sandwich",
    "cheese", "hummus", "yogurt", "apple", "banana",
    "orange", "waffle", "carrots", "bread", "pasta",
    "crackers", "pretzels", "coffee", "soda", "water"]

food_combo1 = QComboBox()
food_combo1.addItems(food_list)
food_combo2 = QComboBox()
food_combo2.addItems(food_list)

# Create two QSpinBox widgets to display prices
self.price_sb1 = QSpinBox()
self.price_sb1.setRange(0, 100)
self.price_sb1.setPrefix("$")
self.price_sb1.valueChanged.connect(
    self.calculateTotal)

self.price_sb2 = QSpinBox()
self.price_sb2.setRange(0, 100)
self.price_sb2.setPrefix("$")
self.price_sb2.valueChanged.connect(
    self.calculateTotal)
```

We create two separate combo boxes, food_combo1 and food_combo2, and add the list of items that we want to be displayed in each of them using the addItems() method. After that, two separate spin boxes are created: price_sb1 and price_sb2.

The setRange() method is used to set upper and lower boundaries for a spin box, and setPrefix() can be used to display other text inside the text box, in this case, a dollar sign. This can be helpful to give the user more information about the widget's purpose.

Finally, as we change the values in the spin boxes, they both send a signal that is connected to the calculateTotal() method. This will dynamically update the value for totals_label that is instantiated in Listing 4-9.

Combining Layouts and Arranging Widgets

The process of combining layouts involves placing one type of layout manager inside of another type. For this example, we'll be combining the two box layouts to gain the benefit of both horizontal and vertical arrangements.

In Listing 4-9, we can arrange the spin boxes and combo boxes from Listing 4-8 into separate horizontal layouts, item1_h_box and item2_h_box.

Note   Since the two QComboBox objects and the two QSpinBox objects each contain the same values, you may have the urge to just try and use them over again rather than creating separate instances. This won't work. When you add an object to a layout, the parent widget takes ownership of the object. This means you cannot add the same object to more than one layout. Instead, you'll need to create a new instance.

Listing 4-9. Creating the nested layout in setUpMainWindow()

```python
# nested.py
        # Create two horizontal layouts for the QComboBox
        # and QSpinBox widgets
        item1_h_box = QHBoxLayout()
        item1_h_box.addWidget(food_combo1)
        item1_h_box.addWidget(self.price_sb1)

        item2_h_box = QHBoxLayout()
        item2_h_box.addWidget(food_combo2)
        item2_h_box.addWidget(self.price_sb2)

        self.totals_label = QLabel("Total Spent: $")
        self.totals_label.setFont(QFont("Arial", 16))
        self.totals_label.setAlignment(
            Qt.AlignmentFlag.AlignRight)

        # Organize widgets and layouts in the main window
        main_v_box = QVBoxLayout()
        main_v_box.addWidget(info_label)
```

```
main_v_box.addLayout(item1_h_box)
main_v_box.addLayout(item2_h_box)
main_v_box.addWidget(self.totals_label)

# Set the layout for the main window
self.setLayout(main_v_box)
```

An additional label, totals_label, will display the summation of the values in the QSpinBox widgets.

At this point, you will have two labels and two QHBoxLayout instances that need to be added to the window. You'll need to create a parent layout to hold these objects. Here, the parent layout is main_v_box. The labels are added with addWidget(), and the layouts are added with addLayout(). This arrangement is depicted in Figure 4-4, where the parent QVBoxLayout is represented with solid lines and the inner QHBoxLayout instances are depicted with dashed lines.

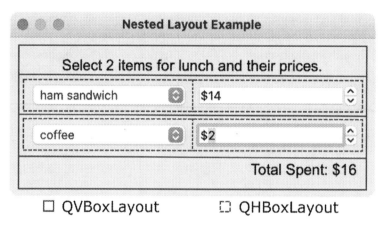

Figure 4-4. *Visualization of the nested layout*

The final task in Listing 4-10 is to create the slot that calculates the values from the spin boxes and updates the text for totals_label.

Listing 4-10. Code for the calculateTotal() slot

```
# nested.py
    def calculateTotal(self, value):
        """Calculate the total price and update
        totals_label."""
```

```
total = self.price_sb1.value() + \
    self.price_sb2.value()
self.totals_label.setText(f"Total Spent: ${total}")
```

At this point, you have finished learning the basics for working with box layouts. Let's move on and take a look at another built-in layout manager.

Arranging Widgets in Grids with QGridLayout

The **QGridLayout** layout manager is used to arrange widgets in rows and columns similar to a spreadsheet or matrix. This layout manager takes the space within its parent window or widget and divides it up according to the sizes of the widgets within that row (or column). Adding space between widgets, creating a border, or stretching widgets across multiple rows or columns is also possible.

Understanding how to add and manipulate widgets using QGridLayout is fairly straightforward. The index values in the grid start at (0,0), which is the top left-most cell. The first value is the row, and the second is the column. To add a widget underneath it (the next row), simply add 1 to the first value, (1,0). To keep moving down rows, keep increasing the first value. To move across columns, increase the second value.

The addWidget() method for QGridLayout has two forms. The first is shown in the following line:

```
addWidget(widget, row, column, alignment)
```

Here, the widget is added to the specified row and column with an optional alignment. The other form allows for widgets to extend across multiple rows, columns, or both:

```
addWidget(widget, fromRow, fromColumn, rowSpan, columnSpan, alignment)
```

The fromRow and fromColumn arguments specify the starting row and column, respectively. The rowSpan and columnSpan arguments take integer values and define how many rows and columns a widget will take up, respectively.

For this section, you'll find out how to use GridLayout to make the daily planner GUI seen in Figure 4-5.

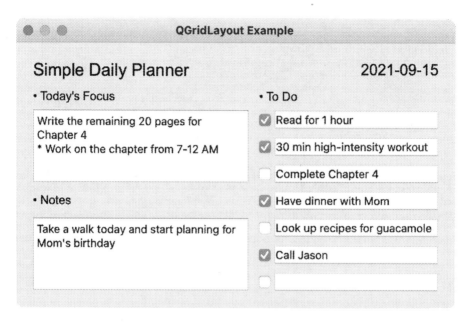

Figure 4-5. *A simple daily planner that uses QGridLayout to organize widgets*

Some to-do lists are broken down by hours of the day, by importance of goals, or by the priority of tasks one may need to do for that day, week, or even month. Once a goal is complete, we need some way to check off a task or remove it.

The application is composed of three parts: an area to write today's most important task, a place to jot down notes, and a section to write daily tasks. We'll also take a brief look at some new PyQt classes for handling large areas of text and for working with dates.

Explanation for QGridLayout

We can begin building the example for using QGridLayout by importing the classes we need and building the MainWindow class in Listing 4-11. You can use the basic_window.py script from Chapter 1 to get you started.

Listing 4-11. Setting up the main window for using QGridLayout

```
# grid.py
# Import necessary modules
import sys, json
from PyQt6.QtWidgets import (QApplication, QWidget, QLabel,
    QLineEdit, QCheckBox, QTextEdit, QGridLayout)
```

```python
from PyQt6.QtCore import Qt, QDate
from PyQt6.QtGui import QFont

class MainWindow(QWidget):

    def __init__(self):
        super().__init__()
        self.initializeUI()

    def initializeUI(self):
        """Set up the application's GUI."""
        self.setMinimumSize(500, 300)
        self.setWindowTitle("QGridLayout Example")

        self.setUpMainWindow()
        self.loadWidgetValuesFromFile()
        self.show()

if __name__ == '__main__':
    app = QApplication(sys.argv)
    window = MainWindow()
    sys.exit(app.exec())
```

To continue building the daily planner interface, we'll need to learn about a widget class that can handle large fields of text.

The QTextEdit Widget

When a user needs an area for entering or editing more than one line of text at a time, the **QTextEdit** class is well suited for modifying either plain or rich text and includes built-in editing features, such as copy, paste, and cut. The widget can handle characters or paragraphs of text. Paragraphs are simply long strings that are word-wrapped into the widget and end with a newline character. QTextEdit is also useful for displaying lists, images, and tables or providing an interface for displaying text using HTML.

We can start building the widgets on the left side of the main window in Listing 4-12, beginning with the header label, the QTextEdit objects, and their corresponding labels.

Listing 4-12. The setUpMainWindow() method for using QGridLayout, part 1

```python
# grid.py
    def setUpMainWindow(self):
        """Create and arrange widgets in the main window."""
        header_label = QLabel("Simple Daily Planner")
        header_label.setFont(QFont("Arial", 20))
        header_label.setAlignment(Qt.AlignmentFlag.AlignLeft)

        # Create widgets for the left side of the window
        today_label = QLabel("· Today's Focus")
        today_label.setFont(QFont("Arial", 14))
        self.today_tedit = QTextEdit()

        notes_label = QLabel("· Notes")
        notes_label.setFont(QFont("Arial", 14))
        self.notes_tedit = QTextEdit()
```

The widgets are now ready to be added to a layout manager.

Adding Widgets and Spanning Rows and Columns in QGridLayout

Since widgets will be placed in a grid-like structure, when you add a new object to the layout, you must specify the row and column values as parameters of the addWidget() or addLayout() method. Take a look at Listing 4-13 to see an example of this.

Listing 4-13. The setUpMainWindow() method for using QGridLayout, part 2

```python
# grid.py
        # Organize the left side widgets into column 0
        # of the QGridLayout
        self.main_grid = QGridLayout()
        self.main_grid.addWidget(header_label, 0, 0)
        self.main_grid.addWidget(today_label, 1, 0)
        self.main_grid.addWidget(self.today_tedit, 2, 0, 3, 1)
        self.main_grid.addWidget(notes_label, 5, 0)
        self.main_grid.addWidget(self.notes_tedit, 6, 0, 3, 1)
```

The header_label object is added to the main_grid layout at the position where row equals 0 and column equals 0, which is also the top-left corner. Then today_label is added directly below header_label by increasing the row value to 1 and leaving the column value equal to 0. The today_tedit object is added to row 2.

What happens if you have a widget in a row or a column that needs to take up more space in the vertical or horizontal direction? Let's look at two different ways for handling these situations.

The first approach involves skipping a few rows or columns to allow certain kinds of widgets, such as QTextEdit, to take up the additional space. If you refer to Figure 4-5, you can see that the QTextEdit widgets use more room in the window than the QLabel or QLineEdit widgets. To allow today_tedit to stretch across three rows, the following widget, notes_label, is placed in row index 5.

The second technique to have widgets utilize space in QGridLayout is to specify the number of rows and columns that you want a widget to **span**. Spanning can be thought of as stretching a widget horizontally or vertically to take advantage of space and help with window organization. Have a look at the following line:

```
self.main_grid.addWidget(self.today_tedit, 2, 0, 3, 1)
```

The extra two parameters at the end, 3 and 1, tell the layout manager that the widget will span three rows and one column. This causes the widget to stretch vertically. The right side of the window is handled in Listing 4-14.

Listing 4-14. The setUpMainWindow() method for using QGridLayout, part 3

```
# grid.py
        # Create widgets for the right side of the window
        today = QDate.currentDate().toString(
            Qt.DateFormat.ISODate)
        date_label = QLabel(today)
        date_label.setFont(QFont("Arial", 18))
        date_label.setAlignment(Qt.AlignmentFlag.AlignRight)

        todo_label = QLabel("· To Do")
        todo_label.setFont(QFont("Arial", 14))
```

```
# Organize the right side widgets into columns 1 and 2
# of the QGridLayout
self.main_grid.addWidget(date_label, 0, 2)
self.main_grid.addWidget(todo_label, 1, 1, 1, 2)

# Create 7 rows, from indexes 2-8
for row in range(2, 9):
    item_cb = QCheckBox()
    item_edit = QLineEdit()
    self.main_grid.addWidget(item_cb, row, 1)
    self.main_grid.addWidget(item_edit, row, 2)

# Set the layout for the main window
self.setLayout(self.main_grid)
```

The date that appears in the top right of the window in Figure 4-5 will change depending upon what day the user is opening the application. This is thanks to the **QDate** class. The current date is retrieved using QDate.currentDate(), converted to a readable string using toString(), and passed to the variable today. The enum Qt.DateFormat is used to set the format for how the date is presented to the user. There are a few different ways to format dates in PyQt, such as TextDate for textual dates or ISODate that uses the ISO 8601 standard style. The today string is displayed in the QLabel, date_label.

For the group of seven QCheckBox and QLineEdit widgets that form the list of to-do items, a for loop is used to create each object and add them to the correct row and column in the main_grid.

We could stop here, but let's go one step further and find out how to use signals and slots to save the values of the text-editing widgets and determine which to-do items to keep for the next day. This can be done by looking at the states of the QCheckBox widgets. To do this, we'll need to find out how to locate child widgets once they have been added to a layout manager.

Finding Child Widgets in a Layout

A common task is to collect the values from widgets, perhaps to update another widget's information or to save data when closing an application. In many cases, instance variables created with self can be used throughout a class to modify and update values. However, as we saw in Listing 4-14, the QCheckBox and QLineEdit widgets were iteratively added to the layout without a clear variable name.

The QWidget class already has methods for finding children widgets, but for this example, we'll learn how child items are located in layout managers, specifically QGridLayout.

For some applications, it may be important to save the information in the window. When a user closes the daily planner, a record is kept of the previous day's notes and unfinished tasks. The MainWindow method for handling these operations, saveWidgetValues(), is constructed in Listing 4-15.

Listing 4-15. Code for the saveWidgetValues() method

```
# grid.py
    def saveWidgetValues(self):
        """Collect and save the widget values."""
        details = {"focus": self.today_tedit.toPlainText(),
                   "notes": self.notes_tedit.toPlainText()}
        remaining_todo = []

        # Check the values of the QCheckBox widgets
        for row in range(2, 9):
            # Retrieve the QLayoutItem object
            item = self.main_grid.itemAtPosition(row, 1)
            # Retrieve the widget (QCheckBox)
            widget = item.widget()
            if widget.isChecked() == False:
                # Retrieve the QLayoutItem object
                item = self.main_grid.itemAtPosition(row, 2)
                # Retrieve the widget (QLineEdit)
                widget = item.widget()
                text = widget.text()
                if text != "":
                    remaining_todo.append(text)
            # Save text from QLineEdit widgets
            details["todo"] = remaining_todo

        with open("details.txt", "w") as f:
            f.write(json.dumps(details))
```

```
def closeEvent(self, event):
    """Save widget values when closing the window."""
    self.saveWidgetValues()
```

The values for the QTextEdit and QLineEdit widgets are stored in a Python dict, simplifying the process for saving data in JSON format. In order to return plain text for both today_tedit and notes_tedit, use the QTextEdit method toPlainText(). If you need to return rich text, use toHtml().

When widgets are added to layouts, they are added as **QLayoutItem** objects. The QGridLayout method itemAtPosition() is used to retrieve items at a given row and column value. By iterating over row indexes 2 to 8, we can find out which QCheckBox widgets are checked with isChecked().

Tip   For box layouts and QFormLayout, you can use the itemAt(index) method, where index is the widget's index in the layout. Note that this returns a **QWidgetItem** object and not the widget itself. Therefore, you'll need to call the widget() method on the returned item to interact with the widget.

Tasks that are completed should be checked. So if a check box is not checked, we'll save the text from the corresponding QLinedEdit in column 2 so long as the QTextEdit field isn't empty. Lastly, the details dictionary is written to a text file. All of this will occur when the window closes using closeEvent().

Loading data into the widgets from a previous session is handled in Listing 4-16. If this is the first time that the application has been run, the try clause is skipped, and the details.txt file is created in the except clause.

Listing 4-16. Code for the saveWidgetValues() method

```
# grid.py
    def loadWidgetValuesFromFile(self):
        """Retrieve previous values from the last session."""
        # Check if file exists first
```

```
try:
    with open("details.txt", "r") as f:
        details = json.load(f)
        # Retrieve and set values for the widgets
        self.today_tedit.setText(details["focus"])
        self.notes_tedit.setText(details["notes"])

        # Set the text for QLineEdit widgets
        for row in range(len(details["todo"])):
            # Retrieve the QLayoutItem object
            item = self.main_grid.itemAtPosition(
                row + 2, 2)
            # Retrieve the widget (QLineEdit)
            widget = item.widget()
            widget.setText(details["todo"][row])
except FileNotFoundError as error:
    # Create the file since it doesn't exist
    f = open("details.txt", "w")
```

Otherwise, the text file is loaded using json.load(). The text values for the
QTextEdit widgets and the QLineEdit from the previous session are set in the try clause.
QLineEdit objects are found using itemAtPosition().

Building Forms with QFormLayout

For situations where you need to create a form to collect information from a user,
PyQt provides the **QFormLayout** class. It is a layout manager that arranges its children
widgets into a two-column layout, the left column consisting of labels and the right one
consisting of entry field widgets such as QLineEdit or QSpinBox. The QFormLayout class
makes designing these kinds of GUIs very convenient.

For the application in Figure 4-6, let's take a look at creating a form that someone
could use to set up an appointment.

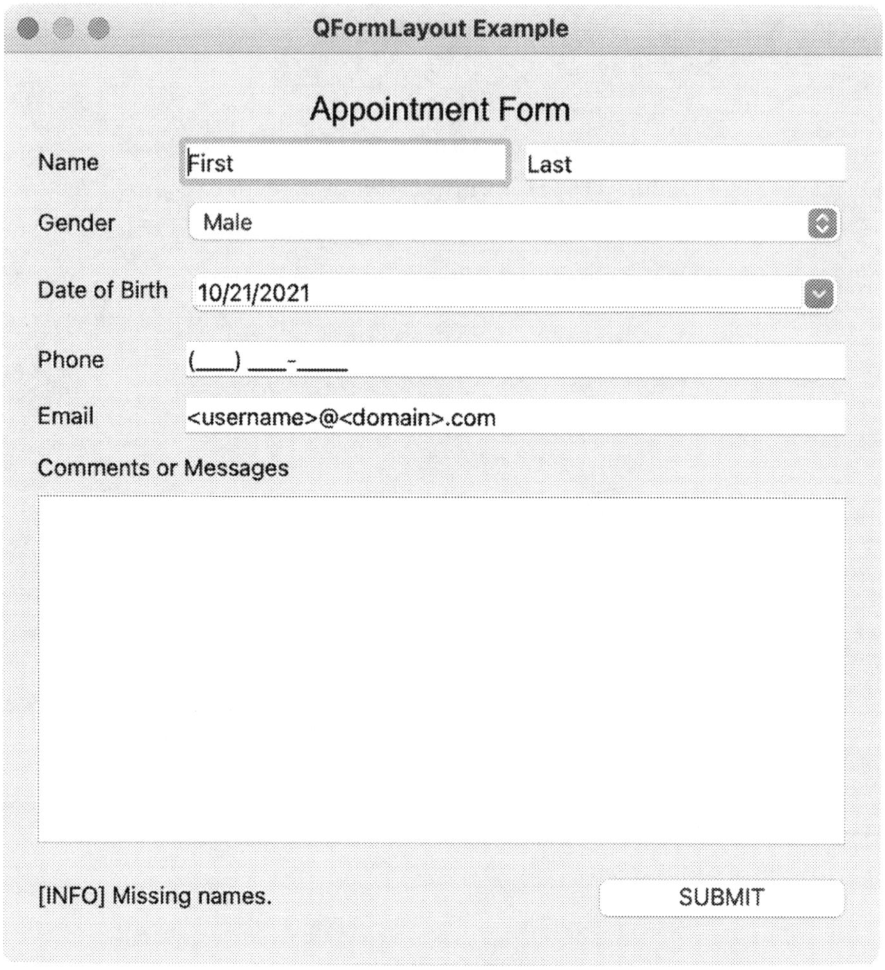

Figure 4-6. *An application form created with QFormLayout*

In this application, you'll also be introduced to the class for matching strings using **regular expressions** in PyQt, which has similar functionality to the Python module re or the third-party module regex.

Explanation for QFormLayout

The application form consists of a number of different widgets, including QLabel, QLineEdit, QComboBox, QTextEdit, and QPushButton. A new class, **QDateEdit**, is similar to QSpinBox but provides specific functionality for selecting and editing dates.

Let's use the basic_window.py script for the basis of the code in Listing 4-17 and get started by importing the necessary PyQt classes. This GUI also contains a few instances of nested layouts, so QHBoxLayout is included.

Listing 4-17. Setting up the main window for using QFormLayout

```python
# form.py
# Import necessary modules
import sys
from PyQt6.QtWidgets import (QApplication, QWidget, QLabel,
    QPushButton, QDateEdit, QLineEdit, QTextEdit, QComboBox,
    QFormLayout, QHBoxLayout)
from PyQt6.QtCore import Qt, QRegularExpression, QDate
from PyQt6.QtGui import QFont, QRegularExpressionValidator

class MainWindow(QWidget):

    def __init__(self):
        super().__init__()
        self.initializeUI()

    def initializeUI(self):
        """Set up the application's GUI."""
        self.setMinimumSize(500, 400)
        self.setWindowTitle("QFormLayout Example")

        self.setUpMainWindow()
        self.show()

if __name__ == '__main__':
    app = QApplication(sys.argv)
    window = MainWindow()
    sys.exit(app.exec())
```

When instantiating the editing fields, be aware that you won't need to create the QLabel widget that typically precedes them. With QFormLayout, two widgets can be added in a row. For now, we'll just set up the text-editing widgets in Listing 4-18.

Listing 4-18. The setUpMainWindow() method for using QFormLayout, part 1

```python
# form.py
    def setUpMainWindow(self):
        """Create and arrange widgets in the main window."""
        header_label = QLabel("Appointment Form")
        header_label.setFont(QFont("Arial", 18))
        header_label.setAlignment(
            Qt.AlignmentFlag.AlignCenter)

        self.first_name_edit = QLineEdit()
        self.first_name_edit.setPlaceholderText("First")
        self.first_name_edit.textEdited.connect(
            self.clearText)
        self.last_name_edit = QLineEdit()
        self.last_name_edit.setPlaceholderText("Last")
        self.last_name_edit.textEdited.connect(self.clearText)

        # Create horizontal layout for names
        name_h_box = QHBoxLayout()
        name_h_box.addWidget(self.first_name_edit)
        name_h_box.addWidget(self.last_name_edit)
```

Even though a Name label exists in front of the first_name_edit and last_name_edit widgets in Figure 4-6, the label has not been created yet. The two QLineEdit widgets are added to a QHBoxLayout manager. Building the clearText() slot is handled in Listing 4-22.

For the second part of setUpMainWindow() in Listing 4-19, more of the application form's widgets are instantiated.

Listing 4-19. The setUpMainWindow() method for using QFormLayout, part 2

```python
# form.py
        # Create additional widgets to be added in the window
        gender_combo = QComboBox()
        gender_combo.addItems(["Male", "Female"])

        self.phone_edit = QLineEdit()
        self.phone_edit.setInputMask("(999) 999-9999;_")
        self.phone_edit.textEdited.connect(self.clearText)
```

```
self.birthdate_edit = QDateEdit()
self.birthdate_edit.setDisplayFormat("MM/dd/yyyy")
self.birthdate_edit.setMaximumDate(
    QDate.currentDate())
self.birthdate_edit.setCalendarPopup(True)
self.birthdate_edit.setDate(QDate.currentDate())
```

The widgets in the previous block of code ask the user to input their gender, phone number, and birthdate using a variety of different widget classes. The gender_combo object is a simple QComboBox.

Any type of character can be typed into the QLineEdit entry field. However, if you want to limit the type, size, or manner in which characters can be input, then you can create an input mask by calling the setInputMask() method. The mask characters in this GUI only allow a user to input integers from 0 to 9. The end of the sequence, ;_, terminates the input mask and sets empty characters to _.

The QDateEdit instance's format for visualizing a date is set with setDisplayFormat(). The maximum range of the widget is set to the date the user opens the application using QDate.currentDate(). QDateEdit has a convenience function, setCalendarPopup(), that will allow a calendar to appear whenever the arrow in the widget is clicked. The initial date that appears in the widget is set with setDate().

The GUI's remaining widgets are set up in Listing 4-20.

Listing 4-20. The setUpMainWindow() method for using QFormLayout, part 3

```
# form.py
        self.email_edit = QLineEdit()
        self.email_edit.setPlaceholderText(
            "<username>@<domain>.com")
        reg_opt = QRegularExpression()
        regex = QRegularExpression(
            "\\b[A-Z0-9._%+-]+@[A-Z0-9.-]+\\.[com]{3}\\b",
            reg_opt.PatternOption.CaseInsensitiveOption)
        self.email_edit.setValidator(
            QRegularExpressionValidator(regex))
        self.email_edit.textEdited.connect(self.clearText)

        extra_info_tedit = QTextEdit()
```

```
self.feedback_label = QLabel()
submit_button = QPushButton("SUBMIT")
submit_button.setMaximumWidth(140)
submit_button.clicked.connect(
    self.checkFormInformation)

# Create horizontal layout for last row of widgets
submit_h_box = QHBoxLayout()
submit_h_box.addWidget(self.feedback_label)
submit_h_box.addWidget(submit_button)
```

Another type of information a user will typically need to include in a form is their email address. A simple QLineEdit would be sufficient, but to handle matching the user's input to the general format of an email address, we can use regular expressions. The **QRegularExpression** class provides the pattern and syntax capabilities we need.

Note   In some documentation, you may come across a Qt class, QRegExp, that has some similarities to QRegularExpression. However, the class is not included in PyQt6 as QRegularExpression contains many improvements over QRegExp.

The expression passed to the regex instance is a basic expression for email addresses. The QRegularExpression.PatternOption enum is used to specify ways that strings can be interpreted, such as CaseInsensitiveOption for case insensitivity or DotMatchesEverythingOption if you need a dot, ., in the pattern string to match any character.

A **validator** is used with some editing widgets to confirm that their contents match constraints specified by the developer. **QRegularExpressionValidator** checks if the string passed to it matches the specified regular expression, in this case, the regex instance.

Lastly, we need to create a few more widgets. The QLabel feedback_label is used to update users about incorrect or missing information. The label and submit_button are added to the submit_h_box layout.

Adding Widgets and Layouts to QFormLayout

Adding widgets to QFormLayout is different from box layouts and QGridLayout. First of all, the method addRow() is used instead of addWidget(). This is also the case when adding other layouts. Secondly, while it is possible to nest layouts into QFormLayout, the layout still fits within the two-column structure.

Let's wrap up building setUpMainWindow() by creating a QFormLayout instance and setting some parameters. First, create a QFormLayout object, main_form, for the main window.

Listing 4-21. Arranging widgets in form layout in setUpMainWindow(), part 4

```
# form.py
    # Organize widgets and layouts in QFormLayout
    main_form = QFormLayout()
    main_form.setFieldGrowthPolicy(
        main_form.FieldGrowthPolicy.AllNonFixedFieldsGrow)
    main_form.setFormAlignment(
        Qt.AlignmentFlag.AlignHCenter | \
        Qt.AlignmentFlag.AlignTop)
    main_form.setLabelAlignment(
        Qt.AlignmentFlag.AlignLeft)

    main_form.addRow(header_label)
    main_form.addRow("Name", name_h_box)
    main_form.addRow("Gender", gender_combo)
    main_form.addRow("Date of Birth", self.birthdate_edit)
    main_form.addRow("Phone", self.phone_edit)
    main_form.addRow("Email", self.email_edit)
    main_form.addRow(QLabel("Comments or Messages"))
    main_form.addRow(extra_info_tedit)
    main_form.addRow(submit_h_box)

    # Set the layout for the main window
    self.setLayout(main_form)
```

Without specifying any parameters or styles, the QFormLayout class will take advantage of a system's native style. To work around this and ensure that the form layout will look the same on different systems, we can set a few parameters.

The enum QFormLayout.FieldGrowthPolicy decides how widgets stretch in the layout. The AllNonFixedFieldsGrow flag ensures that field widgets grow horizontally to fill extra space. The setFormAlignment() method is used to specify how to align a form's contents, and setLabelAlignment() defines the alignment for the labels.

There are a few different ways to add widgets or layouts to a form layout with addRow(). The following list describes them:

- addRow(QWidget(), QWidget()) – Adds two widgets to a row, where the first widget is a *label* and the second is a *field* widget. The first QWidget is typically a QLabel, but it is possible to add other widget types.

- addRow(QWidget(), QLayout()) – Adds a *label* widget and a *layout* to a row.

- addRow(string, QWidget()) – Adds a *string* and a *field* to a row.

- addRow(string, QLayout()) – Adds a *string* and a *layout* to a row.

- addRow(QWidget()) – Adds a single *widget* to a layout.

- addRow(QLayout()) – Nests a single *layout* to the form.

Examples of a few of these can be seen in Listing 4-21. By adding a QLabel and a field widget such as QLineEdit on the same row, you can create a **buddy** for the QLabel.

The slots that the widgets in the form are connected to are created in Listing 4-22. The clearText() slot is used to clear feedback_label whenever the text is edited in one of the form's field widgets.

Listing 4-22. Code for clearText() and checkFormInformation() slots

```
# form.py
    def clearText(self, text):
        """Clear the text for the QLabel that provides
        feedback."""
        self.feedback_label.clear()
```

```
def checkFormInformation(self):
    """Demonstrates a few cases for validating user
    input."""
    if self.first_name_edit.text() == "" or \
        self.last_name_edit.text() == "":
        self.feedback_label.setText(
            "[INFO] Missing names.")
    elif self.phone_edit.hasAcceptableInput() == False:
        self.feedback_label.setText(
            "[INFO] Phone number entered incorrectly.")
    elif self.email_edit.hasAcceptableInput() == False:
        self.feedback_label.setText(
            "[INFO] Email entered incorrectly.")
```

Feedback comes in many forms. In checkFormInformation(), whenever the user presses submit_button in the bottom of the GUI, a series of if conditions are checked. If certain fields don't have acceptable input, then a corresponding message will display in feedback_label.

The next section covers the final built-in layout manager.

Managing Pages with QStackedLayout

For some interfaces, it may be necessary to only show some widgets until certain tasks are complete or to organize widgets into groups and remove clutter. A common example of this is a web browser, where tabs at the top of the window help to separate the different websites.

One way to accomplish this type of layout is by stacking widgets on top of each other using **QStackedLayout**. A single widget added to QStackedLayout serves as a **page**, and other widgets can be appended to that page. With a stacked layout, you also need to include some means to switch between the different pages. Take a look at Figure 4-7 and you will see a QComboBox at the top of the window for changing pages.

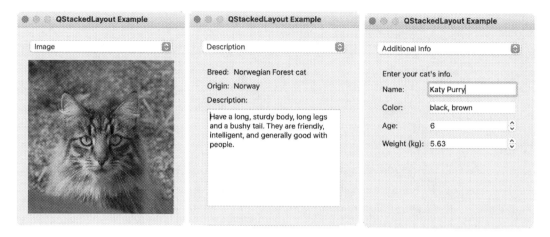

Figure 4-7. *An example of multiple pages in a single window. The image of the cat is from https://pixabay.com*

Tip   PyQt has a convenience class, **QStackedWidget**, which provides the same functionality as QStackedLayout with the additional benefit of QWidget methods. Another widget, QTabWidget (covered in Chapter 6), provides the tabs.

Each page is added to QStackedLayout using addWidget(). Pages that have been added are managed by an internal list of widgets, and accessing each page or widget can be accomplished with the following methods:

- currentIndex() – Returns the index of the visible page. Pages have index values with the beginning index being 0.

- currentWidget() – Retrieves the widget of the visible page.

If a page also contains multiple widgets, those child widgets can be accessed through the widget that currentWidget() returns.

One final note, it is possible to create a dynamic stacked layout where pages are inserted with insertWidget(index, widget) or removed with removeWidget(widget).

Explanation for QStackedLayout

Make sure to download the images folder from the GitHub repository. Starting with the basic_window.py script like before, import the classes like in Listing 4-23 from PyQt and update the MainWindow class for this example.

Listing 4-23. Setting up the main window for using QStackedLayout

```python
# stacked.py
# Import necessary modules
import sys
from PyQt6.QtWidgets import (QApplication, QWidget, QLabel,
    QLineEdit, QTextEdit, QComboBox, QSpinBox, QDoubleSpinBox,
    QStackedLayout, QFormLayout, QVBoxLayout)
from PyQt6.QtCore import Qt
from PyQt6.QtGui import QPixmap

class MainWindow(QWidget):

    def __init__(self):
        super().__init__()
        self.initializeUI()

    def initializeUI(self):
        """Set up the application's GUI."""
        self.setFixedSize(300, 340)
        self.setWindowTitle("QStackedLayout Example")

        self.setUpMainWindow()
        self.show()

if __name__ == '__main__':
    app = QApplication(sys.argv)
    window = MainWindow()
    sys.exit(app.exec())
```

The first widget in Listing 4-24 is the QComboBox object for switching pages. The combo box displays the titles for each page and is connected to the activated signal. The signal is emitted whenever a user selects an item in the QComboBox, and the signal passes the index of the selected page. The switchPage() method is set up in Listing 4-27.

97

Listing 4-24. The setUpMainWindow() method for using QStackedLayout, part 1

```
# stacked.py
    def setUpMainWindow(self):
        """Create and arrange widgets in the main window."""
        # Create and connect the combo box to switch pages
        page_combo = QComboBox()
        page_combo.addItems(["Image", "Description",
            "Additional Info"])
        page_combo.activated.connect(self.switchPage)

        # Create the Image page (Page 1)
        profile_image = QLabel()
        pixmap = QPixmap("images/norwegian.jpg")
        profile_image.setPixmap(pixmap)
        profile_image.setScaledContents(True)
```

Page one contains a single QLabel that displays a QPixmap. The QLabel method setScaledContents() tells the label to use all available space to display its contents.

For page two, we'll use some widgets to display textual information about the image on page one. The widgets are organized in a QFormLayout in Listing 4-25.

Listing 4-25. The setUpMainWindow() method for using QStackedLayout, part 2

```
# stacked.py
        # Create the Profile page (Page 2)
        pg2_form = QFormLayout()
        pg2_form.setFieldGrowthPolicy(
            pg2_form.FieldGrowthPolicy.AllNonFixedFieldsGrow)
        pg2_form.setFormAlignment(
            Qt.AlignmentFlag.AlignHCenter |
            Qt.AlignmentFlag.AlignTop)
        pg2_form.setLabelAlignment(
            Qt.AlignmentFlag.AlignLeft)
```

```
pg2_form.addRow("Breed:",
    QLabel("Norwegian Forest cat"))
pg2_form.addRow("Origin:", QLabel("Norway"))
pg2_form.addRow(QLabel("Description:"))
default_text = """Have a long, sturdy body, long legs
    and a bushy tail. They are friendly, intelligent,
    and generally good with people."""
pg2_form.addRow(QTextEdit(default_text))

pg2_container = QWidget()
pg2_container.setLayout(pg2_form)
```

Refer to the "Building Forms with QFormLayout" section for information about how to arrange widgets in QFormLayout. The layout, however, cannot be added to QStackedLayout. Instead, a **container** widget is created to group all of these widgets together. QWidget can serve as a basic container for other widgets. The layout is then applied to the container using setLayout().

Page three is created in a similar fashion in Listing 4-26, but this time allows for the user to input information using some field widgets.

Listing 4-26. The setUpMainWindow() method for using QStackedLayout, part 3

```
# stacked.py
        # Create the About page (Page 3)
        pg3_form = QFormLayout()
        pg3_form.setFieldGrowthPolicy(
            pg3_form.FieldGrowthPolicy.AllNonFixedFieldsGrow)
        pg3_form.setFormAlignment(
            Qt.AlignmentFlag.AlignHCenter |
            Qt.AlignmentFlag.AlignTop)
        pg3_form.setLabelAlignment(
            Qt.AlignmentFlag.AlignLeft)

        pg3_form.addRow(QLabel("Enter your cat's info."))
        pg3_form.addRow("Name:", QLineEdit())
        pg3_form.addRow("Color:", QLineEdit())
```

```
age_sb = QSpinBox()
age_sb.setRange(0, 30)
pg3_form.addRow("Age:", age_sb)

weight_dsb = QDoubleSpinBox()
weight_dsb.setRange(0.0, 30.0)
pg3_form.addRow("Weight (kg):", weight_dsb)

pg3_container = QWidget()
pg3_container.setLayout(pg3_form)
```

A new widget, QDoubleSpinBox, allows for users to select from a range of floating point values. The three widgets, the label and the two QWidget objects acting as containers, are added to a QStackedLayout object in Listing 4-27.

Listing 4-27. Arrange widgets in setUpMainWindow() using QStackedLayout

```
# stacked.py
        # Create the stacked layout and add pages
        self.stacked_layout = QStackedLayout()
        self.stacked_layout.addWidget(profile_image)
        self.stacked_layout.addWidget(pg2_container)
        self.stacked_layout.addWidget(pg3_container)

        # Create the main layout
        main_v_box = QVBoxLayout()
        main_v_box.addWidget(page_combo)
        main_v_box.addLayout(self.stacked_layout)

        # Set the layout for the main window
        self.setLayout(main_v_box)

    def switchPage(self, index):
        """Slot for switching between tabs."""
        self.stacked_layout.setCurrentIndex(index)
```

Lastly, the switchPage() slot is created to use index from the QComboBox to switch the page using setCurrentIndex().

We've finally looked at all of the different built-in layout managers, but before moving on to the next chapter, now is a good time to talk about a few methods that can be used to manage space in layout managers.

Additional Tips for Managing Space

In this section, you will look at a very brief example that demonstrates a few layout manager methods that can be helpful in ensuring that widgets make the best use of a window's space. When you add widgets to a layout, there are a number of checks that the layout manager performs. These include the following:

- Allocating space based on a widget's `sizeHint()`, the recommended size for a widget, and `sizePolicy()`, which defines the resizing behavior for a widget

- Applying stretch factors, if any are specified

- Additional sizing factors set by a developer, such as setting the minimum or maximum size, height, or width of a widget

For the box layouts, you can adjust the space between items using the following methods:

- `addSpacing(int)` – Creates blank space between widgets specified by `int` (in pixels)

- `addStretch(int)` – Adds a stretchable area of value `int` between widgets that is proportional to the stretch factors of other widgets

Different methods are used for managing the horizontal and vertical spacing between widgets in grid and form layouts, as shown in the following list:

- `setHorizontalSpacing(int)` –Sets the horizontal spacing between widgets (in pixels)

- `setVerticalSpacing(int)` – Sets the vertical spacing between widgets (in pixels)

- `setSpacing(int)` – Sets the horizontal and vertical spacing between widgets (in pixels)

We'll take a look at an example for managing space in `QVBoxLayout` in the following section.

Explanation for Managing Space

For this application, you should create three widgets in the MainWindow class in Listing 4-28 that are organized vertically in the window using QVBoxLayout.

Listing 4-28. Brief demonstration of how spacing works with QVBoxLayout

```
# spacing.py
# Import necessary modules
import sys
from PyQt6.QtWidgets import (QApplication, QWidget,
    QLabel, QPushButton, QLineEdit, QVBoxLayout)

class MainWindow(QWidget):

    def __init__(self):
        super().__init__()
        self.initializeUI()

    def initializeUI(self):
        """Set up the application's GUI."""
        self.setMinimumSize(300, 200)
        self.setWindowTitle("Spacing Example")

        label = QLabel("Enter text")
        line_edit = QLineEdit()
        button = QPushButton("End")

        main_v_box = QVBoxLayout()
        main_v_box.addWidget(label)
        main_v_box.addSpacing(20)
        main_v_box.addWidget(line_edit)
        main_v_box.addStretch()
        main_v_box.addWidget(button)

        self.setLayout(main_v_box)
        self.show()
```

```
if __name__ == '__main__':
    app = QApplication(sys.argv)
    window = MainWindow()
    sys.exit(app.exec())
```

Without adding any spaces or stretching, you will get the left GUI in Figure 4-8. To place a blank, stretchable space in between the QLineEdit and the QPushButton widgets, the addStretch() method is used. An argument does not need to be passed to addStretch() if you want all of the spacing to be the same.

A fixed amount of space is added between the label and line_edit instances using addSpacing(). Have a look at the differences spacing and stretch factor make in the right screenshot in Figure 4-8.

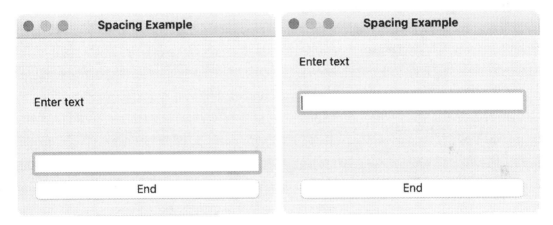

Figure 4-8. *The GUI before adding spacing and stretching (left) and after (right)*

Setting Content Margins

As a final task left for you, add the following line of code in spacing.py to see how it affects the layout:

```
main_v_box.setContentsMargins(40, 30, 40, 30)
```

A **margin** adds space to the outside of a layout. This can be done in PyQt with the setContentMargins() method. Each integer in the code specifies the size of the border in pixels as (left, top, right, bottom).

Summary

Taking the time to learn about layout management will save you time and effort when coding your own GUI applications. In this chapter, we reviewed the many ways of organizing widgets in a PyQt interface. Depending upon the requirements of your application, there are a variety of options, including absolute positioning and any of the built-in Qt layout managers.

The box layouts, `QHBoxLayout` and `QVBoxLayout`, are used to arrange widgets horizontally or vertically. `QFormLayout` is great for building forms. `QGridLayout` is useful for strategically organizing and sizing widgets in a grid-like layout. Last, `QStackedLayout` can be used when you need to manage space in a window by stacking widgets on top of one another. Each class has its own special use case, but the real strength lies in how convenient it is to combine them to create complex arrangements.

The advantages of using a layout manager include having control over the position of child widgets, being able to set default sizes for widgets, ease of use for handling the resizing of widgets, and simplification when it comes to updating content in the window or parent widget when something changes, such as the hiding, showing, or removing of a child widget. Additionally, you can actually design and lay out your interface graphically using Qt Designer. We will take a look at how to do this in Chapter 8.

In Chapter 5, we will take a look at how to build main windows that include menu bars, dock widgets, and more.

CHAPTER 5

Menus, Toolbars, and More

Desktop applications provide means for not only organizing widgets but for arranging and presenting interactive features and tools to the users as well. A **menu** is a list of commands that a computer program can perform presented in a more manageable and organized fashion. Numerous devices and systems include menus for helping the user to navigate and select different options and tasks, and a well-organized menu will make a program easier to use.

In this chapter, you will

- Find out how to create main windows that inherit from QMainWindow

- Create menus, submenus, and checkable menu items using PyQt classes such as QMenuBar and QAction

- Discover how to set and change widget and main window icons

- Learn about PyQt's built-in dialog classes, including QFileDialog, QInputDialog, QColorDialog, and more

- Set up and utilize an application's status bar to provide feedback

- Use the QDockWidget class to build detachable widgets that can display common tools and operations

- Build practical applications that teach additional skills, such as manipulating images using QPixmap and QTransform classes and setting up applications that print images with the QPrinter class

This chapter will create the foundation for completely functioning programs that can either be used right away or as starting points for your own programs.

Let's begin by thinking about common practices used when creating menus.

105

© Joshua M Willman 2022
J. M. Willman, *Beginning PyQt*, https://doi.org/10.1007/978-1-4842-7999-1_5

Common Practices for Creating Menus

The arrangement of GUI menus and **menu items**, or the options in a menu, generally follows a list of standard practices that have been created over the years. Different platforms, such as macOS and Windows, also have their own conventions, and this section will look at the ones common to them all.

- **There is a general pattern for ordering menus.** From left to right, the File menu handles common file and application interactions, the Edit menu contains editing operations, and so on. The Help menu is typically last with application information and instructions.

- **Menus also contain commonly used items.** While it will vary depending upon the type of application you are developing, there are also general items in menus. The most common examples include New, Open, Save, and Print in File and Undo, Redo, Cut, Copy, and Paste in Edit.

- **There are common shortcut keys for performing a task.** Common shortcuts include Ctrl+V for Paste (Command+V on macOS) or Ctrl+X for the Cut item (Command+X on macOS).

- **Separators are used to organize related items.** They are also used to make menus easier to navigate.

Let's begin by putting a few of those ideas into practice in this chapter's first example.

Creating a Simple Menu Bar

For the program in Figure 5-1, you will be taking a look at how to create a simple **menu bar**, which is a set of pull-down menus with a list of commands for interacting with an application. In this GUI, the menu bar will contain one menu, File, with only one command, Quit.

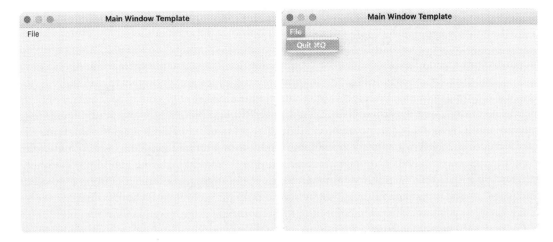

Figure 5-1. *A menu bar is created (left) displaying the File menu. A pull-down menu is displayed (right) with one command, Quit*

Let's create the window that will be the template script for a number of projects throughout this book.

Explanation for Creating a Menu Bar

To begin creating the window in Figure 5-1, we can use the basic_window.py script from Chapter 1 as this GUI's foundation. In Listing 5-1, import the QApplication class like usual, but this time import the class QMainWindow rather than QWidget. The QMainWindow class provides the functionalities for building a main window's key features, such as menu bars and toolbars. In PyQt6, the QAction class is now located in the QtGui module.

Listing 5-1. Creating a class that inherits QMainWindow

```
# main_window_template.py
# Import necessary modules
import sys
from PyQt6.QtWidgets import (QApplication, QMainWindow)
from PyQt6.QtGui import QAction

class MainWindow(QMainWindow):

    def __init__(self):
        super().__init__()
        self.initializeUI()
```

```
    def initializeUI(self):
        """Set up the application's GUI."""
        self.setMinimumSize(450, 350)
        self.setWindowTitle("Main Window Template")

        self.setUpMainWindow()
        self.createActions()
        self.createMenu()
        self.show()

if __name__ == '__main__':
    app = QApplication(sys.argv)
    window = MainWindow()
    sys.exit(app.exec())
```

The MainWindow class in this program inherits from QMainWindow, not QWidget. New class methods, createActions() and createMenu(), will be used to create the menu bar in Listing 5-2.

The following subsection delves a little further into the differences between QMainWindow and QWidget.

QMainWindow vs. QWidget

The **QMainWindow** class focuses on creating and managing the layout for the main window of an application. It allows you to set up a window with a status bar, a toolbar, dock widgets, or other menu features in predefined locations.

The QWidget class is the base class for all user interface objects in Qt, including widgets. The widgets you have used, such as QPushButton and QTextEdit, inherit QWidget, granting them access to a wide array of methods for interacting with an interface or setting the parameters of a widget instance. It is important to note that the QMainWindow and the QDialog classes also inherit QWidget and are special purpose classes focusing on creating main windows and dialogs, respectively.

A **window** in an application is really just a widget that is not placed within a parent widget. This means that a class that inherits QWidget can be considered a window if it does not have a parent. Windows will typically have their own title bar and frame. In Figure 5-2, you can see how the different widgets that QMainWindow can use have areas specifically assigned for them.

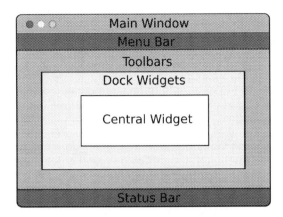

Figure 5-2. *Layout structure for the QMainWindow class (Adapted from* `https://doc.qt.io/`)

The menu bar is fixed horizontally along the top of the window, while the status bar can be found along the bottom. Toolbars can be situated between the menu bar and status bar and are allowed to be placed vertically or horizontally. Dock widgets can be arranged similarly. The central widget in the center of the window must be set if you are going to use `QMainWindow` as your base class. For example, you could use a single `QTextEdit` widget to act as the main widget in the window or create a `QWidget` object with other widgets arranged inside itself.

Creating the Menu Bar and Adding Actions

In the `initializeUI()` method in Listing 5-1, you'll notice three different method calls for setting up the main window and menu. This is done in order to organize and make managing the code easier no matter the size of the application. The first method to create in Listing 5-2, `setUpMainWindow()`, is left here as a placeholder for future projects.

Listing 5-2. Basic structure for creating a menu bar in an application

```python
# main_window_template.py
    def setUpMainWindow(self):
        """Create and arrange widgets in the main window."""
        pass
```

```
def createActions(self):
    """Create the application's menu actions."""
    # Create actions for File menu
    self.quit_act = QAction("&Quit")
    self.quit_act.setShortcut("Ctrl+Q")
    self.quit_act.triggered.connect(self.close)

def createMenu(self):
    """Create the application's menu bar."""
    self.menuBar().setNativeMenuBar(False)

    # Create file menu and add actions
    file_menu = self.menuBar().addMenu("File")
    file_menu.addAction(self.quit_act)
```

The next method, createActions(), sets up the actions for the program's menu. Actions are used to create options in a menu or toolbar, such as Open, Close, and Save. In PyQt, these actions are created from the **QAction** class. Take a look at how the Quit action, quit_act, is created and then added to file_menu.

The Quit action is an instance of the QAction class. Actions must also have a parent, generally passed as the final parameter to the QAction instance. Since the main window is the parent here, we can simply use the self keyword to bind the action to the class. In the next line, the shortcut for the quit_act is set explicitly using the setShortcut() method with the key combination Ctrl+Q. Another way to set the shortcut is to use the ampersand sign, &, in front of the letter you want to use as the shortcut. Depending upon your system, this will display an underscore under the letter that indicates the shortcut key.

Note   On macOS, shortcuts are disabled by default. The best way to set up shortcuts is to use setShortcut().

Actions in menus also use signals and slots. When an action in the menu is selected, it emits a signal that needs to be connected to a slot in order to perform an operation. This is done using the triggered signal.

Sometimes, the same option is displayed in both a menu bar and a toolbar. One common example is the Print operation in a word processor application, where the action can be selected from either the File menu, from the toolbar, or using a shortcut. No matter what causes the signal to be emitted, the QAction class will ensure that the action is performed correctly.

Last, the createMenu() method sets up the menu bar. For this example, there is only a single menu, File. In order to create a horizontal menu bar, you'll need to create an instance of the **QMenuBar** class. Since the MainWindow class inherits QMainWindow, this can be done easily by calling the QMainWindow method menuBar().

Note   Due to guidelines set by macOS, the menu bar will not appear in the GUI. You can change this with self.menuBar().setNativeMenuBar(False). For Windows or Linux users, you can comment this line out or delete it.

Adding menus to the menu bar is also really simple in PyQt:

```
file_menu = self.menuBar().addMenu("File")
```

Here, the addMenu() method is used to add a menu named File to the menu bar. Using addMenu() adds a **QMenu** object. Once again, it is just as simple to use the functions provided by the QMainWindow class.

Since menus, windows, and some widgets can display icons, let's take a moment to find out a little bit more about the QIcon class.

Using Icons and the QIcon Class

Icons can be used as small graphical images in a GUI, or as symbols that can represent actions the user can perform in a menu or on a button. They are useful for helping the user quickly locate common actions and navigate an application. The toolbars in word processing applications are a good example of this concept, containing large amounts of tools, each with an icon or textual description.

Chapter 2 briefly introduced a Qt class for handling images, QPixmap. The **QIcon** class provides methods that can use pixmaps and modify their style or size so that they can be used in an application. One really great use of QIcon is to set the appearance of an icon representing an action to active or disabled.

Explanation for Using Icons

The example seen in Figure 5-3 demonstrates how to

- Set and change icons dynamically on a QPushButton widget

- Reset the application icon in a window's title bar

- Organize and apply the central widget in a QMainWindow instance

---

Note   For this and other examples in this chapter, you will need to download the images folder and its contents from the GitHub repository.

Figure 5-3. *The application icon is not displayed in the title area on macOS systems*

Note   For macOS users, the icon in the application window cannot be applied due to system guidelines. You should still take a look at this program though, as it also shows how to set icons for other widgets in PyQt.

This GUI is a simple exercise in showing how to switch the icon on a QPushButton, which may come in handy when a button's state or purpose has changed. Whenever the user clicks on the button, the fruit that is displayed is randomly selected and the icon is changed. Listing 5-3 sets up the main window and applies a new icon to the title bar in the main window.

Listing 5-3. Code for showing how to set icons for the main window

```
# change_icons.py
# Import necessary modules
import sys, random
from PyQt6.QtWidgets import (QApplication, QMainWindow,
    QWidget, QLabel, QPushButton, QVBoxLayout)
from PyQt6.QtCore import Qt, QSize
from PyQt6.QtGui import QIcon

class MainWindow(QMainWindow):

    def __init__(self):
        super().__init__()
        self.initializeUI()

    def initializeUI(self):
        """Set up the application's GUI."""
        self.setMinimumSize(200, 200)
        self.setWindowTitle("Changing Icons Example")
        self.setWindowIcon(QIcon("images/pyqt_logo.png"))

        self.setUpMainWindow()
        self.show()

if __name__ == '__main__':
    app = QApplication(sys.argv)
    window = MainWindow()
    sys.exit(app.exec())
```

The application icon normally displayed in the top left corner of a window on some systems is changed to the PyQt logo in the right image in Figure 5-4. A window's icon can be set using the setWindowIcon() method and passing it a QIcon object. QIcon takes a path to the image location as an argument. Notice in Figure 5-3 how the application icon is missing in macOS.

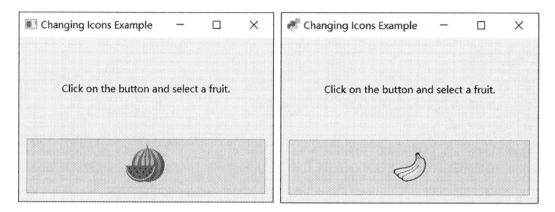

Figure 5-4. *The original application icon in the top left corner of the window (left) can be set to a new icon (right) using the setWindowIcon() method*

The main window created in Listing 5-4 is composed of a QLabel, which provides instruction to the user, and a QPushButton, for selecting one of the fruit images contained in the images list.

Listing 5-4. The setUpMainWindow() method for using icons

```python
# change_icons.py
    def setUpMainWindow(self):
        """Create and arrange widgets in the main window."""
        info_label = QLabel(
            "Click on the button and select a fruit.")
        info_label.setAlignment(Qt.AlignmentFlag.AlignCenter)

        self.images = [
            "images/1_apple.png", "images/2_pineapple.png",
            "images/3_watermelon.png", "images/4_banana.png"]

        self.icon_button = QPushButton()
        self.icon_button.setIcon(
            QIcon(random.choice(self.images)))
        self.icon_button.setIconSize(QSize(60, 60))
        self.icon_button.clicked.connect(
            self.changeButtonIcon)
```

CHAPTER 5   MENUS, TOOLBARS, AND MORE

For the widgets that can display icons, calling the setIcon() method on that widget will allow you to display an icon on it. Here, the icon for icon_button is chosen randomly and passed as an argument to be handled by QIcon. Calling the setIconSize() method on a widget can be used to change the size of the icon. The **QSize** class is used to define the two-dimensional size of a widget. PyQt will handle the sizing and style of the widget based on the parameters you specify.

Finally, the button is connected to the slot in Listing 5-5. In the MainWindow class, create an additional method, changeButtonIcon(), to handle setting the new icon.

Listing 5-5. Creating the changeButtonIcon() slot

```
# change_icons.py
    def changeButtonIcon(self):
        """When the button is clicked, change the icon to
        a different random icon from the images list."""
        self.icon_button.setIcon(
            QIcon(random.choice(self.images)))
        self.icon_button.setIconSize(QSize(60, 60))
```

Whenever icon_button is clicked, setIcon() is used to apply a new icon, and setIconSize() is used to ensure that the icons are all the same size, avoiding any resizing issues.

Setting the Central Widget

The widgets have not been arranged, and the central widget has not been set yet in the main window. Back in the setUpMainWindow() method, the label and button widgets are organized in Listing 5-6 using QVBoxLayout.

Listing 5-6. Setting the central widget in the main window

```
# change_icons.py
        # Create vertical layout and add widgets
        main_v_box = QVBoxLayout()
        main_v_box.addWidget(info_label)
        main_v_box.addWidget(self.icon_button)
```

```
# Set main layout of window
container = QWidget()
container.setLayout(main_v_box)
self.setCentralWidget(container)
```

QWidget can be used as a **container**, providing a means to group and control widgets. Qt has a number of specific widgets that specifically serve as containers, but for now, we'll stick to using QWidget. The widget for the container QWidget is set using setLayout(), and the QMainWindow method setCentralWidget() is used to set the primary widget in the window.

Before building a larger project with menus and QMainWindow, let's first take a look at some of PyQt's built-in dialog classes.

Built-in Dialog Classes in PyQt

Dialogs are great not only for providing feedback but also for interacting with local files or for collecting input from the user. PyQt is able to create native-looking windows, dialogs, and widgets no matter the system. Let's take a moment to get familiar with some of the built-in dialog boxes and see how to use them.

The QFileDialog Class

The **QFileDialog** class can be used to open and select files or directories on your computer. This dialog class is useful for opening, saving, and naming files.

To open a local file, the QFileDialog method getOpenFileName() is used. An example of this is shown in the following snippet of code:

```
file_name, ok = QFileDialog.getOpenFileName(self,
          "Open File", "/Users/user_name/Desktop/",
          "Image Files (*.png *.jpg *.bmp)")
```

The first argument is the parent of the dialog box. If the parent is the main window, then the dialog will appear above it on the screen. Next, you can create a title for the dialog box. This is followed by the directory location that will appear when the dialog opens. Here, the user's Desktop will be displayed. The final argument passed is the filter used to present files with matching patterns given in the string. For the previous code, image files with the extensions .png, .jpg, and .bmp are selectable. You can specify other file types as well.

Saving a file is done in a similar fashion using getSaveFileName():

```
file_name, ok = QFileDialog.getSaveFileName(self,
            "Save File", "/Users/user_name/Desktop/",
            "Text Files (*.txt)")
```

Here, the user is only allowed to save text files with the extension .txt. The look of the dialog box that appears will also reflect the type of system you are using. To change this or other properties, you can include the options parameter:

```
file_name, ok = QFileDialog.getOpenFileName(self,
            "Open File", "/Users/user_name/Desktop/",
            "Image Files (*.png *.jpg *.bmp)",
            options = QFileDialog.Option.DontUseNativeDialog)
```

By default, the system's native style is used.

The QInputDialog Class

QInputDialog is a native dialog in PyQt that can be used to receive input from the user. The input is a single value that can be a string, a number, or an item from a list.

To create a basic input dialog and get text from the user:

```
find_text, ok = QInputDialog.getText(
            self, "Search Text", "Find:")
```

In this example, an input dialog object is created by calling QInputDialog. getText(). Using getText() allows the user to enter a single string into a QLineEdit widget, like in Figure 5-5. The second argument, "Search Text", is the title for the dialog. The third argument is the label that appears next to the QLineEdit widget. An input dialog returns two values: the input from the user, find_text, and a Boolean value, ok. The Boolean value is determined by which budget is pressed in the dialog, True for the OK button and False for Cancel.

Figure 5-5. *Example of a QInputDialog dialog from the Rich Text Notepad GUI*

Other types of input can be collected using one of the following `QInputDialog` methods:

- `getMultiLineText()` – Method to get a multiline string from the user

- `getInt()` – Method to get an integer from the user

- `getDouble()` – Method to get a floating-point number from the user

- `getItem()` – Method to let the user select an item from a list of strings

The QFontDialog Class

QFontDialog provides a dialog box that allows the user to select and manipulate different types of fonts. To create a font dialog box and choose a font, use the `getFont()` method:

```
font, ok = QFontDialog.getFont()
```

The `font` keyword is the particular font returned from `getFont()`, and `ok` is a Boolean variable to check whether the user selected a font and clicked the OK button. The font dialog on macOS is shown in Figure 5-6.

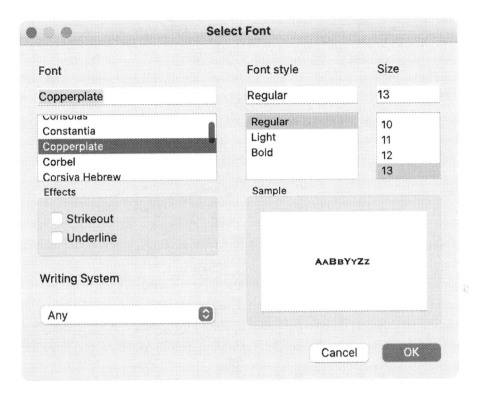

Figure 5-6. *Example of a QFontDialog dialog box*

When the user clicks OK, a font is selected. However, if Cancel is clicked, then the initial font is returned. If you have a default font that you would like to use in case the user does not select OK, you could do the following:

```
font, ok = QFontDialog.getFont(
        QFont("Helvetica", 10), self)
self.text_edit_widget.setCurrentFont(font)
```

In order to change the font if a new one has been chosen, use the `setCurrentFont()` method and change it to the new font.

The QColorDialog Class

The **QColorDialog** class creates a dialog box for selecting colors like the one in Figure 5-7. Selecting colors can be useful for changing the color of the text, the window's background color, and many other tasks.

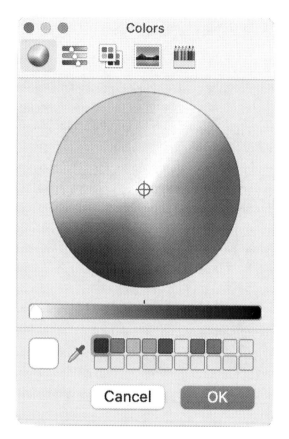

Figure 5-7. *QColorDialog dialog box*

To create a color dialog box and select a color, use the following line of code:

```
color = QColorDialog.getColor()
```

Then check if the user selected a valid color and clicked on the OK button by using the isValid() method.

If so, you could use the QTextEdit method setTextColor() to change the color of the text or use setBackgroundColor() to change the color of the background:

```
if color.isValid():
        self.text_field.setTextColor(color)
```

The final dialog we are going to look at is a static method from QMessageBox.

The About QMessageBox

In many applications, you can often find an About item in the menu. Clicking on this item will open a dialog box that displays information about the application such as the software's logo, title, latest version number, and other legal information.

The QMessageBox class that we looked at in Chapter 3 also provides an about() method for creating a dialog for displaying a title and text. To create an About dialog box, try

```
QMessageBox.about(self, "About Notepad",
    """<p>Beginner's Practical Guide to PyQt</p>
    <p>Project 5.1 - Notepad GUI</p>""")
```

This creates the dialog seen in Figure 5-8. If you have never used HTML before, <p> and </p> around the text are HTML tags that create paragraphs. We'll take a look at using HTML with PyQt in Chapter 6.

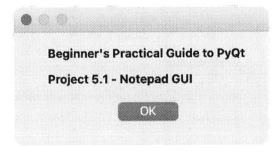

Figure 5-8. *Example About dialog box from the Rich Text Notepad GUI*

You can also display an application icon in the window. If an icon is not provided, the about() method will try and find one from the parent widget. To provide an icon, call the setWindowIcon() method on the QApplication object in the program's main() method.

```
app.setWindowIcon(QIcon("images/app_logo.png"))
```

Next, you'll use what you've learned about menus and dialogs to create a larger application.

Project 5.1 – Rich Text Notepad GUI

For the first project, let's use the concepts learned so far in this chapter to build a notepad application that supports rich text using QTextEdit. Figure 5-9 shows an example of the completed application with text of different sizes, colors, fonts, and highlights.

Figure 5-9. *Notepad GUI with menu bar and QTextEdit widget*

This time we will add a proper menu bar with menus and actions. The user will also have the ability to open and save their text, either as rich text or plain text, and edit the text's font, color, or size to give more functionality and creativity to their notes.

Designing the Rich Text Notepad GUI

It's best to begin building a GUI by mapping out its key features, such as what widgets are used in the main interface and what options can be found in the menu.

For a note-taking application, the layout is relatively simple – a menu bar at the top of the window with different menus for the various functions and tools and an area for displaying and editing text. For the text field, we will be using a QTextEdit widget that will also serve as the central widget for the QMainWindow object. Take a look at Figure 5-10 to see the various menu items that are included in this project.

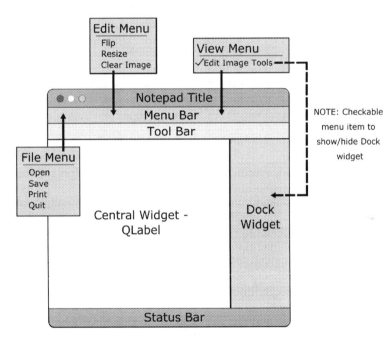

Figure 5-10. *Design showing the layout for the Notepad GUI and the different menus and actions*

This application has four menus in the menu bar: File, Edit, Tools, and Help. Having different menus in the menu bar can help to organize actions under different categories as well as help the user to more easily locate actions they want to use.

Explanation for the Rich Text Notepad GUI

QTextEdit already provides the functionality for writing in either plain text or rich text formats. In this program, you will explore how to use some methods from QTextEdit, such as undo and redo, as well as the different dialog classes to create a notepad application. Use `main_window_template.py` script from the beginning of this chapter to set up Listing 5-7 and the framework for the `MainWindow` class.

Listing 5-7. Setting up the main window for the RichText Notepad GUI

```python
# richtext_notepad.py
# Import necessary modules
import sys
from PyQt6.QtWidgets import (QApplication, QMainWindow,
    QMessageBox, QTextEdit, QFileDialog, QInputDialog,
    QFontDialog, QColorDialog)
from PyQt6.QtCore import Qt
from PyQt6.QtGui import QIcon, QTextCursor, QColor, QAction

class MainWindow(QMainWindow):

    def __init__(self):
        super().__init__()
        self.initializeUI()

    def initializeUI(self):
        """Set up the application's GUI."""
        self.setMinimumSize(400, 500)
        self.setWindowTitle("5.1 - Rich Text Notepad GUI")

        self.setUpMainWindow()
        self.createActions()
        self.createMenu()
        self.show()

if __name__ == "__main__":
    app = QApplication(sys.argv)
    window = MainWindow()
    sys.exit(app.exec())
```

There are quite a few classes to import for the notepad application. From the `QtWidgets` module, we need to import `QMainWindow` for creating the menu bar and menu items. We also need to include the different PyQt dialog classes such as `QFileDialog` and QInputDialog. From QtGui, QIcon is used for handling icons, QTextCursor is used to get information about the cursor in text documents, QColor provides methods to create colors in PyQt, and QAction will create the actions used by the menu.

The MainWindow class inherits QMainWindow. In initializeUI(), the methods for setting up the main window and its menu bar are called. The main window's text edit widget is created in Listing 5-8.

Listing 5-8. The setUpMainWindow() method for the Rich Text Notepad GUI

```
# richtext_notepad.py
    def setUpMainWindow(self):
        """Create and arrange widgets in the main window."""
        self.text_edit = QTextEdit()
        self.text_edit.textChanged.connect(
            self.removeHighlights)
        self.setCentralWidget(self.text_edit)
```

The window consists of a single QTextEdit widget and is set as the central widget for MainWindow. The signal textChanged is emitted when text is edited or pasted into the widget and is connected to the slot removeHighlights(), which is set up in Listing 5-14.

Next, the createActions() method in Listings 5-9 and 5-10 creates the actions for the menu.

Listing 5-9. The createActions() method for the Rich Text Notepad GUI, part 1

```
# richtext_notepad.py
    def createActions(self):
        """Create the application's menu actions."""
        # Create actions for File menu
        self.new_act = QAction(
            QIcon("images/new_file.png"), "New")
        self.new_act.setShortcut("Ctrl+N")
        self.new_act.triggered.connect(self.clearText)

        self.open_act = QAction(
            QIcon("images/open_file.png"), "Open")
        self.open_act.setShortcut("Ctrl+O")
        self.open_act.triggered.connect(self.openFile)
```

125

```
self.save_act = QAction(
    QIcon("images/save_file.png"), "Save")
self.save_act.setShortcut("Ctrl+S")
self.save_act.triggered.connect(self.saveToFile)

self.quit_act = QAction(
    QIcon("images/exit.png"), "Quit")
self.quit_act.setShortcut("Ctrl+Q")
self.quit_act.triggered.connect(self.close)
```

There are four menus in the notepad's menu bar. The actions for the first menu, File, include New for clearing all of the text, Open for opening an existing rich or plain text file, Save for saving the QTextEdit widget's current text, and Quit. Let's look at the first one, since the others are set up similarly.

The new_act variable is assigned to a QAction object. QIcon is used to set an icon next to the action's text in the menu. Then the action is given text to display, "New". Many of the actions in the notepad program are given a textual shortcut using setShortcut(). Finally, we connect the signal that is emitted when new_act is clicked on to a slot, in this case, clearText().

Listing 5-10 creates the actions for the Edit, Tools, and Help menus.

Listing 5-10. The createActions() method for the Rich Text Notepad GUI, part 2

```
# richtext_notepad.py
    # Create actions for Edit menu
    self.undo_act = QAction(
        QIcon("images/undo.png"), "Undo")
    self.undo_act.setShortcut("Ctrl+Z")
    self.undo_act.triggered.connect(self.text_edit.undo)

    self.redo_act = QAction(
        QIcon("images/redo.png"), "Redo")
    self.redo_act.setShortcut("Ctrl+Shift+Z")
    self.redo_act.triggered.connect(self.text_edit.redo)

    self.cut_act = QAction(QIcon("images/cut.png"), "Cut")
    self.cut_act.setShortcut("Ctrl+X")
    self.cut_act.triggered.connect(self.text_edit.cut)
```

```python
self.copy_act = QAction(
    QIcon("images/copy.png"), "Copy")
self.copy_act.setShortcut("Ctrl+C")
self.copy_act.triggered.connect(self.text_edit.copy)

self.paste_act = QAction(
    QIcon("images/paste.png"), "Paste")
self.paste_act.setShortcut("Ctrl+V")
self.paste_act.triggered.connect(self.text_edit.paste)

self.find_act = QAction(
    QIcon("images/find.png"), "Find All")
self.find_act.setShortcut("Ctrl+F")
self.find_act.triggered.connect(self.searchText)

# Create actions for Tools menu
self.font_act = QAction(
    QIcon("images/font.png"), "Font")
self.font_act.setShortcut("Ctrl+T")
self.font_act.triggered.connect(self.chooseFont)

self.color_act = QAction(
    QIcon("images/color.png"), "Color")
self.color_act.setShortcut("Ctrl+Shift+C")
self.color_act.triggered.connect(self.chooseFontColor)

self.highlight_act = QAction(
    QIcon("images/highlight.png"), "Highlight")
self.highlight_act.setShortcut("Ctrl+Shift+H")
self.highlight_act.triggered.connect(
    self.chooseFontBackgroundColor)

# Create actions for Help menu
self.about_act = QAction("About")
self.about_act.triggered.connect(self.aboutDialog)
```

QTextEdit already has predefined slots, such as cut(), copy(), and paste(), that create standard text-editing functionalities. For most of the actions in the Edit menu, their signals are connected to these special slots rather than creating new ones, with the exception being find_act.

The actions created in the Tools menu call slots that open dialogs. These actions are used for altering the appearance of the text. The about_act is used to display an About dialog.

With the actions created, the next step is to create the corresponding menu items in Listing 5-11.

Listing 5-11. The createMenu() method for the Rich Text Notepad GUI

```
# richtext_notepad.py
    def createMenu(self):
        """Create the application's menu bar."""
        self.menuBar().setNativeMenuBar(False)

        # Create File menu and add actions
        file_menu = self.menuBar().addMenu("File")
        file_menu.addAction(self.new_act)
        file_menu.addSeparator()
        file_menu.addAction(self.open_act)
        file_menu.addAction(self.save_act)
        file_menu.addSeparator()
        file_menu.addAction(self.quit_act)
        # Create Edit menu and add actions
        edit_menu = self.menuBar().addMenu("Edit")
        edit_menu.addAction(self.undo_act)
        edit_menu.addAction(self.redo_act)
        edit_menu.addSeparator()
        edit_menu.addAction(self.cut_act)
        edit_menu.addAction(self.copy_act)
        edit_menu.addAction(self.paste_act)
        edit_menu.addSeparator()
        edit_menu.addAction(self.find_act)

        # Create Tools menu and add actions
        tool_menu = self.menuBar().addMenu("Tools")
```

```
tool_menu.addAction(self.font_act)
tool_menu.addAction(self.color_act)
tool_menu.addAction(self.highlight_act)

# Create Help menu and add actions
help_menu = self.menuBar().addMenu("Help")
help_menu.addAction(self.about_act)
```

The different actions are added to the appropriate menus in the `MainWindow` class's menu bar with the `addMenu()` method. To add a divider between categories in a menu, use `addSeparator()`. The menu bar can be seen in Figure 5-11.

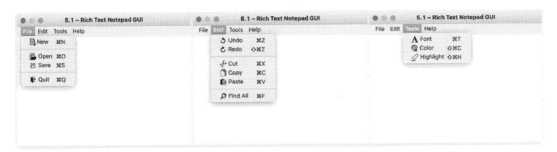

Figure 5-11. *The Notepad GUI and its menus – File (left), Edit (middle), and Tools(right)*

There are a number of slots that are called on when a menu item is clicked. Some of them open a dialog box and return some kind of input from the user, such as a new file, text or background color, or a keyword for searching the text.

Listing 5-12 begins constructing the slots for the File menu.

Listing 5-12. The clearText() and openFile() slots for the File menu

```
# richtext_notepad.py
    def clearText(self):
        """Clear the QTextEdit field."""
        answer = QMessageBox.question(self, "Clear Text",
            "Do you want to clear the text?",
            QMessageBox.StandardButton.No | \
            QMessageBox.StandardButton.Yes,
            QMessageBox.StandardButton.Yes)
```

```
        if answer == QMessageBox.StandardButton.Yes:
            self.text_edit.clear()

    def openFile(self):
        """Open a text or html file and display its contents
        in the text edit field."""
        file_name, _ = QFileDialog.getOpenFileName(
            self, "Open File", "",
            "HTML Files (*.html);;Text Files (*.txt)")

        if file_name:
            with open(file_name, "r") as f:
                notepad_text = f.read()
            self.text_edit.setText(notepad_text)
```

Rather than closing a window and opening a new one when the user selects New from the File menu, the text is simply cleared in clearText(). A QMessageBox is presented, and the QTextEdit method clear() removes all of the current text if the user clicks Yes.

A QFileDialog is shown to the user when Open is clicked. The user can select either HTML or text files on their computer. With the file selected, the QTextEdit.setText() is used to apply the text in the QTextEdit widget.

The slot for saving text, saveToFile(), is created in Listing 5-13.

Listing 5-13. The saveToFile() slot for the File menu

```
# richtext_notepad.py
    def saveToFile(self):
        """If the save button is clicked, display dialog
        asking user if they want to save the text in the text
        edit field to a text or rich text file."""
        file_name, _ = QFileDialog.getSaveFileName(
            self, "Save File", "",
            "HTML Files (*.html);;Text Files (*.txt)")

        if file_name.endswith(".txt"):
            notepad_text = self.text_edit.toPlainText()
            with open(file_name, "w") as f:
                f.write(notepad_text)
```

```
    elif file_name.endswith(".html"):
        notepad_richtext = self.text_edit.toHtml()
        with open(file_name, "w") as f:
            f.write(notepad_richtext)
    else:
        QMessageBox.information(
            self, "Not Saved", "Text not saved.",
            QMessageBox.StandardButton.Ok)
```

The user can choose between two file extensions, .html or .txt. If .txt is selected, QTextEdit.toPlainText() is used to convert the text to plain text. The text is then written to a file. Otherwise, the QTextEdit method toHtml() is used to save the rich text to a file.

The only menu item in the Edit menu that doesn't call a built-in QTextEdit slot is the Find All option, created in Listing 5-14.

Listing 5-14. The searchText() slot for the Edit menu

```
# richtext_notepad.py
    def searchText(self):
        """Search for text."""
        # Display input dialog to ask user for text to find
        find_text, ok = QInputDialog.getText(
            self, "Search Text", "Find:")

        if ok:
            extra_selections = []
            # Set the cursor to the beginning
            self.text_edit.moveCursor(
                QTextCursor.MoveOperation.Start)
            color = QColor(Qt.GlobalColor.gray)

            while(self.text_edit.find(find_text)):
                # Use ExtraSelection() to mark the text you
                # are searching for as gray
                selection = QTextEdit.ExtraSelection()
                selection.format.setBackground(color)
```

131

```
                # Set the cursor of the selection
                selection.cursor = self.text_edit.textCursor()
                extra_selections.append(selection)

            # Highlight all selections in the QTextEdit widget
            self.text_edit.setExtraSelections(
                extra_selections)

    def removeHighlights(self):
        """Reset extra selections after editing text."""
        self.text_edit.setExtraSelections([])
```

The QInputDialog in Figure 5-5 allows the user to enter a string. If the user presses OK in the dialog, the cursor for the text_edit moves back to the beginning of the text with moveCursor() and the QTextCursor flag Start. QTextEdit already has a method for finding matches, find(). However, it only finds the first match and stops. The searchText() slot will iterate over the text, searching for all matches, and highlight them gray.

When a match is found, the QTextEdit structure ExtraSelection() is used to specify the character format and cursor for a selection of text in QTextEdit. The setExtraSelections() method allows for more than one match to be highlighted.

The removeHighlights() slot is used to reset the extra selections to an empty list, consequently removing the gray highlight.

Listing 5-15 sets up the slots for the Tools menu. Each slot will open a dialog for changing the appearance of the text.

Listing 5-15. Various slots for the Tools menu

```
# richtext_notepad.py
    def chooseFont(self):
        """Select a font from the QFontDialog."""
        current = self.text_edit.currentFont()

        opt = QFontDialog.FontDialogOption.DontUseNativeDialog
        font, ok = QFontDialog.getFont(current, self,
            options=opt)
        if ok:
            self.text_edit.setCurrentFont(font)
```

```python
def chooseFontColor(self):
    """Select a font from the QColorDialog."""
    color = QColorDialog.getColor()
    if color.isValid():
        self.text_edit.setTextColor(color)
def chooseFontBackgroundColor(self):
    """Select a color for text's background."""
    color = QColorDialog.getColor()
    if color.isValid():
        self.text_edit.setTextBackgroundColor(color)
```

Refer back to the "Built-in Dialog Classes in PyQt" section for an explanation about the various methods.

The last step is to create the About dialog in Listing 5-16 that appears when the user selects the About option in the Help menu.

Listing 5-16. Various slots for the Tools menu

```python
# richtext_notepad.py
    def aboutDialog(self):
        """Display the About dialog."""
        QMessageBox.about(self, "About Notepad",
            """<p>Beginner's Practical Guide to PyQt</p>
            <p>Project 5.1 - Notepad GUI</p>""")
```

Refer to the subsection "The About QMessageBox" and Figure 5-8.

The QMainWindow provides convenience methods and other means for creating professional and well-rounded GUIs.

Expanding the Features in a Main Window

In this section, you will learn about some additional widgets and features that you can use when constructing menus and main windows in GUI applications, including

- The QDockWidget class

- The QStatusBar class

- Menu features such as submenus and checkable menu items

These topics will be demonstrated while constructing the GUI in Figure 5-12.

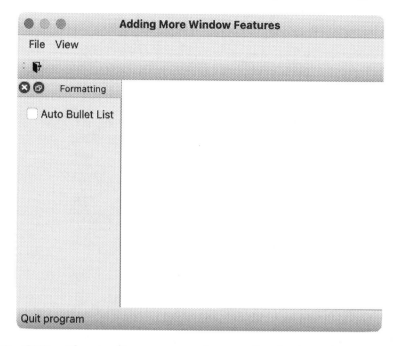

Figure 5-12. *GUI with a toolbar, a status bar, and a dock widget. The status bar on the bottom displays the text "Quit program" when the mouse hovers over the Quit icon in the toolbar*

Explanation for Expanding the Features

Copy the contents of main_window_template.py into a new Python script, and let's begin creating the main window in Listing 5-17.

Listing 5-17. Setting up the main window with additional functionalities

```
# main_window_extras.py
# Import necessary modules
import sys
from PyQt6.QtWidgets import (QApplication, QMainWindow,
    QWidget, QCheckBox, QTextEdit, QDockWidget, QToolBar,
    QStatusBar, QVBoxLayout)
from PyQt6.QtCore import Qt, QSize
from PyQt6.QtGui import QIcon, QAction
```

```python
class MainWindow(QMainWindow):

    def __init__(self):
        super().__init__()
        self.initializeUI()

    def initializeUI(self):
        """Set up the application's GUI."""
        self.setMinimumSize(450, 350)
        self.setWindowTitle("Adding More Window Features")

        self.setUpMainWindow()
        self.createDockWidget()
        self.createActions()
        self.createMenu()
        self.createToolBar()
        self.show()

if __name__ == '__main__':
    app = QApplication(sys.argv)
    window = MainWindow()
    sys.exit(app.exec())
```

A few new classes from the QtWidgets module are imported including QStatusBar, QToolBar, and QDockWidget. Be sure to add the additional method calls for createDockWidget() and createToolBar().

Let's set up the main window and the status bar in Listing 5-18.

Listing 5-18. The setUpMainWindow() method for the main window with additional functionalities

```python
# main_window_extras.py
    def setUpMainWindow(self):
        """Create and arrange widgets in the main window."""
        # Create and set the central widget
        self.text_edit = QTextEdit()
        self.setCentralWidget(self.text_edit)

        # Create the status bar
```

```
self.setStatusBar(QStatusBar())
```

Similar to the Rich Text Notepad, this application's central widget is also QTextEdit. The QMainWindow method setStatusBar() allows for the quick creation of the GUI's status bar. Let's find out a little more about QStatusBar.

The QStatusBar Class

At the bottom of the GUI in Figure 5-12, there is horizontal bar with the text "Quit program" displayed inside of it. This bar is known as the status bar and is created from the **QStatusBar** class. This widget is very useful for displaying feedback, extra information about a widget, or the outcome of a process. The first time the method setStatusBar() is called, it creates the status bar. Following calls will return the status bar object.

In order to display a message in the status bar when the mouse hovers over an icon or a widget, you need to call the setStatusTip() method on an action object. For example:

```
exit_act.setStatusTip("Quit program")
```

This displays the text "Quit program" when the mouse is over the exit_act icon or menu command. To display text in the status bar when the program begins or when a function is called, use the showMessage() method:

```
self.statusBar().showMessage("Welcome back!")
```

Status tips are added to the menu items in Listing 5-19. Let's construct the menu and actions in the next section.

Creating Submenus with Checkable Menu Items

As an application becomes more complex, its menus can also begin to turn into a cluttered mess. With **submenus**, you can organize similar categories together and simplify the menu system. Figure 5-13 displays an example of a submenu.

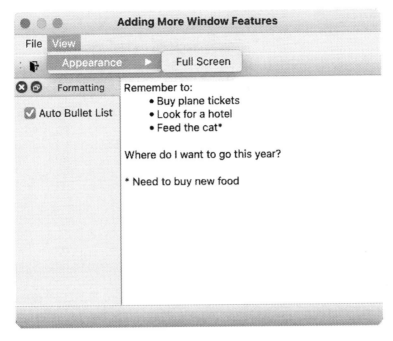

Figure 5-13. *The submenu also contains a checkable action to enter fullscreen mode*

First, we'll need to create the actions for the menu in Listing 5-19.

Listing 5-19. The createActions() method for the main window with additional functionalities

```python
# main_window_extras.py
    def createActions(self):
        """Create the application's menu actions."""
        # Create actions for File menu
        self.quit_act = QAction(
            QIcon("images/exit.png"), "Quit")
        self.quit_act.setShortcut("Ctrl+Q")
        self.quit_act.setStatusTip("Quit program")
        self.quit_act.triggered.connect(self.close)

        # Create actions for View menu
        self.full_screen_act = QAction(
            "Full Screen", checkable=True)
```

```
    self.full_screen_act.setStatusTip(
        "Switch to full screen mode")
    self.full_screen_act.triggered.connect(
        self.switchToFullScreen)
```

Menu items can also be created so that they act just like switches, being able to be turned on and off. To create a checkable menu item, include the argument checkable=True in the QAction parameters. An example of this can be seen with full_screen_act. It is also possible for checkable menu items to be checked from the start by calling the trigger() method on the action.

Next, create the menu bar in Listing 5-20.

Listing 5-20. The createMenu() method for the main window with additional functionalities

```
# main_window_extras.py
    def createMenu(self):
        """Create the application's menu bar."""
        self.menuBar().setNativeMenuBar(False)

        # Create file menu and add actions
        file_menu = self.menuBar().addMenu("File")
        file_menu.addAction(self.quit_act)

        # Create View menu, Appearance submenu and add actions
        view_menu = self.menuBar().addMenu("View")
        appearance_submenu = view_menu.addMenu("Appearance")
        appearance_submenu.addAction(self.full_screen_act)

    def switchToFullScreen(self, state):
        """If state is True, display the main window in full
        screen. Otherwise, return the the window to normal."""
        if state: self.showFullScreen()
        else: self.showNormal()
```

Creating a submenu is similar to creating a regular menu. First, use the addMenu() method to create the View menu. The appearance_submenu is then created and added to the View menu using addMenu(), but this time called from the view_menu instance. Don't forget to also add an action to the submenu using the addAction() method.

The appearance_submenu in the example has a full_screen_act action added to it that allows the user to switch between full screen and normal screen modes. Take a moment to also code the switchToFullScreen() slot in MainWindow.

The next step is to create the application's toolbar.

The QToolBar Class

When the user is performing a number of routine tasks, having to open up the menu to select an action multiple times can become tedious. Luckily, the **QToolBar** class provides ways to create a toolbar with icons, text, or standard Qt widgets for quick access to frequently used commands.

Toolbars are generally located under the menu bar like in Figure 5-12 but can also be placed vertically or at the bottom of the main window above the status bar. Refer to the image in Figure 5-2 for an idea of how to arrange toolbars in the main window.

A GUI can only have one menu bar, but it can have multiple toolbars. First, create a toolbar object with the QToolBar class like in Listing 5-21 and give it a title.

Listing 5-21. The createToolBar() method for the main window with additional functionalities

```
# main_window_extras.py
    def createToolBar(self):
        """Create the application's toolbar."""
        toolbar = QToolBar("Main Toolbar")
        toolbar.setIconSize(QSize(16, 16))
        self.addToolBar(toolbar)

        # Add actions to the toolbar
        toolbar.addAction(self.quit_act)
```

Add it to the main window using the QMainWindow method addToolBar(). You can also set the size of the icons in the toolbar using the setIconSize() method to avoid extra padding when PyQt tries to figure out the placement by itself. To add an action to the toolbar, use addAction(). The same icon will appear in both the toolbar and in the menu. To add a widget to a toolbar, use addWidget().

Let's wrap up this section by learning how to create dock widgets.

The QDockWidget Class

The **QDockWidget** class is used to create detachable or floating tool palettes or widget panels. Dock widgets are secondary windows that provide additional functionality to GUI windows.

To create a dock widget object, create an instance of QDockWidget and set the widget's title using the setWindowTitle() method like in Listing 5-22.

Listing 5-22. The createDockWidget() method for the main window with additional functionalities

```
# main_window_extras.py
    def createDockWidget(self):
        """Create the application's dock widget."""
        dock_widget = QDockWidget()
        dock_widget.setWindowTitle("Formatting")
        dock_widget.setAllowedAreas(
            Qt.DockWidgetArea.AllDockWidgetAreas)

        # Create widget examples to add to the dock
        auto_bullet_cb = QCheckBox("Auto Bullet List")
        auto_bullet_cb.toggled.connect(
            self.changeTextEditSettings)

        # Create layout for dock widget
        dock_v_box = QVBoxLayout()
        dock_v_box.addWidget(auto_bullet_cb)
        dock_v_box.addStretch(1)

        # Create a QWidget that acts as a container to
        # hold other widgets
        dock_container = QWidget()
        dock_container.setLayout(dock_v_box)

        # Set the main widget for the dock widget
        dock_widget.setWidget(dock_container)
```

```
    # Set initial location of dock widget in main window
    self.addDockWidget(
        Qt.DockWidgetArea.LeftDockWidgetArea, dock_widget)

def changeTextEditSettings(self, checked):
    """Change formatting features for QTextEdit."""
    if checked:
        self.text_edit.setAutoFormatting(
            QTextEdit.AutoFormattingFlag.AutoBulletList)
    else:
        self.text_edit.setAutoFormatting(
            QTextEdit.AutoFormattingFlag.AutoNone)
```

When the dock widget is docked inside of the main window, Qt handles the resizing of the dock widget and the central widget. You can also specify the areas you want the dock to be placed in the main window using setAllowedAreas().

A QDockWidget can be placed on any of the four sides of the window. To limit the allowable dock areas, specify a single area or a combination of them separated by a pipe character:

- LeftDockWidgetArea – Arrange the dock widget on the left side

- RightDockWidgetArea – Arrange the dock widget on the right side

- TopDockWidgetArea – Arrange the dock widget in the top area

- BottomDockWidgetArea – Arrange the dock widget in the bottom area

This project's dock widget contains a single QCheckBox that allows the user to add bulleted text to the main QTextEdit widget. The slot that is called when the checkbox is toggled is changeTextEditSettings(). When checked, the user can type an asterisk to create a bulleted list.

In order to place multiple widgets inside the dock, you need to use a container such as QWidget to serve as the parent for multiple child widgets and arrange them using one of the layout managers. Then pass the QWidget object as the argument to setWidget().

Finally, set the dock and its initial location in the main window with addDockWidget().

In this application, if the dock widget is closed, we cannot get it back. In Project 5.2, we will take a look at how to use checkable menu items to hide or show the dock widget.

Project 5.2 – Simple Photo Editor GUI

Nowadays, it is quite common to edit images. Some photo editors are very simple, allowing the user to rotate, crop, or add shapes. Others let the user change the contrast and exposure, reduce noise, or even add special effects.

In this project, you will take a look at how to create a basic photo editor, shown in Figure 5-14.

Figure 5-14. *Photo Editor GUI. Landscape image from* `https://pixabay.com`

The GUI contains a menu bar at the top, a toolbar with icons underneath the menu bar, the central widget that displays the image, the status bar on the bottom, and the dock widget on the right containing simple tools for editing the photo.

Designing the Photo Editor GUI

Similar to Project 5.1, this GUI also has a menu bar that will contain various menus – File, Edit, and View. Have a look at the schematic for the GUI in Figure 5-15. Under the menu bar is the toolbar created using the QToolBar class and contains icons that represent actions the user can take for opening a file, saving a file, and printing.

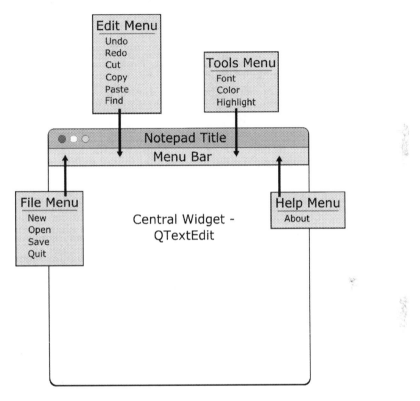

Figure 5-15. *Layout for the Photo Editor GUI. The main window is much busier, containing a toolbar, a dock widget, and a status bar*

Explanation for the Photo Editor GUI

This project will introduce you to a number of new classes and acts as a means to continue learning and applying concepts to build larger, more complex GUIs. Just like before, use the main_window_template.py as the starting point for Listing 5-23, and begin by importing some additional PyQt classes.

Listing 5-23. Setting up the main window for the Photo Editor GUI

```python
# photo_editor.py
# Import necessary modules
import sys
from PyQt6.QtWidgets import (QApplication, QMainWindow,
    QWidget, QLabel, QPushButton, QDockWidget, QDialog,
    QFileDialog, QMessageBox, QToolBar, QStatusBar,
    QVBoxLayout)
from PyQt6.QtCore import Qt, QSize, QRect
from PyQt6.QtGui import (QIcon, QAction, QPixmap, QTransform,
    QPainter)
from PyQt6.QtPrintSupport import QPrinter, QPrintDialog

class MainWindow(QMainWindow):

    def __init__(self):
        super().__init__()
        self.initializeUI()

    def initializeUI(self):
        """Set up the application's GUI."""
        self.setFixedSize(650, 650)
        self.setWindowTitle("5.2 - Photo Editor GUI")

        self.setUpMainWindow()
        self.createToolsDockWidget()
        self.createActions()
        self.createMenu()
        self.createToolBar()
        self.show()

if __name__ == '__main__':
    app = QApplication(sys.argv)
    app.setAttribute(
        Qt.ApplicationAttribute.AA_DontShowIconsInMenus, True)
    window = MainWindow()
    sys.exit(app.exec())
```

The application imports an assortment of new classes from different modules. From the QtGui module, we use QPixmap for handling images, **QTransform** for performing transformations on images, and **QPainter** for drawing and painting widgets.

QRect, from QtCore, is used for creating the rectangular shape of widgets. This will be used in the printImage() method where the **QtPrintSupport** module and its classes provide cross-platform support for accessing printers and printing documents.

The window is initialized like before except this time the setFixedSize() method is used to set the window's geometry so that it cannot be resized. Various method calls will set up the menu, window, toolbar, and dock widget.

Unlike previous examples, this application's menu won't display icons; only the toolbar will show them. Qt has a number of special flags in the Qt Namespace for specifying the parameters of windows and menus. One in particular is AA_DontShowIconsInMenus, which is used to hide the icons in the menus. You can use the QApplication method setAttribute() to specify the flags you want to use.

This GUI's main window, constructed in Listing 5-24, will consist of a QLabel widget for displaying images.

Listing 5-24. The setUpMainWindow() method for the Photo Editor GUI

```python
# photo_editor.py
  def setUpMainWindow(self):
        """Create and arrange widgets in the main window."""
        self.image = QPixmap()

        self.image_label = QLabel()
        self.image_label.setAlignment(
            Qt.AlignmentFlag.AlignCenter)
        self.setCentralWidget(self.image_label)

        # Create the status bar
        self.setStatusBar(QStatusBar())
```

The QPixmap instance, image, is used to display an image on the QLabel, image_label. The pixmap is instantiated in setUpMainWindow() to avoid issues with the buttons that manipulate the image. You can avoid this instance here if you disable all editing buttons and actions when the application starts and only enable them when an image is set in image_label.

The actions for the File menu – Open, Save, Print, and Quit – are handled in Listing 5-25.

Listing 5-25. The createActions() method for the Photo Editor GUI, part 1

```python
# photo_editor.py
    def createActions(self):
        """Create the application's menu actions."""
        # Create actions for File menu
        self.open_act = QAction(
            QIcon("images/open_file.png"),"Open")
        self.open_act.setShortcut("Ctrl+O")
        self.open_act.setStatusTip("Open a new image")
        self.open_act.triggered.connect(self.openImage)

        self.save_act = QAction(
            QIcon("images/save_file.png"),"Save")
        self.save_act.setShortcut("Ctrl+S")
        self.save_act.setStatusTip("Save image")
        self.save_act.triggered.connect(self.saveImage)

        self.print_act = QAction(
            QIcon("images/print.png"), "Print")
        self.print_act.setShortcut("Ctrl+P")
        self.print_act.setStatusTip("Print image")
        self.print_act.triggered.connect(self.printImage)
        self.print_act.setEnabled(False)

        self.quit_act = QAction(
            QIcon("images/exit.png"), "Quit")
        self.quit_act.setShortcut("Ctrl+Q")
        self.quit_act.setStatusTip("Quit program")
        self.quit_act.triggered.connect(self.close)
```

Setting the setEnabled() method on print_act to False shows a disabled menu item and icon in the menu and the toolbar. The print_act only becomes enabled when an image is set on image_label.

The actions for the Edit menu are created in Listing 5-26. These actions also appear in the application's toolbar in Listing 5-27.

Listing 5-26. The createActions() method for the Photo Editor GUI, part 2

```python
# photo_editor.py
        # Create actions for Edit menu
        self.rotate90_act = QAction("Rotate 90°")
        self.rotate90_act.setStatusTip(
            "Rotate image 90° clockwise")
        self.rotate90_act.triggered.connect(
            self.rotateImage90)

        self.rotate180_act = QAction("Rotate 180°")
        self.rotate180_act.setStatusTip(
            "Rotate image 180° clockwise")
        self.rotate180_act.triggered.connect(
            self.rotateImage180)

        self.flip_hor_act = QAction("Flip Horizontal")
        self.flip_hor_act.setStatusTip(
            "Flip image across horizontal axis")
        self.flip_hor_act.triggered.connect(
            self.flipImageHorizontal)

        self.flip_ver_act = QAction("Flip Vertical")
        self.flip_ver_act.setStatusTip(
            "Flip image across vertical axis")
        self.flip_ver_act.triggered.connect(
            self.flipImageVertical)

        self.resize_act = QAction("Resize Half")
        self.resize_act.setStatusTip(
            "Resize image to half the original size")
        self.resize_act.triggered.connect(
            self.resizeImageHalf)
```

```
    self.clear_act = QAction(
        QIcon("images/clear.png"), "Clear Image")
    self.clear_act.setShortcut("Ctrl+D")
    self.clear_act.setStatusTip("Clear the current image")
    self.clear_act.triggered.connect(self.clearImage)
```

The actions for the Edit menu are used to rotate the image, flip the image, resize the image by half, and clear the image. Except for clear_act, the actions are also added to the dock widget in Listing 5-28.

The method for creating the menu bar is found in Listing 5-27.

Listing 5-27. The createMenu() method for the Photo Editor GUI

```
# photo_editor.py
    def createMenu(self):
        """Create the application's menu bar."""
        self.menuBar().setNativeMenuBar(False)

        # Create File menu and add actions
        file_menu = self.menuBar().addMenu("File")
        file_menu.addAction(self.open_act)
        file_menu.addAction(self.save_act)
        file_menu.addSeparator()
        file_menu.addAction(self.print_act)
        file_menu.addSeparator()
        file_menu.addAction(self.quit_act)

        # Create Edit menu and add actions
        edit_menu = self.menuBar().addMenu("Edit")
        edit_menu.addAction(self.rotate90_act)
        edit_menu.addAction(self.rotate180_act)
        edit_menu.addSeparator()
        edit_menu.addAction(self.flip_hor_act)
        edit_menu.addAction(self.flip_ver_act)
        edit_menu.addSeparator()
        edit_menu.addAction(self.resize_act)
        edit_menu.addSeparator()
        edit_menu.addAction(self.clear_act)
```

```
# Create View menu and add actions
view_menu = self.menuBar().addMenu("View")
view_menu.addAction(self.toggle_dock_tools_act)
```

The View menu contains an action for toggling the dock widget's visibility. If the dock is ever closed, it can be reopened using the menu. This action was not created in createActions(), but rather in the createToolsDockWidget() method in Listing 5-29. This is also the reason that createToolsDockWidget() is called before createActions() in initializeUI(), since createActions() relies on the toggle_dock_tools_act to be created already.

The toolbar and its actions are added to the application in Listing 5-28.

Listing 5-28. Creating the toolbar for the Photo Editor GUI

```
# photo_editor.py
    def createToolBar(self):
        """Create the application's toolbar."""
        tool_bar = QToolBar("Photo Editor Toolbar")
        tool_bar.setIconSize(QSize(24,24))
        self.addToolBar(tool_bar)

        # Add actions to the toolbar
        tool_bar.addAction(self.open_act)
        tool_bar.addAction(self.save_act)
        tool_bar.addAction(self.print_act)
        tool_bar.addAction(self.clear_act)
        tool_bar.addSeparator()
        tool_bar.addAction(self.quit_act)
```

The dock widget in Listing 5-29 displays the editing options from the Edit menu. It is restricted to only the left and right sides of the application using setAllowedAreas(). After this step, create the QPushButton widgets for editing images.

Listing 5-29. Creating the dock widget for the Photo Editor GUI

```
# photo_editor.py
    def createToolsDockWidget(self):
        """Create the application's dock widget. Use View ->
        Edit Image Tools menu to show/hide the dock."""
```

149

```python
dock_widget = QDockWidget()
dock_widget.setWindowTitle("Edit Image Tools")
dock_widget.setAllowedAreas(
    Qt.DockWidgetArea.LeftDockWidgetArea |
    Qt.DockWidgetArea.RightDockWidgetArea)

# Create buttons for editing images
self.rotate90 = QPushButton("Rotate 90°")
self.rotate90.setMinimumSize(QSize(130, 40))
self.rotate90.setStatusTip(
    "Rotate image 90° clockwise")
self.rotate90.clicked.connect(self.rotateImage90)

self.rotate180 = QPushButton("Rotate 180°")
self.rotate180.setMinimumSize(QSize(130, 40))
self.rotate180.setStatusTip(
    "Rotate image 180° clockwise")
self.rotate180.clicked.connect(self.rotateImage180)

self.flip_horizontal = QPushButton("Flip Horizontal")
self.flip_horizontal.setMinimumSize(QSize(130, 40))
self.flip_horizontal.setStatusTip(
    "Flip image across horizontal axis")
self.flip_horizontal.clicked.connect(
    self.flipImageHorizontal)

self.flip_vertical = QPushButton("Flip Vertical")
self.flip_vertical.setMinimumSize(QSize(130, 40))
self.flip_vertical.setStatusTip(
    "Flip image across vertical axis")
self.flip_vertical.clicked.connect(
    self.flipImageVertical)
self.resize_half = QPushButton("Resize Half")
self.resize_half.setMinimumSize(QSize(130, 40))
self.resize_half.setStatusTip(
    "Resize image to half the original size")
self.resize_half.clicked.connect(self.resizeImageHalf)
```

```
# Create layout for dock widget
dock_v_box = QVBoxLayout()
dock_v_box.addWidget(self.rotate90)
dock_v_box.addWidget(self.rotate180)
dock_v_box.addStretch(1)
dock_v_box.addWidget(self.flip_horizontal)
dock_v_box.addWidget(self.flip_vertical)
dock_v_box.addStretch(1)
dock_v_box.addWidget(self.resize_half)
dock_v_box.addStretch(10)

# Create QWidget that acts as a container and
# set the layout for the dock
tools_container = QWidget()
tools_container.setLayout(dock_v_box)
dock_widget.setWidget(tools_container)

# Set initial location of dock widget
self.addDockWidget(
    Qt.DockWidgetArea.RightDockWidgetArea,
    dock_widget)

# Handle the visibility of the dock widget
self.toggle_dock_act = dock_widget.toggleViewAction()
```

Add the widgets you create to a layout, add that layout to a QWidget container, and then add it to the dock using addDockWidget(). To handle when the dock widget is checked or unchecked in the menu or if the user has closed the dock widget using its close button, use the QDockWidget method toggleViewAction() to create the action.

Handling Images in the Photo Editor GUI

This section looks at the methods in MainWindow for interacting with local image files. A QFileDialog is presented when the user wants to open or save an image in Listing 5-30.

Listing 5-30. Creating slots for loading and saving images in the Photo Editor GUI

```python
# photo_editor.py
    def openImage(self):
        """Open an image file and display its contents on the
        QLabel widget."""
        image_file, _ = QFileDialog.getOpenFileName(
            self, "Open Image", "",
            "JPG Files (*.jpeg *.jpg );;PNG Files (*.png);;\
                Bitmap Files (*.bmp);;GIF Files (*.gif)")

        if image_file:
            self.image = QPixmap(image_file)

            self.image_label.setPixmap(
                self.image.scaled(self.image_label.size(),
                Qt.AspectRatioMode.KeepAspectRatio,
                Qt.TransformationMode.SmoothTransformation))
        else:
            QMessageBox.information(self, "No Image",
                "No Image Selected.",
                QMessageBox.StandardButton.Ok)
        self.print_act.setEnabled(True)

    def saveImage(self):
        """Display QFileDialog to select image location and
        save the image."""
        image_file, _ = QFileDialog.getSaveFileName(
            self, "Save Image", "",
            "JPG Files (*.jpeg *.jpg );;PNG Files (*.png);;\
                Bitmap Files (*.bmp);;GIF Files (*.gif)")

        if image_file and self.image.isNull() == False:
            self.image.save(image_file)
        else:
            QMessageBox.information(self, "Not Saved",
                "Image not saved.",
                QMessageBox.StandardButton.Ok)
```

If the user selects a local image, the image instance is updated with a new pixmap, image. The new pixmap is then applied to image_label with setPixmap(), where image is scaled to fit the current size of image_label. Its size is determined using the size() method and will vary if the dock widget is open or closed. When resizing a pixmap, other parameters can be specified. How an image will use the available space can be specified with the enum Qt.AspectRatioMode. The aspect ratio can either be

- Ignored so that the image takes up all available space without regard for aspect ratio (IgnoreAspectRatio)

- Preserved, but also scaled to fit within the label (KeepAspectRatio)

- Preserved, but able to expand beyond the label (KeepAspectRatioByExpanding)

When an image is scaled to fit the label's current size, the textures of the image will need to be smoothed to avoid distortion of the image. Smoothing of an image is specified using the parameter SmoothTransformation. The other option is FastTransformation, where no smoothing occurs.

If the user wants to save the image, the QPixmap method save() is used in saveImage().

Slots for clearing and rotating images are called whenever an operation is selected in the menu, toolbar, or dock. An example of an image being rotated is shown in Figure 5-16. The slots are created in Listing 5-31.

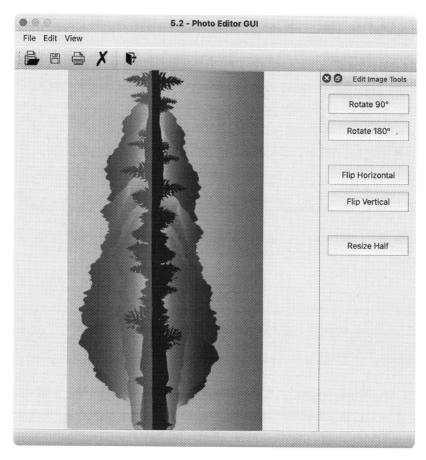

Figure 5-16. *Example of 90° rotation in the Photo Editor GUI. The image is stretched horizontally to fit in the main window*

Listing 5-31. Creating slots for clearing and rotating images in the Photo Editor GUI

```
# photo_editor.py
    def clearImage(self):
        """Clears current image in the QLabel widget."""
        self.image_label.clear()
        self.image = QPixmap() # Reset pixmap
        self.print_act.setEnabled(False)

    def rotateImage90(self):
        """Rotate image 90° clockwise."""
```

```python
    if self.image.isNull() == False:
        transform90 = QTransform().rotate(90)
        pixmap = QPixmap(self.image)
        mode = Qt.TransformationMode.SmoothTransformation
        rotated = pixmap.transformed(transform90,
            mode=mode)

        self.image_label.setPixmap(
            rotated.scaled(self.image_label.size(),
            Qt.AspectRatioMode.KeepAspectRatio,
            Qt.TransformationMode.SmoothTransformation))
        self.image = QPixmap(rotated)
        self.image_label.repaint() # Repaint the label

def rotateImage180(self):
    """Rotate image 180° clockwise."""
    if self.image.isNull() == False:
        transform180 = QTransform().rotate(180)
        pixmap = QPixmap(self.image)
        mode = Qt.TransformationMode.SmoothTransformation
        rotated = pixmap.transformed(transform180,
            mode=mode)

        self.image_label.setPixmap(
            rotated.scaled(self.image_label.size(),
            Qt.AspectRatioMode.KeepAspectRatio,
            Qt.TransformationMode.SmoothTransformation))
        # In order to keep from being allowed to rotate
        # the image, set the rotated image as self.image
        self.image = QPixmap(rotated)
        self.image_label.repaint() # Repaint the label
```

The clearImage() slot clears image_label, creates an empty pixmap for image, and disables print_act.

Image **transforms** occur when a function is applied to an image and alters that image in some way. Transformations include rotation, scaling, and smoothing. QTransform is used to manipulate graphics in 2D space. For both rotateImage90()

and rotateImage180(), the QTransform class is used to rotate the images. The QPixmap method transformed() is used to return a transformed pixmap. The rotated pixmap is then set on the label.

The method repaint() is important as it ensures that the contents of the image_ label are updated after the transformation.

Listing 5-32 continues to use the QTransform for flipping images.

Listing 5-32. Creating slots for flipping images in the Photo Editor GUI

```python
# photo_editor.py
    def flipImageHorizontal(self):
        """Mirror the image across the horizontal axis."""
        if self.image.isNull() == False:
            flip_h = QTransform().scale(-1, 1)
            pixmap = QPixmap(self.image)
            flipped = pixmap.transformed(flip_h)

            self.image_label.setPixmap(
                flipped.scaled(self.image_label.size(),
                Qt.AspectRatioMode.KeepAspectRatio,
                Qt.TransformationMode.SmoothTransformation))
            self.image = QPixmap(flipped)
            self.image_label.repaint()

    def flipImageVertical(self):
        """Mirror the image across the vertical axis."""
        if self.image.isNull() == False:
            flip_v = QTransform().scale(1, -1)
            pixmap = QPixmap(self.image)
            flipped = pixmap.transformed(flip_v)

            self.image_label.setPixmap(
                flipped.scaled(self.image_label.size(),
                Qt.AspectRatioMode.KeepAspectRatio,
                Qt.TransformationMode.SmoothTransformation))
            self.image = QPixmap(flipped)
            self.image_label.repaint()
```

The process for flipping images across the horizontal and vertical axes is similar to the code for rotations. The key difference is the use of `Transform.scale()` for scaling images along the horizontal and vertical axes. A negative value passed to scale() will flip the image in that direction. A value of 1 means that the size of the image does not change, whereas a value of 0.5 would shrink the image by half. This is demonstrated in Listing 5-33.

Listing 5-33. Creating slots for resizing images in the Photo Editor GUI

```
# photo_editor.py
    def resizeImageHalf(self):
        """Resize the image to half its current size."""
        if self.image.isNull() == False:
            resize = QTransform().scale(0.5, 0.5)
            pixmap = QPixmap(self.image)
            resized = pixmap.transformed(resize)

            self.image_label.setPixmap(
                resized.scaled(self.image_label.size(),
                Qt.AspectRatioMode.KeepAspectRatio,
                Qt.TransformationMode.SmoothTransformation))
            self.image = QPixmap(resized)
            self.image_label.repaint()
```

The last step to take care of is creating the method for printing.

The QPrinter Class

The Photo Editor includes a method for printing images. The `QPrinter` class is used to create a page for printing documents. A number of parameters can be set for the page, including its orientation and the paper size.

For this example, we want to use `QPrinter` to print the image on `image_label`. To do so, we will also need to use the `QPainter` class to specify what to paint on the page that we want to print, which is the image. This is all handled in Listing 5-34.

Listing 5-34. Creating the slot for printing images in the Photo Editor GUI

```python
# photo_editor.py
    def printImage(self):
        """Print image and use QPrinter to select the
        native system format for the printer dialog."""
        printer = QPrinter()
        # Configure the printer
        print_dialog = QPrintDialog(printer)

        if print_dialog.exec() == QDialog.DialogCode.Accepted:
            # Use QPainter to output a PDF file
            painter = QPainter()
            painter.begin(printer)
            # Create QRect object to hold the painter's
            # current viewport, which is the image_label
            rect = QRect(painter.viewport())

            # Get the size of image_label and use it to set
            # the size of the viewport
            size = QSize(self.image_label.pixmap().size())
            size.scale(rect.size(),
                Qt.AspectRatioMode.KeepAspectRatio)
            painter.setViewport(rect.x(), rect.y(),
                size.width(), size.height())
            painter.setWindow(
                self.image_label.pixmap().rect())
            # Scale image_label to fit the rect source (0, 0)
            painter.drawPixmap(0, 0,
                self.image_label.pixmap())
            painter.end()
```

With the QPrinter object defined, the next step is to open a native-looking QPrintDialog for the user to configure the printer's settings. If the user clicks the Print button in the dialog (which refers to QDialog.DialogCode,Accepted), a QPainter object is created, and the printer object is passed to it. From there, we can acquire the size of the label and scale painter to the size of the pixmap.

The QPainter method setViewport() specifies the size of the printing device's coordinates, while setWindow() defines the logical coordinates. Using QPainter, we need to map the logical coordinates of the label to physical coordinates before printing. The image is sent to the printer when end() is called.

The user can now perform simple edits, save, and print their images using the Photo Editor GUI.

Summary

In this chapter, you were able to see the benefit of using the QMainWindow class to construct your application's main window. QMainWindow provides the functionalities and interactions necessary for integrating toolbars, menus, dock widgets, and status bars easily into your GUIs. There is still tons more to learn when it comes to using menus, such as creating context menus and displaying widgets in the status bar. As you follow along in this book, you'll continue to learn and apply many of these concepts in practical examples.

A menu bar can consist of several menus, each of which can be broken down into several commands. Each of these commands could themselves also be checkable or even submenus. The QAction class ensures that the correct action is executed no matter what triggered the action, whether from a menu, a toolbar, shortcut keys, or a widget. Toolbars are often composed of icons that allow the user to locate commonly used commands. The QDockWidget class creates movable and floating panels for organizing and displaying different tools, widgets, or commands to the user. Status bars establish a space to give further textual information about widgets or provide feedback.

In Chapter 6, you will learn how to modify the appearance and style of widgets using style sheets.

CHAPTER 6

Styling Your GUIs

The GUIs you have created up until now have mainly focused on functionality and less on appearance and customization. Creating an interactive, coherent, and professional-looking GUI can be achieved not only with widgets and layout managers but also by modifying the look and behavior of each object in the interface. Choosing the right style, colors, fonts, and subtle forms of feedback can help create a consistent, easy-to-navigate, user-friendly experience.

In this chapter, you will

- Find out about styling PyQt applications

- Learn how to customize the appearance of widgets with Qt Style Sheets and HTML

- Use new PyQt widgets and classes, including QRadioButton, QGroupBox, and QTabWidget

- Use containers and tabbed widgets for organizing and managing groups of widgets

Let's start by learning about what styles are in PyQt. After that, you'll find out how to customize the look of an application's windows and widgets.

What Are Styles in PyQt?

When you use PyQt, the appearance of your applications are handled by Qt's **QStyle** class. QStyle contains a number of subclasses that imitate the look of the system on which an application is being run. This makes your GUI look like a native macOS, Linux, or Windows application. Custom styles can be made either by modifying existing QStyle classes, creating your own classes, or using Qt Style Sheets.

© Joshua M Willman 2022
J. M. Willman, *Beginning PyQt*, https://doi.org/10.1007/978-1-4842-7999-1_6

Without specifying a style in your code, PyQt will automatically choose a style that makes a GUI look like a native application. There are a number of built-in styles as well. You can use Listing 6-1 to discover what styles are available on your operating system.

Listing 6-1. Finding out what styles are available on your local system

```python
# styles.py
# Import necessary modules
import sys
from PyQt6.QtWidgets import QApplication, QStyleFactory

# Find out your OS's available styles
print(f"Keys: {QStyleFactory.keys()}")

# Find out the default style applied to an application
app = QApplication(sys.argv)
print(f"Default style: {app.style().name()}")
```

Running this short script will print out the following in a macOS shell:

```
Keys: ['macOS', 'Windows', 'Fusion']
Default style: macos
```

On Windows, you will probably get a different set of keys (['windowsvista', 'Windows', 'Fusion']) and style (windowsvista). Linux should also produce different outputs as well.

The **QStyleFactory** class is used to create a QStyle object. Printing the QStyleFactory keys will return a list of all possible styles available on your OS. The output will change if you are on Windows or Linux. The Windows and Fusion styles are typically included on all systems.

Changing the Default Style

It is possible to change the style being used by an application using the QApplication method setStyle(). Be sure to pass one of the available styles as an argument. For example:

```python
app.setStyle("Fusion")
```

Styles can also be specified in the command line when running an application by including the -style option and a style type, such as

```
$ python3 food_order.py -style Fusion
```

You should take a moment and try changing the style of previous programs. Be sure to include the -style option or use the setStyle() method and notice the differences in appearance.

In the following sections, we will take a look at how you can customize the look of widgets in user interfaces.

Modifying Widget Appearances

If you are going to modify the native styles given to widgets in PyQt, it is important to consider a few principles:

1. **Consistency** is concerned with making sure widgets and other components of a GUI look and behave the same way.

2. **Visual hierarchy** can be created through color, layout, size, or even depth.

3. **Relationships** between different widgets can be established by how widgets are arranged or aligned. Widgets closer to one another or arranged vertically or horizontally in a line are generally perceived as related.

4. **Emphasis** can be used to direct the user's attention to specific widgets or parts of a window or dialog. This can be achieved using visual contrast, perhaps through different sizes or fonts.

5. **Patterns** in the design of a GUI can be used to reduce the time it takes for a user to perform a task, maintain consistency, and create unity within an interface.

In PyQt, it is possible to use **HyperText Markup Language** (**HTML**) for modifying the look of text and **Cascading Style Sheets** (**CSS**) for customizing the appearance of widgets and text. As of publishing, Qt is still using a subset of HTML4.[1] We'll look more at these languages in the following sections.

Using HTML to Change the Look of Text

For classes in PyQt that can display rich text, such as QLabel and QLineEdit, HTML can be used to edit the appearance of text. To demonstrate, we'll create a simple window in Listing 6-2. The GUI displays two QLabel widgets – one where the text is not modified and another with changes to the text. You can use the basic_window.py script from Chapter 1 to get started creating this example.

Listing 6-2. Styling the text in a QLabel widget using HTML

```
# html_ex.py
# Import necessary modules
import sys
from PyQt6.QtWidgets import (QApplication, QWidget, QLabel,
    QVBoxLayout)

class MainWindow(QWidget):

    def __init__(self):
        super().__init__()
        self.initializeUI()

    def initializeUI(self):
        """Set up the application's GUI."""
        self.setMinimumSize(300, 100)
        self.setWindowTitle("HTML Example")
```

---

[1] Higher levels of HTML currently exist, such as HTML5. For more information about HTML4, have a look at www.w3.org/TR/html401/.

```python
        no_style_label = QLabel(
            """Have no fear of perfection
            - you'll never reach it.
            - Salvador Dali""")
        style_label = QLabel("""
            <p><font color='#DB8D31' face='Times' size='+2'>
            Have no fear of perfection -
            you'll never reach it.</font></p>
            <p align='right'>
            <b> - <i>Salvador Dali</i></b></p>""")

        v_box = QVBoxLayout()
        v_box.addWidget(no_style_label)
        v_box.addWidget(style_label)
        self.setLayout(v_box)
        self.show()

if __name__ == '__main__':
    app = QApplication(sys.argv)
    window = MainWindow()
    sys.exit(app.exec())
```

Setting up the main window is similar to previous programs, so we'll focus more on the two QLabel instances, no_style_label and style_label, in this example. The no_style_label instance is similar to other QLabel widgets we have created before. By using triple quotes, the text displayed in the label can also span across multiple lines. You can see this in Figure 6-1.

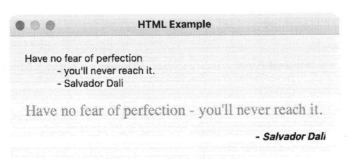

Figure 6-1. *Two QLabel widgets display the same text, but the bottom label has been modified*

For `style_label`, various HTML tags and attributes are used to describe the look of the text. **Tags** are used to define individual sections of text, while **attributes** are used to describe additional characteristics of a tag. Tags will typically consist of a starting tag, for example, `<p>`, and a corresponding ending tag, `</p>`. The p tag is used to define a single block of text within a larger section.

Note   Since Qt still uses HTML4, you are still able to use some tags that are deprecated in HTML5. In many cases, it may be more efficient to use HTML tags along with CSS formatting. (We'll cover CSS in a little more detail in the next section.) This section merely provides one method for manipulating text.

The style changes here are defined **inline**, meaning that the HTML code isn't loaded from an external file but is instead directly specified for each widget. Doing it this way is useful for small adjustments to text or widgets. However, as we shall see in later examples, creating a separate variable or even file to store the styles is a better practice. Table 6-1 describes the tags and attributes used in Listing 6-2.

Table 6-1. *Some HTML4 tags and attributes that can be used in PyQt*

Tag	Description
p	Defines a paragraph. Attributes such as `align` can be used to modify the tag
font	Used to specify the look of a font using the `color`, `face`, and `size` attributes
b	Specifies bold text
i	Specifies italic text

More information about using HTML and the supported tags in Qt can be found at `https://doc.qt.io/qt-6/richtext-html-subset.html#using-html-markup-in-text-widgets`. The following section will discuss how to use the subset of CSS properties that are available in Qt.

Using Qt Style Sheets to Change the Look of Widgets

CSS is a language that can be used alongside HTML to define how the different components of an application should be styled. Properties in CSS style sheets are applied in a "cascading" manner, meaning that properties are applied sequentially in a style sheet. Conflicts can sometimes arise depending on the order of the style sheet or between parent and child widgets, so you will need to pay attention to how you organize your style sheets. You will also face issues when you have multiple objects of the same widget type in a window but want to apply different styles.

With **Qt Style Sheets**, you can customize a number of different widget properties, including background color, font size and color, border type, width, or style, as well as add padding to widgets. You can also modify **pseudostates**, which define special states of a widget, such as when a mouse hovers over a widget or when a widget changes states from active to disabled. **Subcontrols** can also be modified, allowing you to access a widget's sub-elements and change their appearance, location, or other properties. For example, you could change the look of the indicator for QCheckBox to have a different color or icon when checked or unchecked.

Customizations can be applied either to individual widgets or to an application's QApplication instance using setStyleSheet(). For a list of widgets that can be styled or for a reference to all of the different properties supported in Qt, have a look at https://doc.qt.io/qt-6/stylesheet-reference.html. Examples for using Qt Style Sheets are found at https://doc.qt.io/qt-6/stylesheet-examples.html.

Let's look at a few examples before jumping into building an application. Changing the background color of a widget is quite common. To change the color from the standard gray color to blue, you could use the following line of code:

```
line_edit.setStyleSheet("background-color: blue")
```

Pass a CSS property and a value separated by a colon as a string to setStyleSheet(). Here, the background color for line_edit is set to blue using the CSS property background-color. This string that specifies the changes is called a **declaration**. If you are adjusting multiple properties in a single statement, separate each property with a semicolon.

Colors in a style sheet can be specified using either hexadecimal, RGB, or color keyword formats. To change the foreground color (the text color) of a widget, have a look at the following code:

```
line_edit.setStyleSheet("color: rgb(244, 160, 25") # orange
```

For windows and some widgets, you could even set a background image. To add a background image to the main window class, you could use the following code:

```
self.setStyleSheet("background-image: url(images/logo.png)")
```

You'll need to use the `url()` syntax and pass a file location as an argument. A useful link regarding style sheet syntax is found at `https://doc.qt.io/qt-5/stylesheet-syntax.html`.

The first example GUI you will build can be seen in Figure 6-2. The application consists of `QLabel` and `QPushButton` widgets, and styles are applied inline.

Figure 6-2. *Customized QLabel and QPushButton widgets*

For comparison, have a look at the same GUI in Figure 6-3 where style sheets have not been applied.

Figure 6-3. *PyQt GUI without style sheets*

Let's see how to apply the concepts you've learned to build the application in the following section.

Explanation for Using "Inline" Qt Style Sheets

In Listings 6-3 to 6-5, you will take a brief look at seeing how to customize individual widget properties. Let's start by creating a new file using the basic_window.py script, include the additional QtWidgets imports at the top, and modify the settings in initializeUI(). This GUI serves to demonstrate how to style widgets, so widgets are not connected to any signals. Be sure to download the images folder from this chapter's GitHub repository.

Listing 6-3. Setting up the main window for using Qt Style Sheets

```
# style_sheet_ex.py
# Import necessary modules
import sys
from PyQt6.QtWidgets import (QApplication, QWidget, QLabel,
    QPushButton, QVBoxLayout)
class MainWindow(QWidget):

    def __init__(self):
        super().__init__()
        self.initializeUI()

    def initializeUI(self):
        """Set up the application's GUI."""
        self.setMinimumSize(200, 200)
        self.setWindowTitle("Style Sheets Example")
        self.show()

if __name__ == '__main__':
    app = QApplication(sys.argv)
    window = MainWindow()
    sys.exit(app.exec())
```

The code in Listing 6-4 is placed before the show() method call in Listing 6-3. The label created uses a combination of HTML and CSS to modify its appearance.

Listing 6-4. Customizing the appearance for a QLabel widget in initializeUI()

```
# style_sheet_ex.py
        label = QLabel("<p align=center>Give me a like!</p>")
        label.setStyleSheet("""
            background-color: skyblue;
            color: white;
            border-style: outset;
            border-width: 3px;
            border-radius: 5px;
            font: bold 24px 'Times New Roman'""")
```

The label's text is arranged in the center using the HTML attribute `align`. For the style sheet, the background is set to `skyblue`, and the text color is `white`. We can specify different border styles, widths, and radius values of the corners using CSS properties. Some commonly used border styles include `outset`, `inset`, and `solid`. Finally, the font style, weight, and size can also be set. A table of typically used properties can be found toward the end of the chapter in the "CSS Properties Reference" section.

You should have a try and change the different pixel and color values and notice the differences. Refer to the Qt Style Sheets documentation for ideas about different properties that you can manipulate.

Customizing Styles to React to Interactions

When you use the general style settings for widgets, you will notice that they have their own ways of reacting to a user's interaction. However, when you change some aspects of a widget using style sheets, other features may no longer work properly. In many instances, you'll also need to style them as well. One common example is handling button presses after editing a button's style.

Let's start by adding a `QPushButton` like in Listing 6-5 after `label`.

Listing 6-5. Customizing the appearance for a QPushButton widget in initializeUI()

```
# style_sheet_ex.py
        like_button = QPushButton()
        like_button.setStyleSheet("""
            QPushButton {background-color: lightgrey;
```

```
        padding: 5px;
        border-style: inset;
        border-width: 1px;
        border-radius: 5px;
        image: url(images/like_normal.png);
        qproperty-iconSize: 20px 20px;}

QPushButton:pressed {background-color: grey;
                padding: 5px;
                border-style: outset;
                border-width: 1px;
                border-radius: 5px;
                image: url(images/like_clicked.png);
                qproperty-iconSize: 20px 20px;}""")

v_box = QVBoxLayout()
v_box.addWidget(label)
v_box.addWidget(like_button)
self.setLayout(v_box)
```

We want to be able to handle the pseudostate when the button is being pressed. Unlike this GUI's QLabel object, we'll need to specify the **selector**, which is the widget type affected by the change (here, it is QPushButton), in order to access the :pressed state. By altering the normal look of the button, specifically the borders, the button will no longer display feedback when being pressed.

Several properties that can be edited are common among many widgets, such as background-color, border, and padding. The padding property is used to add space around the text or image within the widget. If you wanted to add extra space outside of the widget, you can use the margin property.

An image is also used for like_button, and its size is adjusted using qproperty-iconSize. The qproperty property is used to modify specific aspects of a widget class. A simple example would be the text() getter from QLabel. If you wanted to use style sheets to specify the text of a label, you could use the following bit of code:

```
label.setStyleSheet("qproperty-text: 'example text'")
```

For the :pressed state, a darker background color, a darker image, and a different border style are used to convey to the user that the button is being pressed. The last step is to add the widgets to a layout and set the layout for the window.

A list of all pseudostates can be found in Qt's Style Sheet references. Let's check out a more efficient alternative to using inline style sheets in the next section.

Explanation for Using "Embedded" Qt Style Sheets

Embedded style sheets in CSS are used to define the styles for the entire document in one location, usually in the beginning of the script. We can follow a similar pattern when creating PyQt applications. This is especially useful when you have multiple widgets of the same type that all share the same style, allowing you to specify all of the modifications at one time. For example, the following code would set the background color for all QPushButton instances to red:

```
app.setStyleSheet("QPushButton{background-color: #C92108}")
```

Notice how the change is being applied to the QApplication object, app. For the example GUI in Figure 6-4, we are going to take a look at how to use embedded style sheets to apply changes to specific widgets.

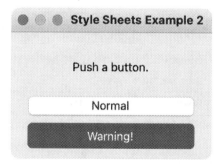

Figure 6-4. *GUI that demonstrates how to apply styles to specific widgets*

The window contains two QPushButton widgets – one with a native style and the other with a modified style.

Applying Changes to Specific Widgets

When you create an object in PyQt, such as a widget, you can give it a name using the QObject method setObjectName(). This can be useful for finding a particular child of a parent widget. When using style sheets, this allows us to give a widget an **ID Selector**, or a specific name, for identifying a particular widget.

Listing 6-6 shows how to use the ID Selector to apply a different style to a specified button.

Listing 6-6. Creating an embedded style sheet

```
# style_sheet_ex2.py
# Import necessary modules
import sys
from PyQt6.QtWidgets import (QApplication, QWidget, QLabel,
    QPushButton, QVBoxLayout)

style_sheet = """
    QPushButton#Warning_Button{
        background-color: #C92108;
        border-radius: 5px;
        padding: 6px;
        color: #FFFFFF
    }
    QPushButton#Warning_Button:pressed{
        background-color: #F4B519;
    }
"""
```

The window is simply composed of a QLabel and two QPushButton widgets. To target one specific widget, use the ID Selector. For this example, that is #Warning_Button. To handle changes when the button is pressed, add the pseudostate :pressed after the ID Selector. These changes are added to the style_sheet variable.

Listing 6-7 shows how to set up the MainWindow class, create the buttons, use setObjectName() to create the ID Selector, and arrange the widgets in a layout.

Listing 6-7. Creating the MainWindow class and applying the style sheet

```python
# style_sheet_ex2.py
class MainWindow(QWidget):

    def __init__(self):
        super().__init__()
        self.initializeUI()

    def initializeUI(self):
        """Set up the application's GUI."""
        self.setMinimumSize(230, 140)
        self.setWindowTitle("Style Sheets Example 2")

        label = QLabel("<p align=center>Push a button.</p>")
        normal_button = QPushButton("Normal")
        warning_button = QPushButton("Warning!")
        # Set ID Selector
        warning_button.setObjectName("Warning_Button")

        v_box = QVBoxLayout()
        v_box.addWidget(label)
        v_box.addWidget(normal_button)
        v_box.addWidget(warning_button)

        self.setLayout(v_box)
        self.show()

if __name__ == '__main__':
    app = QApplication(sys.argv)
    app.setStyleSheet(style_sheet) # Set style of application
    window = MainWindow()
    sys.exit(app.exec())
```

The last task for this program is to apply the style sheet to the application's QApplication object. Before moving on to a larger styling project, let's find out about a few new and useful PyQt classes that are great for organization.

Organizing Widgets with Containers and Tabs

Organization in a GUI can be achieved not only visually, but also by continuing to learn about new tools for structuring widgets. In Chapter 5, you saw how to use QWidget to group widgets together. In this section, you'll

- See how to create **containers** that create boxes around related widgets

- Find out about radio buttons to practically see how relationships can be created and managed when developing GUIs

- Explore the idea of organization in a user interface with tabbed interfaces, allowing for more content to be arranged in a GUI without overloading a user with too much visual information at one time

You'll learn all of this while creating the simple GUI in Figure 6-5.

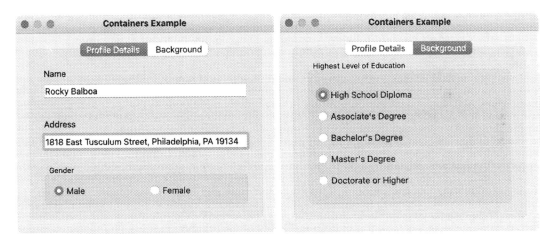

Figure 6-5. *The contact form GUI. The Profile Details tab (left) contains two labels and two line edit widgets as well as a group box with two radio buttons. The Background tab (right) consists of a group box with five radio buttons*

The next few sections will discuss the new PyQt classes that we are going to use to build the application in Figure 6-5.

The QRadioButton Widget

The **QRadioButton** class allows you to create option buttons that can be switched on when checked or off when unchecked. Radio buttons consist of a round button and a corresponding label or icon and are great for situations where you need to provide a user with multiple choices but only one choice can be checked at a time. As the user selects a new radio button, the other radio buttons are unchecked.

To do so, you need to place multiple radio buttons in a parent widget. Those buttons will then become **autoexclusive**, meaning they automatically become members of a mutually exclusive group. If one radio button is checked inside of the parent, all of the other buttons will become unchecked. This functionality can be changed by setting the value of the QRadioButton method setAutoExclusive() to False.

Multiple exclusive groups of radio buttons can also be placed into the same parent widget by using the QButtonGroup class to separate and manage the different groups. Refer back to Chapter 4 for information about QButtonGroup.

Radio buttons are similar to the QCheckBox class when emitting signals. A radio button emits the toggled signal when checked on or off and can be connected to this signal to trigger a slot.

The QGroupBox Class

The **QGroupBox** container is a rectangular frame used for grouping widgets together. A group box has a border with a title on the top. The title can also be checkable so that the child widgets inside the group box can be enabled or disabled when checked or unchecked.

A group box object can contain any kind of widget. Since QGroupBox does not automatically arrange its child widgets, you will also need to apply a layout manager.

The following block of code is a brief example of how to use QGroupBox:

```
# The title for the group box is passed as an argument
effects_gb = QGroupBox("Effects")
# Create two QRadioButton objects to arrange in the group box
effect1_rb = QRadioButton("Strikethrough")
effect2_rb = QRadioButton("Outline")

# Create a layout for the group box
gb_h_box = QHBoxLayout()
```

```
gb_h_box.addWidget(effect1_rb)
gb_h_box.addWidget(effect2_rb)

# Set the layout for the group box
effects_gb.setLayout(gb_h_box)
```

Let's have a look at the final class for creating a tabbed user interface.

The QTabWidget Class

Sometimes, you may need to organize related information onto separate pages rather than creating a cluttered GUI. The **QTabWidget** class provides a tab bar with an area under each tab (referred to as a **page**) to present information and widgets related to each tab. Only one page is displayed at a time, and the user can view a different page by clicking on the tab or by using a shortcut (if one is set for the tab).

There are a few different ways to interact with and keep track of the different tabs. For example, if the user switches to a different tab, the index of the current tab can be returned when the currentChanged signal is emitted. You can also return a current page's index with currentIndex(), or the widget of the current page with currentWidget(). A tab can also be enabled or disabled with the setTabEnabled() method.

Tip   If you want to create an interface with multiple pages, but without the tab bar, then you should consider using a **QStackedWidget**. However, if you do use QStackedWidget, you will need to provide some other means to switch between the windows, such as QComboBox or QListWidget, since there are no tabs.

The following example creates a simple application that includes QRadioButton, QGroupBox, QTabWidget, and a few other classes. The program shows how to set up a tabbed interface and how to organize other widgets on the different pages.

Explanation for Using Containers and Tabs

We'll use the basic_window.py script to get started with this application. Begin by importing the necessary classes in Listing 6-8, including QRadioButton, QTabWidget, and QGroupBox from the QtWidgets module. Next, set up the MainWindow class and initialize its minimum size and title.

Listing 6-8. Setting up the main window for using containers and tabbed widgets

```python
# containers.py
# Import necessary modules
import sys
from PyQt6.QtWidgets import (QApplication, QWidget, QLabel,
    QRadioButton, QGroupBox, QLineEdit, QTabWidget,
    QHBoxLayout, QVBoxLayout)

class MainWindow(QWidget):

    def __init__(self):
        super().__init__()
        self.initializeUI()

    def initializeUI(self):
        """Set up the application's GUI."""
        self.setMinimumSize(400, 300)
        self.setWindowTitle("Containers Example")

        self.setUpMainWindow()
        self.show()

if __name__ == '__main__':
    app = QApplication(sys.argv)
    window = MainWindow()
    sys.exit(app.exec())
```

Following that step, we need to set up the tab widget in setUpMainWindow(). You'll need to first create an instance of QTabWidget. We'll create the object, tab_bar, in Listing 6-9.

Listing 6-9. The setUpMainWindow() method for using containers and tabbed widgets

```python
# containers.py
    def setUpMainWindow(self):
        """Create and arrange widgets in the main window.
        Set up tab bar and different tab widgets."""
        # Create tab bar and different page containers
```

```
tab_bar = QTabWidget(self)
self.prof_details_tab = QWidget()
self.background_tab = QWidget()

tab_bar.addTab(self.prof_details_tab,
    "Profile Details")
tab_bar.addTab(self.background_tab, "Background")

# Call methods to create the pages
self.profileDetailsTab()
self.backgroundTab()

# Create the layout for main window
main_h_box = QHBoxLayout()
main_h_box.addWidget(tab_bar)
self.setLayout(main_h_box)
```

The next task is to create a container for each page. You could use QGroupBox or some other container class. For the purpose of this GUI, let's use QWidget. There are two tabs for this project, prof_details_tab and background_tab. Insert the two pages into tab_bar using addTab(). Be sure to also give each tab an appropriate label.

We'll need to create two methods to create the different pages, profileDetailsTab() and backgroundTab(), and call them in setUpMainWindow(). Finally, arrange tab_bar in the window. Listings 6-10 and 6-11 will set up the pages.

Listing 6-10. Code for the profileDetailsTab() page

```
# containers.py
    def profileDetailsTab(self):
        """Profile page allows the user to enter their name,
        address, and select their gender."""
        # Set up labels and line edit widgets
        name_label = QLabel("Name")
        name_edit = QLineEdit()

        address_label = QLabel("Address")
        address_edit = QLineEdit()
```

```
# Create radio buttons and their layout manager
male_rb = QRadioButton("Male")
female_rb = QRadioButton("Female")

gender_h_box = QHBoxLayout()
gender_h_box.addWidget(male_rb)
gender_h_box.addWidget(female_rb)

# Create group box to contain radio buttons
gender_gb = QGroupBox("Gender")
gender_gb.setLayout(gender_h_box)

# Add all widgets to the profile details page layout
tab_v_box = QVBoxLayout()
tab_v_box.addWidget(name_label)
tab_v_box.addWidget(name_edit)
tab_v_box.addStretch()
tab_v_box.addWidget(address_label)
tab_v_box.addWidget(address_edit)
tab_v_box.addStretch()
tab_v_box.addWidget(gender_gb)

# Set layout for profile details tab
self.prof_details_tab.setLayout(tab_v_box)
```

The first page includes a few widgets for collecting a user's general information. You can refer back to Figure 6-5 to see how each page looks. The labels and line edit widgets are set up like normal. For the QRadioButton objects that ask about the user's gender, they are added to a QGroupBox, gender_gb, to make them mutually exclusive. The last step is to arrange the child widgets in a layout and call the method setLayout() for prof_details_tab to finish creating the page.

The backgroundTab() method in Listing 6-11 uses a for loop to instantiate each QRadioButton and add them to the page's layout.

Listing 6-11. Code for the backgroundTab() page

```python
# containers.py
    def backgroundTab(self):
        """Background page lets users select their educational
        background."""
        # Layout for education_gb
        ed_v_box = QVBoxLayout()

        # Create and add radio buttons to ed_v_box
        education_list = ["High School Diploma",
            "Associate's Degree", "Bachelor's Degree",
            "Master's Degree", "Doctorate or Higher"]
        for ed in education_list:
            self.education_rb = QRadioButton(ed)
            ed_v_box.addWidget(self.education_rb)

        # Set up group box to hold radio buttons
        self.education_gb = QGroupBox(
            "Highest Level of Education")
        self.education_gb.setLayout(ed_v_box)

        # Create and set for background tab
        tab_v_box = QVBoxLayout()
        tab_v_box.addWidget(self.education_gb)

        # Set layout for background tab
        self.background_tab.setLayout(tab_v_box)
```

With a basic understanding of style sheets and a few new PyQt classes, it's now time to apply what you have learned to create a new GUI project.

Project 6.1 – Food Ordering GUI

Food delivery service apps are everywhere. On your phone, on the Internet, and even on kiosks when you go into the actual restaurants themselves. They simplify the ordering process while also giving the user a feeling of control over their choices, asking us to select our own foods and items as we scroll through a list of organized categories.

These types of GUIs may possibly need to contain hundreds of different items that fit into multiple groups. Rather than just throwing all of the products into the interface and letting the user waste their own time sorting through the items, goods are usually placed into categories often differentiated by tabs. These tabs contain titles for the products that can be found on those corresponding pages, such as Frozen Foods or Fruits/Vegetables.

The GUI in this project allows the user to place an order for a pizza. It lays a foundation for a food ordering application using tab widgets to organize items onto separate pages. The project also shows how you can use style sheets to give a GUI made using PyQt a more aesthetic appearance. The tabbed interface can be seen in Figure 6-6.

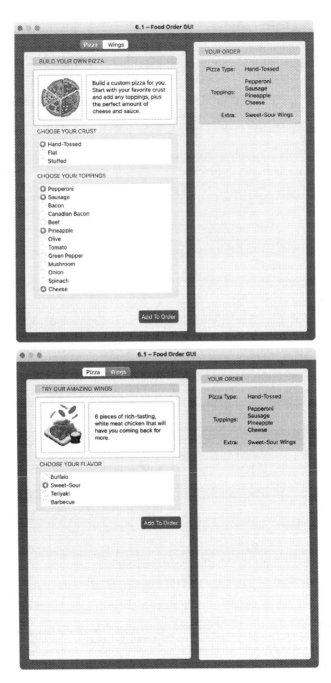

Figure 6-6. *The food ordering GUI. The GUI contains two tabs, Pizza (top) and Wings (bottom), to separate the types of food a customer can see at one time. The choices, which are QRadioButton widgets, that can be selected are separated using QGroupBox widgets. The main window has a red background, and each tab has a tan background. These colors and other styles are created with a style sheet*

Design the Food Ordering GUI

This application consists of two main tabs as seen in Figure 6-7, but more could be easily added. Each tab consists of a QWidget that acts as a container for all the other widgets. The first tab, Pizza, contains an image and text to convey the purpose of the tab to the user. This is followed by two QGroupBox widgets that each consist of a number of QRadioButton widgets. While the radio buttons in the Crust group box are mutually exclusive, the ones in the Toppings group box are not. This is done so that the user can select multiple toppings at one time.

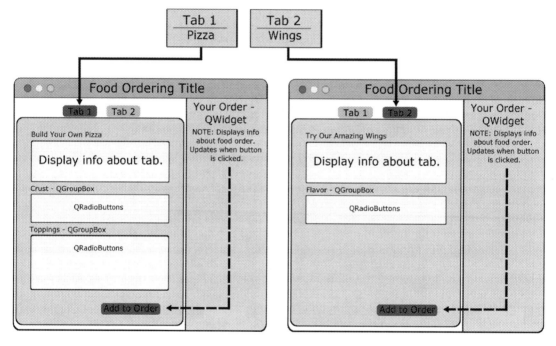

Figure 6-7. *The design for the food ordering GUI*

The second tab, Wings, is set up in a similar fashion with the Flavor radio buttons being mutually exclusive.

At the bottom of each page is an Add to Order QPushButton that will update the user's order in the widget on the right-hand side of the window.

Explanation for the Food Ordering GUI

This GUI does not contain a menu bar, so we'll once again use the basic_window.py script as the foundation for the application and the MainWindow class in Listing 6-12.

Listing 6-12. Setting up the main window for the food ordering GUI

```python
# food_order.py
# Import necessary modules
import sys
from PyQt6.QtWidgets import (QApplication, QWidget, QLabel,
    QPushButton, QRadioButton, QButtonGroup, QTabWidget,
    QGroupBox, QVBoxLayout, QHBoxLayout, QGridLayout)
from PyQt6.QtCore import Qt
from PyQt6.QtGui import QPixmap
class MainWindow(QWidget):

    def __init__(self):
        super().__init__()
        self.initializeUI()

    def initializeUI(self):
        """Set up the application's GUI."""
        self.setMinimumSize(700, 700)
        self.setWindowTitle("6.1 - Food Order GUI")

        self.setUpMainWindow()
        self.show()

if __name__ == '__main__':
    app = QApplication(sys.argv)
    app.setStyleSheet(style_sheet)
    window = MainWindow()
    sys.exit(app.exec())
```

There are quite a few imports for this GUI, but they have all been discussed in this chapter or in previous ones. Notice how the embedded style sheet for the food ordering GUI that we will create in the following section is imported with app. setStyleSheet(style_sheet).

Creating the Style Sheet

If a style sheet is not applied to the food ordering GUI, then it will use your system's native settings to style the application. Figure 6-8 shows what this looks like on macOS.

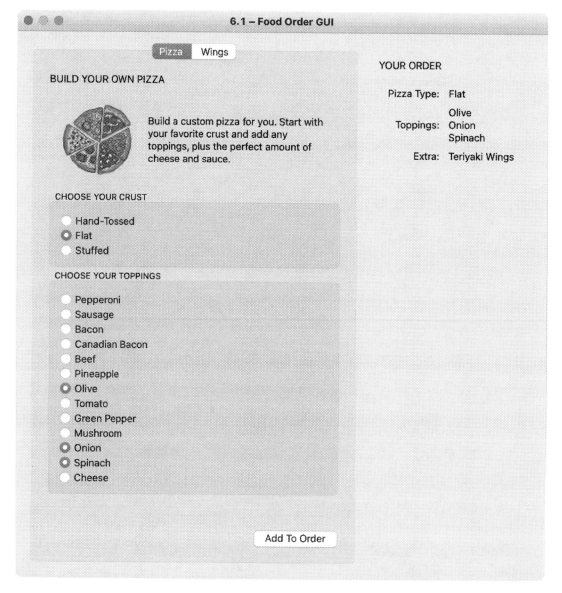

Figure 6-8. *The food ordering GUI before the style sheet is applied*

In the beginning of the program, you will need to create the style_sheet instance that holds all of the different style specifications for the different widgets. To begin, we can specify a general red background color, #C92108, which is used for the main window in Listing 6-13.

Listing 6-13. Setting up the style sheet for the food ordering GUI, part 1

```
# food_order.py
# Set up style sheet for the entire GUI
style_sheet = """
    QWidget{
        background-color: #C92108;
    }

    QWidget#Tabs{
        background-color: #FCEBCD;
        border-radius: 4px
    }

    QWidget#ImageBorder{
        background-color: #FCF9F3;
        border-width: 2px;
        border-style: solid;
        border-radius: 4px;
        border-color: #FABB4C
    }

    QWidget#Side{
        background-color: #EFD096;
        border-radius: 4px
    }
```

But if a QWidget has a specified ID Selector such as #Tabs, then it will get a tan background, #FCEBCD, and rounded corners. Widgets with these properties are used to style the pages for each tab.

The QWidget instances with the ID Selector #ImageBorder are created with an off-white background for containing the labels that display information to the user about each page.

The last QWidget selector with ID Selector #Side defines the settings for the side bar.

In Listing 6-14, create a general style for QLabel widgets, followed by a style for labels that appear as headers on each page. Take note that it is possible to specify a padding value for all four sides of a widget using padding, or for individual sides with padding-left, padding-top, and so on.

Listing 6-14. Setting up the style sheet for the food ordering GUI, part 2

```
# food_order.py
    QLabel{
        background-color: #EFD096;
        border-width: 2px;
        border-style: solid;
        border-radius: 4px;
        border-color: #EFD096
    }

    QLabel#Header{
        background-color: #EFD096;
        border-width: 2px;
        border-style: solid;
        border-radius: 4px;
        border-color: #EFD096;
        padding-left: 10px;
        color: #961A07
    }

    QLabel#ImageInfo{
        background-color: #FCF9F3;
        border-radius: 4px;
    }

    QGroupBox{
        background-color: #FCEBCD;
        color: #961A07
    }
```

```
QRadioButton{
    background-color: #FCF9F3
}

QPushButton{
    background-color: #C92108;
    border-radius: 4px;
    padding: 6px;
    color: #FFFFFF
}

QPushButton:pressed{
    background-color: #C86354;
    border-radius: 4px;
    padding: 6px;
    color: #DFD8D7
}
"""
```

The `QLabel` selectors with `#ImageInfo` are for the informational images and text on each page. To finish off the style sheet, there are styles for the `QGroupBox`, `QRadioButton`, and `QPushButton` objects.

We can now begin to tackle creating the `MainWindow` method `setUpMainWindow()`.

Building the Main Window

To get started, create the structure for the tabs and layout for the main window in Listing 6-15. Set up instances of the `QTabWidget` and `QWidget` objects that will be used for the pages of the tabs. The two tabs are the `pizza_tab`, to display choices for building your own pizza, and the `wings_tab`, to show choices for wing flavors.

Listing 6-15. Setting up the main window for the food ordering GUI, part 1

```
# food_order.py
    def setUpMainWindow(self):
        """Create and arrange widgets in the main window."""
        # Create tab bar, different tabs, and set object names
        self.tab_bar = QTabWidget()
```

```
    self.pizza_tab = QWidget()
    self.pizza_tab.setObjectName("Tabs")
    self.wings_tab = QWidget()
    self.wings_tab.setObjectName("Tabs")

    self.tab_bar.addTab(self.pizza_tab, "Pizza")
    self.tab_bar.addTab(self.wings_tab, "Wings")

    # Call methods that contain the widgets for each tab
    self.pizzaTab()
    self.wingsTab()
```

Some of the widgets in this GUI are given an ID Selector using the setObjectName() method. For example, pizza_tab is given the #Tabs ID Selector. This name is used in the application's style sheet to differentiate this widget from other QWidget objects with a different style.

Listing 6-16 shows how to build the side bar. The side_widget is used to give feedback to users of their choices and can be seen even if the user switches tabs.

Listing 6-16. Setting up the main window for the food ordering GUI, part 2

```
# food_order.py
    # Create side bar in the main window
    self.side_widget = QWidget()
    self.side_widget.setObjectName("Tabs")

    order_label = QLabel("YOUR ORDER")
    order_label.setObjectName("Header")

    items_box = QWidget()
    items_box.setObjectName("Side")
    pizza_label = QLabel("Pizza Type: ")
    self.display_pizza_label = QLabel("")
    toppings_label = QLabel("Toppings: ")
    self.display_toppings_label = QLabel("")
    extra_label = QLabel("Extra: ")
    self.display_wings_label = QLabel("")
```

```
# Set grid layout for objects in side widget
items_grid = QGridLayout()
items_grid.addWidget(pizza_label, 0, 0,
    Qt.AlignmentFlag.AlignRight)
items_grid.addWidget(self.display_pizza_label, 0, 1)
items_grid.addWidget(toppings_label, 1, 0,
    Qt.AlignmentFlag.AlignRight)
items_grid.addWidget(self.display_toppings_label,
    1, 1)
items_grid.addWidget(extra_label, 2, 0,
    Qt.AlignmentFlag.AlignRight)
items_grid.addWidget(self.display_wings_label, 2, 1)
items_box.setLayout(items_grid)
```

Labels that are meant to display a user's choices will initially display an empty string. All of the children for side_widget are arranged in a nested layout and added to the main QHBoxLayout in Listing 6-17.

Listing 6-17. Setting up the main window for the food ordering GUI, part 3

```
# food_order.py
    # Set main layout for side widget
    side_v_box = QVBoxLayout()
    side_v_box.addWidget(order_label)
    side_v_box.addWidget(items_box)
    side_v_box.addStretch()
    self.side_widget.setLayout(side_v_box)

    # Add widgets to main window and set layout
    main_h_box = QHBoxLayout()
    main_h_box.addWidget(self.tab_bar, 1)
    main_h_box.addWidget(self.side_widget)
    self.setLayout(main_h_box)
```

The pizzaTab() method, built in Listings 6-18 and 6-19, creates and arranges the child widgets for the first tab, pizza_tab. The top of the first page gives users information about the purpose of the tab using images and text. The radio buttons that display the pizza crust choices are also instantiated.

Listing 6-18. Code for the pizzaTab() page, part 1

```python
# food_order.py
    def pizzaTab(self):
        """Create the pizza tab. Allows the user to select
        the pizza type and toppings using radio buttons."""
        # Set up widgets and layouts to display information
        # to the user about the page
        tab_pizza_label = QLabel("BUILD YOUR OWN PIZZA")
        tab_pizza_label.setObjectName("Header")
        description_box = QWidget()
        description_box.setObjectName("ImageBorder")
        pizza_image_path = "images/pizza.png"
        pizza_image = self.loadImage(pizza_image_path)
        pizza_desc = QLabel()
        pizza_desc.setObjectName("ImageInfo")
        pizza_desc.setText(
            """<p>Build a custom pizza for you. Start with
            your favorite crust and add any toppings, plus
            the perfect amount of cheese and sauce.</p>""")
        pizza_desc.setWordWrap(True)
        pizza_desc.setContentsMargins(10, 10, 10, 10)

        pizza_h_box = QHBoxLayout()
        pizza_h_box.addWidget(pizza_image)
        pizza_h_box.addWidget(pizza_desc, 1)

        description_box.setLayout(pizza_h_box)

        # Create group box that will contain crust choices
        crust_gbox = QGroupBox()
        crust_gbox.setTitle("CHOOSE YOUR CRUST")

        # The group box is used to group the widgets together,
        # while the button group is used to get information
        # about which radio button is checked
        self.crust_group = QButtonGroup()
        gb_v_box = QVBoxLayout()
```

```
crust_list = ["Hand-Tossed", "Flat", "Stuffed"]
# Create radio buttons for the different crusts and
# add to layout
for cr in crust_list:
    crust_rb = QRadioButton(cr)
    gb_v_box.addWidget(crust_rb)
    self.crust_group.addButton(crust_rb)

crust_gbox.setLayout(gb_v_box)
```

Be sure to follow along with the comments in Listing 6-18 to understand how the page is structured. QRadioButton widgets are grouped together using group boxes. This allows each group to have a title. The QGroupBox class does provide exclusivity to radio buttons, but to get the type of functionality to find out which buttons are checked and return their text values, the QRadioButton objects are also grouped using QButtonGroup. Refer to Chapter 4 for more information about QButtonGroup.

The code in Listing 6-19 sets up the QRadioButton objects that display the pizza topping selections.

Listing 6-19. Code for the pizzaTab() page, part 2

```
# food_order.py
        # Create group box that will contain toppings choices
        toppings_gbox = QGroupBox()
        toppings_gbox.setTitle("CHOOSE YOUR TOPPINGS")

        # Set up button group for toppings radio buttons
        self.toppings_group = QButtonGroup()
        gb_v_box = QVBoxLayout()

        toppings_list = ["Pepperoni", "Sausage", "Bacon",
                    "Canadian Bacon", "Beef", "Pineapple",
                    "Olive", "Tomato", "Green Pepper",
                    "Mushroom", "Onion", "Spinach",
                    "Cheese"]
        # Create radio buttons for the different toppings and
        # add to layout
```

```
    for top in toppings_list:
        toppings_rb = QRadioButton(top)
        gb_v_box.addWidget(toppings_rb)
        self.toppings_group.addButton(toppings_rb)
    self.toppings_group.setExclusive(False)

    toppings_gbox.setLayout(gb_v_box)

    # Create button to add information to side widget
    # when clicked
    add_to_order_button1 = QPushButton("Add To Order")
    add_to_order_button1.clicked.connect(
        self.displayPizzaInOrder)

    # Create layout for pizza tab (page 1)
    page1_v_box = QVBoxLayout()
    page1_v_box.addWidget(tab_pizza_label)
    page1_v_box.addWidget(description_box)
    page1_v_box.addWidget(crust_gbox)
    page1_v_box.addWidget(toppings_gbox)
    page1_v_box.addStretch()
    page1_v_box.addWidget(add_to_order_button1,
        alignment=Qt.AlignmentFlag.AlignRight)

    self.pizza_tab.setLayout(page1_v_box)
```

While only one radio button can be selected in crust_group in Listing 6-18, users need to be able to select more than one topping. This is achieved by using the setExclusive() method to set the exclusivity of toppings_group to False.

The wingsTab() method in Listings 6-20 and 6-21 is set up in a similar manner to pizzaTab().

Listing 6-20. Code for the wingsTab() page, part 1

```
# food_order.py
    def wingsTab(self):
        """Create the wings tab. Allows the user to select
        the pizza type and toppings using radio buttons."""
        # Set up widgets and layouts to display information
```

```
# to the user about the page
tab_wings_label = QLabel("TRY OUR AMAZING WINGS")
tab_wings_label.setObjectName("Header")
description_box = QWidget()
description_box.setObjectName("ImageBorder")
wings_image_path = "images/wings.png"
wings_image = self.loadImage(wings_image_path)
wings_desc = QLabel()
wings_desc.setObjectName("ImageInfo")
wings_desc.setText(
    """<p>6 pieces of rich-tasting, white meat
    chicken that will have you coming back for
    more.</p>""")
wings_desc.setWordWrap(True)
wings_desc.setContentsMargins(10, 10, 10, 10)

wings_h_box = QHBoxLayout()
wings_h_box.addWidget(wings_image)
wings_h_box.addWidget(wings_desc, 1)

description_box.setLayout(wings_h_box)
```

The widgets for selecting wings are organized and added to wings_tab in Listing 6-21.

Listing 6-21. Code for the wingsTab() page, part 2

```
# food_order.py
    wings_gbox = QGroupBox()
    wings_gbox.setTitle("CHOOSE YOUR FLAVOR")

    self.wings_group = QButtonGroup()
    gb_v_box = QVBoxLayout()
    flavors_list = [
        "Buffalo", "Sweet-Sour", "Teriyaki", "Barbecue"]

    # Create radio buttons for the different flavors and
    # add to layout
```

```
    for fl in flavors_list:
        flavor_rb = QRadioButton(fl)
        gb_v_box.addWidget(flavor_rb)
        self.wings_group.addButton(flavor_rb)

    wings_gbox.setLayout(gb_v_box)

    # Create button to add information to side widget
    # when clicked
    add_to_order_button2 = QPushButton("Add To Order")
    add_to_order_button2.clicked.connect(
        self.displayWingsInOrder)

    # create layout for wings tab (page 2)
    page2_v_box = QVBoxLayout()
    page2_v_box.addWidget(tab_wings_label)
    page2_v_box.addWidget(description_box)
    page2_v_box.addWidget(wings_gbox)
    page2_v_box.addWidget(add_to_order_button2,
        alignment=Qt.AlignmentFlag.AlignRight)
    page2_v_box.addStretch()

    self.wings_tab.setLayout(page2_v_box)
```

If users press the add_to_order_button on either page (either 1 or 2), the text from the selected radio buttons on that page are displayed in the side_widget using one of the two methods in Listing 6-22.

Listing 6-22. Code for updating the side bar in the food ordering GUI

```
# food_order.py
    def displayPizzaInOrder(self):
        """Collect the text from the radio buttons that are
        checked on the pizza page. Display text in side
        widget."""
        if self.crust_group.checkedButton():
            text = self.crust_group.checkedButton().text()
            self.display_pizza_label.setText(text)
```

```
        toppings = self.collectToppingsInList()
        toppings_str = '\n'.join(toppings)
        self.display_toppings_label.setText(toppings_str)
        self.update()

    def displayWingsInOrder(self):
        """Collect the text from the radio buttons that are
        checked on the wings page. Display text in side
        widget."""
        if self.wings_group.checkedButton():
            text = self.wings_group.checkedButton().text() +\
                " Wings"
            self.display_wings_label.setText(text)
            self.update()
```

For `displayPizzaInOrder()`, we check to see if any of the radio buttons in the QButtonGroup `crust_group` are selected. If so, the text from the selected button is collected and displayed in `display_pizza_label` using `setText()`. For `display_toppings_label`, all of the selected `toppings` radio buttons are collected and returned using `collectToppingsInList()` in Listing 6-23. The toppings are then depicted in the label. The `update()` method is used to ensure that the text is updated accordingly.

Listing 6-23. Code for collecting information about selected radio buttons in the food ordering GUI

```
# food_order.py
    def collectToppingsInList(self):
        """Create list of all checked radio buttons."""
        toppings_list = [button.text() for i, button in \
            enumerate(self.toppings_group.buttons()) if \
            button.isChecked()]
        return toppings_list
```

The last method to implement in Listing 6-24, `loadImage()`, loads and scales the pizza and wing images used on the two pages.

Listing 6-24. Code for loading images in the food ordering GUI

```
# food_order.py
    def loadImage(self, img_path):
        """Load and scale images."""
        aspect = Qt.AspectRatioMode.KeepAspectRatioByExpanding
        transform = Qt.TransformationMode.SmoothTransformation
        try:
            with open(img_path):
                image = QLabel(self)
                image.setObjectName("ImageInfo")
                pixmap = QPixmap(img_path)
                image.setPixmap(pixmap.scaled(image.size(),
                    aspect, transform))
                return image
        except FileNotFoundError as error:
            print(f"Image not found. Error: {error}")
```

A fairly long project, the food ordering GUI demonstrates just how intensive an interface can be to style. The next step could be to add more tabs and options as a way to practice building stylized tabbed interfaces or even use the Qt documentation to modify the properties of the GUI.

CSS Properties Reference

Table 6-2 lists the CSS properties found throughout this chapter as well as some commonly used properties you may need for your early projects.

Table 6-2. *Commonly used CSS properties in PyQt*

Property	Description
background-color	Sets the background color for the widget
border	Shorthand for setting the border color, style, and width QLabel {border: 2px groove grey}
border-color	Specifies the color of the border for all sides of the widget
border-style	Specifies the pattern for drawing the widget's border. Some of the patterns are dashed, dotted, groove, inset, outset, and solid
border-width	Sets the border width for all sides of the widget (in pixels)
border-radius	Sets the radius of the widget's corners (in pixels)
color	Specifies the color used for text
font	Specifies the font weight, style, size, and family QLabel {font: bold italic small 'Times'}
image	Sets the image used within the widget. Be sure to include url(path_to_file)
margin	Specifies the additional space around the widget (in pixels)
padding	Specifies the additional space inside of the widget (in pixels)

Summary

In this chapter, we saw how to use Qt Style Sheets to modify the appearance of widgets to better fit the purpose and look of an application. We also saw how HTML can be used to manipulate the look of text.

The benefits of using style sheets include easier updates to code, greater consistency in design, simpler way to format the look of widgets, increase in usability, and less difficulty for a developer to control colors, layouts, and other aesthetic aspects of UI design.

Chapter 7 will discuss a very important topic – event handling.

CHAPTER 7

Handling Events in PyQt

Since GUIs need to perform tasks, the widgets, windows, and other aspects of the application need to be able to react to the events that occur. Whether caused by the user or by the underlying system, the events, and possibly data, need to be delivered to their appropriate locations and handled accordingly.

In this chapter, you will

- Find out more about signals, slots, and event handling

- Learn how to modify key press and mouse and enter event handlers

- Explore how to create custom signals using `pyqtSignal`

This chapter is all about handling events and modifying the behaviors of the built-in functions in PyQt.

Event Handling in PyQt

Events in Qt are objects created from the **QEvent** class. The event objects describe different types of interactions that can occur in a GUI as a result of what happens, either caused by a user or by some kind of system activity outside of the application. These events begin once the application's main event loop starts.

Most events, whether the press of a key, click of a mouse, resizing of a window, or dragging and dropping of a widget or data, have their own subclass of `QEvent` that generates an event object and passes it on to the appropriate `QObject` by calling the event() method, which in turn is handled by the suitable event handler. (Recall that `QWidget` inherits `QObject`.) The response from the event is used to determine whether it was accepted or disregarded.

More information about event handling can be found at `https://doc.qt.io/qt-6/eventsandfilters.html`.

© Joshua M Willman 2022
J. M. Willman, *Beginning PyQt*, https://doi.org/10.1007/978-1-4842-7999-1_7

Let's take a look at signals and slots and event handlers in the following subsections and think about their purposes and their differences.

Using Signals and Slots

The concept of signals and slots in PyQt was briefly introduced in Chapter 3. Widgets in PyQt use signals and slots to communicate between objects. Just like events, signals can be generated by a user's actions or by the internal system. Slots are methods that are executed in response to the signal. For example, when a QPushButton is pressed, it emits a clicked signal. This signal could be connected to a built-in PyQt slot, such as close() to allow a user to quit an application, or to a custom-made slot, which is typically a Python function. Signals are also useful because they can be used to send additional data to a slot and provide more information about an event.

The clicked signal is but one of many predefined Qt signals. The type of signals that can be emitted differs according to the widget class. PyQt delivers events to widgets by calling specific, predefined event handling functions. These can range from functions related to window operations such as show() or close(), to GUI appearances with setStyleSheet(), to mouse press and release events, and more.

Have a look at www.riverbankcomputing.com/static/Docs/PyQt6/signals_slots.html for more information about signals and slots in PyQt6.

Using Event Handlers to Handle Events

Event handlers are the functions that respond to an event. While a QEvent subclass is created to deliver the event, a corresponding QWidget method will actually handle the event. If you remember in Chapter 3, the closeEvent() event handler was used to close windows. The class that creates the close event object is **QCloseEvent**.

Note   You may not always be able to handle all of the functionality in an event handler that you modify. When this is the case, you can use an if-else statement. In the if condition, specify how to react to the event, and in the else clause, call the base class's implementation. So for QCloseEvent, you would include super().closeEvent(event) in the else clause. This portion will take care of any default behaviors you did not implement or may have missed.

Difference Between Signals and Slots and Event Handlers

While there is some overlap between the two, signals and slots are typically used for communication between the different widgets and other PyQt classes. Events are generated by an outside activity and delivered through the event loop by QApplication.

Another important difference is that you are notified when a signal is emitted and take action accordingly. Events need to be handled whenever they occur.

Finally, we can use signals with widgets to improve their capabilities, but you will need to reimplement event handlers when modifying a widget's functionalities.

In many cases, you will use signals and slots and event handlers together to complete tasks.

The following section shows a simple example of how to reimplement the keyPressEvent() function.

Handling Key Events

When keys are pressed or released, a **QKeyEvent** is created. Key events are sent to the widget that currently has keyboard focus. We can then reimplement the following QWidget key event handlers to deal with the event:

- keyPressEvent() – Handles a key event when the key is pressed

- keyReleaseEvent() – Handles a key event when the key is released

Figure 7-1 shows the GUI that we'll code, which demonstrates how to modify keyPressEvent().

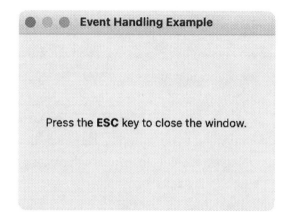

Figure 7-1. *A window that closes when the user presses the Escape key*

Some key names include Key_Escape, Key_Return, Key_Up, Key_Down, Key_Space, Key_0, Key_1, and so on. A full list of Qt.Key enum keyboard codes can be found at https://doc.qt.io/qt-6/qt.html#Key-enum.

Explanation for Handling Key Events

For Listing 7-1, we'll create a simple MainWindow class that inherits QMainWindow. The imports for this application are also fairly simple. The MainWindow class inherits QMainWindow so that we don't have to import any layout managers for the single QLabel object.

Listing 7-1. Code to demonstrate how to modify key event handlers

```
# key_events.py
# Import necessary modules
import sys
from PyQt6.QtWidgets import QApplication, QMainWindow, QLabel
from PyQt6.QtCore import Qt

class MainWindow(QMainWindow):

    def __init__(self):
        super().__init__()
        self.initializeUI()
```

```python
    def initializeUI(self):
        """Set up the application's GUI."""
        self.setGeometry(100, 100, 300, 200)
        self.setWindowTitle("Event Handling Example")
        info_label = QLabel(
            """<p align='center'>Press the <b>ESC</b> key
            to close the window.</p>""")
        self.setCentralWidget(info_label)
        self.show()

    def keyPressEvent(self, event):
        """Reimplement the key press event to close the
        window."""
        if event.key() == Qt.Key.Key_Escape:
            print("Application closed.")
            self.close()

if __name__ == '__main__':
    app = QApplication(sys.argv)
    window = MainWindow()
    sys.exit(app.exec())
```

Whenever a user presses a key on the keyboard, it sends a signal to the computer. If you want to give certain keys abilities, then you will need to use the keyPressEvent().

The keyPressEvent() function checks for events, which in this case are the signals being sent from keys. If the key pressed is the Escape key, then the application calls the close() function to quit the application. Different keys can be accessed using Qt.Key, and you can use those different keys to perform any number of actions.

Handling Mouse Events

Mouse events are handled by the **QMouseEvent** class. For mouse events, we need to be able to find out when a mouse button is pressed, released, and double-clicked and when the mouse moves while clicked. There is also an event class, **QEnterEvent**, that is useful for finding out if the mouse has entered or left the window or a particular widget. Enter events are also useful for collecting information about the mouse cursor's position.

The QWidget mouse event handlers we'll be using include the following:

- mousePressEvent() – Handles events when the mouse button is pressed.

- mouseReleaseEvent() – Handles events when the mouse button is released.

- mouseMoveEvent() – Handles events when the mouse button is pressed and moved. Turn on mouse tracking to enable move events even if a mouse button is not pressed with QWidget. setMouseTracking(True).

- mouseDoubleClickEvent() – Handles events when the mouse button is double-clicked.

For the enter events, we'll use the following event handlers:

- enterEvent() – Handles when the mouse cursor enters a widget

- leaveEvent() – Handles when the mouse cursor leaves a widget

For the GUI in Figure 7-2, there is only the image in the left window without any textual information when the program first starts. When a mouse enters the main window, the image in the window will change to what is shown in the right screenshot in Figure 7-2. If the user clicks or releases the mouse button, a label in the widget will update to let them know which mouse button, left or right, was used. Double-clicking in the window will change the image. Lastly, the x and y coordinates of the mouse's position are displayed on the screen when the mouse is pressed and moving.

Figure 7-2. *The images and information in the window change based on the mouse events. Images from* $https://pixabay.com$

Be sure to download the `images` folder from the GitHub repository for this example.

Explanation for Handling Mouse Events

For this example, we can use the `basic_window.py` script from Chapter 1. In Listing 7-2, let's set up the main window and the `setUpMainWindow()` method. The window consists of three `QLabel` objects, one for displaying images and the other two for relaying information about the mouse events to the user.

Listing 7-2. Code for setting up the main window in the modifying mouse event handlers example

```
# mouse_events.py
# Import necessary modules
import sys
```

```python
from PyQt6.QtWidgets import (QApplication, QWidget, QLabel,
    QVBoxLayout)
from PyQt6.QtCore import Qt
from PyQt6.QtGui import QPixmap

class MainWindow(QWidget):

    def __init__(self):
        super().__init__()
        self.initializeUI()

    def initializeUI(self):
        """Set up the application's GUI."""
        self.setMinimumSize(400, 300)
        self.setWindowTitle("Event Handling Example")

        self.setUpMainWindow()
        self.show()

    def setUpMainWindow(self):
        self.image_label = QLabel()
        self.image_label.setPixmap(QPixmap("images/back.png"))
        self.image_label.setAlignment(
            Qt.AlignmentFlag.AlignCenter)

        self.info_label = QLabel("")
        self.info_label.setAlignment(
            Qt.AlignmentFlag.AlignCenter)

        self.pos_label = QLabel("")
        self.pos_label.setAlignment(
            Qt.AlignmentFlag.AlignCenter)

        main_h_box = QVBoxLayout()
        main_h_box.addStretch()
        main_h_box.addWidget(self.image_label)
        main_h_box.addStretch()
        main_h_box.addWidget(self.info_label)
        main_h_box.addWidget(self.pos_label)
        self.setLayout(main_h_box)
```

```
if __name__ == '__main__':
    app = QApplication(sys.argv)
    window = MainWindow()
    sys.exit(app.exec())
```

The addStretch() method is used before and after image_label in main_h_box to make sure the images stay centered in the window.

Whenever the mouse cursor enters a window, image_label will display a different image. To change the image back, we can use leaveEvent() to check when the mouse has left the widget. This is done in Listing 7-3.

Listing 7-3. Code for the enterEvent() and leaveEvent() event handlers

```
# mouse_events.py
    def enterEvent(self, event):
        self.image_label.setPixmap(
            QPixmap("images/front.png"))

    def leaveEvent(self, event):
        self.image_label.setPixmap(QPixmap("images/back.png"))
```

In PyQt6, QMouseEvent inherits a few methods from **QPointerEvent** that can provide more information about which mouse buttons are clicked or where the mouse is in the window or on the computer screen. These include the following:

- button() – Returns which button caused the event.

- buttons() – Returns the state of the buttons, giving access to which combination of buttons caused the event using an OR operator.

- globalPosition() – Returns the point coordinates of the event on the computer screen.

- position() – Returns the current point coordinates of the mouse relative to the widget that caused the event. The values returned refer to points within the window or widget.

Both globalPosition() and position() have x() and y() methods for collecting horizontal or vertical values. We'll use a few of these methods in Listing 7-4.

Listing 7-4. Code that demonstrates how to modify mouse event handlers

```python
# mouse_events.py
    def mouseMoveEvent(self, event):
        """Print the mouse position while clicked and
        moving."""
        if self.underMouse():
            self.pos_label.setText(
                f"""<p>X:{event.position().x()},
                    Y:{event.position().y()}</p>""")

    def mousePressEvent(self, event):
        """Determine which button was clicked."""
        if event.button() == Qt.MouseButton.LeftButton:
            self.info_label.setText("<b>Left Click</b>")
        if event.button() == Qt.MouseButton.RightButton:
            self.info_label.setText("<b>Right Click</b>")

    def mouseReleaseEvent(self, event):
        """Determine which button was released."""
        if event.button() == Qt.MouseButton.LeftButton:
            self.info_label.setText(
                "<b>Left Button Released</b>")
        if event.button() == Qt.MouseButton.RightButton:
            self.info_label.setText(
                "<b>Right Button Released</b>")

    def mouseDoubleClickEvent(self, event):
        self.image_label.setPixmap(QPixmap("images/boom.png"))
```

The mouse's x and y values are displayed in pos_label using position() in mouseMoveEvent(). For mousePressEvent(), we'll simply update the text of info_label depending upon which mouse button is clicked. The mouseReleaseEvent() will do something similar, but when the button is released. For mouseDoubleClickEvent(), pixmap is updated to look like Figure 7-3. Moving the mouse out of the window causes leaveEvent() to be called, showing the images in Figure 7-2 again.

Figure 7-3. *The image in the screen changes when the mouse is double-clicked*

After seeing how to modify event handlers, now is a good time to learn how to create your own signals.

Creating Custom Signals

We have taken a look at some of PyQt's predefined signals and slots in previous chapters. For many of those applications, we have also seen how to create custom slots to handle the signals emitted from widgets. The custom slots were simply Python functions or methods.

Now let's see how we can create custom signals using pyqtSignal to change a widget's style sheet. Using **pyqtSignal**, new signals can be defined for a class. Just like predefined signals, you can also pass types of information, such as Python strings, integers, dictionaries, or lists, as arguments to the pyqtSignal you create.

211

For the GUI in Figure 7-4, a user can change the background color of the lower QLabel widget by pressing the up or down arrow keys on their keyboard. A **closed** signal, one that takes no arguments, will be emitted when a key is pressed.

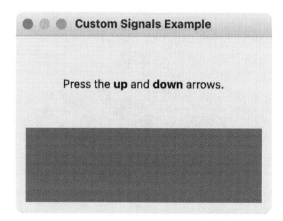

Figure 7-4. *The color of the label will change when the up and down arrows are pressed*

Explanation for Creating Custom Signals

This example creates a simple GUI with a QLabel object as the central widget of the main window. The pyqtSignal factory and QObject classes are imported from the QtCore module. The QtCore module and QObject class provide the mechanics for signals and slots.

Before creating the MainWindow class in Listing 7-5, we'll first create a class, SendSignal, that inherits QObject.

Listing 7-5. Creating a custom signal to change the background color of a QLabel widget

```
# custom_signal.py
# Import necessary modules
import sys
from PyQt6.QtWidgets import (QApplication, QMainWindow,
    QWidget, QLabel, QVBoxLayout)
from PyQt6.QtCore import Qt, pyqtSignal, QObject
```

```python
class SendSignal(QObject):
    """Define a signal, change_style, that takes no
    arguments."""
    change_style = pyqtSignal()

class MainWindow(QMainWindow):

    def __init__(self):
        super().__init__()
        self.initializeUI()

    def initializeUI(self):
        """Set up the application's GUI."""
        self.setGeometry(100, 100, 300, 200)
        self.setWindowTitle("Create Custom Signals")

        self.setUpMainWindow()
        self.show()

if __name__ == '__main__':
    app = QApplication(sys.argv)
    window = MainWindow()
    sys.exit(app.exec())
```

The SendSignal class creates a new signal called change_style from the pyqtSignal factory. To use this signal, we'll first need to create an instance of SendSignal, simply called sig, in Listing 7-6. To use the custom signal you created, call the change_style instance from sig, and use connect() to connect the signal to a slot, in this case, changeBackground().

Listing 7-6. Code for the setUpMainWindow() method

```python
# custom_signal.py
    def setUpMainWindow(self):
        """Create and arrange widgets in the main window."""
        self.index = 0 # Index of items in list
        self.direction = ""
```

213

```
# Create instance of SendSignal class, and
# connect change_style signal to a slot
self.sig = SendSignal()
self.sig.change_style.connect(self.changeBackground)

header_label = QLabel(
    """<p align='center'>Press the <b>up</b> and
    <b>down</b> arrows.</p>""")

self.colors_list = ["red", "orange", "yellow",
                    "green", "blue", "purple"]
self.label = QLabel()
self.label.setStyleSheet(f"""background-color:
    {self.colors_list[self.index]}""")

main_v_box = QVBoxLayout()
main_v_box.addWidget(header_label)
main_v_box.addWidget(self.label)

container = QWidget()
container.setLayout(main_v_box)
self.setCentralWidget(container)
```

The rest of setUpMainWindow() instantiates the two QLabel widgets and creates a list of colors that are used by label to specify the background in its style sheet.

This signal will be emitted whenever the user presses either the up arrow key or the down arrow key in keyPressEvent().

When the user presses Key_Up, direction is set equal to "up", and a change_style signal is emitted. To emit a custom signal, you'll need to call emit() at the point in your application where the signal needs to be triggered. An example for sig is shown in the following line:

```
self.sig.change_style.emit()
```

This signal is connected to the changeBackground() slot that updates the color of the label by checking the index of colors_list and updating the color using setStyleSheet() in Listing 7-7.

Listing 7-7. Code for handling keyPressEvent() and the slot for changing the background color

```python
# custom_signal.py
    def keyPressEvent(self, event):
        """Reimplement how the key press event is handled."""
        if event.key() == Qt.Key.Key_Up:
            self.direction = "up"
            self.sig.change_style.emit()
        elif event.key() == Qt.Key.Key_Down:
            self.direction = "down"
            self.sig.change_style.emit()

    def changeBackground(self):
        """Change the background of the label widget when
        a keyPressEvent signal is emitted."""
        if self.direction == "up" and \
            self.index < len(self.colors_list) - 1:
            self.index = self.index + 1
            self.label.setStyleSheet(f"""background-color:
            {self.colors_list[self.index]}""")
        elif self.direction == "down" and self.index > 0:
            self.index = self.index - 1
            self.label.setStyleSheet(f"""background-color:
            {self.colors_list[self.index]}""")
```

It works in a similar fashion when the down key is pressed. Remember that custom signals can take data types as arguments, so don't worry if you need to pass along information to your other widgets or classes.

Summary

Handling events is a critical component of GUI development. With PyQt, this can be accomplished either through signals and slots or by the event classes and their corresponding event handlers. Either way, you may often find yourself extending the abilities of a widget class by creating custom signals using `pyqtSignal` or reimplementing the base functionality provided by Qt's various event handler methods.

We took a look at both these concepts in this chapter, changing the behaviors of key press and mouse event handlers and creating a custom signal to modify the appearance of a label.

In the next chapter, we'll take a look at using the application Qt Designer to create PyQt applications and simplifying the process for arranging widgets in a GUI window.

## CHAPTER 8

Creating GUIs with Qt Designer

While building GUIs programmatically gives you more control over the design process, some development tasks may require a quicker approach. Fortunately, Qt provides a great interface for arranging widgets and designing main windows, widgets, or dialogs. The graphical development tool, **Qt Designer**, is filled with widgets and other tools for building GUIs. With the application's drag-and-drop interface, you are able to create and customize your own Qt or PyQt applications.

The widgets and other applications you create using Qt Designer can interact with other Qt programs using signals and slots, making it easier to assign behaviors to widgets. This means that more resources can go into coding the functionality and less into layout and design.

In this chapter, you will

- Install the Qt Designer application

- Take a look at the different components that comprise the Qt Designer interface

- Follow along and build an application in Qt Designer, along the way learning how to apply layouts, edit object properties, connect signals and slots, and generate Python code

- Learn about new PyQt classes such as QFrame class for grouping widgets

---

Tip   For references or more help beyond the scope of this chapter, check out the Qt Documentation for Qt Designer at `https://doc.qt.io/qt-6/qtdesigner-manual.html`.

© Joshua M Willman 2022
J. M. Willman, *Beginning PyQt*, https://doi.org/10.1007/978-1-4842-7999-1_8

This chapter serves as an introduction to Qt Designer, providing you with the fundamentals you need to get started using the application.

Getting Started with Qt Designer

In this section, we'll first consider two methods for installing Qt Designer on your computer. After that, we'll discuss the layout of the Qt Designer GUI.

Installing Qt Designer

As of writing, there are two approaches to installing the latest version of Qt Designer, and they can vary depending upon how much memory you are willing to use.

Your first option is to download the latest version of Qt Creator for Qt 6 from `www.qt.io/download`. Qt Designer comes *bundled* with Qt Creator, which is Qt's official C++ IDE. Be aware that this method works for macOS, Windows, and Linux, but also means that you will be installing the entire Qt Creator IDE as well.

On the Qt downloads web page, you'll need to locate the option for downloading Qt for open source creators. From there, scroll to the bottom of the page and find the button that says Download the Qt Online Installer. Once the download completes, you'll need to open up the Qt installer software. You'll need to create a Qt Account and then follow along with the prompts to install Qt Creator. One thing to note, if you choose to perform a custom installation, you'll be able to manually select the software you need and save some memory. Once the installation is complete, do a search on your computer to locate Qt Designer.

Another way to install Qt Designer is through PySide6. First, open a shell window and enter the following command to install PySide6:

```
$ pip3 install PySide6
```

Use `pip` instead of `pip3` on Windows.

Next, perform a search on your computer for Qt Designer and open the application. After opening Qt Designer, you will see a graphical user interface for creating your own GUIs like the one in Figure 8-1.

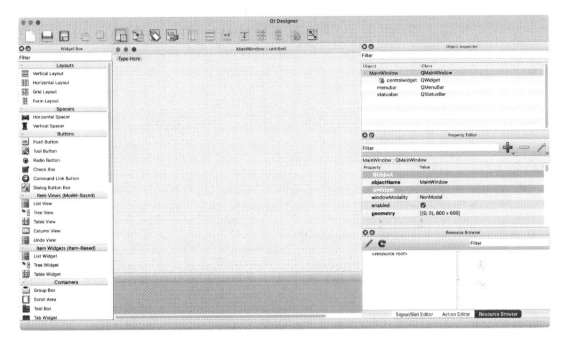

Figure 8-1. *The Qt Designer interface*

Tip   You can change the appearance of the Qt Designer window. In the menu bar, locate the Preferences… menu option, and in the dialog box that appears, look for User Interface Mode. You can select two appearances: Multi Top-Level Windows or Docked Windows. The multilevel layout is great for arranging all of the widgets freely on larger screens.

Before you create your first application, let's get to know the different menus, tools, and modes that are displayed in the main window in Figure 8-1.

Exploring Qt Designer's User Interface

When you first open up Qt Designer, you will notice a dialog in the center of the window with the title New Form. This dialog can be seen in Figure 8-2. From here, you can select a template for creating a main window, a widget, or different kinds of dialog boxes. You can also choose what kinds of widgets to add to your project's layout. Once you have selected a template and the application's size, an empty window, also known as a **form**, will appear for you to modify.

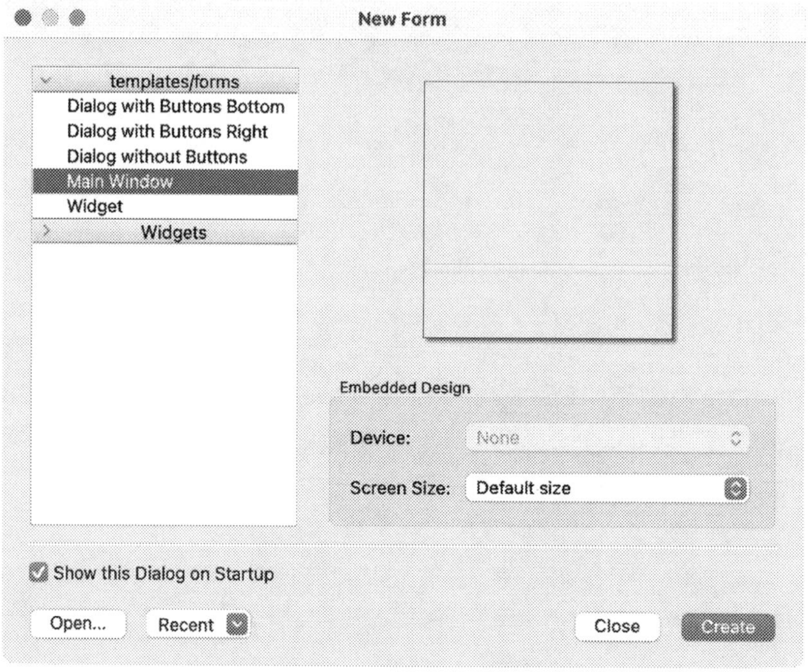

Figure 8-2. *The New Form dialog box for selecting what type of form to build*

At the top of the main window in Figure 8-1, you will notice Qt Designer's menu bar and toolbar for managing and editing your GUI. On the left side of the main window is the Widget Box dock widget, shown in Figure 8-3, which provides an organized list of layouts and widgets that can be dragged and dropped onto the required locations of your GUI. Other features for tinkering with the form can be accessed by right-clicking and opening up various context menus.

Another very useful dock widget is the Property Editor displayed in Figure 8-4. The properties of windows, widgets, and layouts such as an object's name, size constraints, status tips, and more can all be altered using the Property Editor. Each widget you add to a form will have its own set of properties as well as ones that the widget inherits from other classes. To select a specific widget, you can either click on the object in the form or on the widget's name in the Object Inspector dock widget.

The Object Inspector in Figure 8-5 allows you to view all of the objects that are currently being used as well as their hierarchical layout. You can see how the MainWindow is listed first, followed by the centralwidget, and all of its widgets. If your form also has a menu or toolbar, then they will also be listed in the Object Inspector along with their corresponding actions.

Note   The main layout for your GUI is not displayed in the `Object Inspector`. A broken layout icon (a red circle with a slash) is displayed on the central widget or on containers if no layout has been assigned to them.

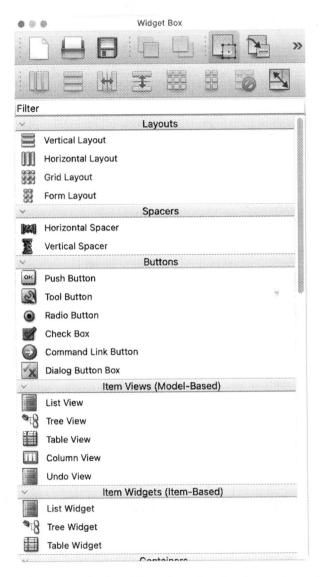

Figure 8-3. *The Widget Box dock widget for selecting layouts and widgets*

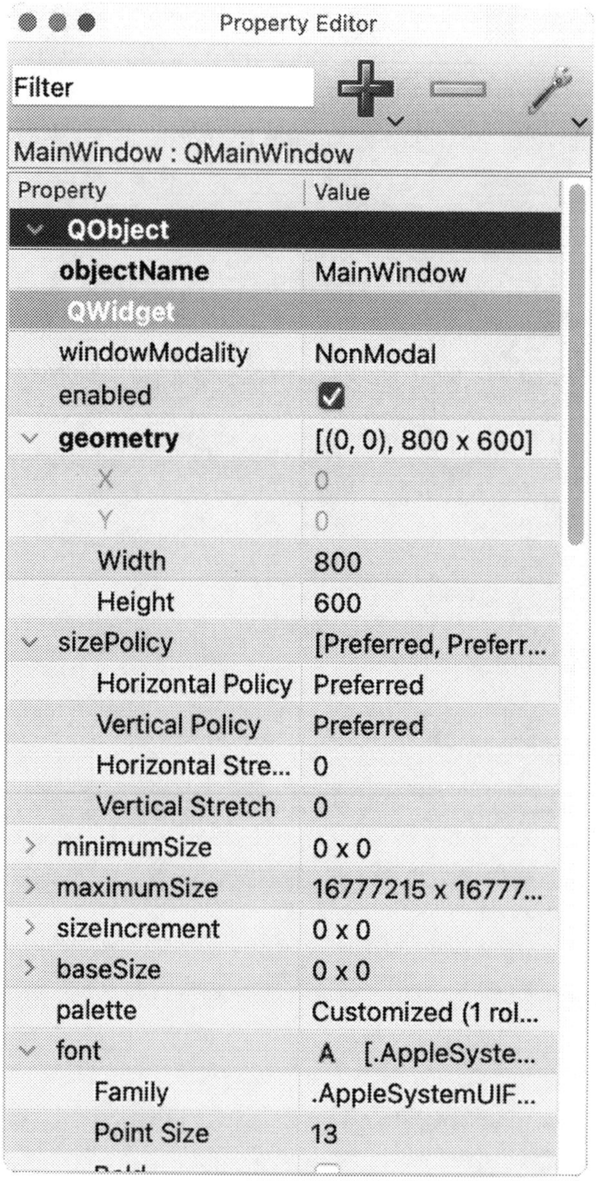

Figure 8-4. *The Property Editor dock widget for setting the attributes of widgets*

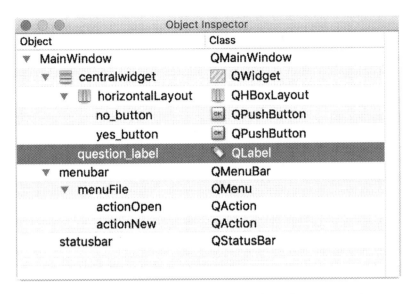

Figure 8-5. *The Object Inspector displays the widget, layout, and menu objects*

In Qt Designer, it is also possible to create, edit, and delete signals and slots between objects using the Signal/Slot Editor. You should be aware that although you can connect signals and slots, you will not always be able to completely configure your widgets and will sometimes need to complete that yourself in code. The Signal/Slot Editor can be seen in Figure 8-6. Qt Designer also provides an editing mode for connecting widgets.

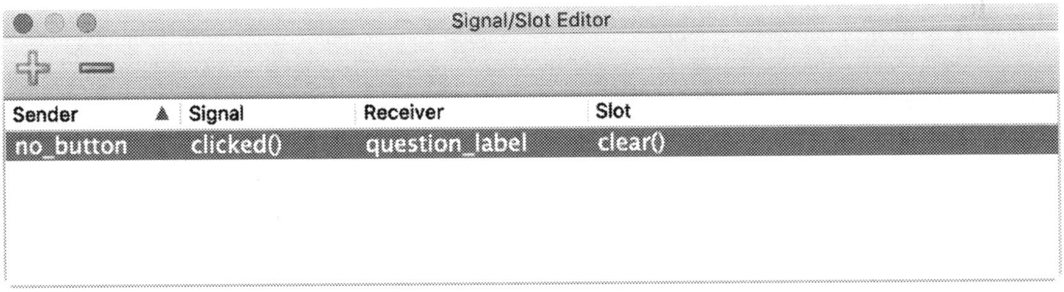

Figure 8-6. *The Signal/Slot Editor for connecting the signals and slots of objects*

Items in a menu, a submenu, or a toolbar are assigned commands by using actions. These actions can then be given a shortcut key, made checkable, and more. The Action Editor seen in Figure 8-7 gives you access to working with actions. For more information about assigning actions, refer to Chapter 5.

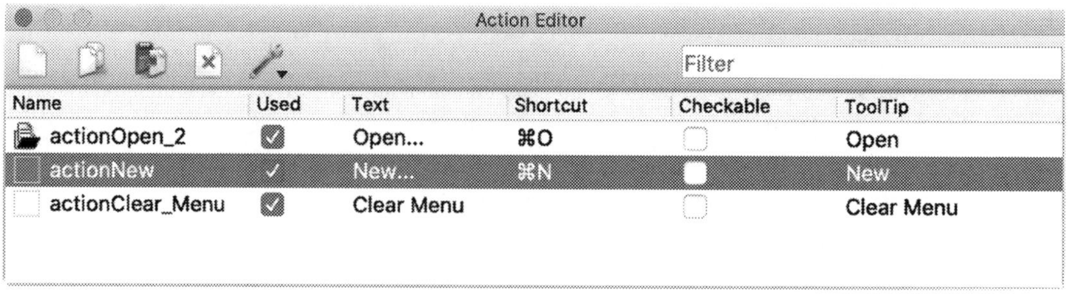

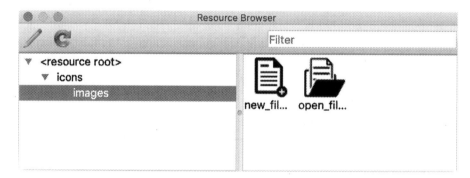

Figure 8-7. *The Action Editor is used to manage the actions of menu items*

Finally, there is the Resource Browser that allows you to specify and manage resources you need to use in your application. These resources can include images and icons. The Resource Browser dock widget can be seen in Figure 8-8.

Figure 8-8. *The Resource Browser for working with resources such as images and icons*

If you need to add resources, you first need to create a new resource file. To do so, click the pencil in the top-left corner of the Resource Browser dock widget. This will open an Edit Resources dialog similar to the one in Figure 8-9.

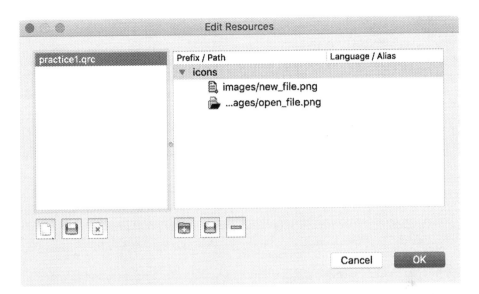

Figure 8-9. *The Edit Resources dialog*

Next, click on the Create New Resource button, navigate to the correct directory, and enter a name for the resource file. The file will be saved with a .qrc file extension, which stands for Qt Resource Collection and contains a list of all the resources used in your program. From here, create a prefix for managing the types of resources and begin adding files such as images and icons. When you are finished, click the OK button, and the files will be added to the Resource Browser.

Note   Support for resources and .qrc files in PyQt6 is different than in PyQt5. To access the resources, you may have to consider using other PyQt classes, such as QFile or QDir, or use the file path to the resource.

Qt Designer's Editing Modes

In Qt Designer, there are four different editing modes that can be accessed either in the Edit menu or from Qt Designer's toolbar. Take a look at Figure 8-10 to help you locate the widgets in the toolbar.

1. Edit Widgets – Widgets can be dragged and dropped to a form, layouts can be applied, and objects can be edited both on the form and in the Property Editor. This is the default mode.

2. Edit Signals/Slots – Connect signals and slots for widgets and layouts. To create connections, click on an object and drag the cursor toward an object that will receive the signal. Items that can be connected will be highlighted as the mouse cursor moves over them. To create the connection, release the mouse button once a line with an arrow connects the two objects. Then configure the signals and slots. Use in conjunction with the Signal/Slot Editor dock widget to edit connections.

3. Edit Buddies – Connect QLabel widgets with shortcuts to input widgets such as QLineEdit or QTextEdit. The input widget becomes the QLabel object's "buddy." When the user enters the label's shortcut key, the focus moves to the input widget.

4. Edit Tab Order – Set the order in which widgets receive focus when the tab key is pressed. This allows the user to navigate through the different widgets, improving your application's usability.

Figure 8-10. *Qt Designer's Editing Modes (outlined in red). (From left to right) Edit Widgets, Edit Signals/Slots, Edit Buddies, Edit Tab Order*

Creating an Application in Qt Designer

When you are creating your GUI's windows and widgets, you will probably continue to make slight adjustments to your application before it is finished. Fortunately, there are a few steps you can follow to simplify the building process.

1. Select a form – In the New Form dialog (shown in Figure 8-2), choose from one of the available templates, Main Window, Widget, or a type of Dialog. You can also add and preview widgets to include in your GUI.

2. Arrange objects on the form – Use Qt Designer's drag-and-drop mechanics to place widgets on the form. Then assign layouts to containers and the main window.

3. Edit the properties of objects – Click on the objects in the form and edit their features in the Property Editor dock widget.

4. Connect signals and slots – Use the Signals/Slots Editing mode to link signals to slots.

5. Preview your GUI – Examine the form before saving it as a UI file with the `.ui` extension.

6. Create and edit Python code – Utilize the `pyuic` compiler to convert the UI file to readable and editable Python code.

The following project will cover these steps in addition to many of the basic concepts for creating GUIs using Qt Designer.

Project 8.1 – Keypad GUI

The GUI in Figure 8-11 should be a familiar one – a keypad.

Figure 8-11. Keypad GUI

Keypads are relatively simple interfaces, with sets of buttons for digits, symbols, or letters used as input devices for passcodes or telephone numbers. They can be found on a number of devices such as calculators, cell phones, and locks.

Explanation for the Keypad GUI

The keypad application is composed of two Python files: keypad_gui.py and keypad_main.py. The keypad_gui.py contains the Python class generated from the UI file built from Qt Designer. In order to use that code, we need to create a customized class in a separate file, keypad_main.py, to import and set up the GUI.

The keypad GUI consists of four QLineEdit widgets to input only numeric values, 12 QPushButton widgets, and a single QLabel to display information about how to use the interface. The asterisk button allows users to clear their current input, and the hash button is for confirming the user's four-digit input.

We'll begin by creating the window in Qt Designer before discussing the code.

Selecting a Form

Begin by opening up Qt Designer. Choose the Widget template from the New Form dialog box. We will use the Default screen size. Select Create. This opens up a blank QWidget form with a grid of dots inside of the Qt Designer interface similar to Figure 8-1 (although that screenshot displays a QMainWindow form).

Arranging Objects on the Form

You could begin by adjusting certain features of the form such as the window size or the background color. Instead, let's first add whatever widgets we need for the project by dragging and dropping them into the main window from the Widget Box dialog on the left of the window.

Locate the QLabel widget (called Label in the dialog) and drag one onto the form. Then drag two QFrame containers (called Frame) onto the form like in Figure 8-12. You can resize the frames by clicking on them and moving the edges of the frame. Then drag four QLineEdit input widgets (called Line Edit) and arrange them in the top QFrame container. They will overlap, but that will be fixed when you apply layouts to the frames and the main window. When an object is dragged on top of a container where it can be placed, the container will be highlighted to indicate that you can drop the widget inside. In addition, place 12 QPushButton widgets (called Push Button) in the bottom frame.

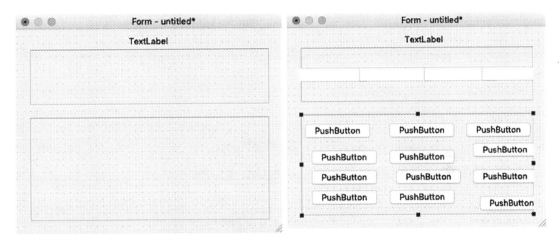

Figure 8-12. *The form with a label and two frames (left) and with the line edit widgets and push buttons added (right)*

Before moving on, let's take a moment to learn more about the QFrame container as it is a very useful element in GUI development.

The QFrame Class

The QFrame class is used as a container to group and surround widgets, or to act as a placeholder in GUI applications. You can also apply a frame style to a QFrame instance to visually separate it from nearby widgets. The following bit of code shows an example of how to create a frame object in a main window, modify its properties, and add a widget.

```
# Create a widget to place in the frame
button = QPushButton("Enter")

grid = QGridLayout()
grid.addWidget(button, 0, 0)
```

```
# Create the frame and set its parameters
frame = QFrame() # Create a QFrame object
size_policy = QSizePolicy(
    QSizePolicy.Policy.Expanding,
    QSizePolicy.Policy.Preferred)
frame.setSizePolicy(size_policy)
frame.setFrameShape(QFrame.Shape.Box)
frame.setFrameShadow(QFrame.Shadow.Raised)
frame.setLineWidth(3)
frame.setMidLineWidth(5)

# Set the layout for the QFrame object
frame.setLayout(grid)
self.setCentralWidget(frame)
```

Using the method setSizePolicy(), we can define how a frame should resize.
A frame object can have a number of different styles of frames, including Box,
Panel, StyledPanel, or NoFrame. The style of the frame can be adjusted using the
setFrameShadow(), setLineWidth(), and setMidLineWidth() methods. Different types
of shadow include Plain, Raised, and Sunken.

For practice, try creating a simple window from the previous code.

Applying Layouts in Qt Designer

The next step is to add layouts to all of the containers and to the main window. This is
an important step that ensures items are placed and resized correctly. Layouts can be
added either from the toolbar or from context menus. It is possible to add more widgets
to existing layouts once they have been set.

Since Qt Designer uses a drag-and-drop interface, you only need to place the objects
on the form close to where you want them to be and then select one of the four layouts –
QGridLayout, QHBoxLayout, QVBoxLayout, or QFormLayout – from the Widget Box dialog,
and Qt Designer will take care of arranging them. For more information about the types
of layouts in PyQt, refer to Chapter 4.

Right-click on the top-most frame to open a context menu (demonstrated in
Figure 8-13). Scroll down to the last option, Lay out, and select Lay Out Horizontally. Do
the same thing for the bottom frame, but this time select Lay Out in a Grid.

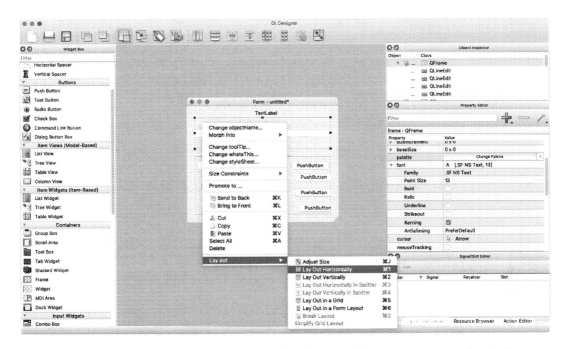

Figure 8-13. *Open a context menu to select layouts for containers and windows*

The top-level layout of a form can be set by right-clicking on the form itself in the main window and locating the layout you want to use. For the keypad GUI, right-click and select Lay Out Vertically. Your GUI should look like Figure 8-14. If the widgets are not aligned properly, you can also open the context menu, select Break Layout, and rearrange the widgets. The option Simplify Grid Layout may also help you arrange items in the grid layout.

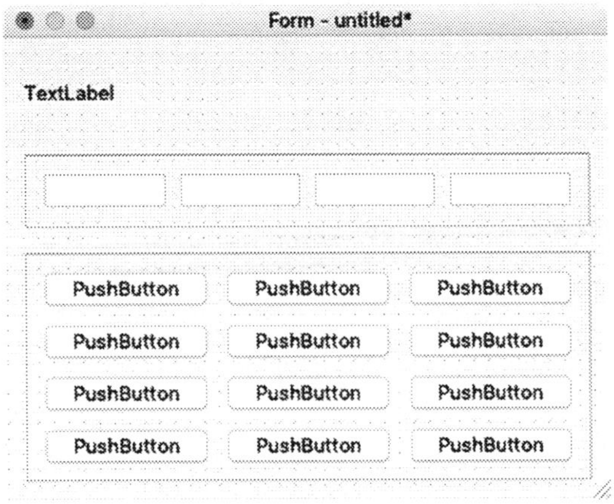

Figure 8-14. *The keypad GUI with layouts*

Editing the Properties of Objects

Once you have the layouts prepared, you should begin editing the features of the objects. This step could also be accomplished earlier when you place objects on the form.

The Property Editor is shown in Figure 8-4. It is organized into two columns: Property and Value. The properties are organized by Qt Classes.

To access and make changes to specific containers, widgets, layouts, or even the main window, you can click on them in the form or in the Object Inspector. If a property is edited in the Property Editor, you can locate it with the following pattern:

Qt Class (Property column) ➤ Property name ➤ (submenu, if any) ➤ Value column ➤ parameter

The following are the steps that you can follow along with to create the keypad GUI in Qt Designer:

1. Change window title: QWidget ➤ windowTitle ➤ 8.1 – Keypad GUI

2. Double-click on the QLabel. Change text to enter a passcode.

3. Change QLabel properties:

   a. QWidget ➤ font ➤ Point Size ➤ 20

   b. To edit palette colors, you will need to locate the palette property that opens a dialog box. Here, you can change the colors for different parts of an object. To change the color of the text in the label object: QWidget ➤ palette ➤ Change Palette ➤ Window Text ➤ white

   c. QLabel ➤ alignment ➤ Horizontal ➤ AlignHCenter

4. Change top frame properties:

   a. QWidget ➤ sizePolicy ➤ Vertical Stretch ➤ 1

   b. QFrame ➤ frameShape ➤ NoFrame

   c. QFrame ➤ frameShadow ➤ Plain

5. For each of the four QLineEdit widgets, modify their properties:

   a. QWidget ➤ sizePolicy ➤ Vertical Policy ➤ Expanding

   b. QWidget ➤ font ➤ Point Size ➤ 30

   c. QLineEdit ➤ alignment ➤ Horizontal ➤ AlignHCenter

6. Change bottom frame properties:

    a. QWidget ➤ sizePolicy ➤ Vertical Stretch ➤ 2

    b. QFrame ➤ frameShape ➤ Box

    c. QFrame ➤ frameShadow ➤ Sunken

    d. QFrame ➤ lineWidth ➤ 2

7. Double-click on each of the buttons and change their text to 0–9, *, and #. (Refer to Figure 8-11.)

8. Edit each of the button's properties:

    a. QWidget ➤ sizePolicy ➤ Vertical Policy ➤ Expanding

    b. QWidget ➤ font ➤ Point Size ➤ 36

9. Resize the main window:

    a. QWidget ➤ geometry ➤ Width ➤ 302

    b. QWidget ➤ geometry ➤ Height ➤ 406

10. Click on the form and change its background color: QWidget ➤ palette ➤ Change Palette ➤ Window ➤ dark gray

11. In the Object Inspector, double-click on each of the default object names for the frames, line edits, and buttons, and edit them. Doing this will be helpful later on so that we can distinguish the buttons when looking at the code. The object name is used to reference the objects.

After you have followed along with each of the steps, the form should look similar to Figure 8-11.

Previewing Your GUI

It is often useful to view and interact with the form before exporting it to code. Not only can this be useful for checking the visual appearance of your GUI, but previewing also helps to make sure the signals and slots, resizing the window, and other functions are working properly.

To preview a form, open the Form menu and select Preview or use the hotkeys Ctrl+R for Windows or Command+R for macOS. If you are satisfied with your form, save it as a UI file with the .ui extension. Qt Designer UI files are written in XML format and contain the widget tree representation for creating a GUI.

Connecting Signals and Slots in Qt Designer

Switch to the Edit Signals/Slots mode by selecting it from the toolbar. Qt Designer has a simple interface for connecting signals and slots. Click on the object that will emit a signal and drag it to the object that will receive the signal. For the keypad GUI, we are only making one set of connections. The remaining signals and slots will be handled by manually coding them.

When the "*" button is clicked, we want to clear all four line edit widgets. Click on the button and drag the red arrow to the first line edit object. A dialog box will appear (displayed in Figure 8-15) that allows you to select the methods for both the signal and the slot.

Tip   When connecting signals and slots, make sure to check the "Show signals and slots inherited from QWidget" checkbox to access more methods.

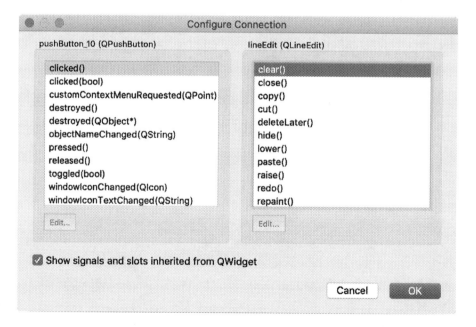

Figure 8-15. *The dialog box for connecting signals and slots*

Select clicked() for the button and clear() for the line edit. Finish connecting the other three line edit widgets. Refer to Figure 8-16 as a guide for connecting the widgets. Make sure to save your work before moving on. For this example, the file is saved as keypad.ui.

Figure 8-16. *The keypad GUI with signal and slot connections*

Creating Python Code from Qt Designer

Qt Designer uses the Qt utility **User Interface Compiler (uic)** to generate code and create the user interface. However, since you are using PyQt6, you must use the uic module, pyuic6, to load .ui files and convert the XML code to Python code. The pyuic6 utility is a command line interface for interacting with uic.

Open up your system's shell and navigate to the directory that contains the UI file. The following line shows the format for XML to Python:

```
$ pyuic6 filename.ui -o filename.py
```

To output a Python file, you need to include the -o flag and the Python file to be written to, filename.py. This command will generate a single Python class.

With your new file created, the best practice is to *create a separate script to inherit from your newly created user interface class.* Another option is to create an executable file that can display the GUI. This can be done by including the -x flag for execute, demonstrated for you in the following code:

```
pyuic6 -x filename.ui -o filename.py
```

Note   If you make changes to the GUI in Qt Designer after creating the Python script, you will need to call pyuic6 again to update the application.

One final note about running the pyuic6 command. If you find that pyuic6 is not found, you can try using the following format:

```
$ python3 -m PyQt6.uic.pyuic filename.ui -o filename.py
```

Change python3 to python on Windows.

Generating Code Using pyuic6

To generate the keypad_gui.py file, navigate to where you saved keypad.ui and run the following line:

```
$ python3 -m PyQt6.uic.pyuic keypad.ui -o keypad_gui.py
```

The following Python code in Listings 8-1 to 8-10 is produced from running the pyuic6 command. It has not been altered so that we can look over what pyuic6 produces. Do note that even if you followed along with the tutorial to make the keypad GUI, your code may not look exactly the same.

Listing 8-1. Python class created from keypad.ui

```python
# keypad_gui.py
from PyQt6 import QtCore, QtGui, QtWidgets

class Ui_Keypad(object):
    def setupUi(self, Keypad):
        Keypad.setObjectName("Keypad")
        Keypad.resize(302, 406)
```

PyQt6 modules are first imported. The Ui_Keypad class inherits object, denoting that this class is the root for all other classes.

From there, the member function setupUi() of the class Ui_Keypad is used to build a widget tree on the Keypad widget. A **widget tree** is used to represent the organization of widgets in a UI. So the setupUi() method is passed a widget that will display the interface (typically QWidget, QDialog, or QMainWindow) and compose the UI based upon the widgets and connections we used to create it along with the parameters it inherits.

Every widget in Qt has a palette that contains information about how they will be drawn in the window. The **QPalette** class contains the color groups for each widget during one of three possible states – Active, Inactive, or Disabled.

Since we altered the palette's background color for the main window to dark gray, those changes will appear in Listing 8-2.

Listing 8-2. Setting up the palette for the keypad GUI

```
# keypad_gui.py
        palette = QtGui.QPalette()
        brush = QtGui.QBrush(QtGui.QColor(255, 255, 255))
        brush.setStyle(QtCore.Qt.BrushStyle.SolidPattern)
        palette.setBrush(QtGui.QPalette.ColorGroup.Active,
            QtGui.QPalette.ColorRole.Base, brush)
        brush = QtGui.QBrush(QtGui.QColor(52, 48, 47))
        brush.setStyle(QtCore.Qt.BrushStyle.SolidPattern)
        palette.setBrush(QtGui.QPalette.ColorGroup.Active,
            QtGui.QPalette.ColorRole.Window, brush)
        brush = QtGui.QBrush(QtGui.QColor(255, 255, 255))
        brush.setStyle(QtCore.Qt.BrushStyle.SolidPattern)
        palette.setBrush(QtGui.QPalette.ColorGroup.Inactive,
            QtGui.QPalette.ColorRole.Base, brush)
        brush = QtGui.QBrush(QtGui.QColor(52, 48, 47))
        brush.setStyle(QtCore.Qt.BrushStyle.SolidPattern)
        palette.setBrush(QtGui.QPalette.ColorGroup.Inactive,
            QtGui.QPalette.ColorRole.Window, brush)
        brush = QtGui.QBrush(QtGui.QColor(52, 48, 47))
        brush.setStyle(QtCore.Qt.BrushStyle.SolidPattern)
        palette.setBrush(QtGui.QPalette.ColorGroup.Disabled,
            QtGui.QPalette.ColorRole.Base, brush)
```

```
brush = QtGui.QBrush(QtGui.QColor(52, 48, 47))
brush.setStyle(QtCore.Qt.BrushStyle.SolidPattern)
palette.setBrush(QtGui.QPalette.ColorGroup.Disabled,
    QtGui.QPalette.ColorRole.Window, brush)
Keypad.setPalette(palette)
```

You can see that even though we only changed the palette color, that change is handled for all three states automatically. The **QBrush** class is used to apply the colors and patterns to widgets. The setPalette() method applies palette to the Keypad class.

The vertical layout for the Keypad class is instantiated in Listing 8-3.

Listing 8-3. Creating the main window's layout manager

```
# keypad_gui.py
        self.verticalLayout = QtWidgets.QVBoxLayout(Keypad)
        self.verticalLayout.setObjectName("verticalLayout")
```

The changes made to the QLabel object are reflected in Listing 8-4. These include modifying the label's palette settings so that the color of the font is white and adding the label to verticalLayout.

Listing 8-4. Creating the header label

```
# keypad_gui.py
        self.label = QtWidgets.QLabel(Keypad)
        palette = QtGui.QPalette()
        brush = QtGui.QBrush(QtGui.QColor(255, 255, 255))
        brush.setStyle(QtCore.Qt.BrushStyle.SolidPattern)
        palette.setBrush(QtGui.QPalette.ColorGroup.Active,
            QtGui.QPalette.ColorRole.WindowText, brush)
        brush = QtGui.QBrush(QtGui.QColor(255, 255, 255))
        brush.setStyle(QtCore.Qt.BrushStyle.SolidPattern)
        palette.setBrush(QtGui.QPalette.ColorGroup.Inactive,
            QtGui.QPalette.ColorRole.WindowText, brush)
        brush = QtGui.QBrush(QtGui.QColor(127, 127, 127))
        brush.setStyle(QtCore.Qt.BrushStyle.SolidPattern)
        palette.setBrush(QtGui.QPalette.ColorGroup.Disabled,
            QtGui.QPalette.ColorRole.WindowText, brush)
```

```python
self.label.setPalette(palette)
font = QtGui.QFont()
font.setPointSize(20)
self.label.setFont(font)
self.label.setAlignment(
    QtCore.Qt.AlignmentFlag.AlignCenter)
self.label.setObjectName("label")
self.verticalLayout.addWidget(self.label)
```

The changes to label instance's font and alignment are also reflected in the code.

The first QFrame container, frame, in Listing 8-5 holds four QLineEdit instances and uses a QHBoxLayout to arrange the widgets.

Listing 8-5. Creating the frame for the QLineEdit widgets in the keypad GUI

```python
# keypad_gui.py
        self.frame = QtWidgets.QFrame(Keypad)
        sizePolicy = QtWidgets.QSizePolicy(
            QtWidgets.QSizePolicy.Policy.Preferred,
            QtWidgets.QSizePolicy.Policy.Preferred)
        sizePolicy.setHorizontalStretch(0)
        sizePolicy.setVerticalStretch(1)
        sizePolicy.setHeightForWidth(
            self.frame.sizePolicy().hasHeightForWidth())
        self.frame.setSizePolicy(sizePolicy)
        self.frame.setFrameShape(
            QtWidgets.QFrame.Shape.NoFrame)
        self.frame.setFrameShadow(
            QtWidgets.QFrame.Shadow.Plain)
        self.frame.setLineWidth(0)
        self.frame.setObjectName("frame")
        self.horizontalLayout = QtWidgets.QHBoxLayout(
            self.frame)
        self.horizontalLayout.setObjectName(
            "horizontalLayout")
```

The adjustments to frame can be seen in the previous code. The vertical stretch is changed to 1, the frame shape is set to NoFrame, and the shadow is set to Plain. The line edits that frame contains are constructed in Listing 8-6.

Listing 8-6. Code for the QLineEdit widgets in the keypad GUI

```
# keypad_gui.py
        self.line_edit1 = QtWidgets.QLineEdit(self.frame)
        sizePolicy = QtWidgets.QSizePolicy(
            QtWidgets.QSizePolicy.Policy.Expanding,
            QtWidgets.QSizePolicy.Policy.Expanding)
        sizePolicy.setHorizontalStretch(0)
        sizePolicy.setVerticalStretch(0)
        sizePolicy.setHeightForWidth(
            self.line_edit1.sizePolicy().hasHeightForWidth())
        self.line_edit1.setSizePolicy(sizePolicy)
        font = QtGui.QFont()
        font.setPointSize(30)
        self.line_edit1.setFont(font)
        self.line_edit1.setAlignment(
            QtCore.Qt.AlignmentFlag.AlignCenter)
        self.line_edit1.setObjectName("line_edit1")
        self.horizontalLayout.addWidget(self.line_edit1)
        self.line_edit2 = QtWidgets.QLineEdit(self.frame)
        sizePolicy = QtWidgets.QSizePolicy(
            QtWidgets.QSizePolicy.Policy.Expanding,
            QtWidgets.QSizePolicy.Policy.Expanding)
        sizePolicy.setHorizontalStretch(0)
        sizePolicy.setVerticalStretch(0)
        sizePolicy.setHeightForWidth(
            self.line_edit2.sizePolicy().hasHeightForWidth())
        self.line_edit2.setSizePolicy(sizePolicy)
        font = QtGui.QFont()
        font.setPointSize(30)
        self.line_edit2.setFont(font)
        self.line_edit2.setAlignment(
            QtCore.Qt.AlignmentFlag.AlignCenter)
```

```python
        self.line_edit2.setObjectName("line_edit2")
        self.horizontalLayout.addWidget(self.line_edit2)
        self.line_edit3 = QtWidgets.QLineEdit(self.frame)
        sizePolicy = QtWidgets.QSizePolicy(
            QtWidgets.QSizePolicy.Policy.Expanding,
            QtWidgets.QSizePolicy.Policy.Expanding)
        sizePolicy.setHorizontalStretch(0)
        sizePolicy.setVerticalStretch(0)
        sizePolicy.setHeightForWidth(
            self.line_edit3.sizePolicy().hasHeightForWidth())
        self.line_edit3.setSizePolicy(sizePolicy)
        font = QtGui.QFont()
        font.setPointSize(30)
        self.line_edit3.setFont(font)
        self.line_edit3.setAlignment(
            QtCore.Qt.AlignmentFlag.AlignCenter)
        self.line_edit3.setObjectName("line_edit3")
        self.horizontalLayout.addWidget(self.line_edit3)
        self.line_edit4 = QtWidgets.QLineEdit(self.frame)
        sizePolicy = QtWidgets.QSizePolicy(
            QtWidgets.QSizePolicy.Policy.Expanding,
            QtWidgets.QSizePolicy.Policy.Expanding)
        sizePolicy.setHorizontalStretch(0)
        sizePolicy.setVerticalStretch(0)
        sizePolicy.setHeightForWidth(
            self.line_edit4.sizePolicy().hasHeightForWidth())
        self.line_edit4.setSizePolicy(sizePolicy)
        font = QtGui.QFont()
        font.setPointSize(30)
        self.line_edit4.setFont(font)
        self.line_edit4.setAlignment(
            QtCore.Qt.AlignmentFlag.AlignCenter)
        self.line_edit4.setObjectName("line_edit4")
        self.horizontalLayout.addWidget(self.line_edit4)
        self.verticalLayout.addWidget(self.frame)
```

There is a lot of repetition in this large block of code. That is because the four line edits all have the same changes made. By looking at one instance, you can understand the other three.

Each of the four line edit widgets has size policies that allow them to stretch if the window resizes in both the vertical and horizontal directions by using QSizePolicy. Policy.Expanding. Changes made to the font size and the alignment also show up. The QLineEdit widgets are then arranged in the horizontalLayout of the frame container. The frame object is finally added to the verticalLayout of the main window.

The bottom frame container is instantiated in Listing 8-7, and its size policy and style attributes are set.

Listing 8-7. Creating the frame for the QPushButton widgets in the keypad GUI

```
# keypad_gui.py
        self.frame_2 = QtWidgets.QFrame(Keypad)
        sizePolicy = QtWidgets.QSizePolicy(
            QtWidgets.QSizePolicy.Policy.Preferred,
            QtWidgets.QSizePolicy.Policy.Preferred)
        sizePolicy.setHorizontalStretch(0)
        sizePolicy.setVerticalStretch(2)
        sizePolicy.setHeightForWidth(
            self.frame_2.sizePolicy().hasHeightForWidth())
        self.frame_2.setSizePolicy(sizePolicy)
        self.frame_2.setFrameShape(QtWidgets.QFrame.Shape.Box)
        self.frame_2.setFrameShadow(
            QtWidgets.QFrame.Shadow.Sunken)
        self.frame_2.setLineWidth(2)
        self.frame_2.setObjectName("frame_2")
        self.gridLayout = QtWidgets.QGridLayout(self.frame_2)
        self.gridLayout.setObjectName("gridLayout")
```

The bottom frame is guaranteed to take up more vertical space since its vertical stretch factor is set to 2. The frame has a Box shape, Sunken shadow, and lineWidth of 2. The layout inside frame_2 holds the 12 buttons and uses a grid layout.

The names of the buttons and the line edit widgets reflect the changes we made in Qt Designer. This makes it easier in the Python script to distinguish the widgets in the keypad interface. Let's take a look at the code for the 12 QPushButton widgets in Listing 8-8.

Listing 8-8. Creating the QPushButton widgets that are arranged in the bottom frame

```
# keypad_gui.py
        self.button_7 = QtWidgets.QPushButton(self.frame_2)
        sizePolicy = QtWidgets.QSizePolicy(
            QtWidgets.QSizePolicy.Policy.Minimum,
            QtWidgets.QSizePolicy.Policy.Expanding)
        sizePolicy.setHorizontalStretch(0)
        sizePolicy.setVerticalStretch(0)
        sizePolicy.setHeightForWidth(
            self.button_7.sizePolicy().hasHeightForWidth())
        self.button_7.setSizePolicy(sizePolicy)
        font = QtGui.QFont()
        font.setPointSize(36)
        self.button_7.setFont(font)
        self.button_7.setObjectName("button_7")
        self.gridLayout.addWidget(self.button_7, 0, 0, 1, 1)
        self.button_8 = QtWidgets.QPushButton(self.frame_2)
        sizePolicy = QtWidgets.QSizePolicy(
            QtWidgets.QSizePolicy.Policy.Minimum,
            QtWidgets.QSizePolicy.Policy.Expanding)
        sizePolicy.setHorizontalStretch(0)
        sizePolicy.setVerticalStretch(0)
        sizePolicy.setHeightForWidth(
            self.button_8.sizePolicy().hasHeightForWidth())
        self.button_8.setSizePolicy(sizePolicy)
        font = QtGui.QFont()
        font.setPointSize(36)
        self.button_8.setFont(font)
        self.button_8.setObjectName("button_8")
        self.gridLayout.addWidget(self.button_8, 0, 1, 1, 1)
        self.button_9 = QtWidgets.QPushButton(self.frame_2)
        sizePolicy = QtWidgets.QSizePolicy(
            QtWidgets.QSizePolicy.Policy.Minimum,
            QtWidgets.QSizePolicy.Policy.Expanding)
```

```
sizePolicy.setHorizontalStretch(0)
sizePolicy.setVerticalStretch(0)
sizePolicy.setHeightForWidth(
    self.button_9.sizePolicy().hasHeightForWidth())
self.button_9.setSizePolicy(sizePolicy)
font = QtGui.QFont()
font.setPointSize(36)
self.button_9.setFont(font)
self.button_9.setObjectName("button_9")
self.gridLayout.addWidget(self.button_9, 0, 2, 1, 1)
self.button_4 = QtWidgets.QPushButton(self.frame_2)
sizePolicy = QtWidgets.QSizePolicy(
    QtWidgets.QSizePolicy.Policy.Minimum,
    QtWidgets.QSizePolicy.Policy.Expanding)
sizePolicy.setHorizontalStretch(0)
sizePolicy.setVerticalStretch(0)
sizePolicy.setHeightForWidth(
    self.button_4.sizePolicy().hasHeightForWidth())
self.button_4.setSizePolicy(sizePolicy)
font = QtGui.QFont()
font.setPointSize(36)
self.button_4.setFont(font)
self.button_4.setObjectName("button_4")
self.gridLayout.addWidget(self.button_4, 1, 0, 1, 1)
self.button_5 = QtWidgets.QPushButton(self.frame_2)
sizePolicy = QtWidgets.QSizePolicy(
    QtWidgets.QSizePolicy.Policy.Minimum,
    QtWidgets.QSizePolicy.Policy.Expanding)
sizePolicy.setHorizontalStretch(0)
sizePolicy.setVerticalStretch(0)
sizePolicy.setHeightForWidth(
    self.button_5.sizePolicy().hasHeightForWidth())
self.button_5.setSizePolicy(sizePolicy)
font = QtGui.QFont()
font.setPointSize(36)
```

```
self.button_5.setFont(font)
self.button_5.setObjectName("button_5")
self.gridLayout.addWidget(self.button_5, 1, 1, 1, 1)
self.button_6 = QtWidgets.QPushButton(self.frame_2)
sizePolicy = QtWidgets.QSizePolicy(
    QtWidgets.QSizePolicy.Policy.Minimum,
    QtWidgets.QSizePolicy.Policy.Expanding)
sizePolicy.setHorizontalStretch(0)
sizePolicy.setVerticalStretch(0)
sizePolicy.setHeightForWidth(
    self.button_6.sizePolicy().hasHeightForWidth())
self.button_6.setSizePolicy(sizePolicy)
font = QtGui.QFont()
font.setPointSize(36)
self.button_6.setFont(font)
self.button_6.setObjectName("button_6")
self.gridLayout.addWidget(self.button_6, 1, 2, 1, 1)
self.button_3 = QtWidgets.QPushButton(self.frame_2)
sizePolicy = QtWidgets.QSizePolicy(
    QtWidgets.QSizePolicy.Policy.Minimum,
    QtWidgets.QSizePolicy.Policy.Expanding)
sizePolicy.setHorizontalStretch(0)
sizePolicy.setVerticalStretch(0)
sizePolicy.setHeightForWidth(
    self.button_3.sizePolicy().hasHeightForWidth())
self.button_3.setSizePolicy(sizePolicy)
font = QtGui.QFont()
font.setPointSize(36)
self.button_3.setFont(font)
self.button_3.setObjectName("button_3")
self.gridLayout.addWidget(self.button_3, 2, 0, 1, 1)
self.button_2 = QtWidgets.QPushButton(self.frame_2)
sizePolicy = QtWidgets.QSizePolicy(
    QtWidgets.QSizePolicy.Policy.Minimum,
    QtWidgets.QSizePolicy.Policy.Expanding)
```

```python
sizePolicy.setHorizontalStretch(0)
sizePolicy.setVerticalStretch(0)
sizePolicy.setHeightForWidth(
    self.button_2.sizePolicy().hasHeightForWidth())
self.button_2.setSizePolicy(sizePolicy)
font = QtGui.QFont()
font.setPointSize(36)
self.button_2.setFont(font)
self.button_2.setObjectName("button_2")
self.gridLayout.addWidget(self.button_2, 2, 1, 1, 1)
self.button_1 = QtWidgets.QPushButton(self.frame_2)
sizePolicy = QtWidgets.QSizePolicy(
    QtWidgets.QSizePolicy.Policy.Minimum,
    QtWidgets.QSizePolicy.Policy.Expanding)
sizePolicy.setHorizontalStretch(0)
sizePolicy.setVerticalStretch(0)
sizePolicy.setHeightForWidth(
    self.button_1.sizePolicy().hasHeightForWidth())
self.button_1.setSizePolicy(sizePolicy)
font = QtGui.QFont()
font.setPointSize(36)
self.button_1.setFont(font)
self.button_1.setObjectName("button_1")
self.gridLayout.addWidget(self.button_1, 2, 2, 1, 1)
self.button_star = QtWidgets.QPushButton(self.frame_2)
sizePolicy = QtWidgets.QSizePolicy(
    QtWidgets.QSizePolicy.Policy.Minimum,
    QtWidgets.QSizePolicy.Policy.Expanding)
sizePolicy.setHorizontalStretch(0)
sizePolicy.setVerticalStretch(0)
sizePolicy.setHeightForWidth(
    self.button_star.sizePolicy().hasHeightForWidth())
self.button_star.setSizePolicy(sizePolicy)
font = QtGui.QFont()
font.setPointSize(36)
```

```
self.button_star.setFont(font)
self.button_star.setObjectName("button_star")
self.gridLayout.addWidget(
    self.button_star, 3, 0, 1, 1)
self.button_0 = QtWidgets.QPushButton(self.frame_2)
sizePolicy = QtWidgets.QSizePolicy(
    QtWidgets.QSizePolicy.Policy.Minimum,
    QtWidgets.QSizePolicy.Policy.Expanding)
sizePolicy.setHorizontalStretch(0)
sizePolicy.setVerticalStretch(0)
sizePolicy.setHeightForWidth(
    self.button_0.sizePolicy().hasHeightForWidth())
self.button_0.setSizePolicy(sizePolicy)
font = QtGui.QFont()
font.setPointSize(36)
self.button_0.setFont(font)
self.button_0.setObjectName("button_0")
self.gridLayout.addWidget(self.button_0, 3, 1, 1, 1)
self.button_hash = QtWidgets.QPushButton(self.frame_2)
sizePolicy = QtWidgets.QSizePolicy(
    QtWidgets.QSizePolicy.Policy.Minimum,
    QtWidgets.QSizePolicy.Policy.Expanding)
sizePolicy.setHorizontalStretch(0)
sizePolicy.setVerticalStretch(0)
sizePolicy.setHeightForWidth(
    self.button_hash.sizePolicy().hasHeightForWidth())
self.button_hash.setSizePolicy(sizePolicy)
font = QtGui.QFont()
font.setPointSize(36)
self.button_hash.setFont(font)
self.button_hash.setObjectName("button_hash")
self.gridLayout.addWidget(
    self.button_hash, 3, 2, 1, 1)
self.verticalLayout.addWidget(self.frame_2)
```

The 12 QPushButton widgets are created. The buttons are able to expand vertically using the Expanding flag, and their font size is set to 36. Every button is then added to the grid layout of frame_2, which is then added to the vertical layout of the main window.

Listing 8-9 connects the signals for the button_star instance to the line edit widgets, clearing the text whenever the button is pressed. This allows the user a way to delete their input and try again.

Listing 8-9. Connecting the signals and slots for the keypad GUI

```
# keypad_gui.py
        self.retranslateUi(Keypad)
        self.button_star.clicked.connect(
            self.line_edit1.clear)
        self.button_star.clicked.connect(
            self.line_edit2.clear)
        self.button_star.clicked.connect(
            self.line_edit3.clear)
        self.button_star.clicked.connect(
            self.line_edit4.clear)
        QtCore.QMetaObject.connectSlotsByName(Keypad)
```

The retranslateUi() method in Listing 8-10 handles how to display text in the GUI in the case that a different language is used.

Listing 8-10. Code for the retranslateUi() method

```
# keypad_gui.py
    def retranslateUi(self, Keypad):
        _translate = QtCore.QCoreApplication.translate
        Keypad.setWindowTitle(
            _translate("Keypad", "8.1 - Keypad GUI"))
        self.label.setText(
            _translate("Keypad", "Enter a passcode"))
        self.button_7.setText(_translate("Keypad", "7"))
        self.button_8.setText(_translate("Keypad", "8"))
        self.button_9.setText(_translate("Keypad", "9"))
        self.button_4.setText(_translate("Keypad", "4"))
        self.button_5.setText(_translate("Keypad", "5"))
```

```
self.button_6.setText(_translate("Keypad", "6"))
self.button_3.setText(_translate("Keypad", "3"))
self.button_2.setText(_translate("Keypad", "2"))
self.button_1.setText(_translate("Keypad", "1"))
self.button_star.setText(_translate("Keypad", "*"))
self.button_0.setText(_translate("Keypad", "0"))
self.button_hash.setText(_translate("Keypad", "#"))
```

QCoreApplication.translate returns the translated text of the second argument passed to the method.

Creating a New Script to Build a GUI

The following section creates the class that inherits Ui_Keypad and sets up the GUI application. In order to utilize the Ui_Keypad class that was created using Qt Designer, we'll create a new Python file, keypad_main.py. The KeypadGUI class created in keypad_main.py will inherit from the Ui_Keypad class.

We begin by importing the modules needed for this project in Listing 8-11, including the Ui_Keypad class and a new PyQt class, QIntValidator. PyQt provides a few classes that can be used to verify the types of input text. **QIntValidator** will be used to check if the values input into the QLineEdit widgets are integers.

Listing 8-11. Setting up the main window for the keypad GUI

```
# keypad_main.py
# Import necessary modules
import sys
from PyQt6.QtWidgets import (QApplication, QWidget,
    QMessageBox)
from PyQt6.QtCore import Qt
from PyQt6.QtGui import QIntValidator
from keypad_gui import Ui_Keypad

class MainWindow(QWidget):
    def __init__(self):
        super().__init__()
        self.ui = Ui_Keypad()
        self.ui.setupUi(self)
```

```
        self.initializeUI()
        self.show()

if __name__ == "__main__":
    app = QApplication(sys.argv)
    Keypad = MainWindow()
    sys.exit(app.exec())
```

The MainWindow class is created using a **single inheritance** approach where it inherits its properties from a single parent class, QWidget. The user interface is set up in the __init__() method in the following lines:

```
        self.ui = Ui_Keypad()
        self.ui.setupUi(self)
```

In the initializeUI() method in Listing 8-12, local modifications are made to the QLineEdit widgets. Here, the line edit widget's focus policy is set to NoFocus so that users can only enter input in the correct order, from left to right.

Listing 8-12. Code for the initializeUI() method in the keypad GUI

```
# keypad_main.py
    def initializeUI(self):
        """Set up the application's GUI."""
        # Update other line_edit features
        # Set the max number of characters allowed
        self.ui.line_edit1.setMaxLength(1)
        # User can only enter ints from 0-9
        self.ui.line_edit1.setValidator(QIntValidator(0, 9))
        # Widget does not accept focus
        self.ui.line_edit1.setFocusPolicy(
            Qt.FocusPolicy.NoFocus)

        self.ui.line_edit2.setMaxLength(1)
        self.ui.line_edit2.setValidator(QIntValidator(0, 9))
        self.ui.line_edit2.setFocusPolicy(
            Qt.FocusPolicy.NoFocus)
```

```
self.ui.line_edit3.setMaxLength(1)
self.ui.line_edit3.setValidator(QIntValidator(0, 9))
self.ui.line_edit3.setFocusPolicy(
    Qt.FocusPolicy.NoFocus)

self.ui.line_edit4.setMaxLength(1)
self.ui.line_edit4.setValidator(QIntValidator(0, 9))
self.ui.line_edit4.setFocusPolicy(
    Qt.FocusPolicy.NoFocus)
```

Then we connect the signals and slots for the button widgets in Listing 8-13. When each button is clicked, it sends a signal that is connected to the numberClicked() slot. Rather than creating a separate method for each button, the **lambda** function is used to reuse a method for signals. lambda calls the numberClicked() function and passes it a new parameter every time, in this case, the specific text from each button.

Listing 8-13. Setting up the signals for the push buttons in the keypad GUI

```
# keypad_main.py
        # 4-digit passcode
        self.passcode = 8618

        # Add signal/slot connections for buttons
        self.ui.button_0.clicked.connect(
            lambda: self.numberClicked(
                self.ui.button_0.text()))
        self.ui.button_1.clicked.connect(
            lambda: self.numberClicked(
                self.ui.button_1.text()))
        self.ui.button_2.clicked.connect(
            lambda: self.numberClicked(
                self.ui.button_2.text()))
        self.ui.button_3.clicked.connect(
            lambda: self.numberClicked(
                self.ui.button_3.text()))
        self.ui.button_4.clicked.connect(
            lambda: self.numberClicked(
                self.ui.button_4.text()))
```

```
self.ui.button_5.clicked.connect(
    lambda: self.numberClicked(
        self.ui.button_5.text()))
self.ui.button_6.clicked.connect(
    lambda: self.numberClicked(
        self.ui.button_6.text()))
self.ui.button_7.clicked.connect(
    lambda: self.numberClicked(
        self.ui.button_7.text()))
self.ui.button_8.clicked.connect(
    lambda: self.numberClicked(
        self.ui.button_8.text()))
self.ui.button_9.clicked.connect(
    lambda: self.numberClicked(
        self.ui.button_9.text()))

self.ui.button_hash.clicked.connect(
    self.checkPasscode)
```

When a user clicks on a button, that button's number needs to appear in the correct line edit widget from left to right. A widget receives focus if its text() value is empty. This is handled in the numberClicked() slot in Listing 8-14.

Listing 8-14. Creating the numberClicked() slot

```
# keypad_main.py
    def numberClicked(self, text_value):
        """When a button with a digit is pressed, check if
        the text for QLineEdit widgets are empty. If empty,
        set the focus to the correct widget and enter text
        value."""
        if self.ui.line_edit1.text() == "":
            self.ui.line_edit1.setFocus()
            self.ui.line_edit1.setText(text_value)
            self.ui.line_edit1.repaint()
```

```python
        elif (self.ui.line_edit1.text() != "") and \
            (self.ui.line_edit2.text() == ""):
            self.ui.line_edit2.setFocus()
            self.ui.line_edit2.setText(text_value)
            self.ui.line_edit2.repaint()
        elif (self.ui.line_edit1.text() != "") and \
            (self.ui.line_edit2.text() != "") and \
            (self.ui.line_edit3.text() == ""):
            self.ui.line_edit3.setFocus()
            self.ui.line_edit3.setText(text_value)
            self.ui.line_edit3.repaint()
        elif (self.ui.line_edit1.text() != "") and \
            (self.ui.line_edit2.text() != "") and \
            (self.ui.line_edit3.text() != "") and \
            (self.ui.line_edit4.text() == ""):
            self.ui.line_edit4.setFocus()
            self.ui.line_edit4.setText(text_value)
            self.ui.line_edit4.repaint()
```

The repaint() method is used to ensure that text is updated in the QLineEdit widgets.

Finally, if the user presses the # button, the slot checkPasscode() in Listing 8-15 checks if the user entered a passcode that matches passcode. If the input does not match, the line edit widgets are reset. This project could be designed so that the password is read from a file or from a database.

Listing 8-15. Creating the checkPasscode() slot

```python
# keypad_main.py
    def checkPasscode(self):
        """Concatenate the text values from the 4 QLineEdit
        widgets, and check to see if the passcode entered by
        user matches existing passcode."""
        entered_passcode = self.ui.line_edit1.text() + \
            self.ui.line_edit2.text() + \
            self.ui.line_edit3.text() + \
            self.ui.line_edit4.text()
```

```
    if len(entered_passcode) == 4 and \
        int(entered_passcode) == self.passcode:
        QMessageBox.information(
            self, "Valid Passcode!", "Valid Passcode!",
            QMessageBox.StandardButton.Ok)
        self.close()
    else:
        QMessageBox.warning(
            self, "Error Message", "Invalid Passcode.",
            QMessageBox.StandardButton.Close)
        self.ui.line_edit1.clear()
        self.ui.line_edit2.clear()
        self.ui.line_edit3.clear()
        self.ui.line_edit4.clear()
        self.ui.line_edit1.setFocus()
```

A QMessageBox appears to inform the user about the outcome of their password. When you run this script, your GUI should look similar to Figure 8-11.

We have only covered some of the features of Qt Designer while building the keypad GUI. In the following section, we'll look at a few other important topics.

Extra Tips for Using Qt Designer

The following section briefly covers three additional topics:

1. Creating GUIs with menus

2. Displaying images in Qt Designer

3. Using style sheets

Setting Up Main Windows and Menus

Open Qt Designer and select the Main Window template from the Form Menu in Figure 8-2. This creates a main window with a menu bar and status bar by default. You can see a main window form displayed in Figure 8-1.

Adding Menus and Submenus in Qt Designer

Adding menus in Qt Designer is simple. Double-click on the Type Here placeholder text in the menu bar and enter the `title` of the menu. This process is shown in Figure 8-17. If you want to create a shortcut, you can also add the ampersand, &, to the beginning of the menu's text. This updates the `menu bar` object in the Object Inspector dialog. You can also edit the menu's properties in the Property Editor.

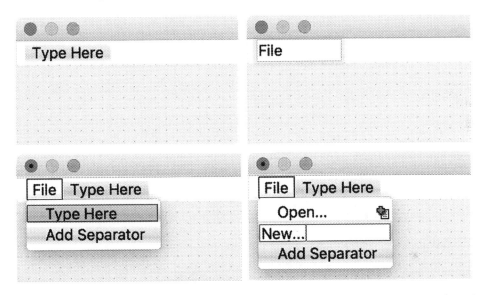

Figure 8-17. *Creating menus and menu entries. Type Here placeholder (top left). Double-click the placeholder and enter the menu's title (top right). Add a new menu entry (bottom left). New menu entry (bottom right)*

From here, you can either add more menus, submenus, or actions. To add a submenu, first create a menu item. Then click on the plus symbol next to the new entry in the menu. This will add a new menu that branches off of the existing menu entry. Double-click on the Type Here placeholder and enter the text for the new item. Refer to Figure 8-18 for help.

Figure 8-18. *Adding submenus. Click on the plus symbol next to the menu entry (left). Add new entry (right)*

Adding Toolbars in Qt Designer

Toolbars can be added to the main window by right-clicking on the form to open a context menu. Click on the Add Tool Bar option.

The actions in toolbars are created as toolbar buttons and can be dragged between the menus and the toolbar. You can also add icons to the toolbar. This topic is covered in Display Images in Qt Designer. An example of the toolbar with an icon is shown in Figure 8-19.

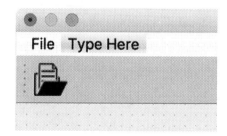

Figure 8-19. *Toolbar with Open File toolbar button*

Adding Actions in Qt Designer

When items are first created in the menu and the toolbar, they are actually actions. Actions can be created, removed, given an icon, designated a shortcut hotkey, and made checkable all in the Action Editor dock widget (shown in Figure 8-7). Actions can also be shared between the menu and the toolbar.

To share an action between the menu and the toolbar so that both objects contain the same item, drag the action from the Action Editor that already exists in the menu onto the toolbar.

Displaying Images in Qt Designer

This section will take a quick look at how you can include images and icons in your application. Whether you are looking to add an image to a QLabel or trying to add icons to your toolbar, the process for adding an image is similar.

For example, if you have a QLabel widget on your form, you can access its properties in the Property Editor. Scroll down until you find the pixmap property. Click on its Value, and from here, you will be able to search for an image file. If you want to add an icon, then you will use the icon property, not pixmap.

You are given two options: Choose Resource... and Choose File.... If you have added resources to your project, then select Choose Resource.... Otherwise, you can search for images on your computer.

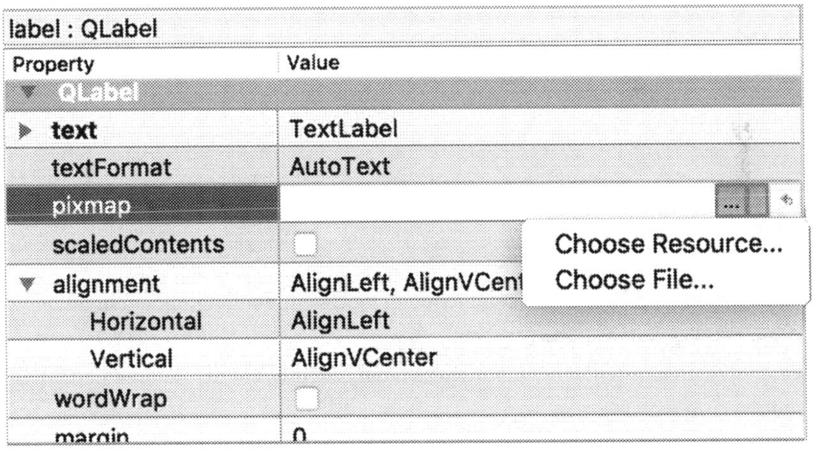

Figure 8-20. *Add images to your application using the pixmap property*

Adding Style Sheets in Qt Designer

Style sheets can also easily be added to each widget by right-clicking on a widget and selecting the Change styleSheet... option from the context menu. A dialog similar to Figure 8-21 will appear.

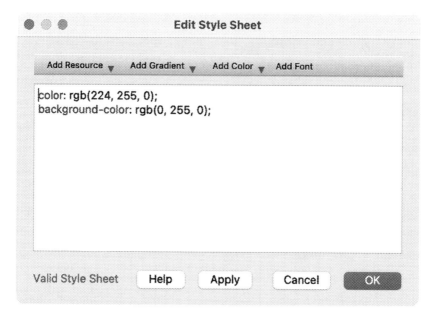

Figure 8-21. *A dialog for creating style sheets*

Here, you can use the drop-down arrows to select different properties and change colors, add resources, or change fonts.

That wraps up this chapter's examination of Qt Designer.

Summary

Qt Designer is definitely a useful tool for creating GUI applications. It provides a drag-and-drop interface that makes it easier to organize widgets; modify the parameters of objects; create menus, toolbars, and dock widgets; add actions to menus; generate code that can be used in Python; and more. Qt Designer can make the design process much quicker and easier.

While this chapter covered a few of the basics for using Qt Designer, there are still other uses, such as creating your own custom widgets or building dialog boxes.

The following chapters will begin to look at more specific PyQt classes and topics that can be used to further improve user interfaces. In the next chapter, you will discover how to use the QClipboard class for copying and pasting data between different applications.

## CHAPTER 9

Working with the Clipboard

One of the major benefits of GUIs is the ability to create programs that can interact with your system and other applications. This concept goes beyond opening and saving files, or printing images.

The **clipboard** is a location in your computer's memory that is used to temporarily store data that you have copied or cut from an application. The clipboard can store a number of different types of data, including text, images, and GIFs. Information that is stored on your system's clipboard can be pasted into other applications as long as the application knows how to work with the type of data stored in the clipboard.

In this chapter, you will

- Use the QClipboard and QMimeData classes to move data between applications
- Find out how to run multiple instances of an application at one time

To get started, let's find out about PyQt's class for interacting with your computer's clipboard.

The QClipboard Class

The **QClipboard** class makes your system's clipboard available so that you can copy and paste data such as text, images, and rich text between applications. Qt widgets that can be used to manipulate textual information, such as QLineEdit and QTextEdit, support using the clipboard. Qt's Model/View classes (which you will learn more about in Chapter 10) also have clipboard support. If you want to paste an image from the clipboard into an application, be sure to use widgets that support graphics, such as QLabel.

© Joshua M Willman 2022
J. M. Willman, *Beginning PyQt*, https://doi.org/10.1007/978-1-4842-7999-1_9

Including the clipboard in your project is pretty straightforward in PyQt. In order to access an application's QClipboard, first create an instance of the clipboard with the following line:

```
self.clipboard = QApplication.clipboard()
```

The following block of code shows one way to retrieve an image that has been copied to the clipboard and apply it to a label:

```
label = QLabel() # Create a label to hold an image
self.clipboard = QApplication.clipboard()
label.setPixmap(self.clipboard.pixmap())
```

This process only works for images, so if you want to paste text or rich text, you'll need to use setText() on a QLabel. Another way to get data is to use the QMimeData class and describe what kind of data is being moved. This topic will be covered in the "Explanation for Using QClipboard" section.

The events that occur between your system and an application built using PyQt are handled by QApplication. The clipboard instance gives you the ability to send or receive data in your application. However, the clipboard can only hold one object at a time. So if you copy an image to the clipboard and then copy text, only the text will be available, and the image will have been deleted.

In this section, you will create a simple GUI, like in Figure 9-1, that shows how to collect text from other applications and then paste it in a PyQt window.

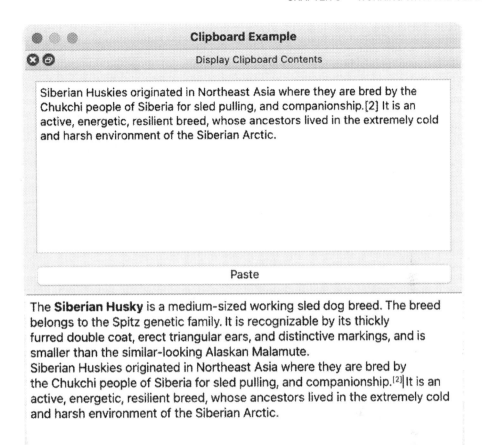

Figure 9-1. *The user can see the contents of the clipboard in the top dock widget*

The top text edit widget displays the current contents of the clipboard. The user can then paste it into the main window, which is the lower text edit widget. In some applications, you may actually want to see the contents of the clipboard in a separate window before pasting it into the main window. A dock widget, especially one that can float separate from the main window, is perfect to use as a clipboard manager.

Explanation for Using QClipboard

In this section, you will see how to set up the clipboard and actually be able to visualize its contents after copying text from another window.

As this project's MainWindow class inherits QMainWindow, you can use the main_window_template.py script from Chapter 5 to get started in Listing 9-1.

Listing 9-1. Setting up the main window for using the clipboard

```python
# clipboard_ex.py
# Import necessary modules
import sys
from PyQt6.QtWidgets import (QApplication, QMainWindow,
    QPushButton, QTextEdit, QDockWidget, QFrame, QVBoxLayout)
from PyQt6.QtCore import Qt

class MainWindow(QMainWindow):
    def __init__(self):
        super().__init__()
        self.initializeUI()

    def initializeUI(self):
        """Set up the application's GUI."""
        self.setMinimumSize(500, 300)
        self.setWindowTitle("Clipboard Example")

        self.setUpMainWindow()
        self.createClipboardDock()
        self.show()

if __name__ == "__main__":
    app = QApplication(sys.argv)
    window = MainWindow()
    sys.exit(app.exec())
```

The upper QTextEdit in Figure 9-1 is placed in a QDockWidget. This is set up in the createClipboardDock() method.

After importing classes and setting up the window in the previous code, let's set the central widget of the main window as a QTextEdit widget in Listing 9-2. The central widget is where the user can edit the text that is pasted from the clipboard.

Listing 9-2. The setUpMainWindow() method for using the clipboard

```python
# clipboard_ex.py
    def setUpMainWindow(self):
        """Create and arrange widgets in the main window."""
```

```
        self.central_tedit = QTextEdit()
        self.setCentralWidget(self.central_tedit)
```

Next, we'll set up the dock widget in Listing 9-3 that is composed of a QTextEdit and a QPushButton arranged in a QVBoxLayout. A QFrame container holds the clipboard_tedit and paste_button widgets.

Listing 9-3. Code for the createClipboardDock() method

```python
# clipboard_ex.py
    def createClipboardDock(self):
        """Set up the clipboard and dock widget to display
        text from the system's clipboard."""
        self.clipboard_tedit = QTextEdit()
        paste_button = QPushButton("Paste")
        paste_button.clicked.connect(self.pasteText)

        dock_v_box = QVBoxLayout()
        dock_v_box.addWidget(self.clipboard_tedit)
        dock_v_box.addWidget(paste_button)

        # Set the main layout for the dock widget,
        # then set the main widget of the dock widget
        dock_frame = QFrame()
        dock_frame.setLayout(dock_v_box)

        # Create a dock widget
        clipboard_dock = QDockWidget()
        clipboard_dock.setWindowTitle(
            "Display Clipboard Contents")
        clipboard_dock.setAllowedAreas(
            Qt.DockWidgetArea.TopDockWidgetArea)
        clipboard_dock.setWidget(dock_frame)

        # Set initial location of dock widget
        self.addDockWidget(
            Qt.DockWidgetArea.TopDockWidgetArea,
            clipboard_dock)
```

```
# Create instance of the clipboard
self.clipboard = QApplication.clipboard()
self.clipboard.dataChanged.connect(
    self.copyFromClipboard)
```

The clipboard_dock widget is set so that it can either float or be attached to the top of the main window. If new text is copied from another application, then clipboard_ tedit will display the text. If the user wants to retain the text, then they can press paste_ button and copy it into central_tedit.

The QClipboard method dataChanged() emits a signal if the contents of the clipboard have changed. If a change has occurred, then the clipboard_tedit widget is updated to display the new clipboard text using the copyFromClipboard() method in Listing 9-4.

Listing 9-4. Code for the copyFromClipboard() and pasteText() slots

```
# clipboard_ex.py
    def copyFromClipboard(self):
        """Get the contents of the system clipboard and
        paste to the window that has focus."""
        mime_data = self.clipboard.mimeData()
        if mime_data.hasText():
            self.clipboard_tedit.setText(mime_data.text())
            self.clipboard_tedit.repaint()

    def pasteText(self):
        """Paste text from clipboard if button is clicked."""
        self.central_tedit.paste()
        self.central_tedit.repaint()
```

To check what kind of data is stored in the clipboard, we use the **QMimeData** class that is used for both the clipboard and the drag-and-drop system in PyQt. The **Multipurpose Internet Mail Extensions (MIME)** format supports not only text but also HTML, URLs, images, and color data. Objects created from the QMimeData class ensure that information can be safely moved between applications and also between objects in the same application.

The method `mimeData()` returns information about the data currently in the clipboard. To check if the object can return plain text, we use the `hasText()` method. If the data is text, then we get the text using `mime_data.text()` and set the text of the `QTextEdit` widget using `setText()`. A similar process is also used to access other kinds of data using `QMimeData`.

Finally, the `QTextEdit` method `paste()` is called in `pasteText()` to fetch the text in the clipboard if the button is pressed. The `repaint()` method is used to force the text of the widget to update.

Project 9.1 – Sticky Notes GUI

Sometimes, you have an idea, a note, or a bit of information that you need to quickly jot down. Maybe you need to remind yourself of an appointment and need to write a note to yourself. You only need a small, temporary, maybe even colorful, area to help brainstorm and organize those ideas. Sticky notes are perfect for those uses and more.

The sticky notes GUI, shown in Figure 9-2, allows you to open as many windows as you want. You can edit the text of each note individually, change the color of a note, and also paste text from the clipboard. This project demonstrates a practical use for the clipboard class and acts as a foundation if you choose to build your own sticky notes application.

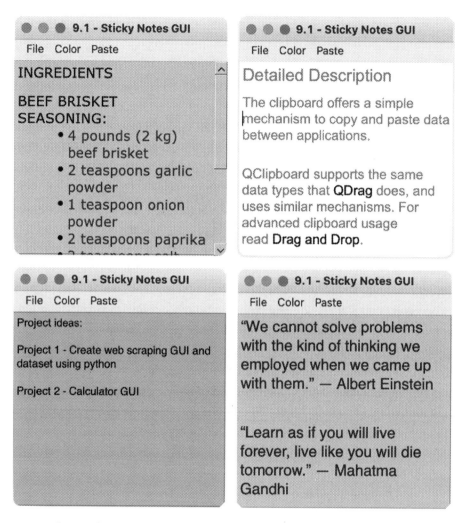

Figure 9-2. *The sticky notes GUI*

The sticky notes GUI is a good project to introduce the concept of **Single Document Interface (SDI)**. SDI is a method that organizes GUIs into individual windows that are handled separately. Even though the sticky note application allows you to create multiple instances of the GUI at the same time, each window is separate and independent from the others. The contrast is **Multiple Document Interface (MDI)**, where a single parent window contains and controls multiple nested child windows. An example of MDI can be found in Chapter 12.

Explanation for the Sticky Notes GUI

The sticky note window is relatively simple, consisting of a single QTextEdit widget that serves as the central widget. The menu bar allows you to create a new note, clear the text in the QTextEdit widget, quit the application, change the background color, and paste text from the clipboard.

Beginning with the main_window_template.py script from Chapter 5, we'll import the classes that we need in Listing 9-5. Since this window contains a menu bar, be sure to import QAction to create actions for the menu.

For this program, the MainWindow class is changed to StickyNote. You don't have to change this, but doing so is just a subtle indication that each instance of StickyNote is its own window.

Listing 9-5. Setting up the main window for the sticky notes GUI

```
# sticky_notes.py
# Import necessary modules
import sys
from PyQt6.QtWidgets import (QApplication, QMainWindow,
    QTextEdit)
from PyQt6.QtGui import QAction

class StickyNote(QMainWindow):
    # Class variables shared by all instances
    note_id = 1
    notes = []

    def __init__(self, note_ref=str()):
        super().__init__()
        self.initializeUI()

    def initializeUI(self):
        """Set up the application's GUI."""
        self.setMinimumSize(250, 250)
        self.setWindowTitle("9.1 - Sticky Notes GUI")

        self.setUpMainWindow()
        self.createActions()
```

```
        self.createMenu()
        self.createClipboard)
        self.show()

if __name__ == "__main__":
    app = QApplication(sys.argv)
    window = StickyNote()
    sys.exit(app.exec())
```

The StickyNote class includes two class variables: note_id, used to give a unique name and reference to each new window, and notes, to keep track of the new windows that are opened by appending them to a list. The class variables are shared by all instances of the class and managed by QApplication.

A QTextEdit widget is set as the central widget in Listing 9-6. In addition, when a new note is created, the instance is appended to the notes list.

Listing 9-6. Code for the SetUpMainWindow() method for the sticky notes GUI

```
# sticky_notes.py
  def setUpMainWindow(self):
        """Create and arrange widgets in the main window."""
        self.notes.append(self)
        self.central_tedit = QTextEdit()
        self.setCentralWidget(self.central_tedit)
```

Listing 9-7 builds the actions for a StickyNote instance. The menu bar includes actions for creating a new instance of StickyNote, changing background colors, and pasting text. You can refer to Chapter 5 for help setting up menu bars and actions.

Listing 9-7. Code for the createActions() method for the sticky notes GUI

```
# sticky_notes.py
    def createActions(self):
        """Create the application's menu actions."""
        # Create actions for File menu
        self.new_note_act = QAction("New Note", self)
        self.new_note_act.setShortcut("Ctrl+N")
        self.new_note_act.triggered.connect(self.newNote)
```

```
self.close_act = QAction("Clear", self)
self.close_act.setShortcut("Ctrl+W")
self.close_act.triggered.connect(self.clearNote)

self.quit_act = QAction("Quit", self)
self.quit_act.setShortcut("Ctrl+Q")
self.quit_act.triggered.connect(self.close)

# Create actions for Color menu
self.yellow_act = QAction("Yellow", self)
self.yellow_act.triggered.connect(
    lambda: self.changeBackground(
        self.yellow_act.text()))

self.blue_act = QAction("Blue", self)
self.blue_act.triggered.connect(
    lambda: self.changeBackground(
        self.blue_act.text()))

self.green_act = QAction("Green", self)
self.green_act.triggered.connect(
    lambda: self.changeBackground(
        self.green_act.text()))

# Create actions for Paste menu
self.paste_act = QAction("Paste", self)
self.paste_act.setShortcut("Ctrl+V")
self.paste_act.triggered.connect(
    self.pasteToClipboard)
```

Depending upon your system, you may see warnings appear in your shell talking about mismatched keys. These are due to the different rules for virtual key codes set by each platform. Other warnings can also arise due to hard-coded key bindings for Qt input widget classes. If you see an error, don't worry at the moment. For this example, the actions will still perform as designated by the specified shortcut keys.

Listing 9-8 creates the File, Color, and Paste menus and their options.

Listing 9-8. Code for the createMenu() method for the sticky notes GUI

```
# sticky_notes.py
    def createMenu(self):
        """Create the application's menu bar."""
        self.menuBar().setNativeMenuBar(False)

        # Create File menu and add actions
        file_menu = self.menuBar().addMenu("File")
        file_menu.addAction(self.new_note_act)
        file_menu.addAction(self.close_act)
        file_menu.addAction(self.quit_act)

        # Create Color menu and add actions
        color_menu = self.menuBar().addMenu("Color")
        color_menu.addAction(self.yellow_act)
        color_menu.addAction(self.blue_act)
        color_menu.addAction(self.green_act)

        # Create Paste menu and add actions
        paste_menu = self.menuBar().addMenu("Paste")
        paste_menu.addAction(self.paste_act)
```

The Color menu allows the user to select a background color for each note. If the user wants to paste text from the clipboard into a widget, they can either use the Paste menu option or the hotkey, Ctrl+V.

The createClipboard() method creates the clipboard object, and the copyToClipboard() slot in Listing 9-9 is triggered when data is changed in the clipboard by the dataChanged signal.

Listing 9-9. Code for setting up the clipboard in the sticky notes GUI

```
# sticky_notes.py
    def createClipboard(self):
        """Set up the clipboard."""
        self.clipboard = QApplication.clipboard()
        self.clipboard.dataChanged.connect(
            self.copyToClipboard)
        self.mime_data = self.clipboard.mimeData()
```

```python
    def copyToClipboard(self):
        """Get the contents of the system clipboard."""
        self.mime_data = self.clipboard.mimeData()

    def newNote(self):
        """Create new instance of StickyNote class."""
        StickyNote().show()
        self.note_id += 1
```

The variable mime_data holds the current data copied to the clipboard and is updated when the data is changed. A new note instance is created in newNote(). Using show(), that new StickyNote instance appears on screen. Each new note is given a reference number, note_id, when it is created. A challenge for you would be to find a PyQt method that allows you to specify the 2D location where the new window will appear.

The other slots in Listing 9-10 allow you to clear with the text, change the background color of central_tedit, or check if mime_data has text and, if so, paste it into central_tedit.

Listing 9-10. Additional slots for the menu items in the sticky notes GUI

```python
# sticky_notes.py
    def clearNote(self):
        """Delete the current note's text."""
        self.central_tedit.clear()

    def changeBackground(self, color_text):
        """Change a note's background color."""
        if color_text == "Yellow":
            self.central_tedit.setStyleSheet(
                "background-color: rgb(248, 253, 145)")
        elif color_text == "Blue":
            self.central_tedit.setStyleSheet(
                "background-color: rgb(145, 253, 251)")
        elif color_text == "Green":
            self.central_tedit.setStyleSheet(
                "background-color: rgb(148, 253, 145)")
```

```
def pasteToClipboard(self):
    """Get the contents of the system clipboard and
    paste into the note."""
    if self.mime_data.hasText():
        self.central_tedit.paste()
```

The sticky note GUI shows one practical use case when copying data between applications can be helpful.

Summary

The QClipboard class allows GUI applications to receive and send data from the system's clipboard. The QMimeData class handles various kinds of data types for both clipboard and drag-and-drop systems, ensuring proper data handling.

Many of PyQt's widgets for editing text already include the ability to interact with the clipboard, so you won't often need to include the code for the clipboard in your program.

In the next chapter, you will learn about Qt's classes for handling data. You will also learn how to apply drag-and-drop functionality in your GUIs so that data can be passed between widgets and other programs.

CHAPTER 10

Presenting Data in PyQt

As a GUI developer, you'll probably find yourself at some point looking for a way to present data, whether textual or visual, in your interface. Before embarking on that adventure, you'll need to keep in mind the user and the purpose of your application. In many cases, the methods for presenting graphical data already follow various standard practices. Many users will have a preexisting notion of how data in tables should be displayed or how items in a list should be added to deleted. Thankfully, Qt has already considered this and created a few classes that make the task of presenting data quicker and simpler.

In this chapter, you will

- Begin thinking about how to handle data in PyQt

- Create a GUI for each of the item-based convenience classes – QListWidget, QTableWidget, and QTreeWidget

- Add drag-and-drop functionality to a GUI

- Create context menus for displaying shortcuts

Let's start by finding out what the convenience classes can do.

Quickly Handling Data in PyQt

The study and collection of data is a great undertaking, especially since information has the potential of improving people's lives, informing decisions, finding solutions, and more. The process of organizing and visualizing data is simplified even more thanks to Qt's **Model/View** design pattern. This topic is covered in more detail in Chapter 14, but what is important to understand here is that the model and view work together to organize, manage, and present data in a GUI. **Models** are used for managing the data, while **views** are used for displaying the data in the GUI.

273

© Joshua M Willman 2022
J. M. Willman, *Beginning PyQt*, https://doi.org/10.1007/978-1-4842-7999-1_10

For this chapter, we'll focus on the **convenience classes** that are derived from the Model/View classes. While this means you'll get less customizability and flexibility, the convenience classes still provide the general functionalities you will need right out of the box. This can be especially helpful when customization is not required for your application.

The three convenience classes use predefined models and views with all of the standard styles, features, and functionalities that you would expect to find in a general item-based interface.

Information about Model/View programming can be found at `https://doc.qt.io/qt-6/model-view-programming.html`.

The QListWidget Class

The **QListWidget** class creates a widget that displays a single column of items, making it simpler for adding and removing items. Items can be added either when the widget is created in code or inserted later through the GUI.

Items in all three of the convenience classes are created using special classes. The **QListWidgetItem** class is used in conjunction with QListWidget to serve as an item that can be used with the list. Figure 10-1 shows the GUI we are going to make for this example.

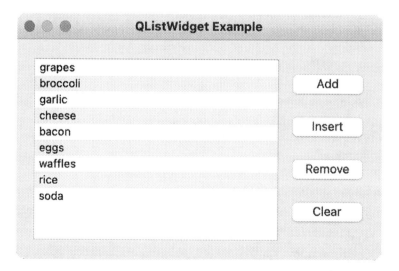

Figure 10-1. *QListWidget can be used to display objects in an inventory or items in a directory*

The QListWidget class includes various methods for creating and manipulating data in the list, including

- addItem(QListWidgetItem) – Adds an item to the end of a list

- currentRow() – Returns the index value of the currently selected row

- insertItem(row, QListWidgetItem) – Inserts an item at the specified row

- takeItem(row) – Removes an item from the specified row

- clear() – Removes and deletes all items from the list

Explanation for Using QListWidget

The following example briefly demonstrates how to add, insert, remove, and clear all items from a QListWidget. To begin, use the basic_window.py script from Chapter 1 to create a new script and set up the MainWindow class and initializeUI() method in Listing 10-1.

Listing 10-1. Setting up the MainWindow class for the QListWidget example

```
# list_widget.py
# Import necessary modules
import sys
from PyQt6.QtWidgets import (QApplication, QWidget,
    QPushButton, QListWidget, QListWidgetItem, QInputDialog,
    QHBoxLayout, QVBoxLayout,)

class MainWindow(QWidget):
    def __init__(self):
        super().__init__()
        self.initializeUI()

    def initializeUI(self):
        """Set up the application's GUI."""
        self.setMinimumSize(400, 200)
        self.setWindowTitle("QListWidget Example")
```

```
        self.setUpMainWindow()
        self.show()

if __name__ == "__main__":
    app = QApplication(sys.argv)
    window = MainWindow()
    sys.exit(app.exec())
```

Be sure to include the QListWidget and QListWidgetItem imports from QtWidgets. QInputDialog will be used when adding or inserting a new row into the QListWidget.

The setUpMainWindow() method for the MainWindow class is built in Listing 10-2. QListWidget is used to manage the data items displayed in the GUI window. For alternating row colors, set the setAlternatingRowColors() method's value to True.

Listing 10-2. Creating the setUpMainWindow() method for the QListWidget example

```
# list_widget.py
    def setUpMainWindow(self):
        """Create and arrange widgets in the main window."""
        self.list_widget = QListWidget()
        self.list_widget.setAlternatingRowColors(True)

        # Initialize the QListWidget with items
        grocery_list = ["grapes", "broccoli", "garlic",
                        "cheese", "bacon", "eggs", "waffles",
                        "rice", "soda"]
        for item in grocery_list:
            list_item = QListWidgetItem()
            list_item.setText(item)
            self.list_widget.addItem(list_item)

        # Create buttons for interacting with the items
        add_button = QPushButton("Add")
        add_button.clicked.connect(self.addListItem)

        insert_button = QPushButton("Insert")
        insert_button.clicked.connect(self.insertItemInList)
```

```
remove_button = QPushButton("Remove")
remove_button.clicked.connect(self.removeOneItem)

clear_button = QPushButton("Clear")
clear_button.clicked.connect(self.list_widget.clear)

# Create layouts
right_v_box = QVBoxLayout()
right_v_box.addWidget(add_button)
right_v_box.addWidget(insert_button)
right_v_box.addWidget(remove_button)
right_v_box.addWidget(clear_button)

main_h_box = QHBoxLayout()
main_h_box.addWidget(self.list_widget)
main_h_box.addLayout(right_v_box)
self.setLayout(main_h_box)
```

To display the string items from grocery_list in list_widget, we'll need to create a QListWidgetItem object for each item, set its text using setText(), and use the addItem() method to add the item to list_widget. These items will populate the list when the program begins. Here, we are merely passing text to QListWidgetItem, but you can also pass an icon as well.

From there, let's create the buttons for each of the actions that can be performed on the QListWidget and connect those buttons to a clicked signal. Whenever a button is clicked, it will emit a signal that connects to a slot for editing the data items in the QListWidget.

The buttons are added to a QVBoxLayout, which are then arranged along with list_widget in the main window's QHBoxLayout.

Listing 10-3 takes care of creating the slot that is triggered by add_button.

Listing 10-3. Code for the addListItem() slot

```
# list_widget.py
    def addListItem(self):
        """Add a single item to the list widget."""
        text, ok = QInputDialog.getText(
            self, "New Item", "Add item:")
```

```
if ok and text != "":
    list_item = QListWidgetItem()
    list_item.setText(text)
    self.list_widget.addItem(list_item)
```

When the user wants to add a new item, a QInputDialog instance like the one seen in Figure 10-2 will appear.

Figure 10-2. *Adding a new item to QListWidget using QInputDialog*

If text has been entered and the user clicks the OK button in the dialog, then a new item is appended to the end of list_widget using addItem().

Using the buttons on the right of the main window, the user can also insert, remove, or clear the list items. We'll need to create two additional slots, insertItemInList() and removeOneItem(), in Listing 10-4. For clear_button, the clicked signal is simply connected to the QListWidget method clear().

Listing 10-4. The remaining slots for the MainWindow class in the QListWidget example

```python
# list_widget.py
    def insertItemInList(self):
        """Insert a single item into the list widget under
        the currently selected row. """
        text, ok = QInputDialog.getText(
            self, "Insert Item", "Insert item:")
        if ok and text != "":
            row = self.list_widget.currentRow()
            row = row + 1 # Select row below current row
```

```
        new_item = QListWidgetItem()
        new_item.setText(text)
        self.list_widget.insertItem(row, new_item)

def removeOneItem(self):
    """Remove a single item from the list widget."""
    row = self.list_widget.currentRow()
    item = self.list_widget.takeItem(row)
    del item
```

A QInputDialog will appear when the user wants to insert a new data item. If the user clicks OK, the currently selected row is determined using currentRow(). Next, the value for row is increased by 1, a new QListWidgetItem is created, and that new item is inserted below the currently selected row. When removing a row, currentRow() is used again to discover which row is selected. The method takeItem() is used to remove the item from the QListWidget. The del keyword is used to permanently delete an item since takeItem() does not actually delete items.

In the following section, you'll continue to use QListWidget to find out how to extend the capabilities of the widget with drag-and-drop functionality.

Drag and Drop in PyQt

The **drag-and-drop** mechanism allows a user to perform tasks in a GUI by selecting items, such as icons or images, and moving them into another window or onto another object. PyQt also makes including this behavior in an application very straightforward. To allow widgets to have basic drag-and-drop functionality, you only need to set the values of setAcceptDrops() and setDragEnabled() methods to True.

With drag-and-drop functionality enabled, you can move items from one text edit, list, or table object to another in PyQt. **QMimeData** can also be used to handle what kind of data can be moved, dragged, or dropped.

Figure 10-3 displays the GUI you'll be creating in this section. Items in the window can be dragged and dropped back and forth between the two QListWidget instances. Be sure to download the images folder from the GitHub repository for this project.

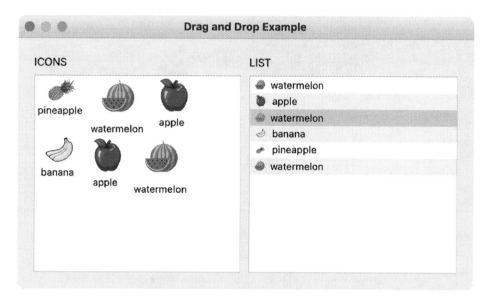

Figure 10-3. *Two QListWidget objects used to demonstrate drag and drop*

Tip   Drag-and-drop mechanics can be applied to a variety of different widgets, not just `QListWidget`. You should have a look at PyQt or Qt documentation to find out which widgets already have built-in drag-and-drop capabilities.

Explanation for Drag and Drop

Start with the `basic_window.py` script and modify the `MainWindow` class in Listing 10-5. We'll continue using the `QListWidget` and `QListWidgetItem` classes in this example to demonstrate drag and drop.

Listing 10-5. Creating the MainWindow class for the drag and drop example

```
# drag_drop.py
# Import necessary modules
import sys, os
from PyQt6.QtWidgets import (QApplication, QWidget, QLabel,
    QListWidget, QListWidgetItem, QGridLayout)
```

```
from PyQt6.QtCore import QSize
from PyQt6.QtGui import QIcon

class MainWindow(QWidget):
    def __init__(self):
        super().__init__()
        self.initializeUI()

    def initializeUI(self):
        """Set up the application's GUI."""
        self.setMinimumSize(500, 300)
        self.setWindowTitle("Drag and Drop Example")

        self.setUpMainWindow()
        self.show()

if __name__ == "__main__":
    app = QApplication(sys.argv)
    window = MainWindow()
    sys.exit(app.exec())
```

There are two instances of the QListWidget class created, icon_widget and list_widget, in Listing 10-6. Items in QListWidget can be viewed either as icons or as text in a list. The icon_widget object displays icons by using the flag IconMode. The default setting is to show items in a list.

Listing 10-6. Code for the setUpMainWindow() method in the drag and drop example

```
# drag_drop.py
    def setUpMainWindow(self):
        """Create and arrange widgets in the main window."""
        icon_label = QLabel("ICONS", self)
        icon_widget = QListWidget()
        icon_widget.setAcceptDrops(True)
        icon_widget.setDragEnabled(True)
        icon_widget.setViewMode(
            QListWidget.ViewMode.IconMode)
```

281

```
    image_path = "images"
    for img in os.listdir(image_path):
        list_item = QListWidgetItem()
        list_item.setText(img.split(".")[0])
        list_item.setIcon(QIcon(os.path.join(image_path,
                            "{0}").format(img)))
        icon_widget.setIconSize(QSize(50, 50))
        icon_widget.addItem(list_item)

    list_label = QLabel("LIST", self)
    list_widget = QListWidget()
    list_widget.setAlternatingRowColors(True)
    list_widget.setAcceptDrops(True)
    list_widget.setDragEnabled(True)

    # create grid layout
    grid = QGridLayout()
    grid.addWidget(icon_label, 0, 0)
    grid.addWidget(list_label, 0, 1)
    grid.addWidget(icon_widget, 1, 0)
    grid.addWidget(list_widget, 1, 1)

    self.setLayout(grid)
```

To set up the drag-and-drop ability for icon_widget, set the values for
setAcceptDrops() and setDragEnabled() to True. The setAcceptDrops() method
allows for drop events to be accepted on the widget, while setDragEnabled() allows for
items to be dragged in and out of the widget. These methods are actually inherited from
QWidget, so most classes that inherit QWidget will also have access to drag-and-drop
functionalities.

When the program begins, only the QListWidget icon_widget will be populated
with items from the images folder. Although the methods setText() and setIcon() are
called to apply the text and icons to the QListWidgetItem instances, these values can
also be passed as arguments when instantiating a QListWidgetItem object.

Next, repeat the process for `list_widget`, but don't change the widget's view mode. When one of the icons that are loaded into `icon_widget` is dragged onto `list_widget`, the list updates its contents to include the new item. Dropping an item from one `QListWidget` to the other adds a new item to that list.

The next section will take a look at the convenience class for creating tables in PyQt.

The QTableWidget Class

The **QTableWidget** class provides a means to display and organize data in tabular form, presenting the information in rows and columns. Using tables arranges data into a more readable format. An example of PyQt's tables can be seen in Figure 10-4.

	ID	First Name	Last Name	Dept.	Start Date	6	7	8	9	10
1	1002	Ken	Sanchez	Executive	2010-05-12					
2	1003	Evelyn	Ye	Executive	2010-04-20					
3	1234	Kalani	Willman	Engineering	2012-08-05					
4	1245	Valorie	Payne	IT	2009-12-09					
5	1657	Steve	Grant	Finance	2013-01-30					
6	1890	Garfield	Adams	Engineering	2016-10-12					
7	2010	Larry	Byrd	Finance	2016-11-01					
8	3501	Mary	Stevenson	HR	2011-08-09					
9										
10										

Figure 10-4. *Example of a table from the QTableWidget class*

QTableWidget provides you with the standard tools that you will need to create tables, including the ability to edit cells, set the number of rows and columns, and add vertical or horizontal header labels. You can also hide headers should you not want them to be visible. QTableWidget also has a number of signals for checking if cells or items have been clicked, double-clicked, or even altered.

For this first example, we will be taking a look at how to use QTableWidget to create the foundation for an application to edit spreadsheets. In addition, this application will teach you how to build a context menu to manipulate the contents of the table widget.

Explanation for Using QTableWidget

For this application, start by building the MainWindow class in Listing 10-7 by using the main_window_template.py script from Chapter 5. Make sure to import QTableWidget and **QTableWidgetItem**, which is used to create items for the table widget. The **QMenu** class will be used to create context menus in the GUI.

Listing 10-7. Setting up the MainWindow class for the QTableWidget example

```python
# table_widget.py
# Import necessary modules
import sys
from PyQt6.QtWidgets import (QApplication, QMainWindow,
    QTableWidget, QTableWidgetItem, QMenu, QInputDialog)
from PyQt6.QtGui import QAction

class MainWindow(QMainWindow):

    def __init__(self):
        super().__init__()
        self.initializeUI()

    def initializeUI(self):
        """Set up the application's GUI."""
        self.setMinimumSize(1000, 500)
        self.setWindowTitle(
            "Spreadsheet - QTableWidget Example")

        # Used for copy and paste actions
        self.item_text = None

        self.setUpMainWindow()
        self.createActions()
        self.createMenu()
        self.show()

if __name__ == "__main__":
    app = QApplication(sys.argv)
    window = MainWindow()
    sys.exit(app.exec())
```

Be sure to create the instance variable, `item_text`, that will hold the text for copy and paste actions. The `QTableWidget` that creates the GUI's spreadsheet is created in Listing 10-8 in `setUpMainWindow()`.

Listing 10-8. Creating the setUpMainWindow() method for the QTableWidget example

```
# table_widget.py
    def setUpMainWindow(self):
        """Create and arrange widgets in the main window."""
        self.table_widget = QTableWidget()

        # Set initial row and column values
        self.table_widget.setRowCount(10)
        self.table_widget.setColumnCount(10)

        # Set focus on cell in the table
        self.table_widget.setCurrentCell(0, 0)

        # When the horizontal headers are double-clicked,
        # emit a signal
        h_header = self.table_widget.horizontalHeader()
        h_header.sectionDoubleClicked.connect(
            self.changeHeader)

        self.setCentralWidget(self.table_widget)
```

When instantiating a `QTableWidget` object, you could pass the number of rows and columns as parameters to the `QTableWidget`, like in the following line:

```
        table_widget = QTableWidget(10, 10)
```

Or you could construct a table using the `setRowCount()` and `setColumnCount()` methods. The `table_widget` instance will start with ten rows and ten columns.

The `setCurrentCell()` method can be used to place focus on a specific cell in the table.

The `QTableWidget` and `QTreeWidget` classes have headers; `QListWidget` does not. To access a table's headers, you can either call the `horizontalHeader()` for horizontal headers or `verticalHeader()` for vertical ones. Changing header labels

285

in QTableWidget can either be done directly in code or by using a slightly indirect approach. Headers for tables are created using **QHeaderView** in the **QTableView** class. We'll cover QTableView and other view classes more in Chapter 14.

Since QTableWidget inherits from the QTableView class, we also have access to its functions. Knowing that, we are able to obtain the QHeaderView object using table_widget.horizontalHeader(). From there, we can connect to the QHeaderView class's signal, sectionDoubleClicked. This signal can be used to check if the user double-clicked a header section. If they did, a signal triggers the changeHeader() slot (created in Listing 10-12).

The menu bar seen in Figure 10-4 contains two menus: File and Table. File contains the action for quitting the application. Table includes actions for adding and deleting rows or columns. We'll set up those actions in Listing 10-9.

Listing 10-9. Code for the createActions() method in the QTableWidget example

```python
# table_widget.py
    def createActions(self):
        """Create the application's menu actions."""
        # Create actions for File menu
        self.quit_act = QAction("Quit", self)
        self.quit_act.setShortcut("Ctrl+Q")
        self.quit_act.triggered.connect(self.close)

        # Create actions for Table menu
        self.add_row_above_act = QAction(
            "Add Row Above", self)
        self.add_row_above_act.triggered.connect(
            self.addRowAbove)

        self.add_row_below_act = QAction(
            "Add Row Below", self)
        self.add_row_below_act.triggered.connect(
            self.addRowBelow)

        self.add_col_before_act = QAction(
            "Add Column Before", self)
        self.add_col_before_act.triggered.connect(
            self.addColumnBefore)
```

```
self.add_col_after_act = QAction(
    "Add Column After", self)
self.add_col_after_act.triggered.connect(
    self.addColumnAfter)

self.delete_row_act = QAction("Delete Row", self)
self.delete_row_act.triggered.connect(self.deleteRow)

self.delete_col_act = QAction("Delete Column", self)
self.delete_col_act.triggered.connect(
    self.deleteColumn)

self.clear_table_act = QAction("Clear All", self)
self.clear_table_act.triggered.connect(
    self.clearTable)
```

The slots that each action is connected to are created in Listing 10-14. The menu items are created in Listing 10-10. Refer to Chapter 5 for more reference on creating actions and menus.

Listing 10-10. Code for the createMenu() method in the QTableWidget example

```
# table_widget.py
    def createMenu(self):
        """Create the application's menu bar."""
        self.menuBar().setNativeMenuBar(False)

        # Create file menu and add actions
        file_menu = self.menuBar().addMenu('File')
        file_menu.addAction(self.quit_act)

        # Create table menu and add actions
        table_menu = self.menuBar().addMenu('Table')
        table_menu.addAction(self.add_row_above_act)
        table_menu.addAction(self.add_row_below_act)
        table_menu.addSeparator()
        table_menu.addAction(self.add_col_before_act)
        table_menu.addAction(self.add_col_after_act)
        table_menu.addSeparator()
```

```
table_menu.addAction(self.delete_row_act)
table_menu.addAction(self.delete_col_act)
table_menu.addSeparator()
table_menu.addAction(self.clear_table_act)
```

The context menu and its actions are generated in the next section.

Creating Context Menus

This application also introduces how to create a **context menu**, sometimes called a pop-up menu, that appears in the window due to a user's interaction, such as when the right mouse button is clicked. A context menu displays a list of general commands, such as Back Page or Reload Page. Context menus can also be set for managing specific widgets.

Since context menus are caused by events, we can reimplement the event handler, contextMenuEvent(). A simple example is shown in the following block of code:

```
def contextMenuEvent(self, event):
    context_menu = QMenu(self)
    context_menu.addAction(self.add_row_above_act)
```

A context menu is typically created using QMenu. You can either use existing actions that are created in the menu bar or the toolbar, or you can create new ones. An example of this application's context menu is shown in Figure 10-5.

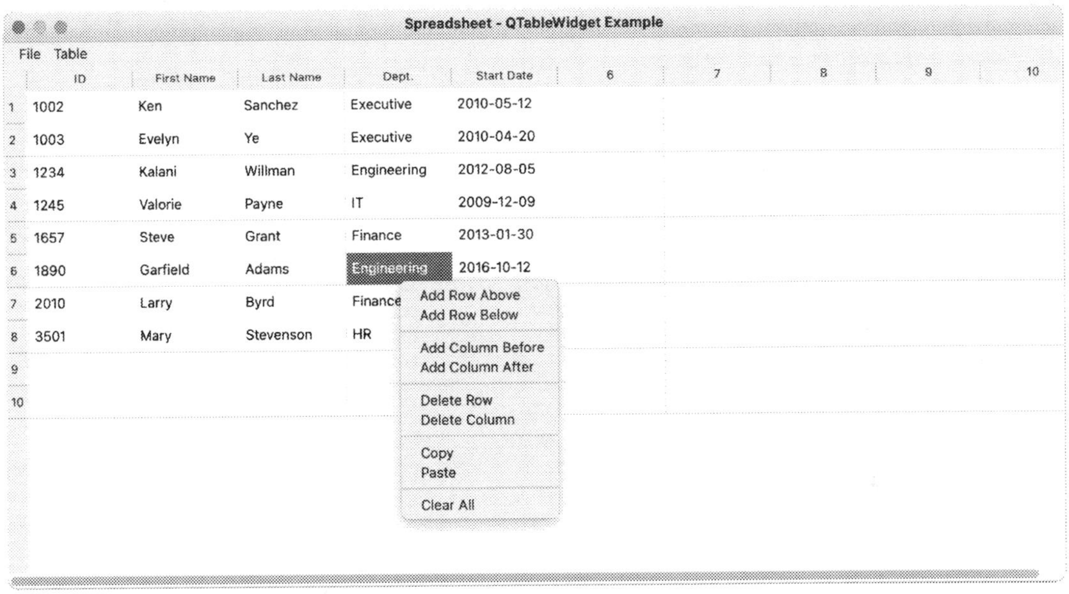

Figure 10-5. *Example of a context menu that displays actions for editing the table widget*

For the context menu in Figure 10-5, all of the menu's actions in Listing 10-9 (except for `quit_act`) are included. Two additional actions are also created specifically for the context menu: `copy_act` and `paste_act`. Those are handled in Listing 10-11.

Listing 10-11. Code for the event handler contextMenuEvent() in the QTableWidget example

```
# table_widget.py
    def contextMenuEvent(self, event):
        """Create context menu and additional actions."""
        context_menu = QMenu(self)
        context_menu.addAction(self.add_row_above_act)
        context_menu.addAction(self.add_row_below_act)
        context_menu.addSeparator()
        context_menu.addAction(self.add_col_before_act)
        context_menu.addAction(self.add_col_after_act)
        context_menu.addSeparator()
```

```
context_menu.addAction(self.delete_row_act)
context_menu.addAction(self.delete_col_act)
context_menu.addSeparator()

# Create actions specific to the context menu
copy_act = context_menu.addAction("Copy")
paste_act = context_menu.addAction("Paste")
context_menu.addSeparator()
context_menu.addAction(self.clear_table_act)

# Execute the context_menu and return the action
# selected. mapToGlobal() translates the position
# of the window coordinates to the global screen
# coordinates. This way we can detect if a right-click
# occurred inside of the GUI and display the context
# menu
action = context_menu.exec(
    self.mapToGlobal(event.pos()))

# Check for actions selected in the context menu that
# were not created in the menu bar
if action == copy_act:
    self.copyItem()
if action == paste_act:
    self.pasteItem()
```

The context menu is displayed using exec(). The value that it returns, action, can be used to determine if the additional actions were clicked on in the context menu. We pass self.mapToGlobal() as an argument to get the coordinates of the mouse within the screen. The position of the mouse is determined with event.pos().

If action is equal to copy_act, we'll call the method copyItem(). For paste_act, the pasteItem() method is called. These are created in Listing 10-13.

Using Built-in QTableWidget Methods to Edit Data

The remaining listings will create the different slots and methods in MainWindow. For Listing 10-12, we'll create changeHeader() that is triggered when a column header is double-clicked.

To get the text for the selected column header, QInputDialog is displayed to get the header label text from the user. Finally, the item for the horizontal header is set using setHorizontalHeaderItem().

Listing 10-12. Code for the changeHeader() slot in the QTableWidget example

```
# table_widget.py
    def changeHeader(self):
        """Change horizontal headers by returning the text
        from input dialog."""
        col = self.table_widget.currentColumn()

        text, ok = QInputDialog.getText(
            self, "Enter Header", "Header text:")
        if ok and text != "":
            self.table_widget.setHorizontalHeaderItem(
                col, QTableWidgetItem(text))
```

Setting horizontal header labels can be accomplished with either setHorizontalHeaderItem() or setHorizontalHeaderLabels(). You can change Horizontal to Vertical in the method calls for vertical headers.

We'll handle the extra methods in the context menu next in Listing 10-13. If the selected cell is not empty, we copy the text to item_text. In the pasteItem() method, the current row and column of the selected cell are collected. We then paste the data using setItem(). The copy and paste actions could also be implemented using the QClipboard.

Listing 10-13. Code for the copyItem() and pasteItem() methods used by the context menu

```
# table_widget.py
    def copyItem(self):
        """If the current cell selected is not empty,
        store the text."""
        if self.table_widget.currentItem() != None:
            text = self.table_widget.currentItem().text()
            self.item_text = text
```

```
def pasteItem(self):
    """Set item for selected cell."""
    if self.item_text != None:
        row = self.table_widget.currentRow()
        column = self.table_widget.currentColumn()
        self.table_widget.setItem(
            row, column, QTableWidgetItem(self.item_text))
```

You can also add items to the table programmatically using the setItem() method. This allows you to specify the row and column values, and an item for the cell using **QTableWidgetItem**. In the following code, the item Kalani is inserted in row 0 and column 0.

```
self.table_widget.setItem(
    1, 0, QTableWidgetItem("Kalani"))
```

QTableWidget includes a few methods for manipulating table objects. The Table menu creates actions that put those methods to use. These actions call slots that utilize built-in QTableWidget methods. The following list describes how these methods are used in the GUI and in Listing 10-14:

- Adding rows above or below the currently selected row using insertRow()

- Adding columns before or after the currently selected column using insertColumn()

- Deleting the current row or column using removeRow() or removeColumn()

- Clearing the entire table, including items and headers with clear()

Listing 10-14. Code for the slots that modify data in the QTableWidget example

```
# table_widget.py
    def addRowAbove(self):
        current_row = self.table_widget.currentRow()
        self.table_widget.insertRow(current_row)
```

```
def addRowBelow(self):
    current_row = self.table_widget.currentRow()
    self.table_widget.insertRow(current_row + 1)

def addColumnBefore(self):
    current_col = self.table_widget.currentColumn()
    self.table_widget.insertColumn(current_col)

def addColumnAfter(self):
    current_col = self.table_widget.currentColumn()
    self.table_widget.insertColumn(current_col + 1)

def deleteRow(self):
    current_row = self.table_widget.currentRow()
    self.table_widget.removeRow(current_row)

def deleteColumn(self):
    current_col = self.table_widget.currentColumn()
    self.table_widget.removeColumn(current_col)

def clearTable(self):
    self.table_widget.clear()
```

Items in a table are accessed using their row and column values. We'll first need to know which row or column is currently selected. For example, when add_row_above_act is clicked, it triggers a signal that calls addRowAbove(). We first find out the row that is selected using currentRow(). A new row is then inserted in the current row's location, causing all other rows to move down. Methods that manipulate columns use the currentColumn() method.

The last program will introduce the QTreeWidget convenience class.

The QTreeWidget Class

The **QTreeWidget** class shares similarities with both QListWidget and QTableWidget. On the one hand, data items can be displayed in a list-like format similar to QListWidget. On the other hand, QTreeWidget can also display multiple columns of data, but not in a tabular format.

What sets QTreeWidget apart is how the class can visually represent the relationships between data in a tree-like structure. It is possible for an item in the tree to be the parent of other items.

The GUI that we will build in this section is shown in Figure 10-6.

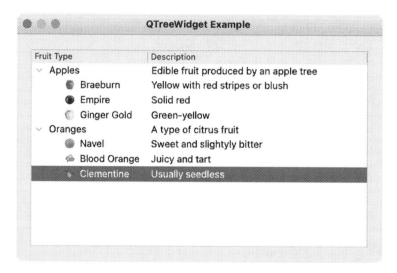

Figure 10-6. *A QTreeWidget is used to present data in a tree-like structure*

Items added to QTreeWidget are created from **QTreeWidgetItem**. For the items in Figure 10-6, there will be two parent items for the types of fruit and a number of child items with icons that are organized under the parents.

Similar to QTableWidget, QTreeWidget also contains horizontal headers for each column. However, there are no vertical headers.

Sorting of column items is also possible with QTreeWidget.

Be sure to download the icons folder from GitHub before beginning this application.

Explanation for Using QTreeWidget

We'll begin with basic_window.py script from Chapter 1, update the imports, and set the window's minimum size and title for the MainWindow class in Listing 10-15.

Listing 10-15. Setting up the MainWindow class for the QTreeWidget example

```
# tree_widget.py
# Import necessary modules
import sys
```

```python
from PyQt6.QtWidgets import (QApplication, QWidget,
    QTreeWidget, QTreeWidgetItem, QVBoxLayout)
from PyQt6.QtGui import QIcon

class MainWindow(QWidget):

    def __init__(self):
        """ Constructor for Empty Window Class """
        super().__init__()
        self.initializeUI()

    def initializeUI(self):
        """"Set up the application's GUI."""
        self.setMinimumSize(500, 300)
        self.setWindowTitle("QTreeWidget Example")

        self.setUpMainWindow()
        self.show()

if __name__ == '__main__':
    app = QApplication(sys.argv)
    window = MainWindow()
    sys.exit(app.exec())
```

After creating the QTreeWidget object in Listing 10-16, we'll need to set the number of columns with the setColumnCount() setter. Next, we'll specify the labels for each of the columns. The method setHeaderLabels() takes an iterable object as an argument. The method setColumnWidth() is used to set the minimum column width of a specified column, ensuring that all of the items are clearly displayed. Here, column 0 is set to a width of 160 pixels.

Listing 10-16. Creating the setUpMainWindow() method for the QTreeWidget example, part 1

```python
# tree_widget.py
    def setUpMainWindow(self):
        """"Create and arrange widgets in the main window."""
        tree_widget = QTreeWidget()
        tree_widget.setColumnCount(2)
```

```
tree_widget.setHeaderLabels(
    ["Fruit Type", "Description"])
tree_widget.setColumnWidth(0, 160)

category_1 = QTreeWidgetItem(tree_widget, ["Apples", \
    "Edible fruit produced by an apple tree"])

apple_list = [
    ["Braeburn", "Yellow with red stripes or blush", \
        "icons/braeburn.png"],
    ["Empire", "Solid red", "icons/empire.png"],
    ["Ginger Gold", "Green-yellow", \
        "icons/ginger_gold.png"]]

for i in range(len(apple_list)):
    category_1_child = QTreeWidgetItem(
        apple_list[i][:2])
    category_1_child.setIcon(
        0, QIcon(apple_list[i][2]))
    category_1.addChild(category_1_child)
```

The category_1 instance is a QTreeWidgetItem for the first parent item in the tree. The parent widget, tree_widget, as well as a list of the information for the two columns is passed to the item. Following that, apple_list is a list of lists. Each list contains an apple type corresponding to the first column, a description to be displayed in the second column, and an icon that is displayed next to the item's name. Each category_1_child is then turned into a QTreeWidgetItem, and its icon is set and at last added to the category_1 parent item in a Python for loop.

The same process is followed to create the second parent item and its children in Listing 10-17.

Listing 10-17. Creating the setUpMainWindow() method for the QTreeWidget example, part 2

```
# tree_widget.py
    category_2 = QTreeWidgetItem(tree_widget,
        ["Oranges", "A type of citrus fruit"])
```

```
orange_list = [
    ["Navel", "Sweet and slightly bitter", \
        "icons/navel.png"],
    ["Blood Orange", "Juicy and tart", \
        "icons/blood_orange.png"],
    ["Clementine", "Usually seedless", \
        "icons/clementine.png"]]

for i in range(len(apple_list)):
    category_2_child = QTreeWidgetItem(
        orange_list[i][:2])
    category_2_child.setIcon(
        0, QIcon(orange_list[i][2]))
    category_2.addChild(category_2_child)

main_v_box = QVBoxLayout()
main_v_box.addWidget(tree_widget)
self.setLayout(main_v_box)
```

With the items created, `tree_widget` is added to the layout of the main window.

With this GUI complete, you have now experienced creating applications for each of the Model/View convenience classes.

Summary

In this chapter, we took a look at the item-based convenience classes that follow standard methods for presenting data. Items are typically presented in a list, in a table, or in a tree. We learned about `QListWidget`, `QTableWidget`, and `QTreeWidget` and discovered how to use some of their features to create unique and practical GUIs. All of the item-based widget classes as well as many other classes that inherit `QWidget` have drag-and-drop capabilities. This system is very useful since it makes moving data between graphical elements in a GUI even simpler.

In the next chapter, we'll explore the graphical aspects of GUIs and begin to see how we can add animation and color to applications.

CHAPTER 11

Graphics and Animation in PyQt

As you design GUIs, you will find out that you can also explore your creative and artistic side through drawing and animating widgets. Since graphics are such an immense part of graphical applications, this chapter is only able to introduce topics related to 2D graphics, including lines, shapes, animations, and painting. If you are interested in creating GUIs that work with 3D visuals, Qt also has support for various graphics APIs, including OpenGL and Vulkan.[1] If you are really interested in graphics in Qt 6, have a look at `https://doc.qt.io/qt-6/topics-graphics.html`.

In this chapter, you will

- Learn about `QPainter` and other classes used for drawing in Qt

- Create tool tips using `QToolTip`

- Use `QPropertyAnimation` to animate widgets

- Animate objects using `QPropertyAnimation` and `pyqtProperty`

- Find out how to use `QGraphicsView` to construct a graphics scene

To begin, let's start with one of the most important classes in PyQt.

---

[1] For information about OpenGL, check out `www.opengl.org`. For Vulkan, check out `www.vulkan.org`.

© Joshua M Willman 2022
J. M. Willman, *Beginning PyQt*, https://doi.org/10.1007/978-1-4842-7999-1_11

Introduction to the QPainter Class

Graphics in Qt are created primarily with the **QPainter** API. Qt's painting system handles drawing for text, images, and vector graphics and can be done on a variety of surfaces, such as QImage, QWidget, and QPrinter. With QPainter, you can enhance the look of existing widgets or even create your own.

The main components of the painting system in PyQt are the QPainter, **QPaintDevice**, and **QPaintEngine** classes. QPainter performs the drawing operations; a QPaintDevice is an abstraction of two-dimensional space that acts as the surface that QPainter can paint on; QPaintEngine is the internal interface used by the QPainter and QPaintDevice classes for drawing.

Whenever you need to draw something in PyQt, you will more than likely need to work with the QPainter class. QPainter provides functions for drawing simple points and lines, complex shapes, text, and pixmaps. We have looked at pixmaps in previous chapters in applications where we needed to display images. QPainter also allows you to customize a variety of its settings, such as rendering quality or changing the painter's coordinate system. Drawing can be done on a **paint device**, which is a two-dimensional object created from the different PyQt classes. These objects can be painted on with QPainter.

Drawing relies on a coordinate system for specifying the position of points and shapes and is typically handled in the paint event of a widget. The default coordinate system for a paint device has the origin at the top-left corner, beginning at (0, 0). The x values increase to the right, and the y values increase going down. Each (x, y) coordinate defines the location of a single pixel.

The GUI created in Figure 11-1 illustrates a few of the QPainter class's drawing functions and tools.

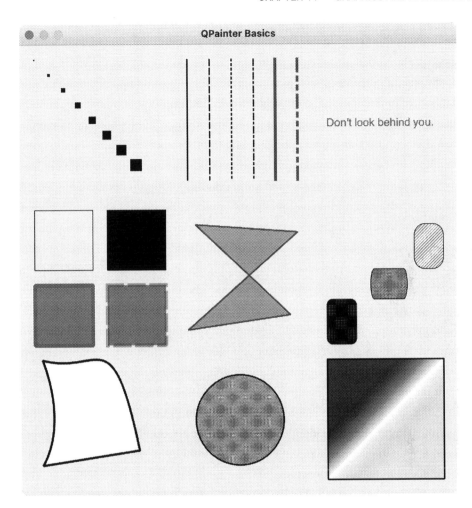

Figure 11-1. *Some of the QPainter class's different painting functions. The GUI includes points, lines, and text in the first row; the second row illustrates shapes and patterns, including rectangles, polygons, and rectangles with rounded corners; the last row displays curves, circles, and painting with gradients*

Explanation for Using the QPainter Class

We'll get started by using the basic_window.py script from Chapter 1. This program introduces quite a few new classes, a majority of them imported from the QtGui module. QtGui provides us with the tools we need for 2D graphics, imaging, and fonts. The **QPoint** and **QRect** classes imported from QtCore in Listing 11-1 are used to define points and rectangles specified by coordinate values in the window's plane.

301

Listing 11-1. Creating the MainWindow class for the QPainter example

```python
# paint_basics.py
# Import necessary modules
import sys
from PyQt6.QtWidgets import QApplication, QWidget
from PyQt6.QtCore import Qt, QPoint, QRect
from PyQt6.QtGui import (QPainter, QPainterPath, QColor,
    QBrush, QPen, QFont, QPolygon, QLinearGradient)

class MainWindow(QWidget):
    def __init__(self):
        super().__init__()
        self.initializeUI()

    def initializeUI(self):
        """Set up the application's GUI."""
        self.setFixedSize(600, 600)
        self.setWindowTitle("QPainter Basics")

        # Create a few pen colors
        self.black = '#000000'
        self.blue = '#2041F1'
        self.green = '#12A708'
        self.purple = '#6512F0'
        self.red = '#E00C0C'
        self.orange = '#FF930A'

        self.show()

if __name__ == '__main__':
    app = QApplication(sys.argv)
    window = MainWindow()
    sys.exit(app.exec())
```

The MainWindow class inherits from QWidget, and all drawing will occur on the widget's surface. It definitely helps to think of widgets as canvases that you will draw and paint patterns and colors on. While the Qt Namespace has the Qt.GlobalColor enum with some standard colors, we'll create a few colors of our own in initializeUI().

You'll probably also notice that there is no setUpMainWindow() method or any other method calls for drawing. That is because the event handler paintEvent() will take care of all of the drawing in the window.

The paintEvent() Event Handler

For general purposes, painting is handled inside the paintEvent() function. Let's look at an example of how to set up QPainter in the following code to draw a simple line:

```
def paintEvent(self, event):
    painter = QPainter() # Construct the painter object
    painter.begin(self)
    painter.drawLine(260, 20, 260, 180)
    painter.end()
```

Drawing occurs between the begin() and end() methods on the paint device, referenced by self. The drawing is handled in between these two methods. Using begin() and end() is not required. You could construct a painter that takes as a parameter the paint device. However, begin() and end() can be used to catch any errors should the painter fail.

Listing 11-2 creates the paintEvent() event handler for MainWindow.

Listing 11-2. Code for the paintEvent() event handler in the QPainter example

```
# paint_basics.py
    def paintEvent(self, event):
        """Reimplement event handler to create a QPainter
        object that is used throughout the example."""
        painter = QPainter()
        painter.begin(self)
        # Use antialiasing to smooth curved edges
        painter.setRenderHint(
            QPainter.RenderHint.Antialiasing)

        self.drawPoints(painter)
        self.drawDiffLines(painter)
        self.drawText(painter)
        self.drawRectangles(painter)
```

```
self.drawPolygons(painter)
self.drawRoundedRects(painter)
self.drawCurves(painter)
self.drawCircles(painter)
self.drawGradients(painter)

painter.end()
```

Other methods can also be called during the paint event. Since only one painter is allowed at a time, we call different methods that all take the painter object as an argument in Listing 11-2.

One of the settings that we can change in QPainter is the rendering quality using render hints. QPainter.RenderHint.Antialiasing creates smoother-looking curved edges.

The QColor, QPen, and QBrush Classes

Some of the settings that can be modified include the color, width, and styles used to draw lines and shapes. The **QColor** class provides access to different color schemes, for example, RGB, HSV, and CMYK values. Colors can be specified by using either RGB hexadecimal strings, "#112233"; predefined color names, such as Qt.GlobalColor.blue or Qt.GlobalColor.darkBlue; or RGB values, (233, 12, 43). QColor also includes an alpha channel used for giving colors transparency, where 0 is completely transparent and 255 is completely opaque.

QPen is used for drawing lines and the outlines of shapes. The following line creates a black pen with a width of 2 pixels that draws dashed lines:

```
pen = QPen(QColor("#000000"), 2, Qt.PenStyle.DashLine)
painter.setPen(pen)
```

The default style is Qt.PenStyle.SolidLine.

QBrush defines how to paint, or rather fill in, shapes. Brushes can have a color, a pattern, a gradient, or a texture. A magenta brush with the Dense5Pattern style is created in the following block:

```
brush = QBrush(Qt.darkMagenta,
    Qt.BrushStyle.Dense5Pattern)
painter.setBrush(brush)
```

The default style is Qt.BrushStyle.SolidPattern.

If you wish to create multiple lines or shapes with different pens and brushes, make sure to call setPen() and/or setBrush() each time they need to be changed. Otherwise, QPainter will continue to use the pen and brush settings from the previous call.

These concepts are all demonstrated in the following sections.

Note   Calling QPainter.begin() will reset all the painter settings to default values.

Drawing Points and Lines

Let's take a look at how to draw points and lines on a widget in Listing 11-3.

Listing 11-3. Code for the drawPoints() and drawDiffLines() methods

```python
# paint_basics.py
    def drawPoints(self, painter):
        """Example of how to draw points with QPainter."""
        pen = QPen(QColor(self.black))
        for i in range(1, 9):
            pen.setWidth(i * 2)
            painter.setPen(pen)
            painter.drawPoint(i * 20, i * 20)

    def drawDiffLines(self, painter):
        """Examples of how to draw lines with QPainter."""
        pen = QPen(QColor(self.black), 2)

        painter.setPen(pen)
        painter.drawLine(230, 20, 230, 180)

        pen.setStyle(Qt.PenStyle.DashLine)
        painter.setPen(pen)
        painter.drawLine(260, 20, 260, 180)
```

```
pen.setStyle(Qt.PenStyle.DotLine)
painter.setPen(pen)
painter.drawLine(290, 20, 290, 180)

pen.setStyle(Qt.PenStyle.DashDotLine)
painter.setPen(pen)
painter.drawLine(320, 20, 320, 180)

# Change the color and thickness of the pen
blue_pen = QPen(QColor(self.blue), 4)

painter.setPen(blue_pen)
painter.drawLine(350, 20, 350, 180)

blue_pen.setStyle(Qt.PenStyle.DashDotDotLine)
painter.setPen(blue_pen)
painter.drawLine(380, 20, 380, 180)
```

The drawPoint() method can be used to draw single pixels. By changing the width of the pen, you can draw wider points. The x and y values can either be explicitly defined or specified with QPoint. A simpler example for drawing a single point of width 3 pixels at point (10, 15) is shown in the following code:

```
pen.setWidth(3)
painter.setPen(pen)
painter.drawPoint(10, 15)
```

Note   The drawPoint() method and other methods are specified using integer values. Some of the drawing methods allow you to also use floating-point values. Rather than importing the QPoint and QRect classes, you would use QPointF and QRectF.

The results of drawPoints() and drawDiffLines() are shown in Figure 11-2.

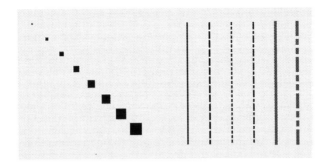

Figure 11-2. *Example of points and lines drawn using QPainter*

For drawing lines, there are the drawLine() and drawLines() methods. Each of the lines shown in Figure 11-2 displays different styles or colors. Lines are created by specifying a set of points, namely, the starting x1 and y1 values and the ending x2 and y2 values. This is demonstrated in the following code:

```
pen.setStyle(Qt.DashLine) # Specify a style
painter.setPen(pen) # Set the pen
painter.drawLine(260, 20, 260, 180) # x1, y1, x2, y2
```

Drawing Text

The drawText() method in Listing 11-4 is used to draw text on the paint device, and we can make use of setFont() to apply different font settings.

Listing 11-4. Code for the drawText() method

```
# paint_basics.py
    def drawText(self, painter):
        """Example of how to draw text with QPainter."""
        text = "Don't look behind you."

        pen = QPen(QColor(self.red))
        painter.setFont(QFont("Helvetica", 15))
        painter.setPen(pen)
        painter.drawText(420, 110, text)
```

The text is drawn by first specifying the top-left coordinates on the paint device (think of text as being placed inside of a rectangle). This is the simplest way to draw text. For multiple lines or for wrapping text, use a QRect object (a rectangle) to contain the text. The results of drawing text are shown in Figure 11-3.

Figure 11-3. *A simple example of drawing text with QPainter*

Drawing Two-Dimensional Shapes

There are a few different ways to draw quadrilaterals using the drawRect() method. For this example, we will specify the top-left corner's coordinates followed by the width and height of the shape.

```
painter.drawRect(120, 220, 80, 80)
```

For each of the squares shown in the top-left corner of Figure 11-4, we begin by setting the pen and brush values before calling drawRect() to draw the shape. The first shape has a black pen with no brush; the second calls setBrush() to fill in the square. The next shape uses a red pen with a green brush. Finally, the last square shows an example of how to set the transparency of the pen object's color to 100.

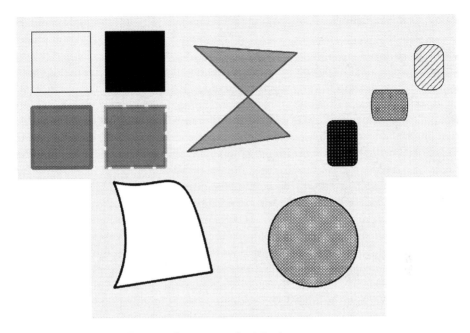

Figure 11-4. *Different shapes drawn with QPainter*

These rectangles are drawn using the `drawRectangles()` method in Listing 11-5.

Listing 11-5. Code for the drawRectangles() method

```
# paint_basics.py
    def drawRectangles(self, painter):
        """Examples of how to draw rectangles with
        QPainter."""
        pen = QPen(QColor(self.black))
        brush = QBrush(QColor(self.black))

        painter.setPen(pen)
        painter.drawRect(20, 220, 80, 80)

        painter.setPen(pen)
        painter.setBrush(brush)
        painter.drawRect(120, 220, 80, 80)

        red_pen = QPen(QColor(self.red), 5)
        green_brush = QBrush(QColor(self.green))
```

```
painter.setPen(red_pen)
painter.setBrush(green_brush)
painter.drawRect(20, 320, 80, 80)

# Demonstrate how to change the alpha channel
# to include transparency
blue_pen = QPen(QColor(32, 85, 230, 100), 5)
blue_pen.setStyle(Qt.PenStyle.DashLine)
painter.setPen(blue_pen)
painter.setBrush(green_brush)
painter.drawRect(120, 320, 80, 80)
```

To draw irregular polygons, the QPolygon class can be used by specifying the point coordinates of each corner. This is handled in Listing 11-6. The order that the points are passed to the QPolygon object is the order in which they are drawn. The polygon object is then drawn using the QPainter method drawPolygon(). The polygon can be seen in the middle of the top row in Figure 11-4.

Listing 11-6. Code for the drawPolygons() method

```
# paint_basics.py
    def drawPolygons(self, painter):
        """Example of how to draw polygons with QPainter."""
        pen = QPen(QColor(self.blue), 2)
        brush = QBrush(QColor(self.orange))

        points = QPolygon([QPoint(240, 240), QPoint(380, 250),
                        QPoint(230, 380), QPoint(370, 360)])

        painter.setPen(pen)
        painter.setBrush(brush)
        painter.drawPolygon(points)
```

QPainter can also draw rectangles with rounded corners. The process for drawing them is similar to drawing normal rectangles, except we need to specify the x and y radius values for the corners. Examples can be seen in Figure 11-4 in the top-right corner. Listing 11-7 shows how to create a rounded rectangle by first creating the QRect object's coordinates, followed by specifying a brush style to fill in the shape.

Listing 11-7. Code for the drawRoundedRects() method

```
# paint_basics.py
    def drawRoundedRects(self, painter):
        """Examples of how to draw rectangles with
        rounded corners with QPainter."""
        pen = QPen(QColor(self.black))
        brush = QBrush(QColor(self.black))

        rect_1 = QRect(420, 340, 40, 60)
        rect_2 = QRect(480, 300, 50, 40)
        rect_3 = QRect(540, 240, 40, 60)

        painter.setPen(pen)
        brush.setStyle(Qt.BrushStyle.Dense1Pattern)
        painter.setBrush(brush)
        painter.drawRoundedRect(rect_1, 8, 8)

        brush.setStyle(Qt.BrushStyle.Dense5Pattern)
        painter.setBrush(brush)
        painter.drawRoundedRect(rect_2, 5, 20)

        brush.setStyle(Qt.BrushStyle.BDiagPattern)
        painter.setBrush(brush)
        painter.drawRoundedRect(rect_3, 15, 15)
```

For drawing abstract shapes, we need to use **QPainterPath**. Objects composed of different components, such as lines, rectangles, and curves, are called **painter paths**. An example of a painter path can be seen in the bottom-left corner of Figure 11-4.

In the drawCurves() method in Listing 11-8, we first create a black pen and a white brush and an instance of QPainterPath. The moveTo() method moves to a position in the window without drawing any other components. We'll start drawing at this position, (30, 420).

Listing 11-8. Code for the drawCurves() method

```
# paint_basics.py
    def drawCurves(self, painter):
        """Examples of how to draw curves with
```

```
QPainterPath."""
pen = QPen(Qt.GlobalColor.black, 3)
brush = QBrush(Qt.GlobalColor.white)

tail_path = QPainterPath()
tail_path.moveTo(30, 420)
tail_path.cubicTo(30, 420, 65, 500, 30, 560)
tail_path.lineTo(163, 540)
tail_path.cubicTo(125, 360, 110, 440, 30, 420)
tail_path.closeSubpath()

painter.setPen(pen)
painter.setBrush(brush)
painter.drawPath(tail_path)
```

The cubicTo() method can be used to draw a parametric curve, also called a Bézier curve, from the starting position, (30, 420), to the ending position, (30, 560). The first two points, (30, 420) and (65, 500), in cubicTo() are used to influence how the line curves between the starting and ending points. The next components of tail_path are a line drawn with lineTo() and another curve drawn with cubicTo(). The abstract shape is closed with closeSubpath(), and the path is drawn using drawPath().

The last shape we are going to look at is the ellipse that is drawn using the QPainter method drawEllipse(). For an ellipse, we need four values, the location of the center, and two radii values for the x and y directions. If the radii values are equal, we can draw a circle like in the bottom right corner of Figure 11-4.

Listing 11-9 shows how to draw an ellipse with a QPoint as the center coordinate, followed by the x and y radius values. The shape could also be drawn by passing a QRect to the QPoint constructor.

Listing 11-9. Code for the drawCircles() method

```
# paint_basics.py
    def drawCircles(self, painter):
        """Example of how to draw ellipses with QPainter."""
        height, width = self.height(), self.width()

        center_x, center_y = (width / 2), height - 100
        radius_x, radius_y = 60, 60
```

```
pen = QPen(Qt.GlobalColor.black, 2,
    Qt.PenStyle.SolidLine)
brush = QBrush(Qt.GlobalColor.darkMagenta,
    Qt.BrushStyle.Dense5Pattern)

painter.setPen(pen)
painter.setBrush(brush)
painter.drawEllipse(QPoint(int(center_x),
    int(center_y)), radius_x, radius_y)
```

Drawing Gradients

Gradients can be used along with QBrush to fill the inside of shapes. There are three different types of gradient styles in PyQt: linear, radial, and conical. For this example, we will use the **QLinearGradient** class to interpolate colors between two start and end points. The result can be seen in Figure 11-5.

Figure 11-5. *Applying a gradient to a square*

The QLinearGradient constructor takes as arguments the area of the paint device where the gradient will occur, specified by the x1, y1, x2, y2 coordinates. An example of this is shown in Listing 11-10.

Listing 11-10. Code for the drawGradients() method

```
# paint_basics.py
    def drawGradients(self, painter):
        """Example of how to fill shapes using gradients."""
```

```
pen = QPen(QColor(self.black), 2)
gradient = QLinearGradient(450, 480, 520, 550)

gradient.setColorAt(0.0, Qt.GlobalColor.blue)
gradient.setColorAt(0.5, Qt.GlobalColor.yellow)
gradient.setColorAt(1.0, Qt.GlobalColor.cyan)

painter.setPen(pen)
painter.setBrush(QBrush(gradient))
painter.drawRect(420, 420, 160, 160)
```

We can create points to start painting and blending colors using `setColorAt()`. This method defines the position where a color starts and what color is used to fill in that area. The position values must be from `0.0` to `1.0`.

The following project combines what we have just learned about drawing in PyQt and combines it with what we know about widgets and windows to build a painting application.

Project 11.1 – Painter GUI

There are many digital art applications out there filled to the brim with tools for drawing, painting, editing, and creating your own art on the computer. With `QPainter`, you could manually code each individual line and shape one by one. However, rather than going through that painstaking process to create digital works of art, the painter GUI project lays the foundation for creating a drawing application that could pave the way for a smoother drawing process. The interface can be seen in Figure 11-6.

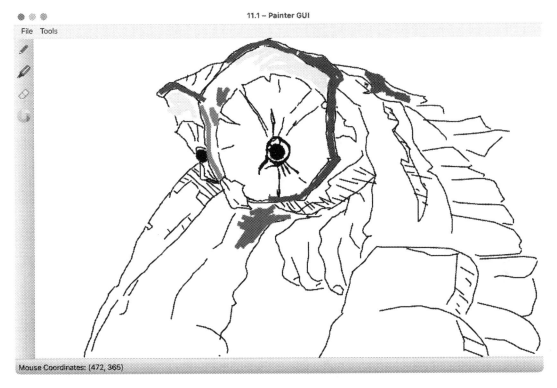

Figure 11-6. *The painter GUI with toolbar on the left side of the window and the mouse's current coordinates displayed in the status bar*

For this first project, we will be looking to combine many of the concepts that you learned in previous chapters, including menu bars, toolbars, status bars, dialog boxes, creating icons, and reimplementing event handlers, and combine them with the QPainter class. On top of it all, we will be sprinkling on a few new ideas, focusing on how to create tool tips and track the mouse's position.

Be sure to get the icons folder from GitHub for this project.

Explanation for the Painter GUI

For the painter GUI, users will be able to draw using either a pencil or a marker tool, erase, and select colors using QColorDialog. The items in the menu allow users to clear the current canvas, save their drawing, quit, and turn on or off antialiasing.

315

To get started, in Listing 11-11, let's use the `main_window_template.py` script from Chapter 5. We'll import a variety of classes from `QtWidgets`, `QtCore`, and `QtGui`. Be sure to include the **QToolTip** class so that we can create informative tool tips for items in the toolbar.

Listing 11-11. Importing PyQt classes for the painter GUI

```
# painter.py
# Import necessary modules
import os, sys
from PyQt6.QtWidgets import (QApplication, QMainWindow,
    QLabel, QToolBar, QStatusBar, QToolTip, QColorDialog,
    QFileDialog)
from PyQt6.QtCore import Qt, QSize, QPoint, QRect
from PyQt6.QtGui import (QPainter, QPixmap, QPen, QColor,
    QIcon, QFont, QAction)
```

The painter GUI allows users to draw images on the canvas area. Unlike in the previous example where painting occurred on the main widget, this example shows how to subclass `QLabel` and reimplement its painting and mouse event handlers. The handling for some of the event handlers in this application was adapted from the Qt document website.[2]

The program contains two classes: the `Canvas` class for drawing and the `MainWindow` class for creating the menu bar and toolbar.

Creating the Canvas Class

Most classes in PyQt can be subclassed in order to modify or expand existing functionalities. The word *most* is used because not all classes are intended to be subclassed, for example, convenience classes like `QListWidget` and `QTableWidget`. For this project, subclassing `QLabel` and reimplementing its `paintEvent()` event handler allow us to create a surface for drawing.

In Listing 11-12, the `Canvas` class inherits `QLabel`, meaning we can create a custom `QLabel` class. We'll also pass the class's `parent` so we have access to its status bar. A different approach could involve using `pyqtSignal` to update the status bar.

---

[2] Link: `https://doc.qt.io/qt-6/qtwidgets-widgets-scribble-example.html`

Listing 11-12. Code for the custom Canvas class

```python
# painter.py
# Creates widget to be drawn on
class Canvas(QLabel):

    def __init__(self, parent):
        super().__init__()
        self.parent = parent
        width, height = parent.width(), parent.height()

        # Create a pixmap object that will act as the canvas
        self.pixmap = QPixmap(width, height)
        self.pixmap.fill(Qt.GlobalColor.white)
        self.setPixmap(self.pixmap)

        # Keep track of the mouse for getting mouse
        # coordinates
        self.mouse_track_label = QLabel()
        self.setMouseTracking(True)

        # Initialize variables
        self.antialiasing_status = False
        self.eraser_selected = False

        self.last_mouse_pos = QPoint()
        self.drawing = False
        self.pen_color = Qt.GlobalColor.black
        self.pen_width = 2
```

Next, we'll create a pixmap object and pass it to setPixmap(). Since QPixmap can be used as a QPaintDevice, using a pixmap makes handling the drawing and displaying of pixels much simpler. Also, using QPixmap means that we can set an initial background color using fill().

Next, we need to initialize a few variables and objects.

- mouse_track_label – A label for displaying the mouse's current position

- eraser_selected – True if the eraser is selected

- antialiasing_status – True if the user has checked the menu item for using antialiasing

- last_mouse_pos – Keeps track of the mouse's last position when the left mouse button is pressed or when the mouse moves

- drawing – True if the left mouse button is pressed, indicating the user might be drawing

- pen_color, pen_width – Variables that hold the initial values of the pen and brush

Since the user will use the mouse to draw in the GUI window, we need to handle the events when the mouse button is pressed or released and when the mouse is moved. We can use setMouseTracking() to keep track of the mouse cursor and return its coordinates in mouseMoveEvent(). The returned coordinates will be displayed in the status bar.

Listing 11-13 creates the selectDrawingTool() slot that determines which drawing tool has been selected in the toolbar. The user has four choices in the toolbar, including a pencil, a marker, an eraser, and a color selector. In addition, the slot also takes care of settling the value of eraser_selected and setting the pen width or color.

Listing 11-13. Code for the selectDrawingTool() slot in the custom Canvas class

```
# painter.py
    def selectDrawingTool(self, tool):
        """Determine which tool in the toolbar has been
        selected."""
        if tool == "pencil":
            self.eraser_selected = False
            self.pen_width = 2
        elif tool == "marker":
            self.eraser_selected = False
            self.pen_width = 8
        elif tool == "eraser":
            self.eraser_selected = True
        elif tool == "color":
            self.eraser_selected = False
            color = QColorDialog.getColor()
```

```
        if color.isValid():
            self.pen_color = color
```

For Listing 11-14, if the user presses the left mouse button while the cursor is in the window, we set `drawing` equal to True and store the current value of the mouse in `last_mouse_pos`. We'll also need to check when the mouse has been released to stop drawing and update the values for `drawing` and `eraser_selected`.

Listing 11-14. Reimplementing mousePressEvent() and mouseReleaseEvent() in the Canvas class

```python
# painter.py
    def mousePressEvent(self, event):
        """Handle when the mouse is pressed."""
        if event.button() == Qt.MouseButton.LeftButton:
            self.last_mouse_pos = event.pos()
            self.drawing = True

    def mouseReleaseEvent(self, event):
        """Handle when the mouse is released.
        Check when the eraser is no longer being used."""
        if event.button() == Qt.MouseButton.LeftButton:
            self.drawing = False
        elif self.eraser_selected == True:
            self.eraser_selected = False
```

Handling Mouse Movement Events

This project displays the mouse's current x and y coordinates in the status bar. You may not want this kind of functionality, so the following code shows the basics for turning mouse tracking on and setting up `mouseMoveEvent()` to return the x and y values:

```python
    # Turn mouse tracking on
    self.setMouseTracking(True)

def mouseMoveEvent(self, event):
    mouse_pos = event.pos()
```

```
    pos_text = "Mouse Coordinates: (
        {}, {})".format(mouse_pos.x(), mouse_pos.y())
    print(pos_text)
```

Mouse move events occur whenever the mouse is moved or when a mouse button is pressed or released.

For mouseMoveEvent() used by the Canvas class in Listing 11-15, we'll call drawOnCanvas() if only the mouse's left button has been clicked. We'll pass the mouse_pos coordinates to mouse_track_label and display them in the status bar.

Listing 11-15. Reimplementing mousePressEvent() and mouseReleaseEvent() in the Canvas class

```python
# painter.py
    def mouseMoveEvent(self, event):
        """Handle mouse movements. Track the coordinates of
        the mouse in the window and display them in the status
        bar."""
        mouse_pos = event.pos()
        if (event.buttons() and Qt.MouseButton.LeftButton) \
            and self.drawing:
            self.drawOnCanvas(mouse_pos)

        self.mouse_track_label.setVisible(True)
        sb_text = f"""<p>Mouse Coordinates: ({mouse_pos.x()},
            {mouse_pos.y()})</p>"""
        self.mouse_track_label.setText(sb_text)
        self.parent.status_bar.addWidget(
            self.mouse_track_label)

    def drawOnCanvas(self, points):
        """Performs drawing on canvas."""
        painter = QPainter(self.pixmap)

        if self.antialiasing_status:
            painter.setRenderHint(
                QPainter.RenderHint.Antialiasing)
```

```
    if self.eraser_selected == False:
        pen = QPen(QColor(self.pen_color), self.pen_width)
        painter.setPen(pen)
        painter.drawLine(self.last_mouse_pos, points)

        # Update the mouse's position for next movement
        self.last_mouse_pos = points
    elif self.eraser_selected == True:
        # Use the eraser
        eraser = QRect(points.x(), points.y(), 12, 12)
        painter.eraseRect(eraser)
    self.update()
```

The actual drawing is handled in drawOnCanvas(). An instance of QPainter is created that draws on the pixmap. We also check a few conditions. These include checking for antialiasing and whether or not eraser_selected is True or False. If its value is False, the user can draw. Otherwise, they can erase.

The Canvas class also includes methods for clearing and saving the pixmap in Listing 11-16.

Listing 11-16. Methods for clearing and saving in the Canvas class

```
# painter.py
    def newCanvas(self):
        """Clears the current canvas."""
        self.pixmap.fill(Qt.GlobalColor.white)
        self.update()

    def saveFile(self):
        """Save a .png image file of current pixmap area."""
        file_format = "png"
        default_name = os.path.curdir + "/untitled." + \
            file_format
        file_name, _ = QFileDialog.getSaveFileName(
            self, "Save As",
            default_name, "PNG Format (*.png)")

        if file_name:
            self.pixmap.save(file_name, file_format)
```

For saving the file, we'll open the current directory and display a default name in a QFileDialog. The QPixmap method save() is used to save the image.

The reimplementation of the paintEvent() in Listing 11-17 creates a painter for the canvas area and draws the pixmap using drawPixmap(). By first drawing on a QPixmap in the drawOnCanvas() method and then copying the QPixmap onto the screen in the paintEvent(), we can ensure that our drawing won't be lost if the window is minimized.

Listing 11-17. Code for the paintEvent() event handler in the Canvas class

```
# painter.py
    def paintEvent(self, event):
        """Create QPainter object.
        This is to prevent the chance of the painting being
        lost if the user changes windows."""
        painter = QPainter(self)

        target_rect = QRect()
        target_rect = event.rect()
        painter.drawPixmap(target_rect,
            self.pixmap, target_rect)
        painter.end()
```

That completes the Canvas class. Let's move onto creating the MainWindow class.

Creating the Painter GUI's MainWindow Class

The MainWindow class in Listings 11-18 to 11-22 creates the main menu, toolbar, and tool tips for each of the buttons in the toolbar as well as an instance of the Canvas class. The base of the MainWindow class is set up in Listing 11-18.

Listing 11-18. Code for painter GUI's MainWindow class

```
# painter.py
class MainWindow(QMainWindow):

    def __init__(self):
        super().__init__()
        self.initializeUI()
```

```python
    def initializeUI(self):
        """Set up the application's GUI."""
        self.setMinimumSize(900, 600)
        self.setWindowTitle("11.1 - Painter GUI")
        # Set a font style used by all tool tips
        QToolTip.setFont(QFont("Helvetica", 12))

        self.setUpMainWindow()
        self.createActions()
        self.createMenu()
        self.createToolbar()
        self.show()

if __name__ == '__main__':
    app = QApplication(sys.argv)
    app.setAttribute(
        Qt.ApplicationAttribute.AA_DontShowIconsInMenus, True)
    window = MainWindow()
    sys.exit(app.exec())
```

The application's central widget is a single Canvas object in Listing 11-19.

Listing 11-19. Code for painter GUI's setUpMainWindow() method

```python
# painter.py
    def setUpMainWindow(self):
        """Create the canvas object that inherits from
        QLabel."""
        self.canvas = Canvas(self)
        self.setCentralWidget(self.canvas)
```

Listing 11-20 builds the actions and menus located in the GUI's menu bar.

Listing 11-20. Code for painter GUI's createActions() and createMenu() methods

```python
# painter.py
    def createActions(self):
        """Create the application's menu actions."""
```

```python
        # Create actions for File menu
        self.new_act = QAction("New Canvas")
        self.new_act.setShortcut("Ctrl+N")
        self.new_act.triggered.connect(self.canvas.newCanvas)

        self.save_file_act = QAction("Save File")
        self.save_file_act.setShortcut("Ctrl+S")
        self.save_file_act.triggered.connect(
            self.canvas.saveFile)

        self.quit_act = QAction("Quit")
        self.quit_act.setShortcut("Ctrl+Q")
        self.quit_act.triggered.connect(self.close)

        # Create actions for Tool menu
        self.anti_al_act = QAction(
            "AntiAliasing", checkable=True)
        self.anti_al_act.triggered.connect(
            self.turnAntialiasingOn)

    def createMenu(self):
        """Create the application's menu bar."""
        self.menuBar().setNativeMenuBar(False)

        # Create File menu and add actions
        file_menu = self.menuBar().addMenu("File")
        file_menu.addAction(self.new_act)
        file_menu.addAction(self.save_file_act)
        file_menu.addSeparator()
        file_menu.addAction(self.quit_act)

        # Create Tools menu and add actions
        file_menu = self.menuBar().addMenu("Tools")
        file_menu.addAction(self.anti_al_act)

        self.status_bar = QStatusBar()
        self.setStatusBar(self.status_bar)
```

The File menu in createMenu() contains actions for clearing the canvas, saving the image, and quitting the application. The Tools menu contains a checkable menu item that turns antialiasing on or off.

The createToolbar() method creates the actions and icons for the drawing tools in the application's toolbar. If a button is pressed, it emits the triggered signal that is connected to the Canvas class's selectDrawingTool() slot. Using a lambda function, we can pass additional information to the slot. For each action, we'll pass a string to selectDrawingTool().

Listing 11-21. Code for painter GUI's createToolbar() method

```
# painter.py
    def createToolbar(self):
        """Create the application's toolbar that contains
        painting tools."""
        tool_bar = QToolBar("Painting Toolbar")
        tool_bar.setIconSize(QSize(24, 24))
        # Set orientation of toolbar to the left side
        self.addToolBar(Qt.ToolBarArea.LeftToolBarArea,
            tool_bar)
        tool_bar.setMovable(False)

        # Create actions and tooltips and add them to the
        # toolbar
        pencil_act = QAction(QIcon("icons/pencil.png"),
            "Pencil", tool_bar)
        pencil_act.setToolTip("This is the <b>Pencil</b>.")
        pencil_act.triggered.connect(
            lambda: self.canvas.selectDrawingTool("pencil"))

        marker_act = QAction(QIcon("icons/marker.png"),
            "Marker", tool_bar)
        marker_act.setToolTip("This is the <b>Marker</b>.")
        marker_act.triggered.connect(
            lambda: self.canvas.selectDrawingTool("marker"))

        eraser_act = QAction(QIcon("icons/eraser.png"),
            "Eraser", tool_bar)
```

```
        eraser_act.setToolTip(
            "Use the <b>Eraser</b> to make it all disappear.")
        eraser_act.triggered.connect(
            lambda: self.canvas.selectDrawingTool("eraser"))

        color_act = QAction(QIcon("icons/colors.png"),
            "Colors", tool_bar)
        color_act.setToolTip(
            "Choose a <b>Color</b> from the Color dialog.")
        color_act.triggered.connect(
            lambda: self.canvas.selectDrawingTool("color"))

        tool_bar.addAction(pencil_act)
        tool_bar.addAction(marker_act)
        tool_bar.addAction(eraser_act)
        tool_bar.addAction(color_act)
```

Creating tool tips is covered in the upcoming subsection, "Creating Tool Tips for Widgets."

The turnAntialiasingOn() slot in Listing 11-22 updates the Canvas class's variable, antialiasing_status. The reimplemented leaveEvent() handles if the mouse cursor moves outside the main window and sets the mouse_track_label's visibility to False.

Listing 11-22. Additional methods used in the painter GUI's MainWindow class

```
# painter.py
    def turnAntialiasingOn(self, state):
        """Turn antialiasing on or off."""
        if state:
            self.canvas.antialiasing_status = True
        else:
            self.canvas.antialiasing_status = False

    def leaveEvent(self, event):
        """QEvent class that is called when mouse leaves
        screen's space. Hide mouse coordinates in status
        bar if mouse leaves the window."""
        self.canvas.mouse_track_label.setVisible(False)
```

Creating Tool Tips for Widgets

A user may often find themselves wondering what a widget or action in a menu or toolbar actually does in an application. Perhaps, additional information is needed to help the user understand how to interact with a tool.

Tool tips are useful little bits of text that can be displayed to inform someone of a widget's function. Tools tips can be applied to any widget by using the setToolTip() method. Tips can display rich text formatted strings as shown in the sample of code from Listing 11-21 and in Figure 11-7.

```
eraser_act.setToolTip(
    "Use the <b>Eraser</b> to make it all disappear.")
```

Figure 11-7. *The tool tip that is displayed when the user hovers over the eraser button*

The font style and appearance of a tool tip can be adapted to fit your preferences.

In the upcoming sections, we'll explore how to animate widgets and other objects in graphical interfaces.

Animating Scenes with QPropertyAnimation

The following project serves as an introduction to Qt's Graphics View Framework and the QAnimationProperty class. With the framework, applications can be created that allow users to interact with the items in the window.

A Graphics View is comprised of three components:

1. A **scene** created from the **QGraphicsScene** class. The scene creates the surface for managing 2D graphical items and must be created along with a view to visualize a scene.

2. **QGraphicsView** provides the **view** widget for visualizing the elements of a scene, creating a scroll area that allows the user to navigate in the scene.

3. **Items** in the scene are based on the **QGraphicsItem** class. Users can interact with graphical items through mouse and key events and drag and drop. Items also support collision detection.

QAnimationProperty is used to animate the properties of widgets and items. Animations in GUIs can be used for animating widgets. For example, you could animate a button that grows, shrinks, or rotates, or text that smoothly moves around in the window, or create widgets that fade in and out or change colors. QAnimationProperty only works with objects that inherit the **QObject** class. QObject is the base class for all objects created in Qt.

Qt provides a number of simple items that inherit QGraphicsItem, including basic shapes, text, and pixmaps. These items already provide support for mouse and keyboard interaction. However, QGraphicsItem does not inherit QObject. Therefore, if you want to animate a graphics item with **QPropertyAnimation**, you must first create a new class that inherits from QObject and define new properties for the item.

Figure 11-8 shows an example of the scene we are going to create in this project.

Figure 11-8. *A scene with a car and tree objects that move in the window*

Before beginning, make sure that you have downloaded the images folder from the GitHub repository.

Explanation for Animating Scenes

In the following application, you will find out how to create new properties for items using **pyqtProperty**, learn how to animate objects using the QPropertyAnimation class, and create a Qt Graphics View for displaying the items and animations.

Since we are going to create a Graphics Scene, we need to import QGraphicsScene, QGraphicsView, and one of the QGraphicsItem classes in Listing 11-23. For this program, we import **QGraphicsPixmapItem** since we will be working with pixmaps. While we can use QPropertyAnimation to animate the properties of widgets, some classes do not have access to some Qt properties. For example, there is no method for changing the color of QLabel text. In those situations, new Qt properties can be made using pyqtProperty. We'll explore this topic more in the "Introduction to Animating Widgets" section.

Listing 11-23. Importing classes for the animation example

```
# animation.py
# Import necessary modules
import sys
from PyQt6.QtWidgets import (QApplication, QGraphicsView,
    QGraphicsScene, QGraphicsPixmapItem)
from PyQt6.QtCore import (QObject, QPointF, QRectF,
    QPropertyAnimation, pyqtProperty)
from PyQt6.QtGui import QPixmap
```

Also, we won't need to import `QMainWindow` or `QWidget` to create the main window since `QGraphicsView` will act as the window for presenting the animation.

`QObject` does not have a position property. Therefore, we'll need to define one with `pyqtProperty` in the `Objects` class in Listing 11-24.

Listing 11-24. Creating the Objects class that inherits QObject

```
# animation.py
# Create Objects class that defines the position property of
# instances of the class using pyqtProperty.
class Objects(QObject):

    def __init__(self, image_path):
        super().__init__()

        item_pixmap = QPixmap(image_path)
        resize_item = item_pixmap.scaledToWidth(150)
        self.item = QGraphicsPixmapItem(resize_item)

    def _set_position(self, position):
        self.item.setPos(position)

    position = pyqtProperty(QPointF, fset=_set_position)
```

`QGraphicsPixmapItem` creates a graphics item from pixmap that can be added into a `QGraphicsScene`. We create a `position` property that allows us to set and update the position of the object using `fset`. The `_set_position()` parameter passes the position to the QGraphicsItem.setPos() method, setting the position of the item as the coordinates specified by QPointF. Underscores in the front of variable, method, or class names are used to denote private instances.

The goal of this project is to animate two items, a car and a tree, in a QGraphicsScene. The code in Listing 11-25 is similar to GUI applications we've made before. However, instead of QWidget, we'll use QGraphicsView to present the objects in the window.

Listing 11-25. Creating the AnimationScene class for visualizing the animations

```python
# animation.py
class AnimationScene(QGraphicsView):

    def __init__(self):
        super().__init__()
        self.initializeView()

    def initializeView(self):
        """Initialize the graphics view and display its
        contents to the screen."""
        self.setMaximumSize(700, 450)
        self.setWindowTitle("Animation Example")

        self.createObjects()
        self.createScene()
        self.show()

if __name__ == '__main__':
    app = QApplication(sys.argv)
    window = AnimationScene()
    sys.exit(app.exec())
```

The createObjects() method is used to create objects, and createScene() will set up the scene.

Let's first create the objects and the animations that will be placed into the scene. For this scene, the two items will move at the same time. Qt provides other classes for handling groups of animations, but for Listing 11-26, QPropertyAnimation and the animations list are used to keep track of the multiple animations.

Listing 11-26. Code for the createObjects() method in the AnimationScene class

```python
# animation.py
    def createObjects(self):
        """Create instances of the Objects class, and set
        up the object animations."""
        # List that holds all of the animations.
        animations = []

        # Create the car object and car animation.
        self.car = Objects("images/car.png")

        self.car_anim = QPropertyAnimation(self.car,
            b"position")
        self.car_anim.setDuration(6000)

        self.car_anim.setStartValue(QPointF(-50, 350))
        self.car_anim.setKeyValueAt(0.3, QPointF(150, 350))
        self.car_anim.setKeyValueAt(0.6, QPointF(170, 350))
        self.car_anim.setEndValue(QPointF(750, 350))

        # Create the tree object and tree animation.
        self.tree = Objects("images/trees.png")

        self.tree_anim = QPropertyAnimation(self.tree,
            b"position")
        self.tree_anim.setDuration(6000)

        self.tree_anim.setStartValue(QPointF(750, 150))
        self.tree_anim.setKeyValueAt(0.3, QPointF(170, 150))
        self.tree_anim.setKeyValueAt(0.6, QPointF(150, 150))
        self.tree_anim.setEndValue(QPointF(-150, 150))

        # Add animations to the animations list, and start the
        # animations once the program begins running.
        animations.append(self.car_anim)
        animations.append(self.tree_anim)

        for anim in animations:
            anim.start()
```

We'll create the car item as an instance of the Objects class and pass car and the position setter to QPropertyAnimation. QPropertyAnimation will update the value of position so that the car moves across the scene. To animate items, use setDuration() to set the amount of time the object moves in milliseconds and specify start and end values of the property with setStartValue() and setEndValue(). The animation for the car is six seconds and starts off-screen going from the left side to the right. The tree is set up in a similar manner, but traveling in the opposite direction.

The setKeyValueAt() method allows us to create key frames at the given steps with the specified QPointF values. Using the key frames, the car and tree will appear to slow down as they pass in the scene. The start() method begins the animation.

Setting up a scene is simple. Create an instance of the scene, set the scene's size, add objects and their animations using addItem(), and then call setScene(). This is handled in Listing 11-27.

Listing 11-27. Code for the createScene() method in the AnimationScene class

```python
# animation.py
    def createScene(self):
        """Create the graphics scene and add Objects instances
        to the scene."""
        self.scene = QGraphicsScene(self)
        self.scene.setSceneRect(0, 0, 700, 450)
        self.scene.addItem(self.car.item)
        self.scene.addItem(self.tree.item)
        self.setScene(self.scene)

    def drawBackground(self, painter, rect):
        """Reimplement QGraphicsView's drawBackground()
        method."""
        scene_rect = self.scene.sceneRect()

        background = QPixmap("images/highway.jpg")
        bg_rectf = QRectF(background.rect())
        painter.drawPixmap(scene_rect, background, bg_rectf)
```

Finally, a scene can be given a background using QBrush. If you want to use a background image, you will need to reimplement the QGraphicView class's drawBackground() method as demonstrated in Listing 11-27.

Introduction to Animating Widgets

We've experienced using widgets and setting their parameters. But what if you were also able to animate the properties, such as size, color, text, and position, of widgets? With the QPropertyAnimation class, we are able to animate Qt properties, such as geometry, size, and text. These properties refer to the getter methods found within each class.

For this introductory example, we'll take a look at how to animate the size of QPushButton and the color of the text of QCheckBox. While size is a built-in property of all PyQt widgets, color is not. For QCheckBox, we'll see how to use pyqtProperty to create a new property.

In Figure 11-9, you'll notice two widgets. When the button is pressed in the left screenshot, its size will grow and shrink. The button will then become disabled, and the QCheckBox widget's text will flash red. When the check box is checked, the state of the window will return back to normal.

Figure 11-9. *Animated widgets that use signals and slots to mutually change states*

The following list contains a few useful methods from **QPropertyAnimation**:

- start() – Starts the animation
- stop() – Stops the animation
- setStartValue(value) – Sets the starting value of the animation
- setEndValue(value) – Sets the ending value of the animation
- setDuration(int) – Sets the duration of the animation (in milliseconds)

- setKeyValueAt(step, value) – Creates a key frame at the given step (from 0.0 to 1.0) with the given value

- setLoopCount(int) – Sets the number of times the animation is repeated; use -1 for infinite times

Many of these methods are inherited from **QVariantAnimation**, one of the base classes for animation classes.

Explanation for Animating Widgets

For this application, we can use the basic_window.py script from Chapter 1 and import a variety of new classes. **QAbstractAnimation** is the base class for all animation classes. **QEasingCurve** is used to define and control the smoothness of an animation.

Two types of classes also exist for grouping multiple animations together:

- **QParallelAnimationGroup** – Runs animations in parallel

- **QSequentialAnimationGroup** – Runs animations as a sequence

For this program, we'll import QSequentialAnimationGroup in Listing 11-28.

Listing 11-28. Code for imports and custom QCheckBox in the animating widgets example

```
# animate_widgets.py
# Import necessary modules
import sys
from PyQt6.QtWidgets import (QApplication, QWidget,
    QPushButton, QCheckBox, QVBoxLayout)
from PyQt6.QtCore import (QAbstractAnimation, QRect, QSize,
    QPoint, QEasingCurve, pyqtProperty,
    QPropertyAnimation, QSequentialAnimationGroup)
from PyQt6.QtGui import QColor

class AnimatedCheckbox(QCheckBox):

    def __init__(self, text):
        """Custom QCheckBox with animated text."""
        super().__init__(text)
```

```
    def _set_color(self, color):
        """Method for the color property of the text using
        style sheets."""
        self.setStyleSheet(
            f"""color: rgb({color.red()}, {color.green()},
                {color.blue()})""")

    color = pyqtProperty(QColor, fset=_set_color)
```

While QCheckBox displays text and has a text property, the class does not have property
for changing the text's color. Therefore, let's create a private method, _set_color(), where
we define the property we want to change. In the method, we can use style sheets to update
the color of the text. The pyqtProperty, color, is the name of our new property.

Listing 11-29 sets up the MainWindow class and builds the setUpMainWindow()
method. The main window consists of two widgets, a check box and a push button,
arranged in a QVBoxLayout.

Listing 11-29. Setting up the MainWindow class and the setUpMainWindow()
method in the animating widgets example

```
# animate_widgets.py
class MainWindow(QWidget):

    def __init__(self):
        super().__init__()
        self.initializeUI()

    def initializeUI(self):
        """Set up the application's GUI."""
        self.setFixedSize(240, 120)
        self.setWindowTitle("Animating Widgets")

        self.setUpMainWindow()
        self.show()

    def setUpMainWindow(self):
        """Create and arrange widgets in the main window."""
        self.update_cb = AnimatedCheckbox("Normal")
        self.update_cb.stateChanged.connect(self.stopFlashing)
```

```python
        self.status_button = QPushButton("Status Changed")
        self.status_button.clicked.connect(
            self.startAnimations)

        # Create animation instances
        self.cb_anim = QPropertyAnimation(
            self.update_cb, b"color")
        self.button_anim = QPropertyAnimation(
            self.status_button, b"geometry")
        self.seq_group = QSequentialAnimationGroup()

        main_v_box = QVBoxLayout()
        main_v_box.addWidget(self.update_cb)
        main_v_box.addWidget(self.status_button)
        self.setLayout(main_v_box)

if __name__ == '__main__':
    app = QApplication(sys.argv)
    window = MainWindow()
    sys.exit(app.exec())
```

The update_cb object displays Normal in the beginning. Its stateChanged signal is connected to the stopFlashing() slot that we'll code in Listing 11-31.

For status_button, clicking the button will start the different animations. There are two property animation objects and one group to manage the animations instantiated in setUpMainWindow().

The cb_anim object animates the color of update_cb, while button_anim takes care of the geometry property for status_button. We'll use geometry to get the x and y coordinates as well as the size of the button. Last, seq_group will manage the animations and play them in order.

A widget's geometry can be collected using the geometry() method. The start_geometry variable in Listing 11-30 holds the initial QPoint and QSize values of status_button. (The geometry() getter actually returns a QRect object, and a rectangle can be broken down into its top-left-corner position and size values.)

Listing 11-30. Code for the startAnimations() slot in the animating widgets example

```python
# animate_widgets.py
    def startAnimations(self):
        """Play the animations and update the states of the
        widgets."""
        # Collect the button's initial geometry values.
        # start_geometry is a QRect object
        start_geometry = self.status_button.geometry()

        # Set up the button's animation for changing its size
        self.button_anim.setEasingCurve(
            QEasingCurve.Type.InOutSine)
        self.button_anim.setDuration(1000)
        self.button_anim.setStartValue(start_geometry)
        self.button_anim.setKeyValueAt(0.5, QRect(QPoint(
            start_geometry.x() - 4, start_geometry.y() - 4),
            QSize(start_geometry.width() + 8,
                start_geometry.height() + 8)))
        self.button_anim.setEndValue(start_geometry)

        # Untoggle the check box if it is toggled
        if self.update_cb.isChecked():
            self.update_cb.toggle()
        self.update_cb.setText("RED ALERT!")

        # Set up the check box's animation for changing its
        # color
        self.cb_anim.setDuration(500)
        self.cb_anim.setLoopCount(-1)
        self.cb_anim.setStartValue(QColor(0, 0, 0))
        self.cb_anim.setEndValue(QColor(255, 0, 0))

        # Start the sequential sequence
        self.seq_group.addAnimation(self.button_anim)
        self.seq_group.addAnimation(self.cb_anim)
        self.seq_group.start()
```

```
# Finally, disable the button
self.status_button.setEnabled(False)
```

With the geometry of the button acquired, we'll specify a few parameters for its animation. **Easing curves** in animation allow smoother visual transitions from one animation to another. QEasingCurve is used along the start, stop, or key frame values to control the transition of the animation. Here, we'll use the QEasingCurve.Type enum to specify an easing curve. The flag InOutSine uses a sinusoidal curve for the button's animation. For a full list of easing curves, take a look at https://doc.qt.io/qt-6/qeasingcurve.html#Type-enum.

The animation will occur for one second. The first argument to setKeyValue() is used to specify a key frame, which is the half-way point for this animation. The QRect object passed to setKeyValue() is used to increase the size of status_button. This will help to keep the button center during the animation. After half a second, the widget will shrink back to its original geometry.

For a single animation, the next step would be to call start(). However, since cb_anim will follow the button's animation, the QSequentialAnimationGroup instance will handle starting the animations.

A few checks are also performed to update the state and text of the QCheckBox. Using cb_anim and a loop count of -1, the check box's text will continue to flash red until the user checks the box. We'll disable the button so the user is forced to do so.

When the check box is finally checked, the stateChanged signal will trigger the stopFlashing() slot in Listing 11-31.

Listing 11-31. Code for the stopFlashing() slot and closeEvent() in the animating widgets example

```
# animate_widgets.py
    def stopFlashing(self):
        """Stop animations when the check box is checked."""
        self.seq_group.stop()
        # Update widgets
        self.update_cb.setText("Normal")
        self.update_cb.setStyleSheet("color: rgb(0, 0, 0)")
        self.status_button.setEnabled(True)
```

```
def closeEvent(self, event):
    """Ensure that animations are stopped when closing
    the window to avoid errors."""
    running = QAbstractAnimation.State.Running
    if self.seq_group.state == running:
        self.seq_group.stop()
    event.accept()
```

The seq_group object will first stop both animations. Next, the values and states of the widgets are returned back to normal. Finally, the closeEvent() stops the animations if they are still running.

While this is only a simple example, the use of painting and animations can be used to draw attention, create engaging interfaces, and clearly and effectively communicate purpose better than any standard or static GUI can.

Summary

PyQt6's graphics and painting system is an extensive topic that could be an entire book by itself. The QPainter class is important for performing the painting on widgets and on other paint devices. QPainter works together with the QPaintEngine and QPaintDevice classes to provide the tools you need for creating two-dimensional drawing applications.

We have taken a look at some of the QPainter class's functions for drawing lines and primitive and abstract shapes. Together with QPen, QBrush, and QColor, QPainter is able to create some rather beautiful digital images. To materialize this concept, we created a simple painting application. Hopefully, you'll improve that application and add even more drawing features.

We also saw how to create properties for objects made from the QObject class and then animate those objects in the Qt Graphics View Framework. It is not covered in this book, but you could use the Graphics View to create a GUI with items that are interactive. We also used QPropertyAnimation to animate widget properties.

In Chapter 12, we'll take a look at how to create custom widgets in PyQt.

CHAPTER 12

Creating Custom Widgets

While most development tasks can be solved with buttons, text editing widgets, and other components provided by PyQt, you may at some point find yourself in a situation where no single widget provides you with the tools or functionality that you need. You might even find yourself needing to use a widget you made in other GUIs and therefore need a way to easily import your custom-made widget into other applications. Thankfully, PyQt allows developers to build and import their own widgets for solving new and unforeseen tasks.

In this chapter, you will

- Find out about creating your own custom widgets in PyQt

- See how to apply the custom widget built in a small example GUI

- Learn about Qt's four image handling classes

- Use a new widget, `QSlider`, for selecting values in a bounded range

Let's learn about the custom widget we'll build in the following sections.

Project 12.1 – RGB Slider Custom Widget

For this chapter's project, we are going to take a look at making a custom, functional widget in PyQt. While PyQt offers a variety of widgets for building GUIs, every once in a while you may find yourself needing to design and build your own. One of the benefits of creating a customized widget is that you can either create a general widget that can be used by many different applications or make an application-specific widget that allows you to solve a specific problem.

There are quite a few techniques that you can use to create your own widgets, most of which we have already seen in previous examples.

341

- Modifying the properties of PyQt's widgets by using built-in methods, such as `setAlignment()`, `setTextColor()`, and `setRange()`

- Creating style sheets to change a widget's existing behavior and appearances

- Subclassing widgets and reimplementing event handlers, or adding properties dynamically to `QWidget` classes

- Creating composite widgets that are made up of two more types of widgets and arranged together using a layout

- Designing a completely new widget that subclasses `QWidget` and has its own unique properties and appearance

The RGB slider, shown in Figure 12-1, actually is created by combining a few of the techniques listed previously. The widget uses Qt's `QSlider` and `QSpinBox` widgets for selecting RGB values and displays the color on `QLabel` widgets. The look of the sliders is modified by using style sheets. All of the widgets are then assembled into a parent widget, which we can then import into other PyQt applications.

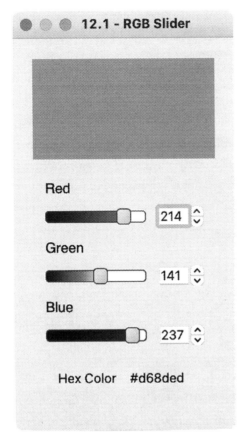

Figure 12-1. *A custom widget used to select colors using sliders and spin boxes*

Before finding out how to make the RGB slider widget, we'll need to learn a little more about some of the classes we will need to build the application.

PyQt's Image Handling Classes

In previous examples, we worked with QPixmap to handle image data. Qt actually provides four different classes for working with images, each with their own special purpose.

QPixmap is the go-to choice for displaying images on the screen. Pixmaps can be presented on a variety of widgets that can display icons, including QLabel and QPushButton. **QImage** is optimized for reading, writing, and manipulating images and is very useful if you need to directly access and modify an image's pixel data. QImage can also act as a paint device. A **paint device** (created by the QPaintDevice class) is a two-dimensional surface that can be drawn on using QPainter. It is also worth noting that QImage inherits QPaintDevice.

Conversion between QImage and QPixmap is also possible. One possibility for using the two classes together is to load an image file with QImage, manipulate the image data, and then convert the image to a pixmap before displaying it on the screen. The RGB slider widget gives an example for converting between the two classes.

QBitmap is a subclass of QPixmap and provides monochrome (1-bit depth) pixmaps. **QPicture** is a paint device that replays QPainter commands, meaning you can create a picture from whatever image format you are painting on. Pictures created with QPicture are resolution independent, appearing the same no matter what image format you use, such as png, svg, or pdf.

The RGB slider uses two types of widgets for selecting RGB values: QSpinBox, which was introduced in Chapter 4, and a new widget.

The QSlider Widget

The **QSlider** class provides a developer with a tool for selecting integer values within a bounded range. Sliders provide users with a convenient means for quickly selecting values or changing settings with only the slide of a simple handle. By default, sliders are arranged vertically (specified by Qt.Orientation.Vertical), but that can be changed by passing the flag Qt.Orientation.Horizontal to the constructor.

The following block of code demonstrates how to create an instance of QSlider, set the slider's maximum range value, and connect to the signal valueChanged that is emitted whenever the slider's value has changed.

```
slider = QSlider(Qt.Horizontal, self)
# Default values are from 0 to 99
slider.setMaximum(200)
slider.valueChanged.connect(self.printSliderValue)

def printSliderValue(self, value):
    print(value)
```

Here, the slider's maximum range is 200, and its value is printed to the shell whenever the slider's position changes.

Explanation for the RGB Slider Widget

The RGB slider is a custom widget created by combining a few of Qt's built-in widgets: QLabel, QSlider, and QSpinBox. The appearance of the sliders is adjusted using style sheets so that they give visual feedback to the user about which RGB value they are adjusting. The sliders and spin boxes are connected together so that their values are in sync and so that the user can see the integer value on the RGB scale. The RGB values are also converted to hexadecimal format and displayed on the widget.

The sliders and spin boxes can be used to either find out the RGB or hexadecimal values for a color or use the reimplemented mousePressEvent() method so that a user can click on a pixel in an image to find out the pixel's RGB value. An example of this is shown in the "RGB Slider Demo" section, where you will also see how to import the RGB slider in a demo application.

We need to import quite a few classes in Listing 12-1. The classes for working with images in PyQt are found in the QtGui module. Another class worth mentioning, **qRgb**, is actually a typedef that creates an unsigned int representing the RGB value triplet (r, g, b). A **typedef** in C++ is a keyword that is used to create a new name for a data type, in this case to represent the RGB value.

Listing 12-1. The imports for the RGB slider

```
# rgb_slider.py
# Import necessary modules
import sys
from PyQt6.QtWidgets import (QApplication, QWidget, QLabel,
    QSlider, QSpinBox, QHBoxLayout, QVBoxLayout, QGridLayout)
from PyQt6.QtGui import QImage, QPixmap, QColor, qRgb, QFont
from PyQt6.QtCore import Qt
```

The style sheet that follows in Listing 12-2 is used to change the appearance of the sliders. We want to modify their appearance so that they give the user more feedback about which RGB values are being changed. Each slider is given an ID Selector using the setObjectName() method in the setUpMainWindow() method. If no ID Selector is used in the style sheet, then that style is applied to all of the QSlider objects.

Listing 12-2. The style sheet for the RGB slider, part 1

```python
# rgb_slider.py
style_sheet = """
    QSlider:groove:horizontal{
        border: 1px solid #000000;
        background: white;
        height: 10 px;
        border-radius: 4px
    }

    QSlider#Red:sub-page:horizontal{
        background: qlineargradient(x1:1, y1:0, x2:0, y2:1,
            stop: 0 #FF4242, stop: 1 #1C1C1C);
        background: qlineargradient(x1:0, y1:1, x2:1, y2:1,
            stop: 0 #1C1C1C, stop: 1 #FF0000);
        border: 1px solid #4C4B4B;
        height: 10px;
        border-radius: 4px;
    }

    QSlider::add-page:horizontal {
        background: #FFFFFF;
        border: 1px solid #4C4B4B;
        height: 10px;
        border-radius: 4px;
    }

    QSlider::handle:horizontal {
        background: qlineargradient(x1:0, y1:0, x2:1, y2:1,
            stop: 0 #EEEEEE, stop: 1 #CCCCCC);
        border: 1px solid #4C4B4B;
        width: 13px;
        margin-top: -3px;
        margin-bottom: -3px;
        border-radius: 4px;
    }
```

```
QSlider::handle:horizontal:hover {
    background: qlineargradient(x1:0, y1:0, x2:1, y2:1,
        stop: 0 #FFFFFF, stop: 1 #DDDDDD);
    border: 1px solid #393838;
    border-radius: 4px;
}
```

The sliders use linear gradients so that users can get a visual representation of how much of the red, green, and blue colors are being used. With linear gradients, the color is interpolated from x1, y1 to x2, y2. The pseudostate horizontal is used to specify that the styles will be applied to horizontal QSlider objects.

The groove subcontrol refers to the long, rectangular part of the slider, which is solid white before moving the handle of the slider. The add-page subcontrol denotes the color of the slider parts before the handle, and sub-page denotes the color after. For the handle, the color will change whenever the mouse hovers over it.

The only changes that need to be made for the Green and Blue sliders are to the sub-page subcontrols. These changes are handled in Listing 12-3. You can also refer back to Chapter 6 for a refresher about style sheets.

Listing 12-3. The style sheet for the RGB slider, part 2

```
# rgb_slider.py
    QSlider#Green:sub-page:horizontal{
        background: qlineargradient(x1:1, y1:0, x2:0, y2:1,
            stop: 0 #FF4242, stop: 1 #1C1C1C);
        background: qlineargradient(x1:0, y1:1, x2:1, y2:1,
            stop: 0 #1C1C1C, stop: 1 #00FF00);
        border: 1px solid #4C4B4B;
        height: 10px;
        border-radius: 4px;
    }

    QSlider#Blue:sub-page:horizontal{
        background: qlineargradient(x1:1, y1:0, x2:0, y2:1,
            stop: 0 #FF4242, stop: 1 #1C1C1C);
        background: qlineargradient(x1:0, y1:1, x2:1, y2:1,
            stop: 0 #1C1C1C, stop: 1 #0000FF);
```

```
        border: 1px solid #4C4B4B;
        height: 10px;
        border-radius: 4px;
    }
"""
```

The RGBSlider class inherits QWidget in Listing 12-4. For this class, the user can pass an image and other arguments as parameters to the constructor.

Listing 12-4. Code to start building the RGBSlider class

```python
# rgb_slider.py
class RGBSlider(QWidget):

    def __init__(self, _image=None, *args, **kwargs):
        super().__init__(*args, **kwargs)
        self._image = _image
        self.initializeUI()

    def initializeUI(self):
        """Set up the application's GUI."""
        self.setMinimumSize(225, 300)
        self.setWindowTitle("12.1 - RGB Slider")

        # Store the current pixel value
        self.current_val = QColor()

        self.setUpMainWindow()
        self.show()

if __name__ == '__main__':
    app = QApplication(sys.argv)
    app.setStyleSheet(style_sheet)
    window = RGBSlider()
    sys.exit(app.exec())
```

The current_val instance variable will be used to keep track of the current RGB color value. The color, of course, will be composed by the slider and spin box values.

In setUpMainWindow() in Listing 12-5, a QImage object is created that will display the color created from the RGB values. Using the QImage method fill(), the first color that will show when the application is run is black. To display the image in the widget, first convert the QImage to a QPixmap using the QPixmap method fromImage() and pass it a QImage instance. Then use setPixmap() to set the QLabel widget's pixmap.

Listing 12-5. Code for the setUpMainWindow() method in the RGBSlider class, part 1

```
# rgb_slider.py
    def setUpMainWindow(self):
        """Create and arrange widgets in the main window."""
        # Image that will display the current color set by
        # slider/spin_box values
        self.color_display = QImage(
            100, 100, QImage.Format.Format_RGBX64)
        self.color_display.fill(Qt.GlobalColor.black)

        self.cd_label = QLabel()
        self.cd_label.setPixmap(
            QPixmap.fromImage(self.color_display))
        self.cd_label.setScaledContents(True)
```

The contents of cd_label are then scaled to fit the window's size.

Updating the Sliders and Spin Boxes

Next, we create the red, green, and blue QSlider and QSpinBox widgets in Listing 12-6. The sliders' maximum values are set to 255, since RGB values are in the range of 0–255. Each slider is also given an object name that is used to identify it in the style sheet.

Listing 12-6. Code for the setUpMainWindow() method in the RGBSlider class, part 2

```
# rgb_slider.py
        # Create RGB sliders and spin boxes
        red_label = QLabel("Red")
        red_label.setFont(QFont("Helvetica", 14))
        self.red_slider = QSlider(Qt.Orientation.Horizontal)
        self.red_slider.setObjectName("Red")
        self.red_slider.setMaximum(255)
```

```
self.red_spinbox = QSpinBox()
self.red_spinbox.setMaximum(255)

green_label = QLabel("Green")
green_label.setFont(QFont("Helvetica", 14))
self.green_slider = QSlider(Qt.Orientation.Horizontal)
self.green_slider.setObjectName("Green")
self.green_slider.setMaximum(255)

self.green_spinbox = QSpinBox()
self.green_spinbox.setMaximum(255)

blue_label = QLabel("Blue")
blue_label.setFont(QFont("Helvetica", 14))
self.blue_slider = QSlider(Qt.Orientation.Horizontal)
self.blue_slider.setObjectName("Blue")
self.blue_slider.setMaximum(255)

self.blue_spinbox = QSpinBox()
self.blue_spinbox.setMaximum(255)
```

The two labels instantiated in Listing 12-7 will display the hexadecimal value of the color. They are then arranged in a QHBoxLayout, which is set as the layout for hex_container.

Listing 12-7. Code for the setUpMainWindow() method in the RGBSlider class, part 3

```
# rgb_slider.py
        # Use the hex labels to display color values in hex
        # format
        hex_label = QLabel("Hex Color ")
        self.hex_values_label = QLabel()

        hex_h_box = QHBoxLayout()
        hex_h_box.addWidget(
            hex_label, Qt.AlignmentFlag.AlignRight)
        hex_h_box.addWidget(self.hex_values_label,
            Qt.AlignmentFlag.AlignRight)
```

```
hex_container = QWidget()
hex_container.setLayout(hex_h_box)

# Create grid layout for sliders and spin boxes
grid = QGridLayout()
grid.addWidget(
    red_label, 0, 0, Qt.AlignmentFlag.AlignLeft)
grid.addWidget(self.red_slider, 1, 0)
grid.addWidget(self.red_spinbox, 1, 1)
grid.addWidget(
    green_label, 2, 0, Qt.AlignmentFlag.AlignLeft)
grid.addWidget(self.green_slider, 3, 0)
grid.addWidget(self.green_spinbox, 3, 1)
grid.addWidget(
    blue_label, 4, 0, Qt.AlignmentFlag.AlignLeft)
grid.addWidget(self.blue_slider, 5, 0)
grid.addWidget(self.blue_spinbox, 5, 1)
grid.addWidget(hex_container, 6, 0, 1, 0)
```

From there, the sliders, spin boxes, and container for the labels are organized in a QGridLayout.

Updating the Colors

QSlider and QSpinBox can both emit the valueChanged signal. We can connect the sliders and spin boxes so that their values change relative to each other. For example, when red_slider emits a signal, it triggers the updateRedSpinBox() slot, which then updates the red_spinbox value using setValue(). A similar process happens for the red_spinbox. This process also happens for the sliders and spin boxes that control the blue and green values.

Take a look at the valueChanged signals in Listing 12-8 for a slider and its corresponding spin box and you will notice that they trigger slots that update each other.

Listing 12-8. Code for the setUpMainWindow() method in the RGBSlider class, part 4

```
# rgb_slider.py
        # The sliders and spin boxes for each color should
        # display the same values and be updated at the same
```

351

```
    # time
    self.red_slider.valueChanged.connect(
        self.updateRedSpinBox)
    self.red_spinbox.valueChanged.connect(
        self.updateRedSlider)

    self.green_slider.valueChanged.connect(
        self.updateGreenSpinBox)
    self.green_spinbox.valueChanged.connect(
        self.updateGreenSlider)

    self.blue_slider.valueChanged.connect(
        self.updateBlueSpinBox)
    self.blue_spinbox.valueChanged.connect(
        self.updateBlueSlider)

    # Create container for rgb widgets
    rgb_widgets = QWidget()
    rgb_widgets.setLayout(grid)

    main_v_box = QVBoxLayout()
    main_v_box.addWidget(self.cd_label)
    main_v_box.addWidget(rgb_widgets)

    self.setLayout(main_v_box)
```

All of the widgets along with cd_label from Listing 12-5 are contained in rgb_widgets and arranged in the main layout.

Let's take a look at the slots in Listing 12-9 for updating the widget values.

Listing 12-9. Code for the slots that update the slider and spin box values

```
# rgb_slider.py
    # The following slots update the red, green and blue
    # sliders and spin boxes
    def updateRedSpinBox(self, value):
        self.red_spinbox.setValue(value)
        self.redValue(value)
```

```
def updateRedSlider(self, value):
    self.red_slider.setValue(value)
    self.redValue(value)

def updateGreenSpinBox(self, value):
    self.green_spinbox.setValue(value)
    self.greenValue(value)

def updateGreenSlider(self, value):
    self.green_slider.setValue(value)
    self.greenValue(value)

def updateBlueSpinBox(self, value):
    self.blue_spinbox.setValue(value)
    self.blueValue(value)

def updateBlueSlider(self, value):
    self.blue_slider.setValue(value)
    self.blueValue(value)
```

When a valueChanged signal triggers a slot, it uses value to update the corresponding slider or spin box and then calls a function that will create a new color from the red, green, or blue values.

We'll take a look at one example since the others are organized in a similar manner. If the value of red_slider is changed, the updateRedSpinBox() slot will be called, and the value of red_spinbox set to value. From there, let's move to Listing 12-10 to handle the creation of new colors.

Listing 12-10. Code for methods that create and update a color

```
# rgb_slider.py
    # Create new colors based upon the changes to the RGB
    # values
    def redValue(self, value):
        new_color = qRgb(value,
            self.current_val.green(), self.current_val.blue())
        self.updateColorInfo(new_color)
```

```python
    def greenValue(self, value):
        new_color = qRgb(self.current_val.red(),
            value, self.current_val.blue())
        self.updateColorInfo(new_color)

    def blueValue(self, value):
        new_color = qRgb(self.current_val.red(),
            self.current_val.green(), value)
        self.updateColorInfo(new_color)

    def updateColorInfo(self, color):
        """Update color displayed in image and set the hex
        values accordingly."""
        self.current_val = QColor(color)
        self.color_display.fill(color)

        self.cd_label.setPixmap(QPixmap.fromImage(
            self.color_display))
        self.hex_values_label.setText(
            f"{self.current_val.name()}")
```

Continuing with red, the redValue() function creates a new qRgb color, using the new red value and the current_val's green() and blue() colors. The variable current_val is an instance of QColor. The **QColor** class has functions that we can use to access an image's RGB (or other color format) values.

The new_color is then passed to updateColorInfo(). Green and blue colors are handled in a similar fashion. Next, we have to create a QColor from the qRgb value and store it in current_val. The QImage color_display is updated with fill(), which is then converted to a QPixmap, and displayed on the cd_label.

The last thing to do is to update the hexadecimal labels using QColor.name(). (Remember that current_val is a QColor object.) This function returns the name of the color in the format "#RRGGBB".

Adding Methods to a Custom Widget

The options for methods that you could create for a custom widget are numerous. One option is to create methods that allow the user to modify the behavior or appearance of your custom widget. Another option is to use the event handlers to check for keyboard or mouse events that could be used to interact with your GUI.

The getPixelValue() method in Listing 12-11 is a reimplementation of the mousePressEvent() event handler. If an image is passed into the RGBSlider constructor, then _image is not None, and the user can click on points in the image to get their corresponding pixel values. QColor.pixel() gets a pixel's RGB values. Then, the value for current_val is updated in order to use the selected pixel's red, blue, and green values. These values are then passed back into the functions that will update the sliders, spin boxes, labels, and QImage.

Listing 12-11. Code for the getPixelValues() method

```
# rgb_slider.py
    def getPixelValues(self, event):
        """The method reimplements the mousePressEvent method.
        To use, set an widget's mousePressEvent equal to
        getPixelValues, like so:
            image_label.mousePressEvent = rgbslider.getPixelValues
        If an _image != None, then the user can select pixels
        in the images, and update the sliders to get view the color,
        and get the rgb and hex values."""
        x = int(event.position().x())
        y = int(event.position().y())

        # valid() returns true if the point selected is a valid
        # coordinate pair within the image
        if self._image.valid(x, y):
            self.current_val = QColor(self._image.pixel(x, y))

            red_val = self.current_val.red()
            green_val = self.current_val.green()
            blue_val = self.current_val.blue()

            self.updateRedSpinBox(red_val)
            self.updateRedSlider(red_val)
            self.updateGreenSpinBox(green_val)
            self.updateGreenSlider(green_val)
            self.updateBlueSpinBox(blue_val)
            self.updateBlueSlider(blue_val)
```

Go ahead and run the script now and see how it operates. Right now, the application is simply its own small GUI. Let's see how to use the custom widget class in another application to utilize the color selecting feature.

RGB Slider Demo

One reason for creating a custom widget is so that it can be used in other applications. The following program is a short example of how to import and set up the RGB slider built in Project 12.1. For this example, an image is displayed in the window alongside the RGB slider. Users can click on points within the image and see the RGB and hexadecimal values change in real time.

This short program's GUI can be seen in Figure 12-2.

Figure 12-2. *An example GUI with the custom RGB slider. Image from* `www.pixilart.com/`

Explanation for the RGB Slider Demo

Be sure to download the image from the images folder in the GitHub repository.

You can use the basic_window.py class from Chapter 1 to get your started with this program. Begin by importing a few classes, including the RGB slider and the style sheet from rgb_slider.py, in Listing 12-12.

Listing 12-12. Code that shows an example for using the RGB slider widget

```python
# rgb_demo.py
# Import necessary modules
import sys
from PyQt6.QtWidgets import (QApplication, QWidget, QLabel,
    QHBoxLayout)
from PyQt6.QtGui import QPixmap, QImage
from PyQt6.QtCore import Qt
from rgb_slider import RGBSlider, style_sheet

class MainWindow(QWidget):

    def __init__(self):
        super().__init__()
        self.initializeUI()

    def initializeUI(self):
        """Set up the application's GUI."""
        self.setMinimumSize(225, 300)
        self.setWindowTitle("12.2 - Custom Widget Example")

        # Load image
        image = QImage("images/duck_pic.png")

        # Create instance of RGB slider widget
        rgbslider = RGBSlider(image)
        image_label = QLabel()
        image_label.setAlignment(Qt.AlignmentFlag.AlignTop)
        image_label.setPixmap(QPixmap().fromImage(image))
        # Reimplement the label's mousePressEvent
        image_label.mousePressEvent = rgbslider.getPixelValues
```

```
        h_box = QHBoxLayout()
        h_box.addWidget(rgbslider)
        h_box.addWidget(image_label)
        self.setLayout(h_box)
        self.show()

if __name__ == '__main__':
    app = QApplication(sys.argv)
    app.setStyleSheet(style_sheet)
    window = MainWindow()
    sys.exit(app.exec())
```

In the MainWindow class, set up the window in initializeUI(), load an image, and create an instance of the RGB slider. The widgets are then arranged in the window.

For this application, we are still creating the image as an instance of QImage and then converting it to a QPixmap. QImage is used so that we have access to the image's pixel information.

To use the getPixelValues() method in the RGBSlider class, we'll need to reimplement the QLabel object's mouse event handler. When the user clicks on a pixel in the image, the x and y coordinates from the event are used to update the values in the RGB slider widget using the getPixelValues() method.

If you only want to use the slider to get different RGB or hexadecimal values, then the application is finished. But you could continue to add other functionalities to the RGB slider to use in your own projects.

Summary

Not every problem can be solved by the widgets that Qt provides. In situations where ingenuity is needed, PyQt is great because it allows developers to design, build, and customize their own widgets. This can be handled in a variety of ways, perhaps by building a new widget from preexisting widgets or by creating completely new widgets from scratch. From there, a new widget can be seamlessly imported into other applications.

In Chapter 13, you will find out how to create modern-looking GUIs using Qt Quick.

CHAPTER 13

Working with Qt Quick

Graphical user interfaces nowadays can be found on a multitude of devices, including desktop computers, mobile devices, and small touchscreens controlled by microcontrollers. While UIs are designed to fit the functional and technical needs of each device, the demands of these platforms have inspired The Qt Company to continue to build a set of scalable, polished, dynamic, and visually stunning tools for building user interfaces.

In this chapter, you will

- Get an overview of the `QtQuick` and `QtQml` modules and the QML programming language

- Learn how to write and run simple applications using QML and PyQt

- Find out how to build QML components and use them in other `.qml` files

- Utilize different methods for arranging `QtQuick` elements using QML

- Experiment with different QML types to create applications

- Use simple transformations to animate objects

This chapter's aim is to provide an overview of `QtQuick` and Qt's QML language. If your aim is to continue using `QtWidgets`, then this chapter may not provide information that is beneficial at this current moment in your development stage. However, for new PyQt developers, the hope is that this chapter can provide some useful ideas and insights about what the latest versions of Qt and PyQt have to offer.

© Joshua M Willman 2022
J. M. Willman, *Beginning PyQt*, https://doi.org/10.1007/978-1-4842-7999-1_13

Note   For those readers using macOS, you may have issues running the applications in this chapter if you are using the Z shell, also known as zsh. The bash shell used to be the default on macOS until recently. If you run into problems due to zsh, you can switch to the bash shell by entering `chsh -s /bin/bash/` in the command line. To switch back to zsh when you are finished, you will need to enter the command `chsh -s /bin/zsh`. Just be aware that when you do switch between shells, you will either need to install PyQt6 from PyPI or edit the paths in bash to locate PyQt6 and your other Python packages.

Outlining QtQuick and QML

While desktop applications are still a large part of Qt, a considerable amount of work has gone into creating a toolkit in Qt 6 that resembles the more fluid, dynamic, and animated UIs of mobile and embedded devices. As you follow along in this chapter (or explore the links within this chapter that lead to even more information about creating GUIs with `QtQuick`), you'll notice a number of similarities with `QtWidgets`. You'll notice visual elements such as buttons and combo boxes. You'll see windows, dialogs, and menus. Layouts, among other methods, are also used in `QtQuick` to arrange elements. We'll even take a brief look at animating objects.

What then is `QtQuick`? Before answering that question, let's first try and clear up some confusion that might occur early on. To build applications, we'll need to clarify three important terms: QML, `QtQuick`, and `QtQml`.

When using `QtQuick`, you'll also hear about the **Qt Modeling Language** (**QML**). QML is the declarative, markup language specifically designed for user interfaces that `QtQuick` is built upon. The language is used to create highly fluid and dynamic interfaces and visual effects similar to those seen on mobile devices. A QML file, also referred to as a **document**,[1] is comprised of a declarative, hierarchical tree of elements and has support for various JavaScript expressions.[2] A QML document can either create a window for an

---

[1] More information about QML documents is found at `https://doc.qt.io/qt-6/qtqml-documents-topic.html`.

[2] For information about JavaScript expressions in QML, refer to `https://doc.qt.io/qt-6/qtqml-javascript-expressions.html`.

application or build a reusable element called a **component**. In essence, QML is used to build the UI objects and specify how they relate to one another.

With the relationships built, the **QtQuick** module is used to describe the look and behaviors of a GUI's elements. It is worth noting that, similar to what we have seen in QtWidgets, QtQuick also contains the classes for the visual canvas, graphical elements, layouts, data models and views, animations, graphics, and so much more!

In addition to QtQuick, we'll leverage the **QtQml** module to provide a **QQmlEngine** object to access the QML content that we create. An engine, along with a **QQmlContext** object for passing data to the QML components, is used to expose Python to the QML code that we create. Luckily, QtQml provides a convenience class, **QQmlApplicationEngine**, that combines the engine and the context. We'll use QQmlApplicationEngine to load our QML files.

By exposing Python to the QML components, we can use QML to write the front-end code and use Python and PyQt to build the back-end logic.

Note   A quick note about the structure of this chapter. To focus on efficiency, we'll first cover how to create a basic QML document, followed by adding simple visual elements such as text and images to get you comfortable. From there, we'll discuss how to organize elements in the GUI. The next step is to find out how to create a QML window, complete with a menu bar and an introduction to signals and slots in QML. Lastly, we'll take a brief glimpse at animating elements.

If after finishing this chapter you find that QtQuick and QML interest you, or if you have any questions along the way, the following links can provide more context and guidance:

- A brief tutorial for QML: `https://doc.qt.io/qt-6/qml-tutorial.html`

- An online QML book provided by The Qt Company: `www.qt.io/product/qt6/qml-book`

- Information for working with PyQt and QML: `www.riverbankcomputing.com/static/Docs/PyQt6/qml.html`

- Information about Qt Quick in Qt 6: `https://doc.qt.io/qt-6/qtquick-index.html`

Before creating any code, let's take a quick look at some common elements and properties we'll be using to create QtQuick applications.

Elements in QtQuick

Elements, also called **types**, are the built-in building blocks used to create GUIs in QtQuick. The term "elements" encapsulates both visual and nonvisual types. Visual elements have geometry and can be arranged in the GUI, while nonvisual elements are typically used to control the visual elements.

To create an instance of a type in QML, simply call the element followed by a pair of braces. An example of creating a `Rectangle` element is shown in the following line:

```
Rectangle {...}
```

Object types will *always* begin with a capital letter. Each element also has a number of particular properties, such as `width`, `height`, `color`, and `text`, that are used to specify different aspects of the element. Properties can also be used to position elements, specify geometric transformations, and handle state changes. These properties are defined between the braces.

Table 13-1 describes some common and interesting elements found in QtQuick. A full list of QML types is found at `https://doc.qt.io/qt-6/qmltypes.html`.

Table 13-1. *Selection of common QtQuick types*

Element	Description
Item	The base element from which all visual elements derive. Does not itself create a visual element. Instead, Item defines the properties for other types. Can also be used as a container for other elements
Rectangle	Inherits Item and adds visual properties, including color, border, and radius
Image	Displays images. Provides the source property to specify the image URL and fillMode for controlling resizing behavior
Text	Displays text. Includes text, font, style, and alignment properties
MouseArea	Nonvisual type that is needed to capture mouse events. MouseArea also includes properties such as width and height
Flickable	Nonvisual type that acts as a draggable and flickable surface for its children. Perfect for showing large numbers of child objects on a scrollable surface
Component	Used along with the Loader type to dynamically create and load components within a component document. Components are typically created and instantiated using separate QML files

Let's take a look at how to use a few of the elements in Table 13-1 to create a QML document with a .qml extension in the following section.

Introduction to the QML Language and Syntax

One of the best ways to get started understanding a new language is to jump right into some code. In this section, we'll take a look at a QML document and break apart the tree-like structure of QML. If you have never coded in JavaScript or any other declarative language, there is no need to worry. There is a very simple pattern to writing QML code.

By creating the simple GUI seen in Figure 13-1, you'll have learned some very important concepts, including how to

- Import QML object types into a document (it is also possible to import JavaScript resources)

- Create QML parent and children elements

- Define properties for different kinds of elements

- Manually arrange elements using the visual canvas's coordinate system

- Create a simple, reusable component

- Understand simple QML syntax concepts

Figure 13-1. *Custom QtQuick component with text*

After working with QtWidgets, you may notice that there is no title in the window's title bar. This is because this example does not actually create a window; instead, we are creating a QML component with Rectangle as the parent object. Not only does

Rectangle not have a `title` property, but by creating a component, we could also instantiate this object in another QML document if we wanted to do so. You'll see an example of this in the "Layout Handling in QML" section.

Explanation for QML Language and Syntax

The first step is to import the object types in Listing 13-1. If you have ever used `QtQuick` before, then you'll know that import statements in Qt 5 also needed a version number. Thankfully, this is no longer necessary in Qt 6,[3] and the version of `QtQuick` will match your version of PyQt6.

Single-line comments in QML use double forward slashes, //. Multi-line comments start with /* and end with */.

To begin, create a new file with the extension `.qml`.

Listing 13-1. Simple QML document that demonstrates basic syntax principles

```
# qml_intro.qml
// Import necessary modules
import QtQuick

Rectangle {
    id: rect
    width: 155; height: 80
    color: "skyblue"

    Text {
        text: "Small Component"
        x: 10; y: 30
        font.pixelSize: 16
        font.weight: Font.DemiBold
        color: "black"
    }
}
```

---

[3] To find out more about `QtQuick` versions in Qt 5 or Qt 6, consult `https://doc.qt.io/qt-6/qtquickcontrols-index.html#versions`. The `QtQuick` versions will be the same even though we are using PyQt.

A QML document contains the hierarchy of objects, where each object can have an id and a name, properties, methods, and even signals and signal handlers. The **root** object is the top-level item in the document.

For this example, there are two objects. The first is the Rectangle element, which acts as the parent for the second, the Text element. One of the benefits of using braces as well as indentation in QML is that you can comprehend the hierarchy of the objects just by looking at the code. Creating parent-child relationships in QML is simply a matter of instantiating an object within the braces of a parent object.

But what happens if you want a child to access the values of other elements other than the parent? To find out, let's have a look at how to specify property values.

Defining Properties of an Element

When a value is assigned to a property in QML, the assignment is denoted with a colon, :, where the left side of the colon is the property name and the right side is its value. For example, the width property of the Rectangle is equal to 155.

You'll notice that the first attribute defined for Rectangle is id, which is an identifier that can be used throughout the QML document to interact with that object. Here, the Rectangle element is identified as rect. Always use lowercase for the first letter of identifiers to avoid confusion between QtQuick elements and other components.

For Rectangle, let's specify its width and height and give it a color other than the default white. Properties that are defined on the same line are separated using a semicolon. The Text element's text, font, and color properties are set. Just like in QtWidgets, you can also style text using HTML tags.

The Coordinate System

The visual canvas in QtQuick is a two-dimensional surface for arranging objects. The top-left pixel of the window is (0, 0). While the canvas is 2D, it also has z-ordering to handle the ordering of objects when they overlap.

What is interesting is that child elements are relative to their parents, meaning that a child inherits the coordinate system of the parent and is arranged based on its parent's top-left corner. An example of this can be found at https://doc.qt.io/qt-6/qtquick-visualcanvas-coordinates.html.

There are a variety of ways to organize elements in the GUI window, many of which will be discussed in the "Layout Handling in QML" section. For this example, we can manually position objects in the window by specifying the x and y values for the Text object.

Tip   If you downloaded Qt Creator back in Chapter 8, then you'll be able to visualize the document at this point. You could either open the file in Qt Creator, or you could locate the qml executable that is included in the Qt directory on your computer. Next, run the following command in the shell:

```
$ <Qt_dir>/Qt/<path-to-qml>/qml qml_intro.qml.
```

Your <path-to-qml> may be similar to 6.0.0/clang_64/bin, where 6.0.0 denotes the Qt version. (Your path and version may also be different.) You can replace qml_intro.qml with any QML document you want to run.

Using what we have learned, let's find out how to continue adding more features to QtQuick UIs and learn how to present documents using Python in the following sections.

Building and Running QML Components

This section is broken down into four major parts:

1. Creating and visualizing QML components using QQuickView

2. Building reusable components

3. Positioning elements in QML

4. Creating and visualizing QtQuick windows using QQmlApplicationEngine

Each one of the examples uses one of two classes to load the QML files. The first is **QQuickView**, which is a convenience class that loads a QML file and provides a window to display QML scenes. QQuickView works for visualizing components.

But what should you do if you want to create a QtQuick application with a window, a menu bar, and other UI elements? That is where QQmlApplicationEngine comes into play. We'll discover in the "Building and Loading QML Windows" section how to build applications with windows.

Along the way, you'll also find out how to

- Add images to your QtQuick applications

- Position objects using anchors

- Enable mouse handling with MouseArea

- Find out how to use JavaScript expressions

- Use QtQuick Controls for creating windows and adding additional components such as buttons and check boxes to GUIs

- See how to use signals and signal handlers in QML

For all of the examples in this chapter, we'll need at least two files: one .qml document for designing the UI and one .py script that handles loading the QML file and possibly the back-end functionality. More complex applications could have multiple components that are called in a main.qml file.

Creating and Loading QML Components

We'll need to create the following two files to build the GUI seen in Figure 13-2:

1. images_and_text.qml – A QML component composed of images and text

2. quick_loader.py – A Python script for quickly loading general QML components

It's amazing!

Figure 13-2. *QtQuick component containing images and text*

Make sure to download the images folder from the GitHub repository before getting started.

Explanation for Creating QML Components

First, create a new QML document. The Item element in Listing 13-2 serves as the root for this component. The id identifier has been assigned as such. The width and height properties are then specified. Since Item types do not display visual content, we'll need to assign the object a child element, perhaps a Rectangle or an Image.

Listing 13-2. Creating a QML document with images and text

```
# images_and_text.qml
// Import necessary modules
import QtQuick

Item {
    id: root
    width: 340; height: 420

    // Create an Image that will serve as the background
    Image {
        anchors.fill: root
        source: "images/background.jpg"
        fillMode: Image.PreserveAspectCrop
    }

    // Create a container Rectangle to hold text and images
    Rectangle {
        id: container
        width: 300; height: 120
        y: 40 // Vertical offset
        /* Comment out the following line and uncomment the
        line after to view the Rectangle */
        color: "transparent"
        //color: "lightgrey"

        anchors.horizontalCenter: root.horizontalCenter
        anchors.topMargin: 40

        Image {
            id: image
            anchors.centerIn: container
            source: "images/qtquick_text.png"
            sourceSize.width: container.width
            sourceSize.height: container.height
        }
```

```
        Text {
            text: "It's amazing!"
            anchors {
                top: image.bottom
                horizontalCenter: image.horizontalCenter
            }
            font.pixelSize: 24
            font.weight: Font.DemiBold
            color: "#3F5674"
        }
    }
}
```

By adding an Image element to the Item as a child, the image can easily be set as the component's background. QtQuick makes this process effortless using anchors.

Positioning Elements with Anchors

Anchors are properties that allow you to arrange objects in a GUI by specifying the relation of one element with respect to its parent or sibling objects. Imagine an object having lines along its left, right, top, and bottom sides as well as lines going vertically and horizontally through its middle. We can use the anchors to define the relationship between the elements and those lines.

The following list describes commonly used anchor properties:

- anchors.fill – Convenience property for one item to have the same geometry as another, thereby filling up the space of the other element (while also preserving aspect ratio and cropping)

- anchors.centerIn – Positions an object in the center of another object

- anchors.left, anchors.right – Positions an object to the left or right of another object

- anchors.top, anchors.bottom – Positions an object on the top or bottom of another object

- anchors.verticalCenter, anchors.horizontalCenter – Arranges an object to the vertical or horizontal center of an another object

There are also ways to add margins between the objects using anchors.

With the first Image type created in Listing 13-2, `anchors.fill: root` binds the Image.anchors property to the root object's size.

A **binding** specifies the value of a property in QML and is denoted with a colon, `:`, similar to assigning a regular value. The difference is that binding creates a dependency between the property and the other object. Bindings in QML can be used to access built-in properties, make function calls, and even use built-in JavaScript objects like Math.

More information about anchors can be found at `https://doc.qt.io/qt-6/qtquick-positioning-anchors.html`.

Adding Images in QtQuick

The `source` property of Image is used to specify the path to a desired image file. The `fillMode` property defines what happens to the image when its size does not match that of the item. The value `PreserveAspectCrop` preserves the image's aspect ratio while also cropping the image, if necessary. Other fillMode values include `Stretch`, `PreserveAspectFit`, `Tile`, and `Pad` (which does not transform the image).

The `Rectangle` type serves as a container for the remaining Image and Text objects. The string `"transparent"` can be assigned to the `color` property. This is a neat little trick to remove the background if you are using PNG images with transparent backgrounds. If you would like to see how the Image and Text types fit within the `container` object, you can switch the comments on the `color` lines.

The `sourceSize` can be used to force an image to scale down or up to a certain size. Here, the size of the `qtquick_text.png` image is forced to remain its original size, but centered in `container`. This prevents distortion of the text.

One thing to note is that you can group properties. You can see this in the Text object. Grouping the properties could have also been done with the `font` and `sourceSize` properties in this example.

With the UI built, we now need a way to load the QML document.

Explanation for Loading QML Components

`QQuickView` provides a window for displaying a QtQuick user interface where all you need to do is to pass the URL of the `.qml` file to `QQuickView`.

In order to make a general Python script that we can pass QML files to as arguments when running the application, we'll also use the Python argparse module[4] in Listing 13-3.

To begin, let's import a few PyQt6 classes into a new Python script. Since we are not using QtWidgets, there's no need to import QApplication. Instead, **QGuiApplication** is used for GUI-related applications that are not using widgets.

Listing 13-3. Code for loading a general QML component using QQuickView

```python
# quick_loader.py
# Import necessary modules
import sys, argparse
from PyQt6.QtCore import QUrl
from PyQt6.QtGui import QGuiApplication
from PyQt6.QtQuick import QQuickView

def parseCommandLine():
    """Use argparse to parse the command line for specifying
    a path to a QML file."""
    parser = argparse.ArgumentParser()
    parser.add_argument("-f", "--file", type=str,
        help="A path to a .qml file to be the source.",
        required=True)
    args = vars(parser.parse_args())
    return args

class MainView(QQuickView):

    def __init__(self):
        """ Constructor for loading QML files """
        super().__init__()
        self.setSource(QUrl(args["file"]))
        # Get the Status enum's value and check for an error
        if self.status().name == "Error":
            sys.exit(1)
```

---

[4] More information about argparse can be found at https://docs.python.org/3.9/howto/argparse.html.

```
    else:
        self.show()

if __name__ == "__main__":
    args = parseCommandLine() # Return command line arguments
    app = QGuiApplication(sys.argv)
    view = MainView()
    sys.exit(app.exec())
```

The QQuickView method setSource() is used to load the QML file. If no errors are found, then show() is used to display the GUI.

You can load either Listing 13-1 or 13-2 and visualize the components. To load a file, run the following command in your shell:

```
$ python3 quick_loader.py -f images_and_text.qml
```

Windows users can use python instead of python3.

To load Listing 13-1, run:

```
$ python3 quick_loader.py -f qml_intro.qml
```

We've just seen how to build a simple component. Now, let's start to find out how to make components that are reusable and interactive.

Creating Reusable Components

Being able to create custom and reusable components is an essential part of GUI development. This holds true even in QtQuick. Figure 13-3 displays a simple custom Rectangle that we're going to build to demonstrate how to use the mouse event handlers.

Figure 13-3. Reusable QtQuick component that changes color when clicked

This is only a taste of the kind of components that you could build. Components can consist of classic UI elements, data views, animations, and more.

Explanation for Creating Custom Components

Listing 13-4 is a new QML document that contains a `Rectangle` type with a single Text child. What sets this component apart from Listing 13-1 is the addition of the MouseArea type.

For this example, create a file called `ColorRect.qml`.

Tip   Be sure to use camelCasing when naming components that you plan to reuse.

Listing 13-4. Code for the ColorRect component

```
# ColorRect.qml
import QtQuick

Rectangle {
    id: root
    width: 80; height: 80
    color: "#1FC6DE" // Cyan-like color
    border.color: "#000000"
    border.width: 4
    radius: 5

    Text {
        text: root.color
        anchors.centerIn: root
    }

    // Click on Rectangle to change the color
    MouseArea {
        anchors.fill: parent
        onClicked: {
            color = '#' + (0x1000000 + Math.random()
                * 0xffffff).toString(16).substr(1, 6);
```

```
        // Uncomment the following line for Listing 13-9
        //root.clicked()
    }
  }
}
```

The current color of the Rectangle is displayed on Text by binding the text property to root.color.

Making an Element Interactive with Mouse Handling

Support for various input devices, including keyboard, mouse, touch, and stylus devices, is possible in QtQuick.

A **MouseArea** is a nonvisual item that is used in conjunction with visual types. Clicking on an item that also includes a MouseArea object could be used to trigger signals, check the location of the cursor, or drag and drop items if drag and drop is enabled.

The anchors.fill property is used so that the user can click anywhere on the parent object (which is the Rectangle). If the Rectangle is clicked, then the clicked signal is emitted, and the onClicked signal handler is called. (**Signal handlers** are methods that handle signals. Their names are simply the signal with on added to the front and camelCased.) We'll explore signals a bit more in the "Signals and Signal Handlers" subsection.

In onClicked, a JavaScript expression is used to select a random color and convert it to a hexadecimal string that represents a new color. The color value is used to update the value of the ColorRect.

Using Listing 13-3 (quick_loader.py), you can run view the ColorRect component by running the following line in the shell:

```
$ python3 quick_loader.py -f ColorRect.qml
```

In the following section, ColorRect will be used to build a few example applications that demonstrate how to organize elements in QtQuick.

Layout Handling in QML

Organizing visual elements in a GUI is important for creating cohesion. Objects in QtQuick can be arranged in a few different fashions. In this section, we'll discuss four of them. A few example documents will also be created to help visualize how to use them in code.

There are a few different approaches for arranging items in QML. The following list talks about each one:

- **Manual positioning** can be used to explicitly specify the x and y coordinates of QtQuick types. This method is extremely efficient for GUIs that are not dynamic. This method was demonstrated in Listing 13-1.

- **Anchoring** uses the boundaries and relative positions of parent and sibling elements to arrange objects. This topic was covered back in the "Positioning Elements with Anchors" subsection.

- **Positioners** are containers that are used to arrange children items in columns, rows, or grids. The "Using Positioners to Position Elements" section gives an overview of positioners.

- **Layout managers** are used to organize items in a UI. The main difference between layout managers and positioners is that layouts also handle resizing. Layouts can be imported into a QML document by using import QtQuick.Layouts. More information about layout managers in QtQuick can be found at https://doc.qt.io/qt-6/qtquicklayouts-index.html.

Using Positioners to Position Elements

Positioners share similar behavior with layout managers. Like layout managers, positioners are used to organize items in a specific form like a row or column. Unlike layout managers, however, positioners act like containers for the widgets that become their children and don't manage the sizes of their children items.

Table 13-2 lists the four commonly used positioners.

Table 13-2. *Four of the standard positioner types*

Positioner	Description
Column	Positions children elements in a single column
Row	Positions children elements in a single row
Grid	Positions children elements in a grid
Flow	Positions children elements side by side, and children can be wrapped top to bottom or left to right

In addition, positioners contain a few properties for managing the spacing between elements, applying padding, and specifying the direction for laying out the items.

More information about positioners is found at `https://doc.qt.io/qt-6/qtquick-positioning-layouts.html`.

Explanation for Using Column and Grid Positioners

A `Column` positioner is used in Figure 13-4 to arrange a few `ColorRect` components from Listing 13-4, (`ColorRect.qml`). The elements are stacked on top of each other and the spacing between each `ColorRect` is set using the `spacing` property.

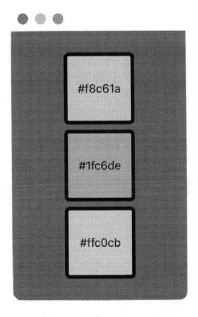

Figure 13-4. *Elements arranged in a Column positioner*

Listing 13-5 creates a simple Rectangle parent in a QML document that contains three ColorRect instances arranged in a Column positioner.

Listing 13-5. Code for the Column positioner example

```
# columns.qml
import QtQuick

Rectangle {
    width: 200; height: 300
    color: "grey"

    Column {
        id: column
        anchors.centerIn: parent
        spacing: 6
        // Add custom components to Column
        ColorRect { }
        ColorRect { }
        ColorRect { color: "pink"}
    }
}
```

Also, if you look at the third ColorRect instance, you'll notice how properties of components can still be modified when instantiating them. Try switching Column to Row or Flow in Listing 13-5 and take a look at the difference in the GUI.

Figure 13-5 is an example of the Grid positioner.

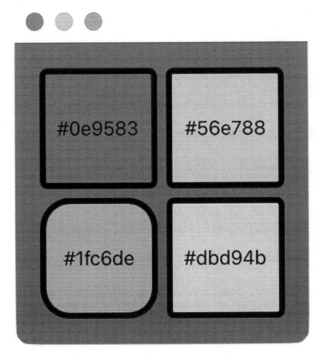

Figure 13-5. *Elements arranged in a Grid positioner*

Listing 13-6 differs only slightly from Listing 13-5. Notice how for the Grid positioner you'll need to specify the number of rows and columns in the grid.

Listing 13-6. Code for the Grid positioner example

```
# grids.qml
import QtQuick

Rectangle {
    width: 200; height: 200
    color: "grey"

    Grid {
        id: grid
        rows: 2; columns: 2
        anchors.centerIn: parent
        spacing: 6
```

```
        // Add custom components to Column
        ColorRect { }
        ColorRect { }
        ColorRect { radius: 20 }
        ColorRect { }
    }
}
```

Even though these two examples use `Rectangle` types to illustrate how to use positioners, they are more efficiently used when arranging buttons, dials, or other UI elements.

In the following section, you'll get closer to creating well-rounded classic desktop applications by finding out how to create menu bars and display dialogs in `QtQuick`.

Building and Loading QML Windows

While `QQuickView` is useful for displaying components, the `QQmlApplicationEngine` class is a more convenient way to load a single QML document where the root object is a window. What this means is that instead of using `Rectangle` or `Item` types as the root, we'll be using the `ApplicationWindow` control. Doing so will provide us with additional tools, such as a menu bar and toolbars.

Note `QQuickView` does not support using window types like `ApplicationWindow` as a root item. To display a scene in a window, you'll need to use `QQmlApplicationEngine`.

For this simple application, we'll create a window that displays local images. The images can be selected through a **FileDialog** instance that is created when selecting the Open menu option. This is shown in Figure 13-6.

Figure 13-6. *An Image Viewer GUI created with QtQuick*

Previous QML documents have only imported QtQuick. In order to include common GUI elements in a QtQuick application, we'll need to import a new class.

QtQuick Controls

Controls are similar to the widgets in QtWidgets. They are the buttons, check boxes, sliders, and other graphical UI elements we have come to expect for interacting with applications.

Table 13-3 lists only a portion of the controls that are available in QtQuick.

Table 13-3. *Selection of common QtQuick.Controls types*

Controls	Description
Action	Describes the actions that can be assigned to menu items and toolbars
ApplicationWindow	Window with additional functionality for adding a menu bar, header, and footer
Button	Push button that can be clicked by the user to perform an action
CheckBox	Check button that can be toggled on and off
ComboBox	Presents a drop-down list for selecting options
Dial	Circular dial that can be rotated to select a value
Dialog	Pop-up dialog box with standard buttons and title
DialogButtonBox	A button box that is used for specifying buttons in a Dialog
Frame	Provides a visual frame for organizing other controls
GroupBox	Provides a visual frame with a title for organizing other controls
MenuBar	Creates a menu bar in a window
RadioButton	Radio buttons that are autoexclusive and can be toggled on and off
Slider	Used for selecting a value using a sliding handle on a track
TabBar	Creates a tab bar for switching between different views
Tumbler	Wheel that can be spun to select values

For a full list of the Controls types, you can check out https://doc.qt.io/qt-6/ qtquick-controls2-qmlmodule.html.

Explanation for Creating QML Windows

For this desktop application, we'll be using a few of the tools that we have used before for creating windowed applications, namely, a menu bar, actions for the menu items, and dialogs for loading image files to be displayed in the GUI's window.

To have access to these tools, we'll need to import some new QtQuick classes into a new QML document like in Listing 13-7. Controls gives us access to the UI elements, while Dialogs is used to create the FileDialog.

Listing 13-7. Creating the QtQuick image viewer GUI to illustrate how to use windows and controls

```
# windows_and_controls.qml
// Import necessary modules
import QtQuick
import QtQuick.Controls
import QtQuick.Dialogs

ApplicationWindow {
    title: "QtQuick Image Viewer"
    width: 800; height: 500
    visible: true

    // Create the menu bar and its actions
    menuBar: MenuBar {
        Menu {
            title: "&File"
            Action {
                text: "&Open"
                onTriggered: openImage()
            }
            MenuSeparator {}
            Action {
                text: "&Quit"
                onTriggered: Qt.quit()}
        }
    }

    // Define the signal for opening images
    signal openImage()

    // Define the signal handler for opening images
    onOpenImage: {
        fileDialog.open()
    }
```

```
    // Define a FileDialog for selecting local images
    FileDialog {
        id: fileDialog
        title: "Choose an image file"
        nameFilters: ["Image files (*.png *.jpg)"]
        onAccepted: {
            // Update displayed image
            image.source = fileDialog.selectedFile
        }
        onRejected: {
            fileDialog.close()
        }
    }

    /* Create a container Rectangle for the image
    in order to add margins around the image's edges */
    Rectangle {
        id: container
        anchors {
            fill: parent
            margins: 10
        }

        Image {
            id: image
            anchors.fill: container
            source: "images/open_image.png"
            fillMode: Image.PreserveAspectFit
        }
    }
}
```

The ApplicationWindow is the root object of the application and will be loaded in the next section with QQmlApplicationEngine. ApplicationWindow also includes the title property. It is most important that you do not forget to include the visible: true line when using QQmlApplicationEngine. If you forget this property, then your window will remain hidden since, by default, an ApplicationWindow is not visible.

An Image element is used in the ApplicationWindow to display the selected image to the user. While an Image can be directly placed in the window, using the anchors. margins property of Rectangle allows for a subtle border to surround the image.

Creating a Menu Bar

The MenuBar control is used to create the window's menu bar. Then Menu is used to create the File menu, and finally Action controls are added to the File menu along with a MenuSeparator control to separate the Open and Quit actions.

Signals and Signal Handlers

The controls in QtQuick.Controls, just like widgets, communicate using signals and slots, referred to as signal handlers in QtQuick. It is easy to figure out which signals are connected to which signal handlers by their names. Signal handlers have an additional on tacked onto the front and are camelCased. For example, the Button control has the clicked signal that triggers the onClicked signal handler whenever the button is clicked.

Take a look at the actions in menuBar. To create a custom signal in a QML type, we need to use the signal keyword. Here, we create a new signal called openImage that has no parameters.

For this example, the ApplicationWindow control's openImage signal is emitted whenever the Open menu item is triggered. This then connects to the onOpenImage signal handler where a fileDialog instance is opened. Just so you know, the onTriggered signal handler could be directly connected to fileDialog.open().

The Quit menu item closes the entire application using Qt.quit().

Using FileDialog to Open Files

Dialogs are used either to gather or to present information to a user. For this example, a FileDialog opens so that the user can select .png or .jpg image files.

The dialog's lower right corner contains two buttons: OK and Cancel. If the user clicks OK, then the accepted signal is handled by onAccepted. This will update the image.source URL and the image using the value of fileDialog.selectedFile. Otherwise, the rejected signal from the Cancel button will connect to onRejected and close the dialog.

Explanation for Loading QML Windows

Similar to Listing 13-3, Listing 13-8 is a Python script for loading general QML documents. The difference is that Listing 13-8 loads the files using QQmlApplicationEngine. This means you can only pass as arguments the path of QML documents where the top-level item is a window, such as ApplicationWindow.

We'll start by importing classes from PyQt6 into a new Python script, including QQmlApplicationEngine from the QtQml module.

Listing 13-8. Code for loading a general QML window using QQmlApplicationEngine

```python
# qml_loader.py
# Import necessary modules
import sys, argparse
from PyQt6.QtCore import Qt, QUrl
from PyQt6.QtGui import QGuiApplication
from PyQt6.QtQml import QQmlApplicationEngine

def parseCommandLine():
    """Use argparse to parse the command line for specifying
    a path to a QML file."""
    parser = argparse.ArgumentParser()
    parser.add_argument("-f", "--file", type=str,
        help="A path to a .qml file to be the source.",
        required=True)
    args = vars(parser.parse_args())
    return args

class MainView(QQmlApplicationEngine):

    def __init__(self):
        super().__init__()
        # Order matters here; need to check if the object was
        # created before loading the QML file
        self.objectCreated.connect(self.checkIfObjectsCreated,
            Qt.ConnectionType.QueuedConnection)
        self.load(QUrl(args["file"]))
```

```
    def checkIfObjectsCreated(self, object, url):
        """Check if QML objects have loaded without errors.
        Otherwise, exit the program."""
        if object is None:
            QGuiApplication.exit(1)

if __name__ == "__main__":
    args = parseCommandLine() # Return command line arguments
    app = QGuiApplication(sys.argv)
    engine = MainView()
    sys.exit(app.exec())
```

The MainView class inherits QQmlApplicationEngine. Once the QML file is passed to the QQmlApplicationEngine method load(), the objectCreated signal will be emitted when all objects have loaded. The enum Qt.ConnectionType.QueuedConnection ensures that the signal is queued until the event loop can deliver it to the slot. This is done to make sure we can check for any errors before loading the file.

If loading is successful, the window will open. Otherwise, an error will return an object with a value of None in the checkIfObjectsCreated() slot.

To load Listing 13-7, run the following command in the shell:

```
$ python3 qml_loader.py -f windows_and_controls.qml
```

In the final section, we'll have a little fun and make some objects spin and change sizes using transforms.

Using Transformations to Animate Objects

A transformation is the general term that refers to manipulating the shape, size, and/ or position of a point, line, or geometric shape. Chapter 11 demonstrated how to use transformations to animate objects in QtWidgets. Now, we'll start to find out how to perform some basic transformations in QtQuick.

Explanation for Simple Transformations

For this first example seen in Figure 13-7, we'll demonstrate how to use the Item type's rotation and scale properties to perform basic transformations on objects.

- rotation – Values passed are in degrees.

- scale – Values less than 1.0 cause the object to render at a smaller size, while values greater than 1.0 render a larger object.

Figure 13-7. *Rotated and scaled objects*

Note   This example reuses the ColorRect component from Listing 13-4. To get this example to work, you'll first need to return to Listing 13-4 and *uncomment the line* that says root.clicked(). This will allow the ColorRect to receive the signals from the ApplicationWindow in Listing 13-8, creating a clickable ColorRect component. Be sure to *comment out the line again* when using ColorRect.qml for other examples.

First, create a new QML file that imports QtQuick and QtQuick.Controls. The top-level object in Listing 13-9 is ApplicationWindow. Be sure that when you load this QML file, you use Listing 13-8. Next, set up the window's properties and make sure visible is set to true.

Listing 13-9. Code for transforming objects using mouse clicks

```
# rotate_and_move.qml
import QtQuick
import QtQuick.Controls

ApplicationWindow {
    title: "Simple Transformations"
    width: 300; height: 300
    visible: true

    MouseArea {
        id: windowMouse
        anchors.fill: parent
        onClicked: {
            // Reset the values of the ColorRect objects
            rect1.rotation = 0
            rect2.scale = 1.0
        }
    }

    ColorRect {
        id: rect1
        x: 20; y: 20
        antialiasing: true
        signal clicked

        onClicked:{
            // Rotate the rect 20° when clicked
            rotation += 20
        }
    }
```

```
ColorRect {
    id: rect2;
    x: 200; y: 200
    antialiasing: true
    signal clicked

    onClicked:{
        // Scale the rect when clicked
        scale += .1
    }
}
}
}
```

Next, we'll create a `MouseArea` element to handle clicks on the application window. Since order matters in QML code, creating the `MouseArea` before the other items ensures that the window will also receive clicks and not just the `ColorRect` items.

The two `ColorRect` objects are arranged in the window manually. A new signal, `clicked`, is defined for each of the objects. We can then use the `onClicked` signal handler in each of the `ColorRect` elements to rotate or scale the items using the built-in `Item` properties.

Click anywhere in the window to reset the `ColorRect` values.

To load Listing 13-9, run the following command in the shell:

```
$ python3 qml_loader.py -f rotate_and_move.qml
```

Let's take a look at one final example that demonstrates how to use transformations and a few other `QtQuick` classes to animate elements.

Explanation for Using Transformations to Animate Objects

The GUI in Figure 13-8 builds upon the previous section's concepts of transformations and shows how we can create animations using the **Behavior** QML type. A Behavior defines the default animation that will occur whenever a particular property value changes.

Figure 13-8. *The spin wheel rotates whenever the mouse clicks in the window*

We'll also see how to leverage JavaScript to create functions for adding randomness to our application.

Make sure that you have downloaded the `images` folder from GitHub before starting this application.

Begin by creating a new QML document. We'll need to import `QtQuick.Controls` in Listing 13-10 so that we have access to the `ApplicationWindow` control. Be sure to set the value of `visible` to `true`.

Listing 13-10. Code for the spin wheel QtQuick GUI

```
# transforms.qml
import QtQuick
import QtQuick.Controls
```

```
ApplicationWindow {
    title: "Spin Wheel Transformations"
    width: 500; height: 500
    visible: true

    /* Get a random number where both the minimum and maximum
    values are inclusive */
    function getRandomIntInclusive(min, max) {
        min = Math.ceil(min);
        max = Math.floor(max);
        return Math.floor(Math.random() *
            (max - min + 1) + min);
    }

    Image {
        id: pointer
        source: "images/pointer.png"
        /* Use the z property to place the pointer above the
        wheel */
        x: parent.width / 2 - width / 2; y: 0; z: 1
    }

    Image {
        id: spinwheel
        anchors.centerIn: parent
        source: "images/spin_wheel.png"
        sourceSize.width: parent.width - 30
        sourceSize.height: parent.height - 30

        // Create a behavior for rotating the spinwheel Image
        Behavior on rotation {
            NumberAnimation {
                duration: getRandomIntInclusive(500, 3000)
                easing.type: Easing.OutSine
            }
        }
```

```
    /* Enable mouse handling and define how the image
    rotates when clicked */
    MouseArea {
        anchors.fill: parent
        onClicked: spinwheel.rotation +=
            getRandomIntInclusive(360, 360 * 4)
    }
  }
}
```

Stand-alone JavaScript functions can be added to QML documents to add extra functionality. The keyword `function` denotes the function called `getRandomIntInclusive()`, which takes as arguments two integer values that represent maximum and maximum limits. Using the two values, a random integer is returned.

The function `getRandomIntInclusive()` will be used on two occasions. The first time is in the `MouseArea` item's signal handler `onClicked`. The random value returned will specify the `rotation` value of `spin wheel`, adding some realism to the GUI so that no spin appears to rotate the same amount.

The second time `getRandomIntInclusive()` is used, we want to describe the animation `Behavior` of the `rotation`. By clicking on the window, the `rotation` value of `spin wheel` will change. The `Behavior on rotation` line means that whenever the value of `rotation` changes, the `NumberAnimation` will run. The `duration` property value denotes how long the rotation will occur, anywhere between half of a second and three seconds.

Finally, the **Easing** type and `easing.type` property denote what kind of easing curve we want to use. Easing curves provide more realistic animations to objects. To find out what kinds of Easing curves are available in `QtQuick`, you should check out `https://doc.qt.io/qt-5/qml-qtquick-propertyanimation.html#easing-prop`.

To load Listing 13-10, run the following command in the shell:

```
$ python3 qml_loader.py -f transforms.qml
```

We've only begun to scratch the surface of the kinds of fluid transformations and animations that exist in `QtQuick`. It is highly recommended that you try and find other examples and experiment with them.

Summary

With the arrival of Qt 6, more emphasis has been put into creating dynamic GUIs that are cross-platform, scalable, easy to maintain, and designed to get the most out of the graphics hardware on any platform. QtQuick, the toolkit that is based on Qt's QML language, defines a wide variety of amazing graphical tools that are great for desktop, mobile, and embedded applications.

There is so much more about QtQuick and QML that can be learned. The goal of this chapter was to provide you with the fundamentals to get you started using QtQuick and, from there, point you in the right direction with links and other useful information.

In this chapter, we've covered how to create a basic window and add QML elements and controls to an application and even discussed how to create reusable QML components that you can use in other applications. Those components were then used to demonstrate other QtQuick concepts like layouts and transformations. We saw how to load QML files with both QQuickView and QQmlApplicationEngine. The last application that we built demonstrated how to animate objects using both Behavior types and JavaScript.

Frankly, a complete guide on QtQuick is necessary to cover and describe all there is to offer in QML. There is so much content and so many possibilities for using QtQuick and QML to build GUIs.

In Chapter 14, we'll return to using QtWidgets and find out how to begin building applications that interact with and manage SQL databases.

Introduction to Handling Databases

Data is fundamental to the ways that modern business, communications, science, and even our personal lives are changing. The information we create from our online shopping, social media posts, search engine queries, and location data is collected, managed, and analyzed and can be used for a number of reasons, including to track consumer patterns, to train artificial intelligence algorithms, or even to study the geographic distribution of particular events such as diseases.

In this chapter, we are going to

- Learn about Qt's Model/View architecture for creating GUIs that work with data

- Use the `QTableView` class to build data-handling applications

- See how to work with CSV files in PyQt

- Introduce the `QtSql` module for creating and managing SQL relational databases

Before we begin, let's think a little more about data's usefulness.

Thinking About Data

Data analysis, or the process of organizing, modifying, and modeling data, is an important process, and this chapter will have a look at working with structured data for GUI development. Data can be stored in many different formats, including textual, visual, and multimedia.

© Joshua M Willman 2022
J. M. Willman, *Beginning PyQt*, https://doi.org/10.1007/978-1-4842-7999-1_14

In order to analyze data, we need to organize it into structures that we can store and then access electronically through a computer system. Sometimes, you may only be working with a small dataset consisting of one or two files. Other times, you may need to access certain portions of an entire database filled with private information. A **database** is an organized collection of multiple datasets.

We generally view the data from files and databases in tables. The rows and columns of a table typically work best for handling the style of data in data files. If we had a dataset of employees in a company, each row might represent an individual employee in the company, while each column depicts the different types of attributes for each employee, such as their age, salary, and employee ID number.

This chapter will focus on using PyQt's table classes for displaying and manipulating data. We will see how to use tables to work with CSV files and to build and interact with the SQL database management language. Of course, there are also other formats that you can use for viewing data, namely, lists and trees, should they better fit your application's requirements.

Introduction to Model/View Programming

Qt, and therefore PyQt, needs a system to access, display, and manage data that can be presented to the user. An older technique used for managing the relationship between data and its visual representation for user interfaces is the **Model-View-Controller** (**MVC**) software design pattern. MVC divides a program's logic into three interlinked components: a model, a view, and a controller.

Qt utilizes a similar design pattern that is based on MVC: the Model/View paradigm.

The Components of the Model/View Architecture

Model/View programming, similar to MVC, also separates the logic between three components but combines the view and the controller objects and introduces a new element – a delegate. A diagram of the architecture can be seen in Figure 14-1.

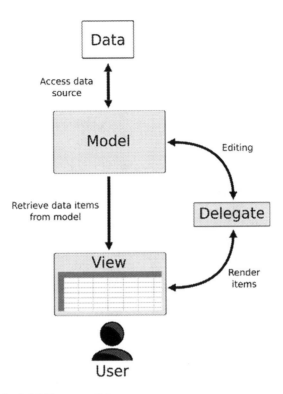

Figure 14-1. *The Model/View architecture*

- Model – The class that communicates with the data source, accessing the data, and provides a point of connection between the data and the view and delegate.

- View – The class that is responsible for displaying the data to the user, either in list, table, or tree formats, and for retrieving items of data from the model using model indexes. The view also has similar functionality to the **controller** in the MVC pattern, which handles the input from a user's interaction with items displayed in the view.

- Delegate – The class that is in charge of painting items and providing editors in the view. The delegate also communicates back to the model if an item has been edited.

Using the model/view structure has quite a few benefits, specifically being ideal for developing large-scale applications, giving more flexibility and control over the appearance and editing of data items, simplifying the framework for displaying data, and offering the ability to display multiple views of a model at the same time.

PyQt's Model/View Classes

As we saw in Chapter 10, Qt provides a few convenience classes for working with data. These classes greatly streamline a developer's work and provide all of the functionality needed for basic data applications. The following is a quick recap:

- `QTreeWidget` – Creates a table of items

- `QListWidget` – Displays a list of items

- `QTreeWidget` – Provides a hierarchical tree-like structure

What these widgets provide are all the tools necessary to work with data and already include the view, model, and delegate classes grouped together into single classes. However, these classes are more focused on item-based interfaces and are less flexible than working with the Model/View structure. It is also worth noting that each of these widgets inherits behavior from the abstract item view class, **QAbstractItemView**, creating the behavior for selecting items and managing headers.

An **abstract class** provides the points of connection, referred to as an **interface**, between other components, providing the class methods, functionality, and default implementation of features. They are the basis used for creating other classes. Qt's abstract data classes can also be used to create custom models, views, or delegates.

Let's take a moment to try and understand a little more about the model, view, and delegate classes that Qt provides:

- Models – All models are based on the **QAbstractItemModel** class, defining the interface used by both views and delegates to access data. They can be used to handle lists, tables, or trees. Data can take on a number of forms, including Python data structures, separate classes, files, or databases. Some other model classes are `QStandardItemModel`, **QFileSystemModel**, and SQL-related models.

- Views – All views are based on `QAbstractItemView` and are used to display data items from a data source, including `QListView`, `QTableView`, and `QTreeView`.

- Delegates – The base class is **QAbstractItemDelegate**, responsible for drawing items from the model and providing an editor widget for modifying items. For example, while editing a cell in a table, an editor widget, such as `QLineEdit`, is placed directly on top of the item.

In this section, we are going to create a GUI that demonstrates how to use the Model/View classes for displaying data in tables. For the GUI in Figure 14-2, data that is contained in a CSV file will be loaded and displayed in the table. In this example, we will also take a look at using the **QStandardItemModel** class, which provides a general model for storing data. This example will also demonstrate how we can connect a model for managing data to a view that will display the data.

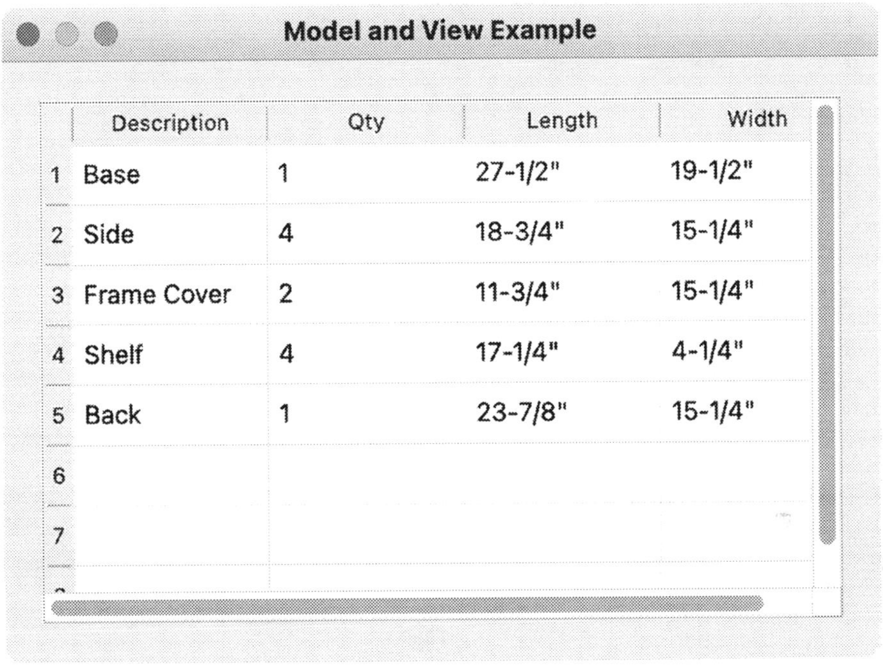

Figure 14-2. *Table created using the Model/View architecture*

Communication between the models, views, and delegates is handled by signals and slots. The model uses signals to notify the view about changes to the data. The view generates signals that provide information about how a user interacts with items. For a simple GUI, you may not need to interact with a delegate, but it is important to know that signals from the delegate are emitted while editing an item in the view. This, in turn, informs the model and view about the state of the editor widget.

Explanation for Introduction to Model/View

Be sure to download the files folder from the GitHub repository before beginning this program. Listings 14-1 to 14-3 illustrate how to use Model/View programming to display the contents of a small CSV file in a table view. In Listing 14-1, we'll use the basic_ window.py script from Chapter 1 to begin setting up the MainWindow class.

Listing 14-1. Code for setting up the MainWindow class in the introductory Model/View example

```
# model_view_ex.py
# Import necessary modules
import sys, csv
from PyQt6.QtWidgets import (QApplication, QWidget,
    QTableView, QAbstractItemView, QVBoxLayout)
from PyQt6.QtGui import (QStandardItemModel, QStandardItem)

class MainWindow(QWidget):
    def __init__(self):
        super().__init__()
        self.initializeUI()

    def initializeUI(self):
        """Set up the application's GUI."""
        self.setGeometry(100, 100, 450, 300)
        self.setWindowTitle("Model and View Example")

        self.setupMainWindow()
        self.loadCSVFile()
        self.show()

if __name__ == '__main__':
    app = QApplication(sys.argv)
    window = MainWindow()
    sys.exit(app.exec())
```

Tables are great for organizing and displaying various types of textual (and sometimes graphical) data, such as employee or inventory information.

We begin by importing classes, including QTableView from the QtWidgets module and the QStandardItemModel and QStandardItem classes from QtGui. QStandardItemModel will supply the item-based model we need to work with the data; **QStandardItem** creates the items that are used in the model.

Setting Up the Model, View, and Selection Modes

For the setUpMainWindow() method in Listing 14-2, instances of both the model using QStandardItemModel and the QTableView class are created. The loadCSVFile() method for loading the data into the table is handled in Listing 14-3.

Listing 14-2. Code for the setUpMainWindow() method in the introductory Model/View example

```
# model_view_ex.py
    def setupMainWindow(self):
        """Create and arrange widgets in the main window."""
        self.model = QStandardItemModel()

        table_view = QTableView()
        table_view.setSelectionMode(
            QAbstractItemView.SelectionMode.ExtendedSelection)
        table_view.setModel(self.model)

        # Set initial row and column values
        self.model.setRowCount(3)
        self.model.setColumnCount(4)

        main_v_box = QVBoxLayout()
        main_v_box.addWidget(table_view)
        self.setLayout(main_v_box)
```

There are different ways that users can select items in the table view. The setSelectionMode() setter, along with the QAbstractItemView.SelectionMode enum, specifies how the view responds to user selections. The following list describes the different flags:

- SingleSelection – A user can select only a single item at any given time. The item that was previously selected will become unselected.

- ExtendedSelection – Allows for normal selection and also for a user to select multiple items by pressing the Ctrl key (Cmd on MacOS) while clicking an item in the view or to select several items using the Shift key.

- ContiguousSelection – Allows for normal selection and also for a user to select multiple items by pressing the Shift key.

- MultiSelection – The user can select and deselect multiple items by clicking and dragging the mouse in the table.

- NoSelection – Selection of items is disabled.

To set up the view to display data from the model, you'll need to call the setModel() method and pass the model you instantiated. The model used for this example is QStandardItemModel.

In Chapter 10 where we looked at QTableWidget, the setRowCount() and setColumnCount() methods were called on the table widget. When using QTableView, these methods are not built-in and instead are called on the model like in the following line of code from Listing 14-2:

```
self.model.setRowCount(3)
```

The table_view widget is added to the QVBoxLayout.

Working with CSV Files

In initializeUI() from Listing 14-1, the next step is to call loadCSVFile() and read the contents of the data file. The items are then added to the model to be displayed in the view. The contents of the file are displayed in Figure 14-3.

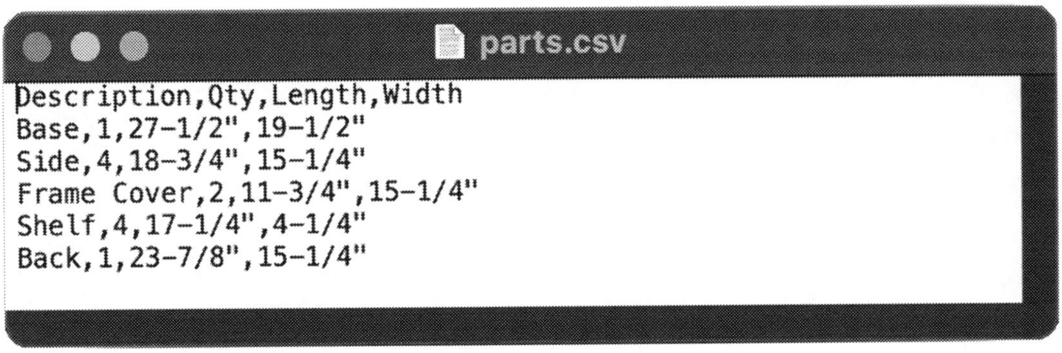

```
Description,Qty,Length,Width
Base,1,27-1/2",19-1/2"
Side,4,18-3/4",15-1/4"
Frame Cover,2,11-3/4",15-1/4"
Shelf,4,17-1/4",4-1/4"
Back,1,23-7/8",15-1/4"
```

📄 **parts.csv**

Figure 14-3. *Example of the data stored in a CSV file*

In the loadCSVFile() method in Listing 14-3, we can see how to read headers and data from a CSV file. **Comma-Separated Values** (**CSV**) is a very common format used for storing the data of spreadsheets and datasets.

Listing 14-3. Code for the loadCSVFile() method in the introductory Model/ View example

```python
# model_view_ex.py
    def loadCSVFile(self):
        """Load header and rows from CSV file."""
        file_name = "files/parts.csv"

        with open(file_name, "r") as csv_f:
            reader = csv.reader(csv_f)
            header_labels = next(reader)
            self.model.setHorizontalHeaderLabels(
                header_labels)
            for i, row in enumerate(csv.reader(csv_f)):
                items = [QStandardItem(item) for item in row]
                self.model.insertRow(i, items)
```

We'll open the file, set up the reader object to read the sequences in the file, get the header labels, and skip to the next line using next(). For this example, we'll assume that the CSV file will have header labels. The horizontal labels for model are set using the list of items from the first row in the file, which are stored in header_labels.

For the remaining rows, we use a list comprehension to read the items for each row into a list. Items created for QStandardItemModel need to be instances of QStandardItem. The insertRow() method is used to insert the list of items into the ith row.

With a fundamental understanding of how to create a model and a view, we can move onto creating GUIs that handle larger datasets. While the rest of this chapter will focus on SQL-based classes and models, you do not have to use SQL. All you need is some form of structured data in order to use the Model/View classes.

Working with SQL Databases in PyQt

Now that we have looked at PyQt's Model/View architecture and the QTableView class, let's see how to use SQL for handling structured data.

What Is SQL?

Structured Query Language (**SQL**) is a programming language designed for communication with databases. The data stored in databases is organized into a set of tables. The rows of the tables are referred to as **records**, and the columns are referred to as **fields**. Each column can only store a specific kind of information, such as names, dates, or numbers.

With SQL, we can **query** the data stored in **relational databases** – a collection of data items that have predefined relationships across multiple tables, marked by a unique identifier known as a **foreign key**. In a relational database, multiple tables comprise a **schema**, more than one schema makes up a database, and those databases are stored on a server. Relational databases allow for multiple users to handle the data at the same time. For this reason, accessing a database often requires a user to log in with a username and password in order to connect to the database.

This section will focus solely on using SQL along with classes from PyQt's QtSql module for creating a very basic database management system interface.

Working with Database Management Systems

The **QtSql** module provides **drivers** for a number of **Relational Database Management Systems** (**RDBMS**), including MySQL, Oracle, Microsoft SQL Server, PostgreSQL, and SQLite versions 2 and 3. An RDBMS is the software that allows users to interact with relational databases using SQL. More information about Qt SQL drivers can be found at `https://doc-snapshots.qt.io/qt6-dev/sql-driver.html`.

For the following examples, we will be using SQLite 3 since the library already comes shipped with Python and is included with Qt. SQLite is not a client-server database engine, so we do not need a database server. In addition, SQLite operates on a single file and is mainly used for small desktop applications.

Getting Familiar with SQL Commands

The SQL language already has its own commands for generating queries from databases. Using these commands, a user can perform a number of different actions for interacting with database tables. For example, the SQL SELECT statement can be used to retrieve records from a table. If you had database for a dog identification registry that contained a table called dog_registry, you could select all of the records in the table with the following statement:

```
SELECT * FROM dog_registry
```

The asterisk, *, means all columns in the table. When you are creating a query, you should consider where you are getting your data from, including which database or table. You should keep in mind what fields you will use. Also be mindful of any conditions in the selection. For example, do you need to display all of the pets in the database or only a specific breed of dog? An example of this using the dog_registry is shown in the following line:

```
SELECT name FROM dog_registry WHERE breed = 'shiba inu'
```

Using different drivers will more than likely entail using different SQL syntax, but PyQt can handle the differences. Table 14-1 lists a few common SQLite 3 commands that will be used in this chapter's examples.

Table 14-1. *A list of common SQLite keywords and functions that can be found in this chapter*[1]

SQLite Keywords	Description
AUTOINCREMENT	Generates a unique number automatically when a new record is inserted into the table
CREATE TABLE	Creates a new table in the database
DELETE	Deletes a row from the table
DROP TABLE	Deletes a table that already exists in the database
FOREIGN KEY	Constraint that links two tables together
FROM	Specifies the table to interact with when selecting or deleting data
INTEGER	Signed integer datatype
INSERT INTO	Inserts new rows into the table
MAX()	Function that finds the maximum value of a specified column
NOT NULL	Constraint that ensures a column will not accept NULL values
PRIMARY KEY	Constraint that uniquely identifies a record in the table
REFERENCES	Used with FOREIGN KEY to specify another table that has relation with the first table
SELECT	Selects data from a database
SET	Identifies which columns and values should be updated
UNIQUE	Constraint that ensures all values in a column are unique
UPDATE	Updates existing values in a row
VALUES	Defines the values of an INSERT INTO statement
VARCHAR	Variable character datatype for strings
WHERE	Filters the results of a query to include only records that satisfy specific conditions

In the following sections, we will work toward creating a user interface that can be used to view and manage a database's information in a table view.

---

[1] A full list of SQLite keywords can be found at `www.sqlite.org/lang_keywords.html`.

Project 14.1 – Account Management GUI

For this project, we are going to take a different approach to designing the account management GUI. This section builds up to the final project by working through a number of smaller example programs. There is a good deal of information to unpack, and if this is your first time working with SQL, especially to build an interface in PyQt, then the process for working with databases can become a little unclear.

Imagine you have a business and you want to create a database to keep track of your employees' information. You want to include information such as their first and last names, employee IDs, email addresses, departments, and the countries where they work. (This could be extended to include more information such as salaries, phone numbers, and dates of hire.) In the beginning, a small database is okay. However, as your workforce builds, so will the information. Some employees may have the same first or last name or even work in the same country. You need a way to manage all of those employees so that fields in the database are populated with the correct information and data types.

Using a relational database, we can avoid issues with the data's integrity. We could set up multiple tables, one for the different employees' accounts and one for the countries. For this example, we only use repeating country names to demonstrate how to use PyQt's classes for working with relational databases. Figure 14-4 displays the account management GUI.

	ID	Employee ID	First	Last	E-mail	Dept.	Country
6	7	1140	Charlotte	Jackson	jacksonc@job.com	R&D	USA
7	8	1846	Amelia	Moore	moorea@job.com	Engineering	India
8	9	1958	Evelyn	Taylor	taylore@job.com	Production	USA
9	10	2092	Abigail	Thomas	thomasa@job.com	Engineering	France
10	11	1924	Valorie	Anderson	andersonv@job.c...	Marketing	India
11	12	1556	Teesha	Wilson	wilsont@job.com	Marketing	Germany
12	13	2249	Jazzmin	Gonzalez	gonzalezj@job.com	Production	Germany
13	14	1631	Liam	Lopez	lopezl@job.com	Managerial	Germany
14	15	1269	Noah	Hernandez	hernandezn@job....	Managerial	Germany
15	16	2238	William	Martinez	martinezw@job.c...	Managerial	Germany
16	17	2327	James	Rodriguez	rodriguezj@job.com	Engineering	China
17	18	1415	Logan	Davis	davisl@job.com	Finance	USA
18	19	2346	Benjamin	Miller	millerb@job.com	Finance	India
19	20	2398	Mason	Garcia	garciam@job.com	Production	France
20	21	1173	Elijah	Jones	jonese@job.com	Marketing	Germany
21	22	1473	Oliver	Brown	browno@job.com	Marketing	India
22	23	1490	Jason	Williams	williamsj@job.com	Production	Germany
23	24	2492	Lucas	Johnson	johnsonl@job.com	Engineering	Germany
24	25	2391	Michael	Smith	smithm@job.com	Marketing	India
*	26	1234	Francis	Michael	michaelf@job.com	Engineering	China

Figure 14-4. *The account management GUI. The last row of the table displays a new record being added to the database*

This project is broken down into the following parts:

1. Introduce how to use QSqlDatabase to connect to databases and QSqlQuery for creating queries.

2. A few examples of how to use QSqlQuery for editing database items.

3. Introduce QSqlTableModel for creating editable data models that work with tables that do not contain foreign keys.

4. Show how use to QSqlRelationalTableModel for creating editable data models that work with tables that do have foreign key support.

5. Create the account management GUI.

Let's get started!

Explanation for Working with the QtSql Module

In this first example, we are going to see how to use QSqlQuery to create a small database that we will be able to view in the account management GUI. The database has two tables, accounts and countries. The two tables are linked together through the country_id field in accounts and the id field in countries.

Note   This program does not create a GUI. Rather, it demonstrates how to get started with QSqlDatabase for connecting to a database and how to use QSqlQuery to create entries and in a database. It also creates the database, accounts.db, that is used throughout the remainder of the chapter.

Creating a Connection to a Database

Since this program does not create a GUI, we'll only need to import the QSqlDatabase and QSqlQuery classes from QtSql. We will use **QSqlDatabase** to create the connection that allows access to a database; **QSqlQuery** will be used to perform SQL statements in PyQt.

The connection to the database is made in Listing 14-4.

Listing 14-4. Connecting to a database with QSqlDatabase

```python
# create_database.py
# Import necessary modules
import sys, random
from PyQt6.QtSql import QSqlDatabase, QSqlQuery

class CreateEmployeeData:
    """Create a sample database for the project.
    Class demonstrates how to connect to a database, create
    queries, and create tables and records in those tables."""
    # Create connection to database. If db file does not
    # exist, a new db file will be created
    # Use the SQLite version 3 driver
    database = QSqlDatabase.addDatabase("QSQLITE")
    database.setDatabaseName("files/accounts.db")
```

```
if not database.open():
    print("Unable to open data source file.")
    sys.exit(1) # Error code 1 - signifies error
```

We begin by creating a connection to the database in the CreateEmployeeData class. The addDatabase() function allows you to specify the SQL driver that you want to use. The examples in this chapter use SQLite 3 so we pass QSQLITE. Once the database object is created, we can set the other connection parameters, including which database we are going to use, the username, password, host name, and the connection port. For SQLite 3, we only need to specify the name of the database with setDatabaseName(). You can also create multiple connections to a database by passing an additional argument, a connection name, to addDatabase() after the driver argument.

Note   A connection is referenced by its name, not by the name of the database. If you want to give your database a name, pass it as an argument after the driver in the addDatabase() method. If no name is specified, then a *default* connection will be used.

If accounts.db does not already exist, then it will be created. Once the parameters are set, you must call open() to activate the connection to the database. A connection cannot be used until it is opened.

Building a Dataset with QSqlQuery

Now that the connections are established in CreateEmployeeData, we can begin querying our database. You typically might start with databases that already have data in them, but in this example, we are going to see how we can create a database using SQL commands. To query a database using PyQt, we first need to create an instance of QSqlQuery. This is handled in Listing 14-5.

Listing 14-5. Building a dataset with QSqlQuery in the CreateEmployeeData class

```
# create_database.py
    query = QSqlQuery()
    # Erase database contents
```

```
query.exec("DROP TABLE accounts")
query.exec("DROP TABLE countries")

query.exec("""CREATE TABLE accounts (
    id INTEGER PRIMARY KEY AUTOINCREMENT UNIQUE NOT NULL,
    employee_id INTEGER NOT NULL,
    first_name VARCHAR(30) NOT NULL,
    last_name VARCHAR(30) NOT NULL,
    email VARCHAR(40) NOT NULL,
    department VARCHAR(20) NOT NULL,
    country_id VARCHAR(20) REFERENCES countries(id))""")

# Positional binding to insert records into the database
query.prepare("""INSERT INTO accounts (
    employee_id, first_name, last_name,
    email, department, country_id)
    VALUES (?, ?, ?, ?, ?, ?)""")
```

The exec() method is used to execute the SQL queries in PyQt. In the following lines, we want to create a query object and delete the table accounts:

```
query = QSqlQuery()
query.exec("DROP TABLE accounts")
```

Let's next create a new accounts table using exec() and the SQL command CREATE TABLE accounts. Each table entry will have its own unique id by using AUTOINCREMENT. The accounts table will include information for an employee's id, first name, last name, email, department, and the country where they are located. We also create a countries table that holds the names of the employee's countries and is linked to the accounts table using the following line:

```
country_id VARCHAR(20) REFERENCES countries(id))
```

The country_id references the countries table's id. Figure 14-5 shows the connection between the two tables.

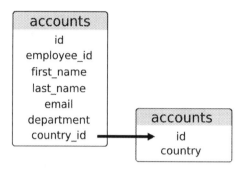

Figure 14-5. *The relations between the accounts and countries tables*

The next task is to insert records into the tables. We could continue to use exec() to execute queries, but this would become tedious if we have a large database. To insert multiple records at the same time, we separate the query from the actual values being inserted using placeholders and the prepare() method. The placeholder will act as a temporary variable, allowing users to supply different data using the same SQL query. In the following code, the **positional placeholders** are the ?. PyQt supports two placeholder syntaxes: the ODBC style, which uses ?, and the Oracle style, which uses :field_name.

```
query.prepare("""INSERT INTO accounts (
            employee_id, first_name, last_name,
            email, department, country_id)
            VALUES (?, ?, ?, ?, ?, ?)""")
```

Each field, such as employee_id or first_name, is associated with one of the placeholders. Since we used AUTOINCREMENT for id, we do not have to include the field or a placeholder in the query.

The prepare() method gets the query ready for execution. If the query is prepared successfully, then values can be **bound** to the fields using the addBindValue() method. For information about executing SQL statements in Qt, have a look at https://doc. qt.io/qt-6/sql-sqlstatements.html. Different approaches for binding values are found at https://doc.qt.io/qt-6/sql-sqlstatements.html.

Next, we'll create the values for the first_name, last_name, and other fields in the SQL tables using Python lists and dictionaries in Listings 14-6 and 14-7.

Listing 14-6. Creating the values for the example dataset in the
CreateEmployeeData class, part 1

```python
# create_database.py
    first_names = ["Emma", "Olivia", "Ava", "Isabella",
        "Sophia", "Mia", "Charlotte", "Amelia", "Evelyn",
        "Abigail", "Valorie", "Teesha", "Jazzmin", "Liam",
        "Noah", "William", "James", "Logan", "Benjamin",
        "Mason", "Elijah", "Oliver", "Jason", "Lucas",
        "Michael"]

    last_names = ["Smith", "Johnson", "Williams", "Brown",
        "Jones", "Garcia", "Miller", "Davis", "Rodriguez",
        "Martinez", "Hernandez", "Lopez", "Gonzalez",
        "Wilson", "Anderson", "Thomas", "Taylor", "Moore",
        "Jackson", "Martin", "Lee", "Perez", "Thompson",
        "White", "Harris"]

    # Create data for the first table, account
    employee_ids = random.sample(
        range(1000, 2500), len(first_names))

    countries = {"USA": 1, "India": 2, "China": 3,
        "France": 4, "Germany": 5}
    country_names = list(countries.keys())
    country_codes = list(countries.values())

    departments = ["Production", "R&D", "Marketing", "HR",
                    "Finance", "Engineering", "Managerial"]

    for f_name in first_names:
        l_name = last_names.pop()
        email = (l_name + f_name[0]).lower() + "@job.com"
        country_id = random.choice(country_codes)
        dept = random.choice(departments)
        employee_id = employee_ids.pop()
        query.addBindValue(employee_id)
        query.addBindValue(f_name)
```

```
query.addBindValue(l_name)
query.addBindValue(email)
query.addBindValue(dept)
query.addBindValue(country_id)
query.exec()
```

A for loop is then used where we bind the values to the placeholders. The exec() method is called at the end of each iteration to insert the values into the accounts table. The countries table is prepared in a similar manner in Listing 14-7.

Listing 14-7. Creating the values for the example dataset in the CreateEmployeeData class, part 2

```
# create_database.py
    # Create data for the second table, countries
    country_query = QSqlQuery()
    country_query.exec("""CREATE TABLE countries (
        id INTEGER PRIMARY KEY AUTOINCREMENT UNIQUE NOT NULL,
        country VARCHAR(20) NOT NULL)""")

    country_query.prepare(
        "INSERT INTO countries (country) VALUES (?)")

    for name in country_names:
        country_query.addBindValue(name)
        country_query.exec()

    print("[INFO] Database successfully created.")

if __name__ == "__main__":
    CreateEmployeeData()
    sys.exit(0)
```

Once the tables are populated, we call sys.exit(0) to exit the program. There is no QApplication instance since there is no GUI.

Visualizing SQL Data Using SQLite

If you want to create a readable SQLite file from `accounts.db` in order to visualize the data, there are a few options. The first is to use available tools, such as SQLiteStudio at `https://sqlitestudio.pl/`, for browsing databases.

Another option is to use the SQLite library. If you are using macOS or Linux, this should already be installed on your system. For Windows, you may have to follow along with the following additional steps (macOS and Linux users should be able to skip this list):

1. On the SQLite download page, `www.sqlite.org/download.html`, download the Precompiled Binaries for Windows. Look for the option that includes command-line tools. Locate where the files have downloaded on your computer. Inside the folder, you'll notice three files, one of which is `sqlite3.exe`.

2. Open a shell window and navigate to `C:\>`. Next, `mkdir sqlite`.

3. Move the three files from step 1 to your new `sqlite` folder. One way to do this is by opening the folder with `start .\sqlite` and dragging and dropping the files.

4. So that you'll be able to use SQLite no matter what folder you are in, you'll need to add the `sqlite` folder you made to your PATH environment variable. On the command line, enter `$env:Path += ";C:\sqlite"`.

5. Finally, run `sqlite3` in the command line, and you should enter the SQLite shell environment. To exit, type `.quit`.

Once you are sure that SQLite is installed, navigate to the `files` folder in your application's directory where `accounts.db` is located, and use the following `sqlite3` command in your shell:

```
$ sqlite3 accounts.db .dump >> accounts.sql
```

You'll see a new file, `accounts.sql`, created in the `files` folder. Also, worth a mention is that SQLite 3 is included as part of the standard Python library, so you can `import sqlite` in your applications if necessary.

In the following section, you'll see how to use `QSqlQuery` to do more than just create tables.

415

Explanation for Querying a Database with QSqlQuery

The program created from Listings 14-8 to 14-10 is not necessary for the accounting manager GUI, but it does give a few more examples for understanding how to input, update, and delete records with SQL in a PyQt application. The purpose of the section is to demonstrate how to open an existing database and modify its contents. We'll do this for the database created in the "Explanation for Working with the QtSql Module" section.

For Listing 14-8, let's import the QSqlDatabase and QSqlQuery classes again. We'll also create a new class called QueryExamples and create two class methods:

- createConnection() – Establishes the connection to the database

- exampleQueries() – Queries the database to acquire and modify existing entries

Listing 14-8. Creating the connection for the QueryExamples class

```python
# query_examples.py
# Import necessary modules
import sys
from PyQt6.QtSql import QSqlDatabase, QSqlQuery

class QueryExamples:

    def __init__(self):
        super().__init__()

        self.createConnection()
        self.exampleQueries()

    def createConnection(self):
        """Create connection to the database."""
        database = QSqlDatabase.addDatabase("QSQLITE")
        database.setDatabaseName("files/accounts.db")

        if not database.open():
            print("Unable to open data source file.")
            sys.exit(1) # Error code 1 - signifies error
```

We start by adding a database using the SQLite 3 driver and a default connection since no connection name is passed to addDatabase(). Next, set the database created in the previous program, accounts.db. Next, we'll complete the connection using open().

In exampleQueries() in Listing 14-9, let's take a look at how to use the QSqlQuery class and the SQL command SELECT to query the database.

Listing 14-9. Demonstrating how to access SQL databases in PyQt

```
# query_examples.py
    def exampleQueries(self):
        """Examples of working with the database."""
        # The QSqlQuery constructor accepts an optional
        # QSqlDatabase object that specifies which database
        # connection to use. In this example, we don't specify
        # any connection, so the default connection is used.
        # If an error occurs, exec() returns false. The error
        # is then available as QSqlQuery::lastError()
        # Executing a simple query
        query = QSqlQuery()
        query.exec("SELECT first_name, last_name FROM \
            accounts WHERE employee_id > 2000")

        # Navigating the result set
        while (query.next()):
            f_name = str(query.value(0))
            l_name = str(query.value(1))
            print(f_name, l_name)
```

We create a new QSqlQuery instance to search for the first and last names of the employees whose employee ids are greater than 2000.

With that query, we could use the values from first_name and last_name to update or delete records. To cycle through the results of the query, we use the QSqlQuery method next(). Other methods that could be used to navigate the results include next(), previous(), first(), and last().

Additional queries are shown in Listing 14-10.

Listing 14-10. Demonstrating how to insert, update, and delete records using SQL and PyQt

```
# query_examples.py
        # Inserting a single new record into the database
        query.exec("""INSERT INTO accounts (
                employee_id, first_name, last_name,
                email, department, country_id)
                VALUES (2134, 'Robert', 'Downey',
                    'downeyr@job.com', 'Managerial', 1)""")

        # Update a record in the database
        query.exec("UPDATE accounts SET department = 'R&D' \
            WHERE employee_id = 2134")

        # Delete a record from the database
        query.exec("DELETE FROM accounts WHERE \
            employee_id <= 1500")
if __name__ == "__main__":
    QueryExamples()
    sys.exit(0)
```

To insert a single record, we can use the INSERT SQL command. In this query, we insert specific values for each field. You could also add multiple records into the database. Refer back to the "Explanation for Working with the QtSql Module" section to see how.

To update records, use UPDATE. We update the department value for the employee that was just inserted. Finally, to delete a record, use DELETE.

This example also has no GUI window. To see the changes, you could run this program after running the program in the "Explanation for Working with the QtSql Module" section and then use the GUI in the next section to visualize the results in a table.

Working with the QSqlTableModel Class

We are finally going to create a GUI for visualizing the database's contents. In the table in Figure 14-6, we are only going to visualize the accounts table to demonstrate the **QSqlTableModel** class, an interface that is useful for reading and writing database records when you only need to use a single table with no links to other tables. The following program will demonstrate how to use Model/View programming to view the contents of a SQL database.

	id	employee_id	first_name	last_name	email	department	country_id
1	2	1980	Olivia	White	whiteo@job.com	HR	2
2	4	1859	Isabella	Perez	perezi@job.com	Managerial	5
3	5	1806	Sophia	Lee	lees@job.com	Production	3
4	7	2031	Charlotte	Jackson	jacksonc@job.com	R&D	3
5	8	1910	Amelia	Moore	moorea@job.com	R&D	2
6	9	1580	Evelyn	Taylor	taylore@job.com	Engineering	4
7	11	1969	Valorie	Anderson	andersonv@job.c...	Engineering	1
8	12	2417	Teesha	Wilson	wilsont@job.com	Managerial	5
9	13	1670	Jazzmin	Gonzalez	gonzalezj@job.com	Engineering	5
10	15	1650	Noah	Hernandez	hernandezn@job....	Engineering	5
11	16	2078	William	Martinez	martinezw@job.c...	Finance	4
12	18	1561	Logan	Davis	davisl@job.com	HR	3
13	19	1926	Benjamin	Miller	millerb@job.com	Production	2
14	21	2137	Elijah	Jones	jonese@job.com	Engineering	1
15	22	1780	Oliver	Brown	browno@job.com	HR	4

Figure 14-6. *The table created using QSqlTableModel*

We could use QSqlQuery to do all of the database work, but combining the class with the Model/View paradigm allows us to design GUIs that make the data management process simpler.

Explanation for Working with QSqlTableModel

Get started by using the basic_window.py script from Chapter 1 and then import the PyQt classes we need, including QSqlTableModel, in Listing 14-11. **QHeaderView** is the class that provides both horizontal and vertical headers for item view classes.

Next, create the MainWindow class for displaying the contents of the database.

419

Listing 14-11. Code for the MainWindow class using QSqlTableModel

```python
# table_model.py
# Import necessary modules
import sys
from PyQt6.QtWidgets import (QApplication, QWidget,
    QTableView, QHeaderView, QMessageBox, QVBoxLayout)
from PyQt6.QtSql import QSqlDatabase, QSqlTableModel

class MainWindow(QWidget):

    def __init__(self):
        super().__init__()
        self.initializeUI()

    def initializeUI(self):
        """Set up the application's GUI."""
        self.setMinimumSize(1000, 500)
        self.setWindowTitle("SQL Table Model")

        self.createConnection()
        self.setUpMainWindow()
        self.show()

if __name__ == "__main__":
    app = QApplication(sys.argv)
    window = MainWindow()
    sys.exit(app.exec())
```

We'll call createConnection() before setUpMainWindow() since the model and view objects in the main window rely on the data from the database. In the createConnection() method in Listing 14-12, we connect to the database and activate the connection with open(). This time, let's check to make sure that the tables we want to use are in the database. If they cannot be found, then a dialog box like the one in Figure 14-7 will be displayed to inform the user and the program will close.

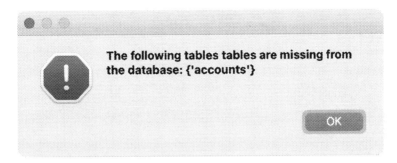

Figure 14-7. *QMessageBox letting users know that the table they want to view is missing*

Listing 14-12. Code for the createConnection() method in the QSqlTableModel example

```
# table_model.py
    def createConnection(self):
        """Set up the connection to the database.
        Check for the tables needed."""
        database = QSqlDatabase.addDatabase("QSQLITE")
        database.setDatabaseName("files/accounts.db")

        if not database.open():
            print("Unable to open data source file.")
            sys.exit(1) # Error code 1 - signifies error

        # Check if the tables we need exist in the database
        tables_needed = {"accounts"}
        tables_not_found = tables_needed - \
            set(database.tables())
        if tables_not_found:
            QMessageBox.critical(None, "Error",
                f"""<p>The following tables are missing
                from the database: {tables_not_found}</p>""")
            sys.exit(1) # Error code 1 - signifies error
```

The instances of the QSqlTableModel and the QTableView are created in the setUpMainWindow() method in Listing 14-13. For QSqlTableModel, we need to set the database table we want to use with setTable(). Here, we'll use the accounts table.

Listing 14-13. Code for the setUpMainWindow() method in the QSqlTableModel example

```python
# table_model.py
    def setUpMainWindow(self):
        """Create and arrange widgets in the main window."""
        # Create the model
        model = QSqlTableModel()
        model.setTable("accounts")

        table_view = QTableView()
        table_view.setModel(model)
        table_view.horizontalHeader().setSectionResizeMode(
            QHeaderView.ResizeMode.Stretch)

        # Populate the model with data
        model.select()

        main_v_box = QVBoxLayout()
        main_v_box.addWidget(table_view)
        self.setLayout(main_v_box)
```

Next, create a QTableView object and set its model using setModel(). To make the table stretch to fit into the view horizontally, we use the following line:

```python
        table_view.horizontalHeader().setSectionResizeMode(
            QHeaderView.Stretch)
```

This line also handles stretching the table when the window resizes.

Finally, the model is populated with data using select(). If you have made changes to the table but have not submitted them, then select() will cause the edited items to return back to their previous states.

Figure 14-6 displays the contents of the database in a table view. Notice how the header labels display the field names used when the database was created. We will see how to set header labels when we actually create the account management GUI. Also, the country_id column currently only displays numbers associated with the different names in the countries table. If you only want to display specific columns, the following code lets you select which ones you want to display:

```
model.setQuery(QSqlQuery("SELECT id, employee_id,
    first_name, last_name FROM accounts"))
```

In the next section, you'll find out how to create and display relations set by foreign keys in the table view.

Working with the QSqlRelationalTableModel Class

Next, we are going to see how to use the `QSqlRelationalTableModel` class for working with relational databases. The **`QSqlRelationalTableModel`** class provides a model for managing and editing data in a SQL table, with additional support for using foreign keys. A foreign key is a SQL constraint used to link tables together.

The application in Figure 14-8 builds upon the GUI in the "Working with the QSqlTableModel Class" section.

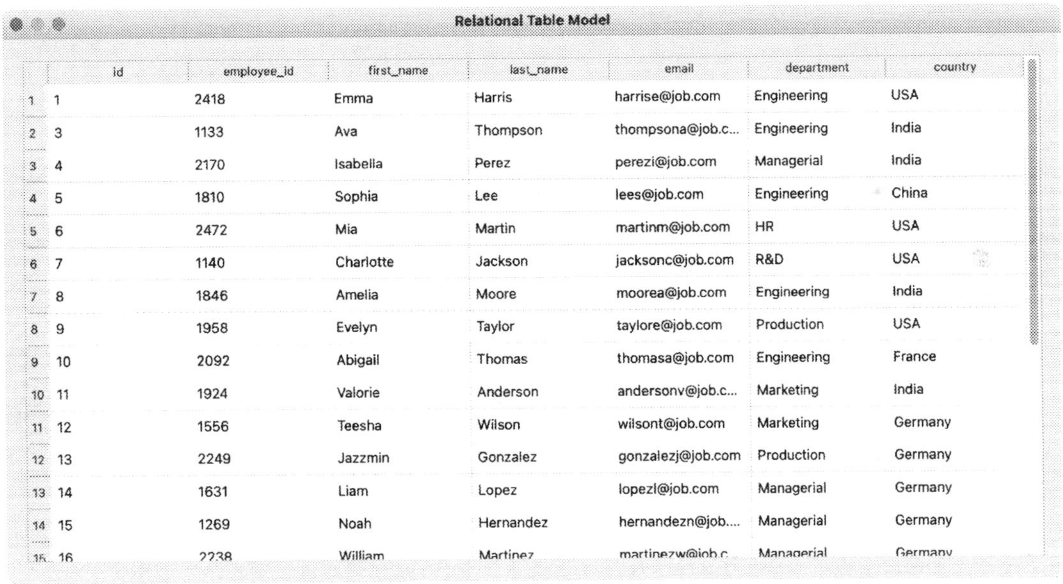

	id	employee_id	first_name	last_name	email	department	country
1	1	2418	Emma	Harris	harrise@job.com	Engineering	USA
2	3	1133	Ava	Thompson	thompsona@job.c...	Engineering	India
3	4	2170	Isabella	Perez	perezi@job.com	Managerial	India
4	5	1810	Sophia	Lee	lees@job.com	Engineering	China
5	6	2472	Mia	Martin	martinm@job.com	HR	USA
6	7	1140	Charlotte	Jackson	jacksonc@job.com	R&D	USA
7	8	1846	Amelia	Moore	moorea@job.com	Engineering	India
8	9	1958	Evelyn	Taylor	taylore@job.com	Production	USA
9	10	2092	Abigail	Thomas	thomasa@job.com	Engineering	France
10	11	1924	Valorie	Anderson	andersonv@job.c...	Marketing	India
11	12	1556	Teesha	Wilson	wilsont@job.com	Marketing	Germany
12	13	2249	Jazzmin	Gonzalez	gonzalezj@job.com	Production	Germany
13	14	1631	Liam	Lopez	lopezl@job.com	Managerial	Germany
14	15	1269	Noah	Hernandez	hernandezn@job....	Managerial	Germany
15	16	2238	William	Martinez	martinezw@job.c...	Managerial	Germany

Figure 14-8. *The table created using QSqlRelationalTableModel*

Explanation for Working with QSqlRelationalTableModel

Start with `basic_window.py` script from Chapter 1. This time we need to import `QSqlRelationalTableModel` since we are working with relational databases and foreign keys. Also, **`QSqlRelation`** is included because we'll need to use the class to store the information about SQL foreign keys. The **QSqlRelationalDelegate** is also needed because we'll need to display editor widgets in the columns that pertain to foreign keys.

Listing 14-14 handles all of this as well as sets up the MainWindow class.

Listing 14-14. Code for the MainWindow class using QSqlRelationalTableModel

```
# relational_model.py
# Import necessary modules
import sys
from PyQt6.QtWidgets import (QApplication, QWidget,
    QTableView, QMessageBox, QHeaderView, QVBoxLayout)
from PyQt6.QtSql import (QSqlDatabase, QSqlRelation,
    QSqlRelationalTableModel, QSqlRelationalDelegate)

class MainWindow(QWidget):

    def __init__(self):
        super().__init__()
        self.initializeUI()

    def initializeUI(self):
        """Set up the application's GUI."""
        self.setMinimumSize(1000, 500)
        self.setWindowTitle("Relational Table Model")

        self.createConnection()
        self.setUpMainWindow()
        self.show()

if __name__ == "__main__":
    app = QApplication(sys.argv)
    window = MainWindow()
    sys.exit(app.exec())
```

We connect to the database in Listing 14-15 just like we did in the QSqlTableModel example, except this time we are checking for both tables, accounts and countries.

Listing 14-15. Code for the createConnection() method in the QSqlRelationalTableModel example

```python
# relational_model.py
    def createConnection(self):
        """Set up the connection to the database.
        Check for the tables needed."""
        database = QSqlDatabase.addDatabase("QSQLITE")
        database.setDatabaseName("files/accounts.db")

        if not database.open():
            print("Unable to open data source file.")
            sys.exit(1) # Error code 1 - signifies error

        # Check if the tables we need exist in the database
        tables_needed = {"accounts", "countries"}
        tables_not_found = tables_needed - \
            set(database.tables())
        if tables_not_found:
            QMessageBox.critical(None, "Error",
                f"""<p>The following tables are missing
                from the database: {tables_not_found}</p>""")
            sys.exit(1) # Error code 1 - signifies error
```

For setUpMainWindow() in Listing 14-16, create instances of the QSqlRelationalTableModel and QTableView classes. The setTable() method causes model to fetch the accounts table's information.

Listing 14-16. Code for the setUpMainWindow() method in the QSqlRelationalTableModel example

```python
# relational_model.py
    def setUpMainWindow(self):
        """Create and arrange widgets in the main window."""
        # Create the model
        model = QSqlRelationalTableModel()
        model.setTable("accounts")
```

```
# Set up relationship for foreign keys
model.setRelation(model.fieldIndex("country_id"),
    QSqlRelation("countries", "id", "country"))

table_view = QTableView()
table_view.setModel(model)
table_view.horizontalHeader().setSectionResizeMode(
    QHeaderView.ResizeMode.Stretch)

# Populate the model with data
model.select()
```

The country_id field in accounts is mapped to countries table's field, id. For the QSqlRelationalTableModel method setRelation(), we'll need to pass the index of the column that contains a foreign key (done with fieldIndex()) and a QSqlRelation object that defines the relationship. For QSqlRelation, the field id of table countries maps to country_id in the accounts table. The final argument, country, specifies which field should be displayed in the accounts table.

If you compare Figure 14-8 to Figure 14-6, you'll notice that data in the last column, country, has been updated to display the names of the countries and that the header has also been changed to country.

Adding Delegates to Edit Relational Data

The purpose of delegates when using Model/View classes becomes more obvious when you either start creating your own custom classes or when you need to use relational classes to select values for fields with foreign keys. With a delegate, an editor widget such as QLineEdit or QComboBox will appear when a user is editing data. You may not have even realized that every time you edit values in the cells of QTableView, you have been using a delegate all along. That's because of how Qt seamlessly blends the view and delegates.

For SQL relational databases, QSqlRelationalDelegate data from a QSqlRelationalTableModel can be viewed and edited.

For the final portion of setUpMainWindow(), let's create a QSqlRelationalDelegate instance and add it to table_view using setItemDelegate() in Listing 14-17.

Listing 14-17. Adding delegates in the QSqlRelationalTableModel example

```
# relational_model.py
        # Instantiate the delegate
        delegate = QSqlRelationalDelegate()
        table_view.setItemDelegate(delegate)

        main_v_box = QVBoxLayout()
        main_v_box.addWidget(table_view)
        self.setLayout(main_v_box)
```

Now if you double-click in the country column, you will see a QComboBox appear containing the list of countries. An example of this is shown in Figure 14-9.

Figure 14-9. *An editor widget (QComboBox) displayed in a column with foreign keys*

The last step is to create and set the layout for the main window.

By this point, you should have a fundamental understanding of how to use model and view classes, use QtSql classes to perform queries, and display foreign key relationships in a table using relational classes. We are now ready to build the account management GUI.

Explanation for the Account Management GUI

The account management GUI uses the QSqlRelationalTableModel for managing the accounts and countries tables. We'll use the concepts we learned in the previous sections to design a GUI with features for managing the database directly rather than programmatically. Refer back to Figure 14-4 to see the interface.

The application lets a user add, delete, and sort the contents of the table. Rows added or deleted will also update the database.

Also, be sure to download the icons folder from GitHub for this project.

For Listing 14-18, let's start with the basic_window.py script from Chapter 1 and import a variety of classes.

Listing 14-18. Code for the MainWindow class in the account management GUI

```
# account_manager.py
# Import necessary modules
import sys, os
from PyQt6.QtWidgets import (QApplication, QWidget, QLabel,
    QPushButton, QComboBox, QTableView, QHeaderView,
    QAbstractItemView, QMessageBox, QHBoxLayout, QVBoxLayout,
    QSizePolicy)
from PyQt6.QtCore import Qt
from PyQt6.QtGui import QIcon
from PyQt6.QtSql import (QSqlDatabase, QSqlQuery,
    QSqlRelation, QSqlRelationalTableModel,
    QSqlRelationalDelegate)

class MainWindow(QWidget):

    def __init__(self):
        super().__init__()
        self.initializeUI()

    def initializeUI(self):
        """Set up the application's GUI."""
        self.setMinimumSize(1000, 600)
        self.setWindowTitle("14.1 - Account Management GUI")
```

```
        self.createConnection()
        self.createModel()
        self.setUpMainWindow()
        self.show()

if __name__ == '__main__':
    app = QApplication(sys.argv)
    window = MainWindow()
    sys.exit(app.exec())
```

For this GUI, a separate method, createModel(), will create the
QSqlRelationalTableModel that is used by the QTableView object in
setUpMainWindow(). This is done to help organize the code.

The next task is to connect to accounts.db just like we have previously done in
createConnections(). This is handled in Listing 14-19.

Listing 14-19. Code for the createConnection() method in the account
management GUI

```
# account_manager.py
    def createConnection(self):
        """Set up the connection to the database.
        Check for the tables needed."""
        database = QSqlDatabase.addDatabase("QSQLITE")
        database.setDatabaseName("files/accounts.db")

        if not database.open():
            print("Unable to open data source file.")
            sys.exit(1) # Error code 1 - signifies error

        # Check if the tables we need exist in the database
        tables_needed = {"accounts", "countries"}
        tables_not_found = tables_needed - \
            set(database.tables())
        if tables_not_found:
            QMessageBox.critical(None, "Error",
                f"""<p>The following tables are missing
                from the database: {tables_not_found}</p>""")
            sys.exit(1) # Error code 1 - signifies error
```

The createModel() method in Listing 14-20 instantiates and sets up model, establishing the foreign key relationship between the two tables with setRelation(). The setHeaderData() method applies labels to each of the columns. We can use the QSqlTableModel method that QSqlRelationalTableModel inherits, fieldIndex(), to specify the index of a field name and modify its value.

Listing 14-20. Code for the createModel() method for the account management GUI

```python
# account_manager.py
    def createModel(self):
        """Set up the model and headers, and populate the
        model."""
        self.model = QSqlRelationalTableModel()
        self.model.setTable("accounts")
        self.model.setRelation(
            self.model.fieldIndex("country_id"),
                QSqlRelation("countries", "id", "country"))

        self.model.setHeaderData(
            self.model.fieldIndex("id"),
                Qt.Orientation.Horizontal, "ID")
        self.model.setHeaderData(
            self.model.fieldIndex("employee_id"),
                Qt.Orientation.Horizontal, "Employee ID")
        self.model.setHeaderData(
            self.model.fieldIndex("first_name"),
                Qt.Orientation.Horizontal, "First")
        self.model.setHeaderData(
            self.model.fieldIndex("last_name"),
                Qt.Orientation.Horizontal, "Last")
        self.model.setHeaderData(
            self.model.fieldIndex("email"),
                Qt.Orientation.Horizontal, "E-mail")
        self.model.setHeaderData(
            self.model.fieldIndex("department"),
                Qt.Orientation.Horizontal, "Dept.")
```

```
self.model.setHeaderData(
    self.model.fieldIndex("country_id"),
        Qt.Orientation.Horizontal, "Country")

# Populate the model with data
self.model.select()
```

The QTableView object, table_view, is created in Listing 14-21 in the setUpMainWindow() method. The GUI's labels, push buttons, and combo box are also instantiated.

Listing 14-21. Code for the setUpMainWindow() method in the account management GUI, part 1

```python
# account_manager.py
    def setUpMainWindow(self):
        """Create and arrange widgets in the main window."""
        icons_path = "icons"

        title = QLabel("Account Management System")
        title.setSizePolicy(QSizePolicy.Policy.Fixed,
            QSizePolicy.Policy.Fixed)
        title.setStyleSheet("font: bold 24px")

        add_product_button = QPushButton("Add Employee")
        add_product_button.setIcon(QIcon(os.path.join(
            icons_path, "add_user.png")))
        add_product_button.setStyleSheet("padding: 10px")
        add_product_button.clicked.connect(self.addItem)

        del_product_button = QPushButton("Delete")
        del_product_button.setIcon(QIcon(os.path.join(
            icons_path, "trash_can.png")))
        del_product_button.setStyleSheet("padding: 10px")
        del_product_button.clicked.connect(self.deleteItem)

        # Set up sorting combobox
        sorting_options = [
            "Sort by ID", "Sort by Employee ID",
```

```
                "Sort by First Name", "Sort by Last Name",
                "Sort by Department", "Sort by Country"]
        sort_combo = QComboBox()
        sort_combo.addItems(sorting_options)
        sort_combo.currentTextChanged.connect(
            self.setSortingOrder)

        buttons_h_box = QHBoxLayout()
        buttons_h_box.addWidget(add_product_button)
        buttons_h_box.addWidget(del_product_button)
        buttons_h_box.addStretch()
        buttons_h_box.addWidget(sort_combo)

        # Widget to contain editing buttons
        edit_container = QWidget()
        edit_container.setLayout(buttons_h_box)
```

The add_product_button and del_product_button objects are used to add and delete items from the table and the model. Each button is connected to a slot using the clicked signal. The slots are created in Listing 14-23.

Items in a view can also be sorted. The sort_combo provides various ways to organize the table's data based on the column names. For the QComboBox, when the selection has changed, the widget can emit a currentTextChanged signal. The signal also passes text that we can use to determine how to set the view's order for displaying records in the setSortingOrder() slot. This is handled in Listing 14-24. The widgets are then arranged in buttons_h_box and added to edit_container.

For table_view, in Listing 14-22, we set its model and a few parameters. These include setting the table's vertical and horizontal headers to stretch and fill the space in the window. For this example, users can only select single items in the table using the flag SingleSelection.

Listing 14-22. Code for the setUpMainWindow() method in the account management GUI, part 2

```
# account_manager.py
        # Create table view and set model
        self.table_view = QTableView()
        self.table_view.setModel(self.model)
```

```
horizontal = self.table_view.horizontalHeader()
horizontal.setSectionResizeMode(
    QHeaderView.ResizeMode.Stretch)
vertical = self.table_view.verticalHeader()
vertical.setSectionResizeMode(
    QHeaderView.ResizeMode.Stretch)

self.table_view.setSelectionMode(
    QAbstractItemView.SelectionMode.SingleSelection)
self.table_view.setSelectionBehavior(
    QAbstractItemView.SelectionBehavior.SelectRows)

# Instantiate the delegate
delegate = QSqlRelationalDelegate()
self.table_view.setItemDelegate(delegate)

# Main layout
main_v_box = QVBoxLayout()
main_v_box.addWidget(
    title, Qt.AlignmentFlag.AlignLeft)
main_v_box.addWidget(edit_container)
main_v_box.addWidget(self.table_view)
self.setLayout(main_v_box)
```

For view classes, the behavior for selecting rows, columns, or single items can be defined using QAbstractItemView.SelectionBehavior. The following list describes the different flags:

- SelectRows – Only rows can be selected

- SelectColumns – Only columns can be selected

- SelectItems – Only individual items can be selected

In Model/View programming, the delegate provides the default tools for painting item data in the view and for providing editor widgets for item models. The appearance and editor widgets of the item delegate can be customized. For the account management GUI, the delegate used is the QSqlRelationalDelegate. This class provides a combo box for editing data in fields that are foreign keys for other tables.

An example of the combo box used by the delegate can be seen in the bottom-right corner of Figure 14-4. The widget appears whenever the user needs to select a country from the countries table that will be displayed in the view.

For addItem() in Listing 14-23, we check how many rows are in the table with rowCount() and use insertRow() to insert an empty row at the end of table view. We query the database to find out the largest id value in the table. If a user does not enter a value for id into the row, then the new record's id is equal to the highest id value plus one. It is also worth noting that if every item in the new row is not filled in, the new record will not be saved to the model upon closing the application.

Listing 14-23. Code for addItem() and deleteItem() slots in the account management GUI

```
# account_manager.py
    def addItem(self):
        """Add a new record to the last row of the table."""
        last_row = self.model.rowCount()
        self.model.insertRow(last_row)

        query = QSqlQuery()
        query.exec("SELECT MAX (id) FROM accounts")
        if query.next():
            int(query.value(0))

    def deleteItem(self):
        """Delete an entire row from the table."""
        current_item = self.table_view.selectedIndexes()
        for index in current_item:
            self.model.removeRow(index.row())
        self.model.select()
```

For deleteItem(), we get the currently selected row's index and delete the row with removeRow(). Then we update the model using select().

The last slot to create in the MainWindow class is setSortingOrder(). We'll use the text that is passed from the currentTextChanged signal to determine how to sort the data. For example, if the user wants to order the items using employee id numbers, they'll first select Sort by Employee ID in the QComboBox. The signal is then emitted, and the value of text is compared in various conditions in setSortingOrder(). The setSort() method is then used to organize the employee_id field in ascending order.

Listing 14-24. Code for setSortingOrder() slot in the account management GUI

```
# account_manager.py
    def setSortingOrder(self, text):
        """Sort the rows in the table."""
        if text == "Sort by ID":
            self.model.setSort(self.model.fieldIndex("id"),
                Qt.SortOrder.AscendingOrder)
        elif text == "Sort by Employee ID":
            self.model.setSort(
                self.model.fieldIndex("employee_id"),
                    Qt.SortOrder.AscendingOrder)
        elif text == "Sort by First Name":
            self.model.setSort(
                self.model.fieldIndex("first_name"),
                    Qt.SortOrder.AscendingOrder)
        elif text == "Sort by Last Name":
            self.model.setSort(
                self.model.fieldIndex("last_name"),
                    Qt.SortOrder.AscendingOrder)
        elif text == "Sort by Department":
            self.model.setSort(
                self.model.fieldIndex("department"),
                    Qt.SortOrder.AscendingOrder)
        elif text == "Sort by Country":
            self.model.setSort(
                self.model.fieldIndex("country"),
                    Qt.SortOrder.AscendingOrder)

        self.model.select()
```

Finally, select() is called to update the model and view with the data.

435

At this point, you should run the application and test it out. If you want to tinker around with the code, first have a look at the different selection modes and selection behaviors. From there, you could go back to the SQL database and try implementing additional fields or create new foreign keys to test out the relational classes.

Summary

PyQt provides convenience classes for lists, tables, and trees. QListWidget, QTableWidget, and QTreeWidget are useful when you need to view data for general situations. While they are practical for creating quick interfaces for editing data, if you need to have more than one widget for displaying a dataset in an application, you must also create a process for keeping the datasets and the widgets in agreement. A better option is to use PyQt's Model/View architecture.

There are different formats available for storing and managing data. One example is the CSV format that is convenient for reading, parsing, and storing smaller datasets. However, for large databases that contain multiple tables with relational characteristics, a Relational Database Management System that uses the SQL language is a more preferable option for managing the data. SQL allows users to select desired information that might be shared between tables as well as insert, update, and delete existing records easily.

Model/View is very useful for working with SQL databases, providing the tools necessary for connecting to a database and viewing its content. Qt provides three models for working with SQL databases. For an editable data model without foreign key support, use `QSqlTableModel`. If you have tables with relational properties, use `QSqlRelationalTableModel`. Finally, the **QSqlQueryModel** is beneficial when you only need to read the results of a query without editing them.

Over the course of this book, we took a look at a few applications that could have benefited greatly from data management. The login GUI in Chapter 3 could connect to a database to retrieve usernames and passwords. There is also the pizza ordering GUI from Chapter 6. You could implement a database for storing customer's information, using a relational database for adding new customers, updating existing ones, and preventing data from being duplicated.

In Chapter 15, we will take a brief look at multithreading in PyQt.

CHAPTER 15

Managing Threads

We have all experienced that moment when running some process such as copying files between directories or launching a new instance of an application causes a program to lag for just a moment and, in some cases, to freeze completely. We are then forced to either wait for the current task to complete or Ctrl+Alt+Delete our way to freedom. When you are creating GUIs, you should be aware of how to handle and have foresight about avoiding these situations.

In this chapter, you will

- Consider techniques to handle time-consuming processes in PyQt

- Learn how to implement threading in GUIs with QThread

- Use the QProgressBar widget for giving visual feedback about a task's progression

The motivation behind this chapter is twofold: to help you design more robust GUI applications while also informing you how you might be able to handle situations where your applications need to run long processes. Any action that causes event processing to come to a standstill is bad for a user's experience.

Introduction to Threading

A computer's performance can be measured by the accuracy, efficiency, and speed at which it can execute program instructions. Modern computers can take advantage of their multicore processors to run those instructions in parallel, thereby increasing the performance of computer applications that have been written to utilize a multicore architecture.

© Joshua M Willman 2022
J. M. Willman, *Beginning PyQt*, https://doi.org/10.1007/978-1-4842-7999-1_15

The idea of performing tasks in a synchronous manner where only one task is processed at a time until completion before moving on to the next task can be inefficient, especially for larger operations. What we need is a way to perform operations concurrently. That is where threads and processes come into play.

Threads and processes are not the same thing. Without going too much into the technical jargon, let's try and understand the differences between the two. A **process** is an instance of an application that requires memory and computer resources to run. Opening up the word processor on your computer to write an essay is one process. While writing your essay, you need to search on the Internet for information. You now have two separate processes running on your computer independently and in parallel. What happens in one process is not influencing the other. Of course, you have multiple tabs open in the web browser, and each tab is loading and updating information; those tabs are working side by side with the web browser. This is where a thread becomes important.

A **thread** is essential to the concurrency within an individual process. When a process begins, it only has one thread, and multiple threads can be started within a single process. These threads, just like the processes, are managed by the central processing unit (CPU). **Multithreading** occurs when the CPU can handle multiple threads of execution concurrently within one process. These threads are independent but also share the process's resources. Using multithreading allows for applications to be more responsive to user's inputs while other operations are occurring in the background and to better utilize a system's resources.

On a system with a CPU with only a single core, true parallelism is actually unachievable. In these instances, the CPU is shared among the processes or threads. To switch between threads, **context switches** are used to interrupt the current thread, save its state, and then restore the next thread's state. This gives the user a false appearance of parallelism.

To achieve true parallelism and create a truly concurrent system, a multicore processor would allow threads in a multithreaded application to be assigned to different processors.

Threading in PyQt

Applications based on Qt are event based. When the event loop is started using exec(), a thread is created. This thread is referred to as the **main thread** of the GUI. Any events that take place in the main thread, including the GUI itself, run synchronously within the main event loop. To take advantage of threading, we need to create a **secondary thread** to offload processing operations from the main thread.

PyQt makes communicating between the main thread and secondary threads, also referred to as **worker threads**, simple with signals and slots. This can be useful for relaying feedback, allowing the user to interrupt a process, and for informing the main thread that a process has finished. Since threads utilize the same address space, they can share data very easily.

Be cautious, though. If multiple threads try to access shared data or resources concurrently, this can cause crashes or memory corruption. Deadlock is another issue that can occur if two threads are blocked because they are waiting for resources. PyQt provides a few classes, for example, `QMutex`, `QReadWriteLock`, and `QSemaphore`, for avoiding these kinds of problems.

Note   Python also has a number of modules for handling threading and processing tasks, including `_thread`, `threading`, `asyncio`, and `multiprocessing`. While you can also use these modules, PyQt's `QThread` and other classes allow you to emit signals between the main and worker threads.

Methods for Processing Long Events in PyQt

While this chapter focuses on using `QThread`, it is also a good idea to keep in mind that there are also other ways that you might want to try before attempting to use threading in your GUI. Implementing threading can lead to problems with concurrency and identifying errors. Combined with signals and slots, PyQt provides a few different ways to handle time-consuming operations.

Choosing which method is best for your application comes down to considering your situation. The following are the main methods, including threading, for handling these kinds of events:

1. If there is a process in your application that is causing it to freeze, check to see if that process can be broken down into smaller steps and perform them sequentially. Manually handle the processing of long operations, and explicitly call `QApplication.processEvents()` to process pending events. This works best if your operations can be processed using a single thread.

2.   With **QTimer** and signals and slots, you can schedule operations to
     be performed at certain intervals in the future.

3.   Use **QThread** to create a worker thread that will perform long
     operations in a separate thread. Derive a class from QThread,
     reimplement run(), and use signals and slots to communicate
     with the main thread. This method can help to avoid blocking the
     main event loop.

4.   The **QThreadPool** and **QRunnable** classes can be used to divide the
     work across the CPU cores on your computer. Create a subclass
     of QRunnable and reimplement the run() function; an instance
     of QRunnable can then be passed to threads that are managed by
     QThreadPool. QThreadPool handles the queuing and execution of
     QRunnable instances for you.

There are even other options that may depend upon your application's
requirements. Keep in mind that while using threads could benefit your application, they
could also slow it down or cause errors if used incorrectly.

Project 15.1 – File Renaming GUI

Creating and labeling datasets often entails writing Python scripts for labeling thousands
of images and data files. Those scripts are generally written to include some kind of
visual feedback to the user about how the process is going in the command line.

For the GUI in Figure 15-1, we are going to create a GUI that will allow us to select
a local directory and edit the names of files in the folder with the specified extension.
The interface includes QTextEdit and QProgressBar widgets as two different means
of feedback about the file labeling process. This application also takes advantage of
the QThread class so that users are still able to interact with the interface while the
operations are being performed in the background.

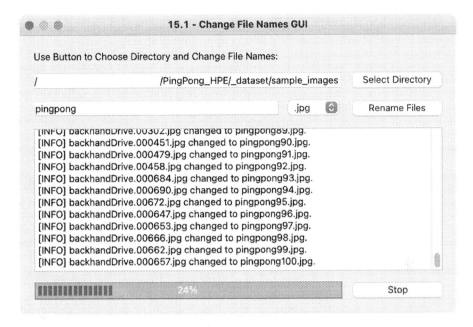

Figure 15-1. *The interface for renaming files in a selected directory*

The QProgressBar Widget

The **QProgressBar** widget visually relays the progress of an extended operation back to the user. This feedback can also be used as reassurance that a process such as a download, installation, or file transfer is still running. Some of the settings that can be controlled include the widget's orientation and range.

Refer to the project in the following sections for setting up a progress bar.

Explanation for File Renaming GUI

The GUI window contains various buttons and editor widgets that allow the user to manage file renaming. The user can select a directory using a QPushButton and the QFileDialog that appears. The new file name can be entered into a QLineEdit widget. Using a QComboBox, the file extension for the files that need to be changed can also be selected.

The application uses threading to update the progress bar, display information about the files being changed in the text edit, and perform the actual renaming operation. This is all done using signals and slots.

Let's start by using the basic_window.py script from Chapter 1 as a template. Next, import the Python and PyQt classes in Listing 15-1. The QThread class is part of QtCore.

Listing 15-1. Code for imports and the style sheet used in the file renaming GUI

```python
# file_rename_threading.py
# Import necessary modules
import os, sys, time
from PyQt6.QtWidgets import (QApplication, QWidget, QLabel,
    QProgressBar, QLineEdit, QPushButton, QTextEdit,
    QComboBox, QFileDialog, QGridLayout)
from PyQt6.QtCore import pyqtSignal, QThread

style_sheet = """
    QProgressBar{
        background-color: #C0C6CA;
        color: #FFFFFF;
        border: 1px solid grey;
        padding: 3px;
        height: 15px;
        text-align: center;
    }

    QProgressBar::chunk{
        background: #538DB8;
        width: 5px;
        margin: 0.5px
    }
"""
```

The style sheet is used to modify the appearance of the QProgressBar. Besides changing the look of the progress bar, we can also edit the appearance of the subcontrol chunk in order to create a blocky look to the bars as they update.

For this GUI, let's create a class that inherits QThread. The Worker class in Listing 15-2 will be used to update the progress bar, update the text edit widget, and actually perform the task of renaming the image files, thereby freeing up the main event loop to perform other tasks. An instance of a QThread class manages only one thread.

Three custom signals are created for updating the progress bar and text edit widgets:

- update_value_signal – Emits a signal that is used to update the integer value of the progress bar

- update_text_edit_signal – Used to update the content of the QTextEdit widget. Passes string information about the old file name and the new file name

- clear_text_edit_signal – Signal that is used to clear the text edit widget if the user stops running the worker thread

Listing 15-2. Creating the Worker class that subclasses QThread

```python
# file_rename_threading.py
# Create worker thread for running tasks like updating
# the progress bar, renaming photos, displaying information
# in the text edit widget.
class Worker(QThread):
    update_value_signal = pyqtSignal(int)
    update_text_edit_signal = pyqtSignal(str, str)
    clear_text_edit_signal = pyqtSignal()

    def __init__(self, dir, ext, prefix):
        super().__init__()
        self.dir = dir
        self.ext = ext
        self.prefix = prefix

    def stopRunning(self):
        """Terminate the thread."""
        self.terminate()
        self.wait()

        self.update_value_signal.emit(0)
        self.clear_text_edit_signal.emit()

    def run(self):
        """The thread begins running from here.
        run() is only called after start()."""
```

```
for (i, file) in enumerate(os.listdir(self.dir)):
    _, file_ext = os.path.splitext(file)
    if file_ext == self.ext:
        new_file_name = self.prefix + str(i) + \
            self.ext
        src_path = os.path.join(self.dir, file)
        dst_path = os.path.join(
            self.dir, new_file_name)

        # os.rename(src, dst): src is original address
        # of file to be renamed and dst is destination
        # location with new name
        os.rename(src_path, dst_path)
        # Uncomment if process is too fast and want to
        # see the updates
        #time.sleep(1.0)

        self.update_value_signal.emit(i + 1)
        self.update_text_edit_signal.emit(
            file, new_file_name)
    else:
        pass
# Reset the value of the progress bar
self.update_value_signal.emit(0)
```

The reimplemented QThread method, run(), begins executing the thread. The time-consuming operations – traversing the directory, renaming files, and emitting the signals for updating the QProgressBar and QTextEdit – are performed in run(). However, this method is not called directly. The QThread method start() is used to communicate with the worker thread and begin executing the thread by calling run(). The start() method is called from the MainWindow class method renameFiles() in Listing 15-8.

The stopRunning() slot is used to end the thread's processes when the user pushes the Stop button in the main window. The terminate() method is used to end the thread, and wait() is used to make sure that the thread ends by blocking the thread.

Listing 15-3 begins creating the MainWindow class that inherits QWidget.

Listing 15-3. Base code for the MainWindow class

```python
# file_rename_threading.py
class MainWindow(QWidget):

    def __init__(self):
        super().__init__()
        self.initializeUI()

    def initializeUI(self):
        """Set up the application's GUI."""
        self.setMinimumSize(600, 250)
        self.setWindowTitle("15.1 - Change File Names GUI")

        self.directory = ""
        self.combo_value = ""

        self.setUpMainWindow()
        self.show()

if __name__ == "__main__":
    app = QApplication(sys.argv)
    app.setStyleSheet(style_sheet)
    window = MainWindow()
    sys.exit(app.exec())
```

The variable directory is used to store the value of the directory selected, and combo_value pertains to the file extension value selected in the QComboBox.

In Listing 15-4, setUpMainWindow() is used to create the label, line edit, and button for selecting a directory. Various widgets in this program also use tooltips to provide more information to the user about a widget's purpose or functionality.

Listing 15-4. Creating the setUpMainWindow() for the file renaming GUI, part 1

```python
# file_rename_threading.py
    def setUpMainWindow(self):
        """Create and arrange widgets in the main window."""
        dir_label = QLabel(
            """<p>Use Button to Choose Directory and
            Change File Names:</p>""")
```

```
        self.dir_edit = QLineEdit()
        dir_button = QPushButton("Select Directory")
        dir_button.setToolTip("Select file directory.")
        dir_button.clicked.connect(self.chooseDirectory)
```

For specifying new file names, text can be entered into change_name_edit in Listing 15-5. The QComboBox is used to determine which file types to change in the selected directory. Only files with the selected extension will be changed while the renaming process is running.

Listing 15-5. Creating the setUpMainWindow() for the file renaming GUI, part 2

```
# file_rename_threading.py
        self.change_name_edit = QLineEdit()
        self.change_name_edit.setToolTip(
            """<p>Files will be appended with numerical
            values. For example: filename<b>01</b>.jpg</p>""")
        self.change_name_edit.setPlaceholderText(
            "Change file names to…")

        file_exts = [".jpg", ".jpeg", ".png", ".gif", ".txt"]
        self.combo_value = file_exts[0]

        # Create combo box for selecting file extensions
        ext_combo = QComboBox()
        ext_combo.setToolTip(
            "Only files with this extension will be changed.")
        ext_combo.addItems(file_exts)
        ext_combo.currentTextChanged.connect(
            self.updateComboValue)

        rename_button = QPushButton("Rename Files")
        rename_button.setToolTip(
            "Begin renaming files in directory.")
        rename_button.clicked.connect(self.renameFiles)
```

The rename_button instance is used to begin the process of renaming files. Clicking the button emits a signal that calls the renameFiles() slot.

Listing 15-6 finishes setting up the main window by creating the text edit and progress bar widgets that provide feedback about the renaming process. In addition, a QPushButton is created that will be enabled after rename_button is pressed and while files are being renamed.

Listing 15-6. Creating the setUpMainWindow() for the file renaming GUI, part 3

```python
# file_rename_threading.py
        # Text edit is for displaying the file names as they
        # are updated
        self.display_files_tedit = QTextEdit()
        self.display_files_tedit.setReadOnly(True)

        self.progress_bar = QProgressBar()
        self.progress_bar.setValue(0)

        self.stop_button = QPushButton("Stop")
        self.stop_button.setEnabled(False)

        # Create layout and arrange widgets
        grid = QGridLayout()
        grid.addWidget(dir_label, 0, 0)
        grid.addWidget(self.dir_edit, 1, 0, 1, 2)
        grid.addWidget(dir_button, 1, 2)
        grid.addWidget(self.change_name_edit, 2, 0)
        grid.addWidget(ext_combo, 2, 1)
        grid.addWidget(rename_button, 2, 2)
        grid.addWidget(self.display_files_tedit, 3, 0, 1, 3)
        grid.addWidget(self.progress_bar, 4, 0, 1, 2)
        grid.addWidget(self.stop_button, 4, 2)

        self.setLayout(grid)
```

The widgets are then organized in a QGridLayout.

The chooseDirectory() slot in Listing 15-7 is called when dir_button is clicked and opens a QFileDialog for selecting directories. Once a directory is chosen, the user can enter the new file names into change_name_edit and select the file extension for the types of files to change in the combo box.

Listing 15-7. Creating the chooseDirectory() slot

```python
# file_rename_threading.py
    def chooseDirectory(self):
        """Choose file directory."""
        file_dialog = QFileDialog(self)
        file_dialog.setFileMode(
            QFileDialog.FileMode.Directory)
        self.directory = file_dialog.getExistingDirectory(
            self, "Open Directory", "",
            QFileDialog.Option.ShowDirsOnly)

        if self.directory:
            self.dir_edit.setText(self.directory)

            # Set the max value of progress bar equal to max
            # number of files in the directory
            num_of_files = len(
                [name for name in os.listdir(self.directory)])
            self.progress_bar.setRange(0, num_of_files)
```

Directories in this application can only be selected by using the chooseDirectory()
slot. We are also able to set the max range of the QProgressBar using the total number of
files in the directory.

Renaming the files could take place in the main thread. This wouldn't be a problem
for a few files. However, if the user wants to work with a large number of files, this
would cause the GUI to be locked until the operations are finished. Therefore, the
process for renaming the files, along with updating the progress bar and the text edit
widgets, is performed in the worker thread. An instance of the Worker class is created in
Listing 15-8.

Listing 15-8. Code for the renameFiles() slot that creates the worker thread

```python
# file_rename_threading.py
    def renameFiles(self):
        """Create instance of worker thread to handle
        the file renaming process."""
        prefix_text = self.change_name_edit.text()
```

```
    if self.directory != "" and prefix_text != "":
        self.worker = Worker(
            self.directory, self.combo_value, prefix_text)
        self.worker.clear_text_edit_signal.connect(
            self.display_files_tedit.clear)

        self.stop_button.setEnabled(True)
        self.stop_button.repaint()
        self.stop_button.clicked.connect(
            self.worker.stopRunning)

        self.worker.update_value_signal.connect(
            self.updateProgressBar)
        self.worker.update_text_edit_signal.connect(
            self.updateTextEdit)
        self.worker.finished.connect(
            self.worker.deleteLater)
        self.worker.start()
```

For Listing 15-9, directory, combo_value, and prefix_text are passed to the newly created worker thread. The worker_clear_text_signal is then connected to display_files_text instance's clear() method.

If stop_button is clicked at this point, it will call the Worker class's stopRunning() slot, causing the thread to end and resetting the progress bar and text edit. The other Worker signals are also connected to the slots in Listing 15-9.

QThread also has a finished signal that is emitted when the read stops running. The finished signal is connected to the QObject method deleteLater(), which is used to delete the worker object and release objects that were created while the thread was running.

Listing 15-9. Code for the slots that update widget values

```
# file_rename_threading.py
    def updateComboValue(self, text):
        """Change the combo box value. Values represent
        the different file extensions."""
        self.combo_value = text
        print(self.combo_value)
```

```
def updateProgressBar(self, value):
    self.progress_bar.setValue(value)

def updateTextEdit(self, old_text, new_text):
    self.display_files_tedit.append(
        f"[INFO] {old_text} changed to {new_text}.")
```

The updateProgressBar() and updateTextEdit() slots are connected to the worker thread's signals.

You can now run the program and locate a local folder. If you find that the process is too fast and want to see the processes actually running, you can uncomment time. sleep(1.0) in the Worker class to slow down the process.

Summary

Preventing GUIs from becoming frozen while processing long operations is important for a user's experience. There are a few options for effectively handling blocking in your application, including using timers and threads. Qt provides a class, QThread, that, combined with signals and slots, can be used for handling additional processes in GUI applications. However, you must be careful when using QThread to ensure that threads protect access to their own data. While not displayed in this chapter's short project, QThread also has methods, such as started(), finished(), wait(), and quit(), for managing threads.

In Chapter 16, we will build multiple example projects to learn and practice a variety of concepts not covered in previous chapters.

CHAPTER 16

Extra Projects

Throughout this book, we have aimed to take a practical approach for creating applications in order to help you learn the fundamentals of GUI development. As you continue to use PyQt6 and Python, you will find yourself learning about other modules and classes that will also prove useful.

In some cases, this book has only scratched the surface of what you can do with PyQt. With so many modules, classes, and possibilities for customization provided by Qt, the potential for building GUIs is endless. To expand your experience with PyQt, this chapter takes a look at some additional Qt classes that we couldn't fit into earlier chapters.

In this chapter, you will create projects for

1. Displaying directories and files using QFileSystemModel and QTreeView

2. Making a GUI that takes photos using QCamera and demonstrates how to make custom dialogs using QDialog

3. Creating a simple clock GUI with QDate and QTime

4. Exploring the QCalendarWidget class

5. Building Hangman with QPainter and other PyQt classes

6. Building the framework for a web browser using the QtWebEngineWidgets module

7. Creating tri-state QComboBox widgets

The explanations for each project will not go into great lengths of detail. Rather, they will focus on explaining the key points of each program and leave it up to you to research the details that you are unsure about, either by finding the answers in a different chapter or by searching online for help.

451

© Joshua M Willman 2022
J. M. Willman, *Beginning PyQt*, https://doi.org/10.1007/978-1-4842-7999-1_16

Project 16.1 – Directory Viewer GUI

For every operating system, there needs to be some method for a user to access the data and files located within it. The drives, directories, and files are stored in a hierarchical file system and presented to the user so that they only view the files that they are interested in seeing.

Whether you use a command line interface or a graphical user interface, there needs to be some way to create, remove, and rename files and directories. However, if you are already interacting with one interface, it may be more convenient to locate files or directories that you need in the application's main window rather than opening new windows or other programs.

This project shows you how to set up an interface for viewing the files on your local system. There are two key classes that will be introduced in this project: **QFileSystemModel**, which grants you access to the file system on your computer, and **QTreeView**, which provides a visual representation of data using a tree-like structure. The directory viewer application can be seen in Figure 16-1.

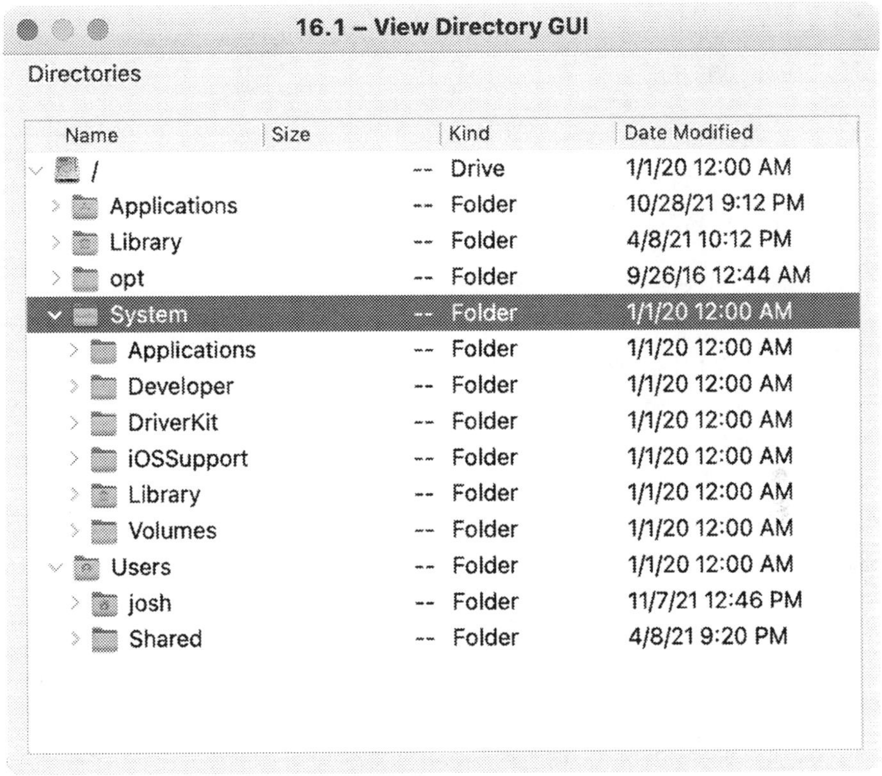

Figure 16-1. *Directory viewer displaying the local system's directories*

Explanation for the Directory Viewer GUI

Begin by using the main_window_template.py script from Chapter 5, and then import the necessary modules for this GUI. For this project, we will need to use the Model/View paradigm to view the data on your computer. For more information about Model/View programming, refer to Chapter 10. The code for the directory viewer is found in Listing 16-1.

Listing 16-1. Code for the directory viewer GUI

```
# directory_viewer.py
# Import necessary modules
import sys
from PyQt6.QtWidgets import (QApplication, QMainWindow,
    QTreeView, QFrame, QFileDialog, QVBoxLayout)
```

```python
from PyQt6.QtGui import QFileSystemModel, QAction

class MainWindow(QMainWindow):

    def __init__(self):
        super().__init__()
        self.initializeUI()

    def initializeUI(self):
        """Set up the application's GUI."""
        self.setMinimumSize(500, 400)
        self.setWindowTitle("16.1 - View Directory GUI")

        self.setUpMainWindow()
        self.createActions()
        self.createMenu()
        self.show()

    def setUpMainWindow(self):
        """Set up the QTreeView in the main window to
        display the contents of the local filesystem."""
        self.model = QFileSystemModel()
        self.model.setRootPath("")

        self.tree = QTreeView()
        self.tree.setIndentation(10)
        self.tree.setModel(self.model)

        # Set up container and layout
        frame = QFrame()
        frame_v_box = QVBoxLayout()
        frame_v_box.addWidget(self.tree)
        frame.setLayout(frame_v_box)

        self.setCentralWidget(frame)
    def createActions(self):
        """Create the application's menu actions."""
        # Create actions for Directories menu
        self.open_dir_act = QAction("Open Directory...")
```

```python
        self.open_dir_act.triggered.connect(
            self.chooseDirectory)

        self.root_act = QAction("Return to Root")
        self.root_act.triggered.connect(
            self.returnToRootDirectory)

    def createMenu(self):
        """Create the application's menu bar."""
        self.menuBar().setNativeMenuBar(False)

        # Create file menu and add actions
        dir_menu = self.menuBar().addMenu("Directories")
        dir_menu.addAction(self.open_dir_act)
        dir_menu.addAction(self.root_act)

    def chooseDirectory(self):
        """Slot for selecting a directory to display."""
        file_dialog = QFileDialog(self)
        file_dialog.setFileMode(
            QFileDialog.FileMode.Directory)
        directory = file_dialog.getExistingDirectory(
            self, "Open Directory",
            "", QFileDialog.Option.ShowDirsOnly)

        self.tree.setRootIndex(self.model.index(directory))

    def returnToRootDirectory(self):
        """Slot for redisplaying the contents of the root
        directory."""
        self.tree.setRootIndex(self.model.index(""))

if __name__ == '__main__':
    app = QApplication(sys.argv)
    window = MainWindow()
    sys.exit(app.exec())
```

The QFileSystemModel class provides the model we need to access data on the local file system. For PyQt6, this class is now located in QtGui. While not included in this project, you could also use QFileSystemModel to rename or remove files and directories, create new directories, or use it with other display widgets as part of a browser.

The QTreeView class will be used to display the contents of the model in a hierarchical tree view.

For this GUI, we will create a Directories menu with actions that will either let the user view a specific directory or return back to the root directory. A screenshot of the menu bar can be seen in Figure 16-2.

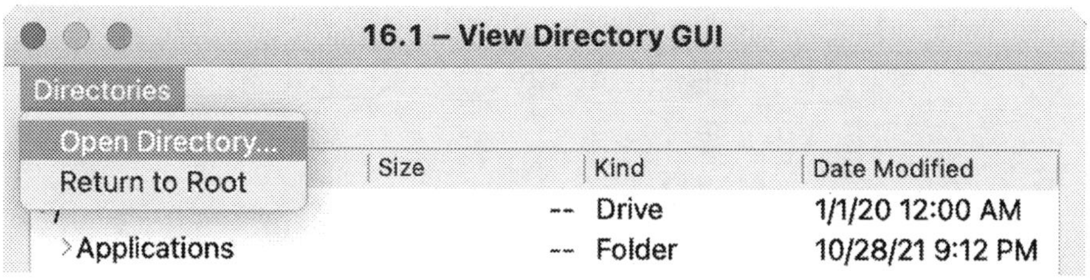

Figure 16-2. *The menu for the directory viewer GUI*

Create an instance of the QFileSystemModel class, model, and set the directory to the root path by passing an empty string to setRootPath(). You can set a different directory by passing a different path to setRootPath().

Finally, let's set the model for the tree object to show the contents of the file system using setModel(). To choose a different directory, the user can select Open Directory... from the menu, and a file dialog will appear. A new directory can then be selected in the chooseDirectory() slot and set as the new root path to be displayed in the tree object using the QTreeView method setRootIndex().

If a new directory has been selected, you can use the slot, returnToRootDirectory(), that is triggered by root_act to redisplay the root directory.

Project 16.2 – Camera GUI

PyQt can do more than handle images, as it also includes modules for working with videos, audio, and other kinds of media. For this GUI, we'll create a simple window that opens your computer's webcam and displays its contents in a window. If the user presses the space bar, a custom QDialog appears, displaying the screenshot and prompting the user to save or reject the video. The main window is shown in Figure 16-3.

Figure 16-3. *The camera GUI*

Before beginning this project, make sure your version of PyQt6 is version 6.2 or higher. The multimedia classes were not included in version 6.1 and earlier. To check your version of PyQt6, open the Python shell and enter the following commands:

```
>>> import PyQt6
>>> from PyQt6.QtCore import PYQT_VERSION_STR
>>> print(PYQT_VERSION_STR)
6.2.1
>>> help(PyQt6)
```

You should see at least 6.2.1 appear as output in the shell. If you don't, you can upgrade your version of PyQt6 by running the following command:

```
$ pip3 install PyQt6 --upgrade
```

Use `pip` instead of `pip3` on Windows. You can use the Python `help()` function to get a list of all of the PyQt6 modules. Look through them and you should see `QtMultimedia` listed among the different modules.

Another way to make sure that the multimedia classes were installed is to open your Python shell and run the following code:

```
>>> from PyQt6 import QtMultimedia
```

Note   For those readers using macOS, you may have issues running this application if you are using the Z shell, also known as zsh. The bash shell used to be the default on macOS until recently. If you run into problems due to zsh, you can switch to using bash by entering `chsh -s /bin/bash/` in the command line. If you want to switch back to zsh when you are finished, you will need to enter the command `chsh -s /bin/zsh`. Just be aware that when you do switch between shells, you will also need to install PyQt6 from PyPI or edit the paths in bash to locate PyQt6 and your other Python packages.

Explanation for the Camera GUI

Let's take a look at how to use the multimedia classes to create a GUI for taking photos in Listing 16-2. To begin, we'll use `basic_window.py` from Chapter 1.

To build a custom dialog that will display the images taken using the webcam, we'll need QDialog and QDialogButtonBox from QtWidgets. The widget **QDialogButtonBox** is used to easily create and arrange standard buttons in dialog boxes. Have a look in the Appendix at the "QDialog" subsection for more information about button types.

There have been numerous updates when it comes to the multimedia classes in PyQt6. The **QtMultimedia** module provides access to a number of multimedia tools that can handle audio, videos, and cameras. The **QCamera** class provides the interface to work with camera devices. We can use QImageCapture to record or take pictures of media objects, such as QCamera. **QMediaDevices** supplies information about available cameras or audio devices.

From the **QtMultimediaWidgets** module, the **QVideoWidget** class sets up and displays the camera or video object's output.

Listing 16-2. Example code that shows how to use the QCamera class and build custom dialogs

```python
# camera.py
# Import necessary modules
import os, sys
from PyQt6.QtWidgets import (QApplication, QWidget, QLabel,
    QDialog, QDialogButtonBox, QVBoxLayout)
from PyQt6.QtCore import Qt, QDate
from PyQt6.QtGui import QPixmap
from PyQt6.QtMultimedia import (QCamera, QImageCapture,
    QMediaDevices, QMediaCaptureSession)
from PyQt6.QtMultimediaWidgets import QVideoWidget

class ImageDialog(QDialog):

    def __init__(self, id, image):
        """Custom QDialog that displays the image taken."""
        super().__init__()
        self.id = id
        self.setWindowTitle(f"Image #{id}")
        self.setMinimumSize(400, 300)

        self.pixmap = QPixmap().fromImage(image)
        image_label = QLabel()
        image_label.setPixmap(self.pixmap)

        # Create the buttons that appear in the dialog
        self.button_box = QDialogButtonBox(
            QDialogButtonBox.StandardButton.Save | \
            QDialogButtonBox.StandardButton.Cancel)
        self.button_box.accepted.connect(self.accept)
        self.button_box.rejected.connect(self.reject)

        dialog_v_box = QVBoxLayout()
        dialog_v_box.addWidget(image_label)
        dialog_v_box.addWidget(self.button_box)
        self.setLayout(dialog_v_box)
```

```python
    def accept(self):
        """Reimplement accept() method to save the image
        file in the images directory."""
        file_format = "png"
        today = QDate().currentDate().toString(
            Qt.DateFormat.ISODate)

        file_name = f"images/image{self.id}_{today}.png"
        self.pixmap.save(file_name, file_format)
        super().accept()

class MainWindow(QWidget):

    def __init__(self):
        super().__init__()
        self.initializeUI()

    def initializeUI(self):
        """Set up the application's GUI."""
        self.setMinimumSize(500, 400)
        self.setWindowTitle("16.2 - Camera GUI")

        self.setUpMainWindow()
        self.show()

    def setUpMainWindow(self):
        """Create and arrange widgets in the main window."""
        # Create the image output directory
        exists = os.path.exists("images")
        if not exists:
            os.makedirs("images")

        info_label = QLabel(
            "Press 'Spacebar' to take pictures.")
        info_label.setAlignment(Qt.AlignmentFlag.AlignCenter)

        # Create the camera that uses the computer's
        # default camera
        self.camera = QCamera(
            QMediaDevices.defaultVideoInput())
```

```
        # Create an instance of the class used to capture
        # images
        self.image_capture = QImageCapture(self.camera)
        self.image_capture.imageCaptured.connect(
            self.viewImage)

        video_widget = QVideoWidget(self)

        # QMediaCaptureSession handles playing and capturing
        # video and audio
        self.media_capture_session = QMediaCaptureSession()
        self.media_capture_session.setCamera(self.camera)
        self.media_capture_session.setImageCapture(
            self.image_capture)
        self.media_capture_session.setVideoOutput(
            video_widget)

        self.camera.start()

        main_v_box = QVBoxLayout()
        main_v_box.addWidget(info_label)
        main_v_box.addWidget(video_widget, 1)
        self.setLayout(main_v_box)

    def viewImage(self, id, preview):
        """Open a dialog to preview the image."""
        self.image_dialog = ImageDialog(id, preview)
        self.image_dialog.open()

    def keyPressEvent(self, event):
        """Reimplement to capture the image when the space
        bar is pressed."""
        if event.key() == Qt.Key.Key_Space:
            self.image_capture.capture()

    def closeEvent(self, event):
        if self.camera.isActive():
            self.camera.stop()
        event.accept()
```

```
if __name__ == '__main__':
    app = QApplication(sys.argv)
    window = MainWindow()
    sys.exit(app.exec())
```

In order to create a customized dialog, you'll need to create a new class that inherits QDialog. An instance of ImageDialog will display the image taken from the camera on a QLabel. The argument id refers to the id value returned by QImageCapture when a picture is taken. Since QImageCapture also returns a QImage object, we'll need to change image to a pixmap using the QPixmap method fromImage() before setting the picture on the label.

The button_box instance is a QDialogButtonBox that contains Save and Cancel keys. The two buttons are added to button_box and separated by a pipe key, |. When a button is clicked, it emits a signal. Generally, those signals are accepted or rejected when working with dialog buttons. We'll attach those signals to built-in slots, accept() and reject(). While these are standard slots, you could also connect the accepted or rejected signals to custom slots and perform other operations. We'll do just that for accept() but use the default functionality for reject().

For this example, we'll reimplement accept() to save the pixmap to a folder called images. The file extension, .png, still needs to be included to avoid issues with saving images (especially on Windows).

An example of ImageDialog along with its buttons can be seen in Figure 16-4.

Figure 16-4. *A custom QDialog instance that displays the image taken by the camera*

The last step is to arrange the widgets in a layout just like you normally do with other windows.

Moving on to setUpMainWindow() in the MainWindow class, let's first create the images directory for saving images if it does not already exist. The window consists of a label for providing instructions and a QVideoWidget object for showing the camera's contents.

QMediaDevices can be used to specify a camera to use or provide a list of possible devices to the user. For cameras, we'll need to use QCameraDevice to detect available cameras. The QMediaDevices method defaultVideoInput() locates a computer's default QCameraDevice. You can then pass that camera device to QCamera when creating the camera instance.

Using QImageCapture, the user is able to take pictures. The imageCaptured signal is used to detect when a picture is taken. Image capturing for this GUI is handled by keyPressEvent(). When the space bar is pressed, QImageCapture.capture() takes a picture, thereby emitting the imageCaptured signal. This calls ViewImage(), where the picture's id and QImage object, preview, are passed to an ImageDialog instance.

The open() method is used to open the dialog. If the user clicks the Save button, the image is converted to a pixmap and saved in the images folder (handled in the accept() slot of ImageDialog).

Back in setUpMainWindow(), QMediaCaptureSession will manage the capturing of the camera that is displayed in video_widget.

Project 16.3 – Simple Clock GUI

PyQt6 also provides classes for dealing with dates, **QDate**, or time, **QTime**. The **QDateTime** class supplies functions for working with both dates and time. All three of these classes include methods for handling time-related features.

Let's take a brief look at the QDateTime class. The following snippet of code creates an instance of QDateTime that prints the current date and time using the currentDateTime() method:

```
now = QDateTime.currentDateTime()
print(now.toString("MMMM dd, yyyy hh:mm:ss AP"))
```

The current date and time is printed to the screen with the following format:

```
November 07, 2021 03:34:11 PM
```

This format is used to display the time in GUI in Figure 16-5.

Figure 16-5. *The clock GUI displaying the current calendar date and clock time*

In PyQt6, you can also use the enum Qt.DateFormat to utilize standard date and time format types. These include ISO 8601 format (using the flag ISODate) and RFC 2822 (using the flag RFC2822Date). The toString() method returns the date and time as a string. QDateTime also handles daylight saving time, different time zones, and the manipulation of times and dates such as adding or subtracting months, days, or hours.

If you only need to work with the individual dates and times, QDate and QTime also provide similar functions as you shall see in the following example.

Explanation for the Clock GUI

We'll use the basic_window.py from Chapter 1 as the base for this program. Start by importing the necessary modules, including QDate, QTime, and QTimer from the QtCore module in Listing 16-3.

The QTimer class will be used to create a timer object to keep track of the time that has passed and update the labels that hold the date and time accordingly. The timer is set up in initializeUI(), and its timeout signal is connected to the updateDateTime() slot. The timeout signal is emitted every second.

Listing 16-3. Code for the clock GUI

```python
# clock.py
# Import necessary modules
import sys
from PyQt6.QtWidgets import (QApplication, QWidget, QLabel,
    QVBoxLayout)
from PyQt6.QtCore import Qt, QDate, QTime, QTimer

class DisplayTime(QWidget):

    def __init__(self):
        super().__init__()
        self.initializeUI()

    def initializeUI(self):
        """Set up the application's GUI."""
        self.setGeometry(100, 100, 250, 100)
        self.setWindowTitle("16.3 - QDateTime Example")
        self.setStyleSheet("background-color: black")

        self.setUpMainWindow()
```

```python
        # Create timer object
        timer = QTimer(self)
        timer.timeout.connect(self.updateDateTime)
        timer.start(1000)

        self.show()

    def setUpMainWindow(self):
        """Create labels that will display current date and
        time in the main window."""
        current_date, current_time = self.getDateTime()

        self.date_label = QLabel(current_date)
        self.date_label.setStyleSheet(
            "color: white; font: 16px Courier")
        self.time_label = QLabel(current_time)
        self.time_label.setStyleSheet(
            """color: white;
            border-color: white;
            border-width: 2px;
            border-style: solid;
            border-radius: 4px;
            padding: 10px;
            font: bold 24px Courier""")

        # Create layout and add widgets
        v_box = QVBoxLayout()
        v_box.addWidget(self.date_label,
            alignment=Qt.AlignmentFlag.AlignCenter)
        v_box.addWidget(self.time_label,
            alignment=Qt.AlignmentFlag.AlignCenter)

        self.setLayout(v_box)

    def getDateTime(self):
        """Returns current date and time."""
        date = QDate.currentDate().toString("MMMM dd, yyyy")
        time = QTime.currentTime().toString("hh:mm:ss AP")
        return date, time
```

```
    def updateDateTime(self):
        """Slot that updates date and time values."""
        date = QDate.currentDate().toString("MMMM dd, yyyy")
        time = QTime.currentTime().toString("hh:mm:ss AP")

        self.date_label.setText(date)
        self.time_label.setText(time)
        return date, time

if __name__ == '__main__':
    app = QApplication(sys.argv)
    window = DisplayTime()
    sys.exit(app.exec())
```

In order to get the current date and time, the values are retrieved using the currentDate() and currentTime() methods in the getDateTime() method. These are then returned and set as the current_date and current_time.

The values for date and time are both set using a sequence of characters to create a format string. For date, we'll present the full month's name (MMMM), the day (dd), and the full year (yyyy). The time instance will display hours (hh), minutes (mm), seconds (ss), and AM or PM (AP).

The labels that will display the date and time are then instantiated, styled, and added to the layout in setUpMainWindow(). The values of the labels are updated using the updateDateTime() slot that is connected to timer.

Project 16.4 – Calendar GUI

This project takes a look at how to set up the **QCalendarWidget** class and use a few of its functions. PyQt makes adding a monthly calendar to your applications rather effortless. The calendar can be seen in Figure 16-6.

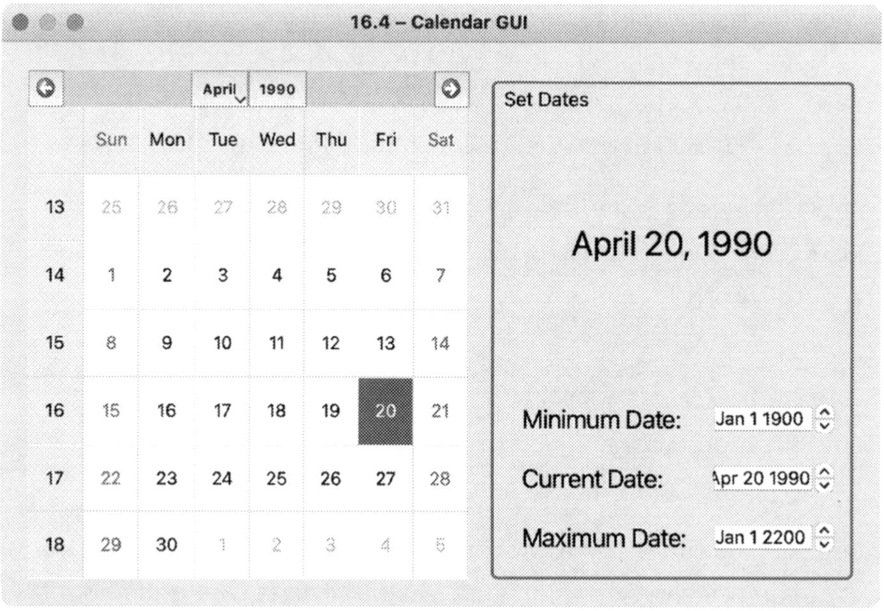

Figure 16-6. *The calendar GUI that displays the calendar, the current date, and the widgets that allow the user to search for dates within a specified time range*

The QCalendarWidget class provides a calendar that already has a number of other useful widgets and functions built-in. For example, the calendar already includes a horizontal header that includes widgets for changing the month and the year and a vertical header that displays the week number. The class also includes signals that are emitted whenever the dates, months, and years on the calendar are changed. The look of your calendar will vary depending upon the platform that you are using to run the application.

The **QDateEdit** widget is used in this application to restrict the date range a user can select, specified by minimum and maximum values.

Explanation for the Calendar GUI

We can start with basic_window.py script from Chapter 1. After importing the modules needed for the calendar GUI in Listing 16-4, the styles for the QLabel and QGroupBox widgets are prepared using style_sheet.

Listing 16-4. The calendar GUI code

```python
# calendar.py
# Import necessary modules
import sys
from PyQt6.QtWidgets import (QApplication, QWidget, QLabel,
    QCalendarWidget, QDateEdit, QGroupBox, QHBoxLayout,
    QGridLayout)
from PyQt6.QtCore import Qt, QDate

style_sheet = """
    QLabel{
        padding: 5px;
        font: 18px
    }

    QLabel#DateSelected{
        font: 24px
    }

    QGroupBox{
        border: 2px solid gray;
        border-radius: 5px;
        margin-top: 1ex;
        font: 14px
    }
"""

class MainWindow(QWidget):

    def __init__(self):
        super().__init__()
        self.initializeUI()

    def initializeUI(self):
        """Set up the application's GUI."""
        self.setMinimumSize(500, 400)
        self.setWindowTitle("16.4 - Calendar GUI")
```

```
        self.setUpMainWindow()
        self.show()

    def setUpMainWindow(self):
        """Create and arrange widgets in the main window."""
        self.calendar = QCalendarWidget()
        self.calendar.setGridVisible(True)
        self.calendar.setMinimumDate(QDate(1900, 1, 1))
        self.calendar.setMaximumDate(QDate(2200, 1, 1))

        # Connect to newDateSelection() slot when currently
        # selected date is changed
        self.calendar.selectionChanged.connect(
            self.newDateSelection)

        current = QDate.currentDate().toString(
            "MMMM dd, yyyy")
        self.current_label = QLabel(current)
        self.current_label.setObjectName("DateSelected")

        # Create current, minimum, and maximum QDateEdit
        # widgets
        min_date_label = QLabel("Minimum Date:")
        self.min_date_edit = QDateEdit()
        self.min_date_edit.setDisplayFormat("MMM d yyyy")
        self.min_date_edit.setDateRange(
            self.calendar.minimumDate(),
            self.calendar.maximumDate())
        self.min_date_edit.setDate(
            self.calendar.minimumDate())
        self.min_date_edit.dateChanged.connect(
            self.minDatedChanged)

        current_date_label = QLabel("Current Date:")
        self.current_date_edit = QDateEdit()
        self.current_date_edit.setDisplayFormat("MMM d yyyy")
        self.current_date_edit.setDate(
            self.calendar.selectedDate())
```

```
self.current_date_edit.setDateRange(
    self.calendar.minimumDate(),
    self.calendar.maximumDate())
self.current_date_edit.dateChanged.connect(
    self.selectionDateChanged)

max_date_label = QLabel("Maximum Date:")
self.max_date_edit = QDateEdit()
self.max_date_edit.setDisplayFormat("MMM d yyyy")
self.max_date_edit.setDateRange(
    self.calendar.minimumDate(),
    self.calendar.maximumDate())
self.max_date_edit.setDate(
    self.calendar.maximumDate())
self.max_date_edit.dateChanged.connect(
    self.maxDatedChanged)

# Add widgets to group box and add to grid layout
dates_gb = QGroupBox("Set Dates")
dates_grid = QGridLayout()
dates_grid.addWidget(self.current_label, 0, 0, 1, 2,
    Qt.AlignmentFlag.AlignAbsolute)
dates_grid.addWidget(min_date_label, 1, 0)
dates_grid.addWidget(self.min_date_edit, 1, 1)
dates_grid.addWidget(current_date_label, 2, 0)
dates_grid.addWidget(self.current_date_edit, 2, 1)
dates_grid.addWidget(max_date_label, 3, 0)
dates_grid.addWidget(self.max_date_edit, 3, 1)
dates_gb.setLayout(dates_grid)

# Create and set main window's layout
main_h_box = QHBoxLayout()
main_h_box.addWidget(self.calendar)
main_h_box.addWidget(dates_gb)
self.setLayout(main_h_box)
```

```python
    def selectionDateChanged(self, date):
        """Update current_date_edit when the calendar's
        selected date changes. """
        self.calendar.setSelectedDate(date)

    def minDatedChanged(self, date):
        """Update the calendar's minimum date.
        Update max_date_edit to avoid conflicts with
        maximum and minimum dates."""
        self.calendar.setMinimumDate(date)
        self.max_date_edit.setDate(
            self.calendar.maximumDate())

    def maxDatedChanged(self, date):
        """Update the calendar's maximum date.
        Update min_date_edit to avoid conflicts with
        minimum and maximum dates."""
        self.calendar.setMaximumDate(date)
        self.min_date_edit.setDate(
            self.calendar.minimumDate())

    def newDateSelection(self):
        """Update date in current_label and current_date_edit
        widgets when a new date is selected."""
        date = self.calendar.selectedDate().toString(
            "MMMM dd, yyyy")
        self.current_date_edit.setDate(
            self.calendar.selectedDate())
        self.current_label.setText(date)

if __name__ == '__main__':
    app = QApplication(sys.argv)
    app.setStyleSheet(style_sheet)
    window = MainWindow()
    sys.exit(app.exec())
```

Creating an instance of QCalendarWidget is very simple.

```python
        self.calendar = QCalendarWidget()
```

Next, we set a few of the `calendar` object's parameters. Setting `setGridVisible()` to `True` will make the grid lines visible. In order to specify the date range that a user can select in the calendar, we set the minimum and maximum date values using the `QCalendar` methods `setMinimumDate()` and `setMaximumDate()`.

Whenever a date is selected in the `calendar` widget, it emits a `selectionChanged` signal. This signal is connected to the `newDateSelection()` slot that updates the date on `current_label` and in `current_date_edit`. Selecting a value in `current_date_edit` widget will also change the other values.

The `QCalendarWidget` class also has a number of functions that allow you to configure its behaviors and appearance. For this project, we create three `QDateEdit` widgets that will allow the user to change the minimum and maximum values for the date range, as well as the current date selected in the calendar. These widgets can be seen on the right side of the GUI in Figure 16-6.

A displayed format for the date in the `QDateEdit` widget can be set using `setDisplayFormat()`. The date edit objects are also given a date range using `setDateRange()`. The following line of code is an example of how to set the `min_date_edit` widget's date range by using ranges set earlier for the `calendar` object:

```
self.min_date_edit.setDateRange(
    self.calendar.minimumDate(),
    self.calendar.maximumDate())
```

When a date is changed in a date edit widget, it generates a `dateChanged` signal. Each one of the `QDateEdit` widgets is connected to a corresponding slot that will update the calendar's minimum, maximum, or current date values depending upon which date edit widget is changed. The method for changing the dates is adapted from the Qt document website.[1]

Finally, the label and date edit widgets are arranged in a `QGroupBox`, added to a `QGridLayout` instance, and nested into the main window's layout in `setUpMainWindow()`.

Project 16.5 – Hangman GUI

PyQt can be used to create a variety of different kinds of applications. Throughout this book, we have looked at quite a few ideas for building GUIs. For this next project,

---

[1] Link: `https://doc.qt.io/qt-6/qtwidgets-widgets-calendarwidget-example.html`

we will take a look at how to use QPainter and a few other classes to build a game –
Hangman. While Hangman is a simple game to play, it can be used to teach a few of the
fundamental concepts for using PyQt to create games. The Hangman interface can be
seen in Figure 16-7.

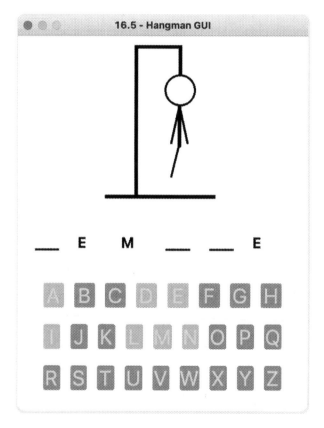

Figure 16-7. *The Hangman application. Can you save him?*

For this application, the player can select from one of the 26 English letters to guess
a letter in an unknown word. As each letter is chosen, they will become disabled in
the window. If the letter is correct, it will be revealed to the player. Otherwise, a part
of the Hangman figure's body is drawn on the screen. If all of the letters are correctly
guessed, then the player wins. There are a total of six turns. Whether or not the player
wins or loses, a dialog will be displayed to inform the player and allow them to quit or to
continue playing.

Be sure to download words.txt from the files folder in the GitHub repository
before beginning this project.

Explanation for the Hangman GUI

A variety of classes are used in the Hangman GUI in Listing 16-5, including different widgets from QtWidgets, as well as classes used for drawing from QtCore and QtGui. The style sheet used is to change the style properties of the widgets and to handle the appearance of the buttons when they are pressed.

Listing 16-5. Code for the Hangman GUI

```python
# hangman.py
# Import necessary modules
import sys, random
from PyQt6.QtWidgets import (QApplication, QMainWindow,
    QWidget, QPushButton, QLabel, QFrame, QButtonGroup,
    QHBoxLayout, QVBoxLayout, QMessageBox, QSizePolicy)
from PyQt6.QtCore import Qt, QRect, QLine
from PyQt6.QtGui import QPainter, QPen, QBrush, QColor

style_sheet = """
    QWidget{
        background-color: #FFFFFF
    }

    QLabel#Word{
        font: bold 20px;
        qproperty-alignment: AlignCenter
    }

    QPushButton#Letters{
        background-color: #1FAEDE;
        color: #D2DDE1;
        border-style: solid;
        border-radius: 3px;
        border-color: #38454A;
        font: 28px
    }
```

```
    QPushButton#Letters:pressed{
        background-color: #C86354;
        border-radius: 4px;
        padding: 6px;
        color: #DFD8D7
    }

    QPushButton#Letters:disabled{
        background-color: #BBC7CB
    }
"""

class DrawingLabel(QLabel):

    def __init__(self):
        """The hangman is drawn on a QLabel object, rather
        than on the main window. This class handles the
        drawing."""
        super().__init__()
        self.height = 200
        self.width = 300

        self.incorrect_letter = False
        self.incorrect_turns = 0

        self.wrong_parts_list = []

    def drawHangmanBackground(self, painter):
        """Draw the gallows for the GUI."""
        painter.setBrush(QBrush(QColor("#000000")))
        # drawRect(x, y, width, height)
        painter.drawRect(int(self.width / 2) - 40,
            self.height, 150, 4)
        painter.drawRect(int(self.width / 2), 0, 4, 200)
        painter.drawRect(int(self.width / 2), 0, 60, 4)
        painter.drawRect(int(self.width / 2) + 60, 0, 4, 40)

    def drawHangmanBody(self, painter):
        """Create and draw body parts for hangman."""
```

```
if "head" in self.wrong_parts_list:
    head = QRect(int(self.width / 2) + 42, 40, 40, 40)
    painter.setPen(QPen(QColor("#000000"), 3))
    painter.setBrush(QBrush(QColor("#FFFFFF")))
    painter.drawEllipse(head)
if "body" in self.wrong_parts_list:
    body = QRect(int(self.width / 2) + 60, 80, 2, 55)
    painter.setBrush(QBrush(QColor("#000000")))
    painter.drawRect(body)
if "right_arm" in self.wrong_parts_list:
    right_arm = QLine(int(self.width / 2) + 60, 85,
        int(self.width / 2) + 50,
        int(self.height / 2) + 30)
    pen = QPen(Qt.GlobalColor.black, 3,
        Qt.PenStyle.SolidLine)
    painter.setPen(pen)
    painter.drawLine(right_arm)
if "left_arm" in self.wrong_parts_list:
    left_arm = QLine(int(self.width / 2) + 62, 85,
        int(self.width / 2) + 72,
        int(self.height / 2) + 30)
    painter.drawLine(left_arm)
if "right_leg" in self.wrong_parts_list:
    right_leg = QLine(int(self.width / 2) + 60, 135,
        int(self.width / 2) + 50,
        int(self.height / 2) + 75)
    painter.drawLine(right_leg)
if "left_leg" in self.wrong_parts_list:
    left_leg = QLine(int(self.width / 2) + 62, 135,
        int(self.width / 2) + 72,
        int(self.height / 2) + 75)
    painter.drawLine(left_leg)

# Reset variable
self.incorrect_letter = False
```

```python
    def paintEvent(self, event):
        """Create QPainter object and handle painting
        events."""
        painter = QPainter()
        painter.begin(self)

        self.drawHangmanBackground(painter)
        if self.incorrect_letter == True:
            self.drawHangmanBody(painter)

        painter.end()

class Hangman(QMainWindow):

    def __init__(self):
        super().__init__()
        self.initializeUI()

    def initializeUI(self):
        """Set up the application's GUI."""
        self.setFixedSize(400, 500)
        self.setWindowTitle("16.5 - Hangman GUI")

        self.newGame()
        self.show()

    def newGame(self):
        """Create new Hangman game. Sets up the objects
        for the main window."""
        self.setUpHangmanBoard()
        self.setUpWord()
        self.setUpBoard()

    def setUpHangmanBoard(self):
        """Set up label object to display hangman."""
        self.hangman_label = DrawingLabel()
        self.hangman_label.setSizePolicy(
            QSizePolicy.Policy.Expanding,
            QSizePolicy.Policy.Expanding)
```

```python
def setUpWord(self):
    """Open words file and choose random word.
    Create labels that will display '_' depending
    upon length of word."""
    words = self.openFile()
    self.chosen_word = random.choice(words).upper()
    #print(self.chosen_word)

    # Keep track of correct guesses
    self.correct_counter = 0

    # Keep track of label objects.
    # Is used for updating the text on the labels
    self.labels = []

    word_h_box = QHBoxLayout()

    for letter in self.chosen_word:
        self.letter_label = QLabel("___")
        self.labels.append(self.letter_label)
        self.letter_label.setObjectName("Word")
        word_h_box.addWidget(self.letter_label)

    self.word_frame = QFrame()
    self.word_frame.setLayout(word_h_box)

def setUpBoard(self):
    """Set up objects and layouts for keyboard and main
    window."""
    top_row_list = ["A", "B", "C", "D", "E",
        "F", "G", "H"]
    mid_row_list = ["I", "J", "K", "L", "M",
        "N", "O", "P", "Q"]
    bot_row_list = ["R", "S", "T", "U", "V",
        "W", "X", "Y", "Z"]

    # Create buttongroup to keep track of letters
    self.keyboard_bg = QButtonGroup()
```

```python
# Set up keys in the top row
top_row_h_box = QHBoxLayout()

for letter in top_row_list:
    button = QPushButton(letter)
    button.setObjectName("Letters")
    top_row_h_box.addWidget(button)
    self.keyboard_bg.addButton(button)

top_frame = QFrame()
top_frame.setLayout(top_row_h_box)

# Set up keys in the middle row
mid_row_h_box = QHBoxLayout()

for letter in mid_row_list:
    button = QPushButton(letter)
    button.setObjectName("Letters")
    mid_row_h_box.addWidget(button)
    self.keyboard_bg.addButton(button)

mid_frame = QFrame()
mid_frame.setLayout(mid_row_h_box)

# Set up keys in the bottom row
bot_row_h_box = QHBoxLayout()

for letter in bot_row_list:
    button = QPushButton(letter)
    button.setObjectName("Letters")
    bot_row_h_box.addWidget(button)
    self.keyboard_bg.addButton(button)

bot_frame = QFrame()
bot_frame.setLayout(bot_row_h_box)

# Connect buttons in button group to slot
self.keyboard_bg.buttonClicked.connect(
    self.buttonPushed)
```

```
        keyboard_v_box = QVBoxLayout()
        keyboard_v_box.addWidget(top_frame)
        keyboard_v_box.addWidget(mid_frame)
        keyboard_v_box.addWidget(bot_frame)

        keyboard_frame = QFrame()
        keyboard_frame.setLayout(keyboard_v_box)

        # Create main layout and add widgets
        main_v_box = QVBoxLayout()
        main_v_box.addWidget(self.hangman_label)
        main_v_box.addWidget(self.word_frame)
        main_v_box.addWidget(keyboard_frame)

        # Create central widget for main window
        central_widget = QWidget()
        central_widget.setLayout(main_v_box)
        self.setCentralWidget(central_widget)

    def buttonPushed(self, button):
        """Handle buttons from the button group and
        game logic."""
        button.setEnabled(False)

        body_parts_list = ["head", "body", "right_arm",
            "left_arm", "right_leg", "left_leg"]

        # When the user guesses incorrectly and the number of
        # incorrect turns is not equal to 6 (the number of
        # body parts)
        if button.text() not in self.chosen_word and \
            self.hangman_label.incorrect_turns <= 5:
            self.hangman_label.incorrect_turns += 1
            index = self.hangman_label.incorrect_turns - 1
            self.hangman_label.wrong_parts_list.append(
                body_parts_list[index])
            self.hangman_label.incorrect_letter = True
```

```python
        # When a correct letter is chosen, update labels and
        # correct counter
        elif button.text() in self.chosen_word and \
            self.hangman_label.incorrect_turns <= 5:
            self.hangman_label.incorrect_letter = True
            for i in range(len(self.chosen_word)):
                if self.chosen_word[i] == button.text():
                    self.labels[i].setText(button.text())
                    self.correct_counter += 1

        # Call update before checking winning conditions
        self.update()

        # User wins when the number of correct letters equals
        # the length of the word
        if self.correct_counter == len(self.chosen_word):
            self.displayDialogs("win")

        # Game over if number of incorrect turns equals
        # the number of body parts. Reveal word to user
        if self.hangman_label.incorrect_turns == 6:
            for i in range(len(self.chosen_word)):
                self.labels[i].setText(self.chosen_word[i])
            self.displayDialogs("game_over")

    def openFile(self):
        """Open words.txt file."""
        try:
            with open("files/words.txt", 'r') as f:
                word_list = f.read().splitlines()
                return word_list
        except FileNotFoundError:
            print("File Not Found.")
            ex_list = ["nofile"]
            return ex_list

    def displayDialogs(self, text):
        """Display win and game over dialog boxes."""
```

```
        if text == "win":
            message = QMessageBox().question(self, "Win!",
                "You Win!\nNEW GAME?",
                QMessageBox.StandardButton.Yes | \
                QMessageBox.StandardButton.No,
                QMessageBox.StandardButton.No)
        elif text == "game_over":
            message = QMessageBox().question(
                self, "Game Over",
                "Game Over\nNEW GAME?",
                QMessageBox.StandardButton.Yes | \
                QMessageBox.StandardButton.No,
                QMessageBox.StandardButton.No)

        if message == QMessageBox.StandardButton.No:
            self.close()
        else:
            self.newGame()

if __name__ == '__main__':
    app = QApplication(sys.argv)
    app.setStyleSheet(style_sheet)
    window = Hangman()
    sys.exit(app.exec())
```

This program contains two classes: DrawingLabel and Hangman.

Creating the Drawing Class

The DrawingLabel class inherits from QLabel and handles the different paint events that will be drawn on the label object in the main window. The paintEvent() function is called in a class that inherits from QLabel so that way the paint events occur on the label and are not covered up by the main window.

In order to use the DrawingLabel() class, an instance is created in the Hangman class method setupHangmanBoard():

```
        self.hangman_label = DrawingLabel()
```

The paintEvent() function sets up QPainter and handles the two painting methods: drawHangmanBackground(), which draws the gallows of the Hangman game onto the label, and drawHangmanBody(), which only draws the body parts if they are contained in the part_list.

Creating the Main Window Class

The Hangman class starts by initializing the GUI window and calling the newGame() method. First, the Hangman board is created as an instance of the DrawingLabel class. Then, setUpBoard() selects a random word from the words.txt file. The labels that will represent the letters of the chosen word are replaced with underscore characters, appended to the labels list, and added to the horizontal layout of the word_frame object.

Finally, we need to set up the keyboard push buttons, layouts, and the game logic in setUpBoard(). Three rows of push buttons that represent the letters of the alphabet are controlled by one QButtonGroup object, keyboard_bg.

When one button is pushed, it generates a signal that calls the buttonPushed() slot. When a push button is pressed, it is disabled by passing False to setEnabled().

The list of body parts, body_parts_list, contains the six body part names. If the player guesses an incorrect letter, the name is appended to the wrong_parts_list and checked for in the DrawingLabel method drawHangmanBody() function. Using this method ensures that all necessary parts are drawn with their different styles when paintEvent() is called. Otherwise, the labels are updated to display the correct letters in the appropriate positions if the player guesses correctly.

If the player wins or loses, a QMessageBox will appear and allow the user to close the application or continue. If Yes is selected, newGame() is called.

Project 16.6 – Web Browser GUI

A web browser is a graphical user interface that allows access to information on the World Wide Web. A user can enter a Uniform Resource Locator (URL) into an address bar and request content for a website from a web server to be displayed on their local device, including text, image, and video data. URLs are generally prefixed with http, a protocol used for fetching and transmitting requested web pages, or https, for encrypted communication between browsers and websites.

Qt provides quite a few classes for network communication, WebSockets, support for accessing the World Wide Web, and more. This project introduces PyQt's classes for adding web integration into GUIs.

For the following project, we will take a look at Qt's WebEngine core classes, specifically the **QtWebEngineWidgets** module for creating widget-based web applications. The WebEngine core classes provide a web browser engine that can be used to embed web content into your applications. The **QtWebEngineCore** module uses Chromium as its back end. Chromium is an open source software from Google that can be used to create web browsers.

The web browser GUI that we will create in Figure 16-8 serves as a framework for creating your own web browser and includes the following features:

- Ability to open multiple windows and tabs, either by using the application's menu or shortcut hotkeys

- A navigation bar that is made up of back, forward, refresh, stop and home buttons, and the address bar for entering URLs

- The web engine view widget created using QWebEngineView

- A status bar

- A progress bar that relays feedback to the user about loading web pages

Figure 16-8. *The web browser GUI displaying the menu bar, toolbar, different tabs, the logo for my blog, redhuli.io, and the progress bar at the bottom*

Note   You will need to install the QtWebEngineWidgets module. To do so, enter the following command into the command line: pip3 install PyQt6-WebEngine (use pip for Windows).

In addition, make sure that you download the icons folder from this chapter's GitHub repository.

Explanation for Web Browser GUI

You can begin with main_window_template.py from Chapter 5 as your foundation for this application. Two new classes are introduced in Listing 16-6: **QUrl** is used for managing and constructing URLs, and **QWebEngineView** is used for creating the main component for rendering content from the Web, the web engine view (denoted as web_view in the code).

Listing 16-6. Code for the web browser GUI

```python
# web_browser.py
# Import necessary modules
import os, sys
from PyQt6.QtWidgets import (QApplication, QMainWindow,
    QWidget, QLabel, QLineEdit, QTabWidget, QToolBar,
    QProgressBar, QStatusBar, QVBoxLayout)
from PyQt6.QtCore import QSize, QUrl
from PyQt6.QtGui import QIcon, QAction
from PyQt6.QtWebEngineWidgets import QWebEngineView

style_sheet = """
    QTabWidget:pane{
        border: none
    }
"""

class WebBrowser(QMainWindow):
    def __init__(self):
        super().__init__()
        # Create lists that will keep track of the new
        # windows, tabs and urls
        self.window_list = []
        self.list_of_web_pages = []
        self.list_of_urls = []

        self.initializeUI()

    def initializeUI(self):
        self.setMinimumSize(300, 200)
        self.setWindowTitle("16.6 - Web Browser")
        self.setWindowIcon(QIcon(os.path.join("icons",
            "pyqt_logo.png")))

        self.sizeMainWindow()
        self.createToolbar()
        self.setUpMainWindow()
```

```python
        self.createActions()
        self.createMenu()
        self.show()

    def setUpMainWindow(self):
        """Create the QTabWidget object and the different
        pages for the main window. Handle when a tab is
        closed."""
        self.tab_bar = QTabWidget()
        # Add close buttons to tabs
        self.tab_bar.setTabsClosable(True)
        # Hides tab bar when less than 2 tabs
        self.tab_bar.setTabBarAutoHide(True)
        self.tab_bar.tabCloseRequested.connect(self.closeTab)

        # Create a tab
        self.main_tab = QWidget()
        self.tab_bar.addTab(self.main_tab, "New Tab")

        # Call method that sets up each page
        self.setUpTab(self.main_tab)
        self.setCentralWidget(self.tab_bar)

        self.status_bar = QStatusBar()
        self.setStatusBar(self.status_bar)

    def createActions(self):
        """Create the application's menu actions."""
        # Create actions for File menu
        self.new_window_act = QAction("New Window", self)
        self.new_window_act.setShortcut("Ctrl+N")
        self.new_window_act.triggered.connect(
            self.openNewWindow)

        self.new_tab_act = QAction("New Tab", self)
        self.new_tab_act.setShortcut("Ctrl+T")
        self.new_tab_act.triggered.connect(self.openNewTab)
```

```python
        self.quit_act = QAction("Quit Browser", self)
        self.quit_act.setShortcut("Ctrl+Q")
        self.quit_act.triggered.connect(self.close)

    def createMenu(self):
        """Create the application"s menu bar."""
        self.menuBar().setNativeMenuBar(False)

        # Create File menu and add actions
        file_menu = self.menuBar().addMenu("File")
        file_menu.addAction(self.new_window_act)
        file_menu.addAction(self.new_tab_act)
        file_menu.addSeparator()
        file_menu.addAction(self.quit_act)

    def createToolbar(self):
        """Set up the navigation toolbar."""
        tool_bar = QToolBar("Address Bar")
        tool_bar.setIconSize(QSize(30, 30))
        self.addToolBar(tool_bar)

        # Create toolbar actions
        back_page_button = QAction(
            QIcon(os.path.join("icons", "back.png")),
            "Back", self)
        back_page_button.triggered.connect(
            self.backPageButton)
        forward_page_button = QAction(
            QIcon(os.path.join("icons", "forward.png")),
            "Forward", self)
        forward_page_button.triggered.connect(
            self.forwardPageButton)

        refresh_button = QAction(
            QIcon(os.path.join("icons", "refresh.png")),
            "Refresh", self)
        refresh_button.triggered.connect(self.refreshButton)
```

```
home_button = QAction(
    QIcon(os.path.join("icons", "home.png")),
    "Home", self)
home_button.triggered.connect(self.homeButton)

stop_button = QAction(
    QIcon(os.path.join("icons", "stop.png")),
    "Stop", self)
stop_button.triggered.connect(self.stopButton)

# Set up the address bar
self.address_line = QLineEdit()
# addAction() is used here to merely display the icon
# in the line edit
self.address_line.addAction(
    QIcon("icons/search.png"),
    QLineEdit.ActionPosition.LeadingPosition)
self.address_line.setPlaceholderText(
    "Enter website address")
self.address_line.returnPressed.connect(
    self.searchForUrl)

tool_bar.addAction(home_button)
tool_bar.addAction(back_page_button)
tool_bar.addAction(forward_page_button)
tool_bar.addAction(refresh_button)
tool_bar.addWidget(self.address_line)
tool_bar.addAction(stop_button)

def setUpWebView(self):
    """Create the QWebEngineView object that is used to
    view web docs. Set up the main page, and handle
    web_view signals."""
    web_view = QWebEngineView()
    web_view.setUrl(QUrl("https://google.com"))

    # Create page loading progress bar that is displayed
    # in the status bar.
```

```
        self.page_load_pb = QProgressBar()
        self.page_load_label = QLabel()
        web_view.loadProgress.connect(self.updateProgressBar)

        # Display url in address bar
        web_view.urlChanged.connect(self.updateUrl)

        ok = web_view.loadFinished.connect(
            self.updateTabTitle)
        if ok:
            # Web page loaded
            return web_view
        else:
            print("The request timed out.")

    def setUpTab(self, tab):
        """Create individual tabs and widgets. Add the
        tab"s url and web view to the appropriate list.
        Update the address bar if the user switches tabs."""
        # Create the web view that will be displayed on the
        # page
        self.web_page = self.setUpWebView()

        # Append new web_page and url to the appropriate lists
        self.list_of_web_pages.append(self.web_page)
        self.list_of_urls.append(self.address_line)
        self.tab_bar.setCurrentWidget(self.web_page)

        # If user switches pages, update the url in the
        # address to reflect the current page.
        self.tab_bar.currentChanged.connect(self.updateUrl)

        tab_v_box = QVBoxLayout()
        # Sets the left, top, right, and bottom margins to
        # use around the layout.
        tab_v_box.setContentsMargins(0,0,0,0)
        tab_v_box.addWidget(self.web_page)
        tab.setLayout(tab_v_box)
```

```python
    def openNewWindow(self):
        """Create new instance of the WebBrowser class."""
        new_window = WebBrowser()
        new_window.show()
        self.window_list.append(new_window)

    def openNewTab(self):
        """Create a new web tab."""
        new_tab = QWidget()
        self.tab_bar.addTab(new_tab, "New Tab")
        self.setUpTab(new_tab)

        # Update the tab_bar index to keep track of the new
        # tab. Load the url for the new page
        tab_index = self.tab_bar.currentIndex()
        self.tab_bar.setCurrentIndex(tab_index + 1)
        self.list_of_web_pages[
            self.tab_bar.currentIndex()].load(
                QUrl("https://google.com"))

    def updateProgressBar(self, progress):
        """Update progress bar in status bar.
        This provides feedback to the user that page is
        still loading."""
        if progress < 100:
            self.page_load_pb.setVisible(progress)
            self.page_load_pb.setValue(progress)
            self.page_load_label.setVisible(progress)
            self.page_load_label.setText(
                f"Loading Page... ({str(progress)}/100)")
            self.status_bar.addWidget(self.page_load_pb)
            self.status_bar.addWidget(self.page_load_label)
        else:
            self.status_bar.removeWidget(self.page_load_pb)
            self.status_bar.removeWidget(self.page_load_label)
```

```python
def updateTabTitle(self):
    """Update the title of the tab to reflect the
    website."""
    tab_index = self.tab_bar.currentIndex()
    title = self.list_of_web_pages[
        self.tab_bar.currentIndex()].page().title()
    self.tab_bar.setTabText(tab_index, title)
def updateUrl(self):
    """Update the url in the address to reflect the
    current page being displayed."""
    url = self.list_of_web_pages[
        self.tab_bar.currentIndex()].page().url()
    formatted_url = QUrl(url).toString()
    self.list_of_urls[
        self.tab_bar.currentIndex()].setText(
            formatted_url)

def searchForUrl(self):
    """Make a request to load a url."""
    url_text = self.list_of_urls[
        self.tab_bar.currentIndex()].text()

    # Append http to url
    url = QUrl(url_text)
    if url.scheme() == "":
        url.setScheme("http")

    # Request url
    if url.isValid():
        self.list_of_web_pages[
            self.tab_bar.currentIndex()].page().load(url)
    else:
        url.clear()

def backPageButton(self):
    tab_index = self.tab_bar.currentIndex()
    self.list_of_web_pages[tab_index].back()
```

```python
    def forwardPageButton(self):
        tab_index = self.tab_bar.currentIndex()
        self.list_of_web_pages[tab_index].forward()

    def refreshButton(self):
        tab_index = self.tab_bar.currentIndex()
        self.list_of_web_pages[tab_index].reload()

    def homeButton(self):
        tab_index = self.tab_bar.currentIndex()
        self.list_of_web_pages[tab_index].setUrl(
            QUrl("https://google.com"))
    def stopButton(self):
        tab_index = self.tab_bar.currentIndex()
        self.list_of_web_pages[tab_index].stop()

    def closeTab(self, tab_index):
        """Slot is emitted when the close button on a tab is
        clicked. index refers to the tab that should be
        removed."""
        self.list_of_web_pages.pop(tab_index)
        self.list_of_urls.pop(tab_index)

        self.tab_bar.removeTab(tab_index)

    def sizeMainWindow(self):
        """Use QApplication.primaryScreen() to access
        information about the screen and use it to size the
        main window when starting a new application."""
        desktop = QApplication.primaryScreen()
        size = desktop.availableGeometry()
        screen_width = size.width()
        screen_height = size.height()
        self.setGeometry(0, 0, screen_width, screen_height)

if __name__ == '__main__':
    app = QApplication(sys.argv)
    app.setStyleSheet(style_sheet)
```

```
window = WebBrowser()
app.exec()
```

Before calling `initializeUI()`, we need to instantiate a few lists that will contain the new windows, web pages viewed, and URLs for each tab. This project also calls `setWindowIcon()` to include an application icon, but it will not be displayed on macOS due to system guidelines.

There are several methods that are called in `initializeUI()`. The first one is `sizeMainWindow()`, which demonstrates how to use `QApplication` to access information about the computer's screen size. The second, `createToolbar()`, sets up the toolbar for navigating web pages. Methods `createActions()` and `createMenu()` set up the main menu. The menu includes actions and shortcuts for creating new windows and new tabs and closing the application. The application's status bar is created in `setUpMainWindow()`, along with the `QTabWidget` for managing the open web pages.

In the `createToolbar()` method, the `tool_bar` instance includes buttons for navigating between web pages and a `QLineEdit` widget for entering and displaying URLs. Each button emits a signal when `triggered` that is connected to an appropriate slot. For example, if the `back_page_button` is pressed, the `backPageButton()` slot will be called, which we can see in the following block of code:

```
def backPageButton(self):
    tab_index = self.tab_bar.currentIndex()
    self.list_of_web_pages[tab_index].back()
```

The current index of the tab we are viewing is stored in `tab_index`. The `back()` method is then called on the `web_view` object for that current tab. If the `tab_index` is not 0, then the user can navigate back through previously viewed web pages. The `back()` method is but one of several functions included in the `QWebEngineView` class. Other methods for navigation include `forward()`, `reload()`, and `stop()`, and these are also utilized for the other `tool_bar` buttons.

When the user enters a web address in the `QLineEdit` widget and presses the return key, we check to see if the URL begins with the correct scheme (such as `http`, `https`, or `file`) in `searchForUrl()`. If a valid scheme is not present, `http` is appended to the beginning of the URL. If the URL conforms to standard encoding rules, a request is then sent to `load()` the website.

Creating Tabs for the Web Browser

The setUpMainWindow() is used to handle creating the tab widget and the web view objects. First, we need to create the QTabWidget that will display each individual tab's web view. Refer back to Chapter 6 for more details on setting up tab widgets.

A few of the tab_bar widget's parameters are changed so that each tab includes a close button, and if only one tab remains, then the tab bar will not be displayed. This helps to make sure that there is always at least one tab in the main window. If a tab is closed, the closeTab() slot is called. The corresponding URLs and web view items for that tab are also removed from the list_of_urls and list_of_web_pages lists.

The first tab, main_tab, is created, added to the tab_bar, and then passed to the setUpTab() method. The tab_bar widget is set as the central widget for the main window. To set up a tab to display a web page, we first need to create a web view object.

Creating the Web View

The setUpWebView() method creates an instance of the QWebEngineView class, web_view, and sets the web view's URL to display the Google web page:

```
web_view.setUrl(QUrl("https://google.com"))
```

To create a basic instance of a web view in an application, you only need to create a QWebEngineView object, use the load() method to load the web page onto the web view widget, and then call show(). The following code shows the process for setting up a simple web view widget.

```
web_view = QWebEngineView()
web_view.load(QUrl("https://google.com"))
web_view.show()
```

Once the web page has loaded, the urlChanged signal connected to updateUrl() changes the URL displayed in address_line. We can use the loadFinished() signal to tell the current tab to update its title using the updateTabTitle() slot and return the web_view widget.

Next, create the layout to hold the web view widget, append the current tab's URL and web_page object to the list_of_urls and list_of_web_pages lists, and set the layout for the current tab's page. The web_page object is the web_view widget that is returned from setUpWebView() and displayed in the page in setUpTab().

Finally, to handle when a user switches between tabs, QTabWidget has the currentChanged signal. If a different tab is selected, the connected slot, updateUrl(), will change the displayed URL in address_line.

Adding a QProgressBar to the Status Bar

In setUpWebView(), a progress bar and label are also created that will be used to display the loading progress of a web page in the browser's status bar. When the loadProgress signal is generated, the updateProgressBar() slot is called.

The loadProgress slot includes integer information that we can use to track how much of the page has loaded. While progress is less than 100, the progress bar and the label are both displayed, and their values are set. The code for displaying the progress bar is shown in the following lines:

```
self.page_load_pb.setVisible(progress)
self.page_load_pb.setValue(progress)
```

The widgets are then added to the status bar:

```
self.status_bar.addWidget(self.page_load_pb)
```

When a page is finished loading, we call removeWidget() to remove the progress bar and the label. An example of the progress bar can be seen at the bottom of Figure 16-8.

Note   Creating a web browser is a very extensive task. There are many topics that are not included in this project, such as accessing HTTP cookies with Qt WebEngine Core, working with the browser history with QWebEngineHistory, managing connections and client certificates, proxy support with QNetworkProxy, working with JavaScript, downloading content from websites, and others. You are definitely encouraged to research these topics if you need to use Qt WebEngine for more advanced projects.

Project 16.7 – Tri-state QComboBox

While you may typically work with check boxes that have two states, checked or unchecked, a third state also exists, partially checked. This type of condition is usually influenced by the combo box's children widgets or by the group that the QComboBox is managing. Figure 16-9 shows a simple example of a tri-state combo box where not all of its children are selected.

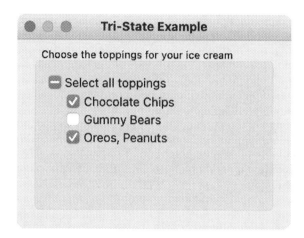

Figure 16-9. *A window that contains a partially checked QComboBox*

If all of the child elements are selected, the parent check box is checked. If some of the children are selected, then the parent is partially checked.

Explanation for the Tri-state QComboBox

For this example, let's begin with the basic_window.py script from Chapter 1. There are no new widgets or other classes introduced in this section. Here, we'll focus on learning what we've learned before in order to learn a new skill. Take a look at the tristate_cb instance in setUpMainWindow() in Listing 16-7. You'll notice that we want to wait for a signal whenever the state of the widget changes using stateChanged.

Listing 16-7. Code for the tri-state QComboBox

```
# tristate.py
# Import necessary modules
import sys
from PyQt6.QtWidgets import (QApplication, QWidget,
    QCheckBox, QGroupBox, QButtonGroup, QVBoxLayout)
from PyQt6.QtCore import Qt
```

```python
class MainWindow(QWidget):

    def __init__(self):
        super().__init__()
        self.initializeUI()

    def initializeUI(self):
        """Set up the application's GUI."""
        self.setMinimumSize(300, 200)
        self.setWindowTitle("Tri-State Example")

        self.setUpMainWindow()
        self.show()

    def setUpMainWindow(self):
        """Create and arrange widgets in the main window."""
        self.tristate_cb = QCheckBox("Select all toppings")
        self.tristate_cb.stateChanged.connect(
            self.updateTristateCb)

        # Create the check boxes with an indentation
        # using style sheets
        topping1_cb = QCheckBox("Chocolate Chips")
        topping1_cb.setStyleSheet("padding-left: 20px")
        topping2_cb = QCheckBox("Gummy Bears")
        topping2_cb.setStyleSheet("padding-left: 20px")
        topping3_cb = QCheckBox("Oreos, Peanuts")
        topping3_cb.setStyleSheet("padding-left: 20px")

        # Create a non-exclusive group of check boxes
        self.button_group = QButtonGroup(self)
        self.button_group.setExclusive(False)
        self.button_group.addButton(topping1_cb)
        self.button_group.addButton(topping2_cb)
        self.button_group.addButton(topping3_cb)
        self.button_group.buttonToggled.connect(
            self.checkButtonState)
```

499

```
        gb_v_box = QVBoxLayout()
        gb_v_box.addWidget(self.tristate_cb)
        gb_v_box.addWidget(topping1_cb)
        gb_v_box.addWidget(topping2_cb)
        gb_v_box.addWidget(topping3_cb)
        gb_v_box.addStretch()

        group_box = QGroupBox(
            "Choose the toppings for your ice cream")
        group_box.setLayout(gb_v_box)

        main_v_box = QVBoxLayout()
        main_v_box.addWidget(group_box)
        self.setLayout(main_v_box)

    def updateTristateCb(self, state):
        """Use the QCheckBox to check or uncheck all boxes."""
        for button in self.button_group.buttons():
            if state == 2: # Qt.CheckState.Checked
                button.setChecked(True)
            elif state == 0: # Qt.CheckState.Unchecked
                button.setChecked(False)

    def checkButtonState(self, button, checked):
        """Determine which buttons are selected and set the
        state of the tri-state QCheckBox."""
        button_states = []

        for button in self.button_group.buttons():
            button_states.append(button.isChecked())

        if all(button_states):
            self.tristate_cb.setCheckState(
                Qt.CheckState.Checked)
            self.tristate_cb.setTristate(False)
        elif any(button_states) == False:
            self.tristate_cb.setCheckState(
                Qt.CheckState.Unchecked)
            self.tristate_cb.setTristate(False)
```

```
        else:
            self.tristate_cb.setCheckState(
                Qt.CheckState.PartiallyChecked)
if __name__ == '__main__':
    app = QApplication(sys.argv)
    window = MainWindow()
    sys.exit(app.exec())
```

If tristate_cb is checked, we'll use the value of state that is passed with the stateChanged signal to check all of the check boxes in checkButtonState(). Otherwise, the widgets are all unchecked.

Next, we'll create the rest of the window, instantiate the children QCheckBox objects, and arrange them in a QButtonGroup. The QButtonGroup signal buttonToggled is emitted whenever any of the widgets are checked or unchecked. If the state of one of the check boxes in the button group changes, the slot checkButtonState() is used to find out which buttons are checked or unchecked. We can access all of the buttons in QButtonGroup using the buttons() method.

Those values are then added to the button_states list. It is here that we take care of updating the parameters of tristate_cb. If all values are True, setCheckState() is used to ensure that tristate_cb only has two states. If all of the buttons are False, then tristate_cb is unchecked. Finally, if there is a mix of True and False values in button_states, tristate_cb is set to tri-state mode using setCheckState() and the PartiallyChecked flag.

Summary

In this chapter, you saw different GUI applications that build the structure for larger projects, such as the camera GUI or the web browser GUI. Other projects introduced components that you may be able to include in other programs, such as the directory viewer GUI, the clock GUI, and the calendar GUI. In the case of the Hangman GUI, we demonstrated how an understanding of QPainter is useful for drawing and customizing the look of widgets. Finally, tri-state QComboBox widgets are useful for managing child elements.

We have explored a variety of topics for designing graphical user interfaces using PyQt6 and Python throughout this book – different types of widgets, classes, and layouts. We saw how to stylize your interfaces, how to add menus, and how to make an application simpler with Qt Designer. Advanced topics such as working with the clipboard, SQL, and multithreaded applications were also covered.

The Appendix will fill in more details about some of the PyQt6 classes used in this book as well as a few other classes that were not included in previous chapters.

Your feedback and questions are always welcome. Thank you so much for joining me on this journey and allowing me to share my knowledge about GUI development with you.

Reference Guide for PyQt6

PyQt is a Python binding for the Qt Application framework maintained by Riverbank Computing Limited. A **binding** is an application programming interface (API) that provides the code to allow a programming language to use other libraries not native to that language. Qt is a set of C++ libraries and development tools, providing access to networking, threads, SQL databases, OpenGL and other graphics tools, XML, GUI development, and a variety of other features. This chapter focuses only on PyQt6, but many of the concepts and methods are still available in PyQt5.

Appendix contains a reference for some of the tools, modules, and classes learned throughout this book, including

- A review of PyQt modules and classes

- An overview of Qt Style Sheets

- A discussion about Qt Namespace

More information about Riverbank Computing Limited and PyQt6 can be found at `https://riverbankcomputing.com/software/pyqt/intro`.

Selected PyQt6 Modules

PyQt provides a range of modules that give you access to a wide array of tools, including basic GUI design, 2D and 3D rendering, multimedia content, networking, global positioning, and more. For basic GUI development, you will primarily use the `QtWidgets`, `QtGui`, and `QtCore` modules. Table A-1 lists the modules covered throughout the book as well as a few extra you should check out.

For a full list of PyQt6's top-level modules, check out the following link:

`www.riverbankcomputing.com/static/Docs/PyQt6/module_index.html`

© Joshua M Willman 2022
J. M. Willman, *Beginning PyQt*, https://doi.org/10.1007/978-1-4842-7999-1

Table A-1. *Table of select PyQt modules*

Module Name	Description
QtWidgets	Provides the widgets and other classes for creating desktop-style UIs
QtCore	Contains a variety of extra classes, including the essential non-GUI classes, such as ones for Qt's signal and slot system
QtGui	Contains classes for 2D graphics and imaging, event handling, and window system integration
QtPrintSupport	Provides cross-platform support for configuring and connecting to printers
QtNetwork	Provides classes for writing communications protocols using UDP or TCP
QtQuick	Contains the classes for creating QML applications with Python
QtMultimedia	Contains the classes for multimedia content, including cameras, images, and audio
QtMultimediaWidgets	Provides additional classes that increase the functionality of multimedia-related widgets
QtWebEngineCore	Contains the core classes used by other Web Engine modules
QtWebEngineWidgets	Classes that can be used to create a Chromium-based web browser
QtSql	Provides classes for working with SQL databases
sip	Tools used for creating Python bindings for C ++ libraries (which is the language Qt is written in)
uic	Contains classes used for handling the .ui files created by Qt Designer

Selected PyQt Classes

There are hundreds of PyQt classes. The following section lists the classes and widgets that can be found throughout this book. Each subsection either lists tables with commonly used methods and signals or a link to where you can find more information about the class.

For a list of all the PyQt classes, check out

`www.riverbankcomputing.com/static/Docs/PyQt6/sip-classes.html`

Although it is written for C++, the Qt classes documentation is generally more detailed. If you want more information about Qt classes, you can also check out

`https://doc.qt.io/qt-6/classes.html`

Just keep in mind that some of the classes that exist in Qt are not available in PyQt. In many cases, this is because Python already includes the functionality that the removed class would provide. One common example is `QList`, which exists in Qt but is not included in Python since it includes the `list` data structure.

Classes for Building a GUI Window

With PyQt, you can create a new class that inherits from any of the widget classes. However, for a general GUI application, you will need to create only one instance of `QApplication` and create a class that inherits from either `QWidget`, `QMainWindow`, or `QDialog` to create the application's main window.

QApplication

`QApplication` is responsible for handling the initialization and finalization of widgets in graphical user interfaces. If you are making `QWidget`-based applications, then you will need to create an instance of `QApplication` before creating any other objects related to the GUI.

Some of the `QApplication` class's responsibilities include initializing an application to conform to a user's desktop settings, event handling, defining the GUI's style, working with the clipboard, and keeping track of all the application's windows.

If you are creating an application that does not need a GUI and can be run through the command line, then you should consider using **QCoreApplication** instead.

QWidget

The `QWidget` class is the base class for all of PyQt's graphical user interface objects. A widget created from the `QWidget` class is able to receive input from mouse, keyboard, and other events and able to paint itself on the screen. Widgets that are not embedded in a parent widget are considered to be a window complete with a title bar and a frame. The `QWidget` class is a subclass of `QObject` and **QPaintDevice** (the class that defines a two-dimensional space for drawing on with `QPainter`). Some helpful `QWidget` methods can be found in Table A-2.

Table A-2. *Selected methods from QWidget*

Method	Description
addAction(action)	Adds an action to the widget
close()	Closes the widget
height()	Retrieves the widget's height
width()	Retrieves the widget's width
move(x, y)	Sets the location of the widget to (x, y)
rect()	Retrieves the geometry of the widget minus the frame
setDisabled(bool)	If True, the widget is disabled
setEnabled(bool)	If True, the widget is enabled
setFont(font)	Sets the font of the widget's text (if the widget can display text)
setLayout(layout)	Sets the layout manager for the widget
setGeometry(x, y, width, height)	Sets the widget's location, (x, y), and its size, width and height
setStyleSheet(styleSheet)	Sets the styleSheet for the widget
setToolTip(text)	Sets the widget's tool tip
repaint()	Repaints the widget immediately by calling paintEvent()
showFullScreen()	Displays the widget in full-screen mode
update()	Updates the widget by scheduling a paint event in the main event loop

Event Handling

Events are typically caused by users or the underlying system. These can include moving a mouse, pressing a key, resizing the window, or a timer delivering events. The widgets in an application need to respond appropriately to the event. The events are generally already handled in the background of simpler applications, but you sometimes may find yourself needing to reimplement event handlers to supply further behavior or content for the widgets. Table A-3 lists a few commonly used event handlers.

Table A-3. *Some event handlers used for supplying behavior to QWidget objects*

Event Handler	Description
paintEvent()	Called whenever a widget needs to be repainted
resizeEvent()	Called when a widget has been resized
mousePressEvent()	Called when a mouse button is pressed while the mouse cursor is inside of the widget. Which mouse button is clicked can be specified in the event
mouseReleaseEvent()	Called when a mouse button is released. A widget that receives this event is dependent on receiving the mouse press event
mouseDoubleClickEvent()	Called when a widget is double-clicked on
mouseMoveEvent()	Called when the mouse moves while the button is held down. If setMouseTracking() is True, events are sent even when no buttons are pressed
enterEvent()	Called when the mouse enters a widget's space
leaveEvent()	Called when the mouse leaves a widget's space
keyPressEvent()	Called when a key is pressed
keyReleaseEvent()	Called when a key is released
focusInEvent()	Called when a widget gets the keyboard focus
focusOutEvent()	Called when a widget loses the keyboard focus
closeEvent()	Called when either a widget or the window is closed

QMainWindow

The QMainWindow class provides the framework for building an application, complete with functions for adding a menu bar, toolbars, a status bar, and dock widgets. Menu and toolbar items are created using QAction. QMainWindow already has its own layout, to which you must add a central widget as the center area of the application's window. Some of the QMainWindow class's methods can be seen in Table A-4.

Table A-4. *Select methods from QMainWindow*

Method	Description
addDockWidget(area, dockwidget)	Creates a dock widget in the main window in the specified area
addToolBar(area, toolbar)	Creates a toolbar for the main window. An area can also be specified
menuBar()	Returns the main window's menu bar
setStatusBar(statusbar)	Creates the status bar for the main window
setCentralWidget(widget)	Sets the window's central widget
setWindowIcon(icon)	Sets the window's icon
setWindowTitle(text)	Sets the window's title. This is a method inherited from QWidget

QDialog

Dialog boxes provide a top-level window that are generally used to quickly obtain feedback from a user. QDialog instances can be modal or modeless. Modal dialogs are often used when selecting an option in the dialog that will return a value. That value could then be used to save a file, close a document, or cancel an action.

QDialog is the base class for other dialog box classes, including QColorDialog, QFileDialog, QFontDialog, QInputDialog, QMessageBox, QProgressDialog, and QErrorMessage. A few methods for setting the mode of the dialog and handling the results of the dialog are in Table A-5.

Table A-5. *Select methods for QDialog*

Method	Description
accept()	Hides the modal dialog and returns True, accepting the actions specified by the dialog
reject()	Hides the modal dialog and returns False, rejecting the actions specified by the dialog
open()	The dialog is shown as a modal dialog and blocks the user from any further action until the dialog is closed
show()	The dialog is a modeless dialog, returning control to the user immediately

Table A-6 lists some common default buttons that are part of the `QMessageBox.StandardButton` or `QDialogButtonBox.StandardButton` enums. These flags are very useful when creating custom dialog boxes. Each one of the buttons returns a specific **ButtonRole**, describing the behavior of the button. For example, **AcceptRole** causes the dialog and its contents to be accepted. This is equivalent to OK. A **RejectRole** rejects the dialog, which is what Cancel does. There are other kinds of roles too. Refer to the table for more information.

Table A-6. *Select standard buttons for QDialogButtonBox and QMessageBox*

Method	Description
Ok	Defines an OK button with an AcceptRole
Open	Defines an Open button with an AcceptRole
Save	Defines a Save button with an AcceptRole
Cancel	Defines a Cancel button with a RejectRole
Close	Defines a Close button with a RejectRole
Yes	Defines a Yes button with a YesRole
No	Defines a No button with a NoRole
Reset	Defines a Reset button with a ResetRole

QPainter

The `QPainter` class is responsible for handling drawing in PyQt, being able to draw simple lines and complex shapes onto widgets and other paint devices. `QPainter` is most commonly used in the `paintEvent()` event handler, as well as for handling pixmaps and images. Table A-7 displays some of the `QPainter` class's methods for drawing.

Table A-7. *Methods selected from QPainter*

Method	Description
begin(device)	Begins painting on the paint device
end()	Ends painting. Resources used while painting are released
save()	Saves the current painter state. save() must be followed by restore(), which returns the current painter state
drawArc(QRectF, startAngle, spanAngle)	Draws an arc defined by the QRectF rectangle, startAngle, and spanAngle
drawChord(QRectF, startAngle, spanAngle)	Draws a chord defined by the QRectF rectangle, startAngle, and spanAngle
drawEllipse(QPointF, x_rad, y_rad)	Draws an ellipse at QPointF center, with radius x_rad and y_rad
drawLine(x1, y1, x2, y2)	Draws a line from point (x1, y1) to (x2, y2)
drawPath(path)	Draws a path specified by QPainterPath path
drawPie(QRectF, startAngle, spanAngle)	Draws a pie defined by the QRectF rectangle, startAngle, and spanAngle
drawPixmap(x, y, pixmap)	Draws a pixmap at (x, y)
drawPoint(x, y)	Draws a point at (x, y)
drawRect(x, y, width, height)	Draws a rectangle at (x, y) with width and height
drawRoundedRect(QRectF, x_rad, y_rad)	Draws a rectangle with rounded corners specified by QRectF, with radius x_rad and y_rad
drawText(QPointF, text)	Draws text at QPointF point
fillRect(QRectF, brush)	Fills in a QRectF rectangle with the brush color
rotate(angle)	Rotates the coordinate system clockwise by angle (in degrees)
setBrush(brush)	Sets the painter's brush
setPen(pen)	Sets the painter's pen
setFont()	Sets the painter's font

Layout Managers

Using PyQt's layout managers makes the process of arranging widgets much easier compared to manually specifying each widget's size, position, or `resizeEvent()` event handler. Using layout managers is generally a good start for positioning widgets, although you may still need to adjust a widget's size policy or add stretching or spacing to a layout.

The following classes inherit from the **QLayout** class, which is the base class for layout managers:

1. `QBoxLayout` – Arranges child widgets into a row (horizontally) or into a column (vertically)

    a. `QHBoxLayout` – Arranges widgets horizontally

    b. `QVBoxLayout` – Arranges widgets vertically

2. `QGridLayout` – Orders widgets in a grid of rows and columns

3. `QFormLayout` – Lays out widgets into a form-like structure with labels and their associated input widgets

4. `QStackedLayout` – Arranges widgets into a stack where only one widget is visible at a time. The convenience `QStackedWidget` class is built on top of the `QStackedLayout`.

Table A-8 lists commonly used methods from the layout classes.

Table A-8. *Selected methods for the different layout managers*

Method	Class	Description
addWidget(widget, stretch, alignment)	QBoxLayout	Adds widget to the end of the layout with stretch factor and alignment
addWidget(widget, row, column, rowSpan, columnSpan alignment)	QGridLayout	Adds widget at row, column with (optional) rowSpan and columnSpan and alignment
addRow(label, field)	QFormLayout	Adds a new row with a given label and field (input widget)
addWidget(widget)	QStackedLayout	Adds a new widget to the end of the layout. This method returns the widget's index in the stack
addLayout(layout, stretch)	QBoxLayout	Adds a layout to the end of the box. Creates a nested layout
addLayout(layout, row, column, alignment)	QGridLayout	Adds a layout at position (row, column). Creates a nested layout
addSpacing(int)	QGridLayout, QBoxLayout	Adds a nonstretchable area (a QSpacerItem) of int value to the layout
addStretch(int)	QBoxLayout	Adds a stretchable area (a QSpacerItem) of int value to the layout
setSpacing(int)	QLayout	Sets the space between widgets in the layout. Inherited from QLayout
setContentMargins(left, top, right, bottom)	QLayout	Sets the left, top, right, and bottom margins around the layout

Button Widgets

Buttons are one of the main tools used in a GUI for interaction, giving an application feedback about a user's decisions. Buttons in PyQt can display text or icons and are checkable. The following classes inherit from the base class for button widgets, **QAbstractButton**:

1. QPushButton – A command button used to tell the computer to perform some action

2. QCheckBox – Provides an option button that is checkable and generally used for enabling/disabling features in an application

3. QRadioButton – Similar to check boxes, but are mutually exclusive

4. QToolButton – Typically used in a toolbar, tool buttons provide quick-access buttons for selecting commands or options

For managing and organizing multiple buttons, the QButtonGroup class can act as a container for creating exclusive buttons (the default setting). Table A-9 lists some of the more commonly used methods for button widgets.

Table A-9. *Selected methods for the different button widgets*

Method	Description
setIcon(icon)	Sets the widget's icon
setText(text)	Sets the widget's text
setAutoExclusive(bool)	Enables autoexclusivity for buttons in a group
setCheckable(bool)	Sets whether the button is a toggle button or not
setChecked(bool)	Sets whether the button is checked or not
isChecked()	Indicates whether the button is checked or not (if setCheckable() is True)
text()	Gets the buttons text

Some signals for the button widget classes are listed in Table A-10.

Table A-10. *Signals for the different button widgets*

Signal	Class	Description
clicked(bool)	QAbstractButton	Signal emitted when the button is pressed and released
pressed()	QAbstractButton	Emitted when the left mouse button clicks on the button
released()	QAbstractButton	Signal emitted when the left mouse button is released
toggled(bool)	QAbstractButton	Emitted when a checkable button changes its state
stateChanged(bool)	QCheckBox	Emitted when the check box's state changes
triggered(action)	QToolButton	Signal emitted when the action is triggered

Input Widgets

There are quite a few widgets that are provided by PyQt for getting input from the user. These widgets provide different means for gathering information, such as text entry or selecting values with sliders, combo boxes, and spin boxes.

Combo Boxes

The QComboBox class presents a user with a list of selectable options in a compact, drop-down menu. Some of the class's methods are found in Table A-11. When the combo box is not being interacted with, all items except for the current item selected are hidden from view. The **QFontComboBox** widget is another type of combo box that inherits QComboBox and is used for selecting a font family.

Table A-11. *Select methods from the QComboBox class*

Method	Description
addItem(text)	Appends an item to the list with text
addItems(list(text))	Appends a list of items to the combo box
currentIndex()	Gets the index of the currently selected item
currentText()	Gets the text of the currently selected item
insertItem(index, text)	Inserts the text into the combo box at the given index
setItemText(index, text)	Sets the text for the item at the given index
removeItem(index)	Removes the item at the given index
clear()	Clears all items from the combo box
setEditable(bool)	If True, the contents of the combo box are editable

Table A-12 displays select signals for the combo box classes.

Table A-12. *Commonly used signals from the QComboBox and QFontComboBox classes*

Signal	Description
currentIndexChanged(index)	Emitted if the current item in the combo box has changed
currentTextChanged(text)	Signal emitted if the current item in the combo box has changed. Returns text
activated(index)	Emitted only if the user interacts with an item
highlighted(index)	Emitted when an item in the combo box is highlighted
textActivated(text)	Signal emitted when the user chooses an item
currentFontChanged(font)	Emitted when the current font changes

QLineEdit

The QLineEdit widget provides a single line for entering and editing plain text. Although not listed in the following tables, QLineEdit includes clear(), selectAll(), cut(), copy(), paste(), undo(), and redo() slots already built-in. Table A-13 displays a few of the QLineEdit class's methods.

Table A-13. *Methods from the QLineEdit class*

Method	Description
text()	Retrieves the current text in the line edit
setAlignment(alignment)	Sets the alignment of the text displayed in the widget
setPlaceholderText(text)	Displays placeholder text while line edit is empty
setEchoMode(mode)	The parameter mode describes how the contents of a line should be displayed. Set mode to QLineEdit. Password to mask characters
setMaxLength(int)	Sets the maximum length of characters
setTextMargins(left, top, right, bottom)	Sets the text margins for the text displayed in the line edit
setDragEnabled(bool)	If True, dragging selected text in the line edit is permitted

A few common signals for QLineEdit can be seen in Table A-14.

Table A-14. *Commonly used signals from the QLineEdit class*

Signal	Description
returnPressed()	Emitted when the Enter key is pressed. If a validator is set, then a signal is only emitted if the text is accepted
textChanged(text)	Signal is emitted when the text changes

Text Editing Widgets

The two text editing classes, QTextEdit and **QPlainTextEdit**, provide tools and functionality for displaying and editing larger bodies of text. QTextEdit also has the added benefit of being able to work with rich text, graphics, and tables. Both classes are similar to QLineEdit, because they already have editing features built-in. A few methods for text editors are found in Table A-15.

Also worth noting is the **QTextBrowser** class, which inherits QTextEdit. QTextBrowser only allows read-only mode but includes hypertext navigation functionality so that users can click on links and follow them.

Table A-15. *Select methods from QTextEdit and QPlainTextEdit*

Method	Description
find(text, flags)	Finds the next occurrence of text in the text edit
print(printer)	Prints the text edit's document to the printer
setPlaceHolderText(text)	Sets placeholder text for text edit
setReadOnly(bool)	If True, the text edit is set to read-only
toPlainText()	Returns the text of the text edit as plain text
zoomIn(range)	Zooms in on the text
zoomOut(range)	Zooms out on the text

Commonly used signals for the text editing widgets can be found in Table A-16.

Table A-16. *Select signals from QTextEdit and QPlainTextEdit*

Signal	Description
selectionChanged()	Signal emitted when the text selected in the text edit changes
textChanged()	Emitted whenever the contents of the text edit change

Spin Box Widgets

Spin boxes allow users to choose values within a given range by clicking up/down buttons to cycle through the widget's values. Users can also manually type in values into the provided line edit. The **QAbstractSpinBox** class is the base class for the following classes:

1. QSpinBox – Handles integers.

2. QDoubleSpinBox – Similar to QSpinBox, but is used for floating-point values.

3. QDateTimeEdit – A spin box widget for selecting dates and times. Use setDisplayFormat() to set the format used for displaying the dates and time.

4. QDateEdit – A spin box that displays only dates. Inherits QDateTimeEdit.

5. QTimeEdit – A spin box that displays only times. Inherits QDateTimeEdit.

Some of the methods for the QSpinBox and QDoubleSpinBox classes are listed in Table A-17. The QDateTimeEdit and other spin box widgets have similar methods.

Table A-17. *Select signals from QSpinBox and QDoubleSpinBox. The value* val *refers to integers for QSpinBox and floating-point numbers for QDoubleSpinBox*

Method	Description
setValue(val)	Sets the value val of the spin box
setMinimum(val)	Sets the minimum value val of the spin box
setMaximum(val)	Sets the maximum value val of the spin box
setPrefix(str)	Adds a prefix to the start of the displayed value
setSuffix(str)	Adds a suffix to the end of the displayed value
setRange(min, max)	Sets the minimum and maximum range values
setSingleStep(val)	The spin box's value is incremented/decremented by val when the arrow keys are pressed

Some QSpinBox and QDoubleSpinBox signals are found in Table A-18.

Table A-18. *Signals from QSpinBox and QDoubleSpinBox*

Signal	Description
valueChanged(val)	Signal emitted when the value changes. Provides the new value's val
textChanged(text)	Signal emitted when the value changes. Provides the new value's text

Slider Widgets

The following widgets are different in appearance but are actually quite similar in functionality. Widgets that inherit from the **QAbstractSlider** class are used for selecting integer values within a bounded range. Classes that inherit QAbstractSlider include the following:

1. QDial – Provides a rounded range controller for selecting or adjusting values. An example of QDial can be seen in Figure A-1.

2. QScrollBar – Provides horizontal or vertical scrollbars that the user can use to access other parts of a document that are wider than the widget used to display it.

3. QSlider – Creates the classic horizontal and vertical sliders widgets for controlling values within a specified range.

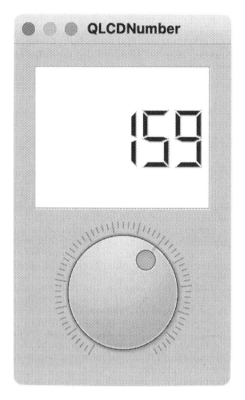

Figure A-1. *Example of the QLCDNumber and QDial widgets. The XML and Python code for this example can be found in the Appendix folder of the GitHub repository*

Table A-19 shows some of the methods of the QAbstractSlider base class.

Table A-19. *Select methods from QAbstractSlider*

Method	Description
value()	Holds the slider's current value
setMinimum(int)	Sets the minimum value of the slider
setMaximum(int)	Sets the maximum value of the slider
setOrientation(orientation)	Sets the orientation, Horizontal or Vertical (provided by the Qt.Orientation enum)
setSingleStep(int)	The slider's value is incremented/decremented by int when the arrow keys are pressed
setTracking(bool)	If True, the slider's position can be tracked
setSliderPosition(int)	Sets the current position of the slider
setValue(int)	Sets the current position of the slider to int. If tracking is enabled, then this has the same value as the value() getter

Signals of the QAbstractSlider class can be found in Table A-20.

Table A-20. *Signals from QAbstractSlider*

Signal	Description
valueChanged(val)	Signal emitted when the value changes. Provides the new value's val
rangeChanged(min, max)	Signal emitted when the range has changed with new minimum and maximum values
sliderMoved(val)	Emitted when the slider is pressed down and the slider moves
sliderPressed()	Emitted when the slider is pressed down
sliderReleased()	Emitted when the slider is released

Display Widgets

The following widgets are all used for different purposes, but each has one major characteristic in common – they are all used for displaying information to the user.

QLabel

QLabel is a versatile widget. Although a label provides no user interaction functionality, QLabel is able to display plain or rich text, pixmaps, and even GIFs. Labels provide a number of methods for configuring their appearance. Table A-21 lists a few of those methods.

Table A-21. *Select methods from QLabel*

Method	Description
setPicture(picture)	Sets the label content to picture
setPixmap(pixmap)	Sets the label content to pixmap
setMovie(movie)	Sets the label content to movie
setText(text)	Sets the label content to text
setAlignment(alignment)	Sets the alignment of the label's content
setIndent(int)	Sets the number of pixels that the label's text is indented
setMargin(int)	Sets the label's margins

QProgressBar

Progress bars are used to give visual feedback to the user about the progress of a computer operation. Progress bars can be displayed vertically or horizontally. Table A-22 shows some of the QProgressBar class's methods.

Table A-22. *Select methods for the QProgressBar class*

Method	Description
value()	Holds the progress bar's current value
setMinimum(int)	Sets the progress bar's minimum value
setMaximum(int)	Sets the progress bar's maximum value
setRange(min, max)	Sets the minimum and maximum values
setOrientation(orientation)	Sets the orientation, Horizontal or Vertical (provided by the Qt.Orientation enum)
setTextVisible(bool)	If True, the current completed percentage is displayed

QProgressBar has one signal, valueChanged(int), that is emitted when the value shown in the progress bar changes.

QGraphicsView

The QGraphicsView class provides a widget for displaying the contents of a QGraphicsScene. As the one part of Qt's Graphics View Framework, the QGraphicsView class's responsibility is to display the items of a graphics scene in a scrollable window. The QGraphicsScene object's duty is to manage the items in a scene. QGraphicsItem (or one of its subclasses) provides the items for a scene.

If you are interested in learning more about the Graphics View Framework, check out https://doc.qt.io/qt-6/graphicsview.html.

QLCDNumber

The **QLCDNumber** widget displays numbers in a seven-segment LCD display. An example of this is shown in Figure A-1. The display can visualize decimal, hexadecimal, octal, and binary numbers. The LCD display can only display certain characters. Note that if a character is passed that the widget cannot display, a space will be presented in place of the character.

Table A-23 lists a few of QLCDNumber class's methods.

Table A-23. *Select methods from the QLCDNumber class*

Method	Description
value()	Retrieves the LCD's displayed value
intValue()	Retrieves the displayed value rounded to the nearest integer value
display(val)	Displays the value val in the display. val can be floating-point, integer, or string types
setMode(mode)	Sets the mode of the LCD to display Bin, Oct, Dec, or Hex values
setSmallDecimalPoint(bool)	If True, the decimal is drawn between two digits

QLCDNumber has the overflow() signal, which is emitted when the widget is asked to display a number or string that is too long.

Item Views

The following model view classes provide the means to display items in lists, tables, or tree structures. They must be used alongside a model class as part of Qt's Model/View framework.

1. QListView – Provides a list and icon view for displaying items from a model

2. QTableView – Provides a table for displaying items from a model

3. QTreeView – Provides a hierarchical tree architecture for displaying items from a model

These classes all inherit from the **QAbstractItemView** class. Using signals and slots, item views created from QAbstractItemView are able to interact with models that use **QAbstractItemModel**. Each of the item views has their own methods for working with rows, columns, headers, and items. Views use indices to manage items. You can find some methods for QAbstractItemView in Table A-24.

Table A-24. *Select methods for the QAbstractItemView base class*

Method	Description
clearSelection()	All items selected are deselected
selectAll()	Selects all the items in the view
setCurrentIndex(index)	Sets the item at index as the current item
update(index)	Updates the area at the given index
setAlternatingRowColors(bool)	If True, the background is drawn with alternating colors
setAcceptDrops(bool)	If True, items can be dropped into the view
setDragEnabled(bool)	If True, items can be dragged around in the view
setIconSize(size)	Sets the size of icons
setItemDelegate(delegate)	Sets an item delegate for the view's Model/View framework
setModel(model)	Sets the model for the view

PyQt also offers convenience item-based classes for each of the different types of views – QListWidget, QTableWidget, and QTreeWidget. Items are added to the widgets by using QListWidgetItem, QTableWidgetItem, or QTreeWidgetItem.

Select signals for QAbstractItemView can be found in Table A-25.

Table A-25. *Select methods for the QAbstractItemView base class*

Signal	Description
activated(index)	Signal emitted when the item at index is activated by the user
clicked(index)	Emitted when the left mouse button is clicked on an item in the view (specified by index)
doubleClicked(index)	Emitted when a mouse button is double-clicked on an item in the view (specified by index)
entered(index)	Signal emitted when the mouse cursor enters the item at index. Turn on mouse tracking to use
pressed(index)	Signal emitted when a mouse button is pressed on an item at index

Container Widgets

PyQt provides a few container widgets for maintaining control over groups of widgets. Containers can be used to manage input widgets, make the process of organizing a group of widgets simpler, or simply as a decorative widget for separating groups of widgets. Once a container is created, a layout manager still needs to be applied to the container widget itself.

Containers with Frames

QFrame widgets can enclose and group widgets as well as function as placeholders in windows. Using frames, you can set the appearance of other widgets to have raised, sunken, or flat appearances. The QFrame class is used as the base class for a few other container classes, including **QToolBox** and **QStackedWidget**. Table A-26 lists a few of the QFrame class's methods.

Table A-26. *Select methods for QFrame*

Method	Description
setFrameRect(QRect)	Sets the rectangle that the frame is drawn in
setFrameShadow(shadow)	Sets the frame's shadow, using flags such as Plain, Raised, or Sunken
setFrameShape(shape)	Sets the frame's shape, using flags such as Box, Panel, HLine, and VLine
setLineWidth(int)	Sets the width of line drawn around the frame

QToolBox widgets provide a series of pages or compartments in a column. To navigate through each of the pages, a tab is included at the top of each page. By clicking on the next tab, the user can view a new tab's contents. Some methods for QToolBox are listed in Table A-27.

Table A-27. *A few of the QToolBox class's methods*

Method	Description
addItem(widget, text)	Adds the widget in a new tab at the bottom of the toolbox
insertItem(index, widget, text)	Inserts the widget in a new tab at the given index
indexOf(widget)	Returns the index of the specified widget
setCurrentIndex(index)	Sets the index to a new item's index
setCurrentWidget(widget)	Makes the widget the current widget displayed in the toolbox

When the item in a QToolBox is changed, the currentChanged(index) signal is emitted.

The QStackedWidget has a similar function to QToolBox, displaying multiple widgets stacked on top of one another to conserve space in a window. However, there is a key difference: QStackedWidget does not provide a means for the user to switch between tabs. Therefore, other widgets, such as a QComboBox or a QListWidget, are used to navigate through the different pages.

The QTabWidget is another container class that is similar to QStackedLayout but provides the tabs necessary to switch pages.

Finally, QGroupBox widgets typically group together collections of radio buttons and checkboxes. The main visual difference from the QFrame class is the addition of a title.

QScrollArea

A scroll area can be added onto a child widget to display the contents within a frame. If the size of the frame changes, the scroll bars will appear, allowing the user to still view the entire child widget. A few class methods are listed in Table A-28. The manner in how the scroll bars appear can be controlled with the **QAbstractScrollArea** class's size policies.

Table A-28. *Select methods for QScrollArea*

Method	Description
ensureVisible(x, y, xmargin, ymargin)	Ensures the specified (x, y) coordinate with margins xmargin and ymargin remains visible in the viewport
setAlignment(alignment)	Sets the alignment of the scroll area's widget
setWidget(widget)	Sets the scroll area's widget
setWidgetResizable(bool)	If False, the scroll area abides by the child widget's size

QMdiArea

For **multiple-windowed GUIs (MDIs)**, the **QMdiArea** class provides the container for displaying multiple windows inside a single application window. **Subwindows** are instances of the **QMdiSubWindow** class and can be arranged in tiled or cascading patterns. The subwindows can work together, relaying information back and forth. A context menu could also be added to the MDI area widget as a means to conveniently switch between windows. Some methods for the MDI widget are found in Table A-29.

Table A-29. *List of select QMdiArea methods*

Method	Description
addSubWindow(widget)	Adds widget as a new subwindow to the MDI area
activeSubWindow()	Returns the active subwindow
cascadeSubWindow()	Arranges subwindows in a cascade pattern
tileSubWindows()	Arranges subwindows in a tiled pattern
removeSubWindow(widget)	Removes widget from the MDI area, where widget is a subwindow
setBackground(background)	Sets the QBrush background for the MDI area
subWindowList(subwindows)	Returns a list of subwindows
setTabsClosable(bool)	If True, close buttons are placed on each tab in the tabbed view
setTabsMovable()	If True, tabs within the tabbed view are movable

QtQuick and QML

As Qt and PyQt continue to evolve with each new version, more focus has gone into creating more dynamic and fluid user interfaces. This is especially true with Qt 6 and PyQt6.

With the QtQuick and QtQml modules, developers are able to use the Qt Modeling Language (QML) to build custom interfaces and components. QtQuick includes a number of classes for building a canvas for visualizing graphical components, handling user input, working with data, and handling graphical effects that are reminiscent of mobile applications.

Note that QtQuick is different from the QtWidgets API that we have used throughout most of this book. The QML syntax that QtQuick uses is based on embedded JavaScript. Using PyQt, we are able to create applications that connect to the QML code using Python. In many instances, you are even able to use classes such as QtCore and QtGui to communicate with the interface built using QML.

There are two links that may help you get started using QtQuick. The first is Qt's Qt Quick documentation at https://doc.qt.io/qt-6/qtquick-index.html. The second is the Riverbank documentation at www.riverbankcomputing.com/static/Docs/PyQt6/qml.html#ref-integrating-qml.

Qt Style Sheets

For a great reference of widgets and properties that can be manipulated with Qt Style Sheets, have a look at https://doc.qt.io/qt-6/stylesheet-reference.html.

Style sheets allow for customizing many aspects and behaviors of widgets. Table A-30 lists many of the properties that can be modified. Widgets support only certain properties, so be sure to check out Qt's documentation if you are not sure about which properties you can change.

Table A-30. *List of properties that can be influenced using Qt Style Sheets*

Property	Description

alternate-background-color	The alternate background color for QAbstractItemView widgets
	QListView{
	alternate-background-color: blue;
	background: grey
	}

Background	Shorthand for setting the background

background-color	Background color used for the widget
	QPushButton{
	background-color: #49DE1F
	}

background-image	The background image used for the widget
	QFrame{
	background-image: url(images/black_cat.png)
	}

Border	Shorthand for setting the widget's border
	QComboBox{
	border: 2px solid magenta
	}

border-top, border-right, border-bottom, border-left	Shorthand for specifying sides of the widget's border
border-color	The color for all sides of the widget's border
border-image	Specifies an image to fill the border

border-radius	The radius of the border's corners
	QTextEdit{
	border-width: 1px;
	border-style: groove;
	border-radius: 3px
	}

(continued)

Table A-30. (*continued*)

Property	Description
border-style	Specifies the style for all of the border's edges
border-width	Specifies the width for all of the border's edges
color	The color used for rendering text

font	Shorthand for defining a widget's font
	QRadioButton{
	font: bold italic large "Helvetica"
	}

font-family, font-size, font-style, font-weight	Other properties used to individually set a font's features
height, width	The height and width of a widget
icon-size	The width and height of a widget's icon
image	The image drawn on a widget. Can use url or svg
margin	Specifies the widget's margins. Just like border, specific sides can also be set
max-height, max-width	The widget's maximum height or width
min-height, min-width	The widget's minimum height or width
outline	The outline draws a widget's border. Can also specify color, style, and radius
padding	Specifies the widget's padding. Just like border, specific sides can also be set
selection-color	The foreground color of selected items to text
spacing	Sets the internal spacing in a widget

text-align	Specifies the alignment of text and icons inside of a widget
	QPushButton{
	text-align: right
	}

Qt Namespace

Throughout this book, you have come across numerous enums and flags that allow you to describe or modify the parameters, states, and appearances of widgets. The `Qt` class in the `QtCore` module organizes the multitude of identifiers in the Qt Namespace. A **namespace** in C++ is essentially used to organize the names of functions and variables into logical groups to prevent errors.

To get an idea of just how extensive Qt Namespace is, have a look at `https://doc.qt.io/qt-6/qt.html`. There you'll find enums related to alignment, cursor style, date format, dock widget areas, keyboard buttons, window states, and more.

Summary

You have already used many of PyQt's foundational classes for building graphical user interfaces while following along with this book. The Appendix provides references to help you analyze the programs found in this book and to learn more about the widgets, layouts, and style sheets used to design and build PyQt applications. The classes and methods contained here act as a guide to get you thinking about ways to build and improve your own programs.

There is simply not enough room to include every class, method, or signal in this guide. As you follow along with the examples, use this Appendix as a resource to help you learn and find out more about the possibilities of PyQt. If the answer isn't provided for you here, follow the links, search on the Internet, or send me an email.

Happy coding!

Index

A

B

© Joshua M Willman 2022
J. M. Willman, *Beginning PyQt*, https://doi.org/10.1007/978-1-4842-7999-1

W, X, Y, Z

Printed in the United States
by Baker & Taylor Publisher Services